Canberra

(P) I said we would do so early in the life of the new parliament.

(P) Mr Speaker, we do so on this the first day of the forty-second parliament of the Commonwealth.

(P) Because it is time — well and truly time — for all the people of our great country Australia; for all our great Commonwealth, for all Australians (those who are saying sorry and those who are not) — to embrace a new future together
why Apologise?

(P) Some have asked "why apologise" to parliament

(P) Let me begin to answer by telling just a little of one person's story — an elegant lady in her eighties, and most eloquent, who has travelled a long way to be here with us in the parliament today, a survivor — a member of the stolen generations, who shared some of her life story with me when I called around to see her on Saturday.

(P) Ola N, as she asked to be called, was born in the 20's outside of Tennant Creek.

(P)

full of life
full of wonderful
and often
funny
stories

FOR THE TRUE BELIEVERS

'No one can claim that success has attended all the Labor Party's efforts, but it may at least be said generally that it has advanced the cause of humanity by another step. It has taught the rank and file to know their strength, and stressed the fact that the golden opportunities existent in Australia have never-ending responsibilities as their necessary accompaniment.'

John (Chris) Watson

The Watson Papers, National Library of Australia

Also by Troy Bramston:

Looking for the Light on the Hill: Modern Labor's Challenges
(Scribe, Melbourne, 2011)

The Wran Era
(The Federation Press, Sydney, 2006)

The Hawke Government: A Critical Retrospective (with Susan Ryan)
(Pluto Press, Melbourne, 2003)

FOR THE TRUE BELIEVERS

Great Labor Speeches that Shaped History

Edited by

Troy Bramston

Foreword by

Graham Freudenberg

THE FEDERATION PRESS
2012

Published in Sydney by
The Federation Press
PO Box 45, Annandale, NSW, 2038.
71 John St, Leichhardt, NSW, 2040.
Ph (02) 9552 2200. Fax (02) 9552 1681.
E-mail: info@federationpress.com.au
Website: http://www.federationpress.com.au

Front and back endpapers: Extracts from Kevin Rudd's handwritten draft apology speech to the
Stolen Generations of Aboriginal Australians

National Library of Australia
Cataloguing-in-Publication entry

Bramston, Troy
For the true believers: great Labor speeches that shaped history / Troy Bramston

ISBN 978 186287 831 0 (hbk)

Australian Labor Party.
Speeches, addresses, etc, Australia.
Australia – Politics and government.

808.85

Typeset by The Federation Press, Leichhardt, NSW.
        Printed by Ligare Pty Ltd, Riverwood, NSW.

Foreword

Graham Freudenberg

The Australian Labor Party was built on speeches. Born in a Golden Age of Argument, everything about the young Labor Party put a premium on speechmaking: the contest of ideas; the mission to 'educate and agitate'; the struggle for authority between and within Conference and Caucus; the competing demands of the industrial and political wings; the jostling for priority of place in the practical 'Fighting Platform' and the more ideological 'General Platform'; the discipline of the solidarity Pledge, designed partly as a curb on personal ambitions; and, above all, the commitment to the parliamentary road to power. A torrent of speeches surged around the eternal question, 'Whose party is it?'

The commitment to Parliament defined decisively the character of 'The Labor Speech'. By the turn of the century, the goal was not just worker representation or George Black's formula of 'support in return for concessions', but a parliamentary majority and government. This changed the key element in any speech – the audience. Conferences and branches still provided the test and training for aspiring politicians; conference still commanded the Platform. But for the elected leadership, the ultimate audience became the 'Men and Women of Australia'.

In this splendid collection, Troy Bramston shows that the hallmarks of the typical Labor speech developed early and persist to this day. The essence of the style and approach is a continuing quest for practical idealism.

Labor leaders have always been vulnerable to accusations of backsliding, from those who, at any given time, claim to the be the custodians of the true faith. On the other hand, the difficulty for the 'true believers' is that there is no received doctrine by which ideological purity can be measured. In his debates with Sir George Reid, WA Holman gave a version of socialism which intentionally ignored Karl Marx. Chris Watson set out the abiding problem for the Labor leadership in a speech in Melbourne in 1904:

> We have everywhere the enthusiast who is prepared to die fighting rather than accept any compromise. I do not wish to undervalue the enthusiastic and the quixotic man. The success of every movement depends on the enthusiast. But we should consider the immediate welfare of the great mass of the people.

Andrew Fisher made a virtue of necessity when he spoke at the Brisbane Trades Hall in September 1908:

> There are two distinct bodies in our movement – the propaganda teacher and the practical politician. The very name of politician, of course, puts the politician outside the sphere of the teacher. The propagandist does not care whether he has two, three, or more with him; the politician does his best for the mass of the people he is serving, otherwise he should not have his place in Parliament.

Few Labor leaders, and not Fisher himself, have accepted this dichotomy of roles. The teacher par excellence, Gough Whitlam, made the point, much more aggressively, at the Melbourne Trades Hall, sixty years after Fisher:

> Certainly, the impotent are pure … This party was not conceived in failure, brought forth by failure or consecrated to failure … So let us have none of this nonsense that defeat is in some way more moral than victory … I did not seek and do not want the leadership of Australia's largest pressure group. I propose to follow the traditions of those of our leaders who have seen the role of our party as striving to achieve, and achieving, the national government of Australia.

Some of the best speeches retrieved by Troy Bramston are not by the leaders and some of the leaders were not the best Labor speakers of their time. In the Watson-Fisher years, Billy Hughes was far and away the most brilliant orator; his subsequent career is a salutary reminder of the destructive power of speech. John Curtin's oratory bore the marks of his Yarra Bank days. A sympathetic critic, Paul Hasluck, wrote in his official history:

> The boldness and resolution of Curtin as a war leader shone brightly when he was among his own people. Those most closely associated with him, either as associates or as officials, agree that the most forceful speeches he ever made during the war – most of them unrecorded – were made at Labor conferences. There he was decisive, determined and eloquent, speaking extempore in the surroundings in which his political life had been nurtured and in a style in which he was at home.[1]

Ben Chifley is the outstanding example of speech as character. The enduring resonance of his 'Light on the Hill' and 'Things Worth Fighting For' speeches comes from the character and integrity of the man who made them. Great issues make for great speeches, but if I am asked to identify the single quality which makes a great oration, I will always say: 'Character, character, character.' Art and eloquence count, and speechwriters can help in this, but the bottom line remains character, in which I include courage, intellect and vision.

---

1 P Hasluck, *Australia in the Second World War*, Volume Two, p 251.

In a parliamentary party that included Kim Beazley Snr, Jim Cairns, Clyde Cameron and Fred Daly, Whitlam may not have held the first place as a debater, but he was the great all-rounder. He saw Parliament as the grand forum in which to develop and explain policy. It may be true that Whitlam, with his tendency to overlay detail upon detail and his determination to instruct and educate, could, on occasion, qualify for Oliver Goldsmith's comment on Edmund Burke: 'He kept on refining while others thought of dining.' Or at least, in the days when we took public meetings seriously in Australia, nipping out to the pub before closing time, Bob Hawke seriously believed that a speech was an act of persuasion. He was convinced that an informed and intelligent audience, by which he genuinely meant the Australian people, could be *persuaded* to see things as he saw them. Paul Keating personified speech as energy and dynamic force. He was very uneven in performance, but at his best, the most electrifying speaker of my time. He is the only federal Labor leader between HV 'Doc' Evatt and Julia Gillard I was never asked to write for. In fact, I wrote Keating's speech for the Sydney 2000 Olympic bid at Monte Carlo in 1993. But this was part of the presentation which included a speech by John Fahey, the Liberal Premier of NSW – the only speech I ever wrote for a non-Labor parliamentarian.

These speakers for the most part found their voice first at party conferences and on the public platform. The public meeting, with all its challenges and opportunities for the development and advocacy of policy and ideas, is disappearing. Don't blame television or the media. Its extinction is being connived at by the politicians, party managers, political staffers and speechwriters. The displacement of the public meeting from its central role in the public discourse has meant not only a loss of spontaneity and oratorical skills. What is being lost is also the bonding between the leadership and the rank-and-file and the sense of public participation, dialogue, and continuity in the public debate. These things are essential to the operation of an effective party system, itself the mainstay of a vigorous parliamentary democracy. Nothing could do more to strengthen it than to restore the genuine public meeting to its former glory. The media treatment of the 2010 campaign would have been transformed if the parties had held authentic public meetings.

The Australian Labor Party is a collective memory in action. These speeches are the chords of that memory. Troy Bramston deserves our thanks for recovering many that have been lost or forgotten and for giving a new lease of life to so many great Labor speeches.

To my son, Angus

Contents

Part 3
The Campaign Trail

CONTENTS

xi

Part 5
War and Conflict

Part 6
Australia and the World

CONTENTS

Part 7
Victory, Defeat, Love and Loss

Preface

This book comes at a time when Labor needs to more effectively define and communicate what it believes in and what it stands for, and is beset by many challenges.

Party membership is at its lowest level in a century and internal party engagement has hollowed out. Trade union membership has declined markedly in recent decades and some unions are supporting rival political parties. Labor is no longer a community-based party that encourages internal participation or public engagement in its affairs. In government, Federal Labor was reduced to a minority status in Parliament after just one term, achieving only 38 per cent of the vote, amid widespread disillusionment with its performance. Today, Labor remains historically unpopular in opinion polls, as voters look to other parties on the left and right of politics to represent their interests.

So, a book that showcases Labor's achievements and presents speeches that animate Labor's enduring values, philosophy and purpose, could not be timelier.

Labor has always been a principled, progressive and pragmatic centre-left political party. It shares in the reformist tradition advanced by the great social democratic political parties of the centre-left throughout the world. It has always been a mass party and, primarily, the party of the working and middle classes, that seeks to govern in the national interest for all Australians.

Labor has been most successful when it has been boldest, with big reforming ideas and making the case for change – however hard – and placing a premium on long-term policy strategy rather than short-term political tactics.

Labor has always been a party of the future, championing hope over fear, expressing its collective roots as a party for the many and not the few, while respecting individual liberty and believing that more can be achieved by working together, rather than apart, at home and abroad.

Labor has always had a core set of enduring values: social and economic justice, equality of opportunity, nation-building, democratic liberalism, internationalism and, more recently, environmental sustainability. Labor saw the levers of government and the collective talents of society as the best way to achieve these goals. The challenge today is to refresh these values for the modern era, reinforce them through policies and articulate them through speeches and other forms of communication.

This book shows how Labor's greatest figures have sought to give voice to this purpose through the power of political speech.

* * *

The idea for this book came while working as Kevin Rudd's principal speechwriter during 2007.

It was, at times, an exhilarating, immensely rewarding and an exceptionally privileged opportunity. Like any experience in politics at the highest levels, it could also be maddeningly frustrating, incredibly stressful and exhausting.

Between January and December 2007, I had the rare opportunity to work directly with Kevin Rudd on hundreds of speeches, speech notes, articles and correspondence – from his first major speech as party leader in January 2007 to the Budget Reply of May 2007 to his election night speech in Brisbane and his first press conference as Prime Minister-elect. (I also wrote several speeches for Julia Gillard during 2007.)

This work was conducted in Parliament House, sitting next to Rudd on planes, while driving in cars, in hotel rooms and hotel foyers, in temporary offices, on the phone and in his front lounge room at his home in Norman Park, Brisbane.

A speechwriter is no more than somebody who provides, in draft form, words, sentences, ideas and arguments arranged in a particular way. The speaker owns the words they speak. Sometimes, Rudd would hardly change a word from the draft presented to him. Most often he blended his own words and ideas into the draft and it became the speech that was delivered. Sometimes he would write or rewrite an entire draft himself. He consulted others, including some of the nation's finest wordsmiths, on some of his speeches, including Graham Freudenberg and Don Watson. Other staff also assisted with speeches, especially in the lead up to and during the election campaign.

Frequently, Rudd would ask for a dissertation on some aspect of party or political history to inform the drafting of a speech. He would seek a quote from a storied Labor Leader that could be applied to modern politics or a rare or insightful bon mot of history to dazzle a crowd, illustrate a point or augment an argument.

Similarly, I was, and still am, asked by Labor MPs for the odd historical reference or quote to furnish their own speeches. I jumped at the offer to contribute to several first speeches by several freshly minted Labor MPs elected in the classes of 2007 and 2010. I enjoyed working with Tony Burke on speeches too when working for him during the Rudd government. After

I left the Rudd office, I was occasionally asked to assist with Rudd's speeches and always enthusiastically agreed to do so.

It was this incredible opportunity to work as a speechwriter which prompted this book – to provide inspiration by recalling the values and achievements of Labor through the words that make up the lingua franca of Australia's oldest and most successful political party. With Labor today in dire political trouble, with the party's true believers deeply disillusioned and with uplifting, informative and persuasive oratory seemingly lost, this collection of great Labor speeches could not be more relevant.

* * *

Despite the collective wisdom, I still believe that Kevin Rudd was one of Labor's most effective political communicators. It is axiomatic to say that no Labor parliamentarian has ever seized the party leadership without being a persuasive and articulate speaker – *without* the support of strategists, focus group research, speechwriters and media advisers. This was undoubtedly the case with Rudd.

Rudd's rise to the Labor leadership was powered by his communication skills: his ability to communicate plainly and persuasively on everyday issues on a weekly basis to the morning television audience watching Seven's *Sunrise* program coupled with an equally effective ability to communicate a detailed and authoritative knowledge of policy matters to a myriad of audiences, providing a clear, articulate and formidable presentation of Labor's policies and a stinging and persuasive critique of the foreign policy approach of his political opponents.

During the 2007 election campaign, his discipline in sticking to Labor's key messages and policies that communicated Labor's core values and the attributes of his leadership was unrivalled. His performance in interviews, on the campaign trail, in the election debate and in speeches was near faultless.

In delivering a formal set-piece speech, he ranged from being able to deliver what was the highest form of political oratory that the Parliament had witnessed for over a decade when he delivered the apology to Australia's indigenous peoples, to captivating small audiences with his charm, humour and knowledge, to delivering turgid, detailed and long-winded speeches and interviews of indecipherable bureaucratise and political-speak. It was a curious mix.

But once in government, as Rudd acknowledged, his political communication skills ran hot and cold. He told Laurie Oakes in February 2010 that 'most of my critics would not say I have a (Tony) Blairite skill for the one-liner. Their criticism would be the reverse'. On pressing the case for an emissions trading scheme to combat climate change, Rudd said, 'Throughout all this, the Australian people were saying "We don't understand you, you need to explain it better". I think that's where I didn't deliver'. It became a fatal flaw and a key reason why his leadership faltered and his support in the Labor caucus fell sharply.

His day-to-day language was replete with a strange mix of clichés ('a fork in the road', 'up hill and down dale', 'not on your nelly', 'fair shake of a sauce bottle'); well-worn and hackneyed phrases ('in due season', 'but you know something', 'I've got to zip', 'when it comes to', 'can I just say', 'I haven't seen the detail', 'the bottom line is this'); and focus-group tested political sound-bites ('working families', 'get the balance right', 'shovel-ready', 'fairness out the back door'). At times, he slipped into impenetrable Rudd-speak: telling an audience abroad that the major economies were unlikely to agree on significant action on climate change 'by way of detailed programmatic specificity' and describing 'a conjointly controlled mechanism' which would manage hospitals under his major health reform package. He told the Brookings Institute in April 2008, 'Therefore, there is, in my argument, on the face of it, a natural complementarity between these two philosophical approaches and a complementarity that could be developed further in the direction of some form of conceptual synthesis'. While many of Rudd's parliamentary colleagues recoiled at his approach to communication, I suspect that the wider public simply saw it as one of the many aspects of his unique and, still, popular appeal.

Rudd delivered more speeches and gave more interviews than any other Prime Minister on an annual, monthly or weekly basis. He was also under far more scrutiny than any other Prime Minister, with penetrating 24-hour media scrutiny – from pay-television to newspapers and radio to internet blogs watching and recording his every public statement. Not all of his prose could be perfectly polished.

But for all this, and for the tortured phrases and mind-boggling statements that fell from the mouth of Kevin Rudd, this does not discount his exceptional skills as a political communicator in a variety of forms. Indeed, in recent times, there has been no finer speech in Australian politics than his apology to Australia's indigenous peoples delivered in the nation's Parliament in 2008. That was a great Labor speech.

Troy Bramston

Acknowledgements

While researching, writing and editing this book, I was humbled that so many people offered their help, advice and encouragement.

First and foremost, my heartfelt thanks go to the nation's greatest speech-writer, Graham Freudenberg, for writing the foreword to this book. Nobody was better suited for this task. Indeed, Graham drafted many of the speeches in this book. For more than a decade, I have been fortunate to be able to call Graham a friend. I cherish his friendship, his counsel and his generous contributions to many of my books.

Thank you to those who have allowed me to reprint their words in this book, and who also provided me with their comments and reflections. In August 2010, I had the great privilege to meet with Gough Whitlam in his office to talk to him about this book. To interview Bob Hawke – Labor's most successful Prime Minister – is, as always, immensely informative. To engage Paul Keating in a long discussion about political communication, his speeches and aspects of his prime ministership was alone worth the many hours that I have put into this book. And to be granted one of the first, wide-ranging and on the record interviews with Kevin Rudd since losing the prime ministership, in October 2010, was not only very generous, but also very insightful. Ambassador Kim Beazley provided me with extensive comments on his speeches in the book. Bill Hayden and Simon Crean also shared with me their reflections on speeches in the book and the challenges and opportunities of leading the Labor Party in opposition. Mark Latham and I occasionally discuss and correspond on matters of Labor politics and I thank him for permission to reproduce one of his speeches.

For permissions, my thanks go also to Claire Bossley, John Cain Jr, Mary Calwell, Andrew Dunstan, Susan Ryan and Neville Wran. Thanks are also due to Sam Dastyari and his predecessor, Matthew Thistlethwaite, from the Australian Labor Party's NSW Branch for their support and for providing funds to reproduce the photographs in this book. I also thank Nick Martin from the Australian Labor Party's National Secretariat, who assert copyright over speeches delivered by Labor MPs outside of Parliament, and who gave me the remaining permissions that I needed. He also provided several photographs in the book.

Many distinguished Australians provided me with their advice, comments and suggestions, when I am sure they had better things to do: Simon Banks, Peter Bastian, Grant Belchamber, Karl Bitar, David Black, Judith Brett, Verity

Burgmann, Tony Burke, Glenn Byres, Bob Carr, Michael Cathcart, Rodney Cavalier, David Clune, Brian Dale, David Day, Tim Dixon, Michael Easson, Michael Egan, Bob Ellis, Michael Fullilove, Dennis Glover, Michael Gordon, Katharine Gelber, Bridget Griffen-Foley, Susan Grusovin, Jim Hagan, Michael Hogan, Johno Johnson, Paul Kelly, Andrew Leigh, Malcolm Mackerras, David McKnight, Iola Mathews, Race Mathews, Ross McMullin, Andrew Moore, Kaila Murnain, Alan Ramsey, Aaron Rule, Jill Saunders, Robert Schlesinger (son of Arthur M Schlesinger Jr), Dennis Shanahan, Marian Simms, Paul Strangio, Peter Stanley, Ken Turner, Barrie Unsworth, John Warhurst and Don Watson. I thank them all very much.

The comments and suggestions of my friends and family were much appreciated: my parents, Jeff and Michele Bramston, and also Martin Breen, John Degen, Ben Heraghty and Matthew Martyn-Jones. I also thank Nicky Seaby, who, as always, was a wellspring of encouragement, assurance, love and support as I worked on this book over several years.

The hunt for speeches, photos and permissions would not have been possible without the support provided by many institutions and libraries: Newspix and Fairfax Syndication; the Australian Labor Party; the Parliaments of Australia (Paul Oglethorpe), New South Wales (Richard Torbay), Victoria (Joel Hallinan) and Queensland (Neil Laurie); The John Curtin Prime Ministerial Library (Lesley Wallace, David Wylie and Kate Roberton); The Bob Hawke Prime Ministerial Library (Margaret Goedhart); The Whitlam Institute (Eric Sidoti, Liz Curach, Amy Sambrooke and Lorraine West); The Evatt Collection at Flinders University Library (Gillian Dooley); The Dunstan Collection at the Flinders University Library (also Gillian Dooley); the NSW Parliamentary Library (Gareth Griffith); the Victorian Parliamentary Library (Marion King); the National Archives of Australia; the NSW State Archives; the National Library of Australia; and the State Libraries of New South Wales, Victoria and Western Australia.

I acknowledge and thank Linda Green, whom I engaged to assist with some of the transcribing and re-typing of speeches.

This is my second book with The Federation Press. It has been a pleasure to again work with Chris Holt, Kathryn Fitzhenry and Di Young, and the rest of the publishing team. They have produced so many quality books of enduring value to all Australians.

Although many people generously helped me with this book, I alone take responsibility for the selection of speeches and any errors there may be in transcribing, editing or interpreting them.

Finally, this book is lovingly dedicated to my son, Angus, who, like his sister, Madison, was never ever far from my mind as I worked to complete it.

Introduction

'With words, we govern', wrote British Prime Minister Benjamin Disraeli. Indeed, the words that join together to make a speech reflect the oldest continuing form of political communication. It is the most effective way to present an argument to the people and to link together policies, programs and philosophies into a framework for political persuasion. It provides a political compass to navigate by. It gives coherence, depth and ballast to the swirling mix of political tactics, strategies, policies and programs that a political leader deals with and the citizenry try to make sense of.

No leader of a political movement, no candidate for political office, no party leader or Prime Minister can really succeed without being an effective speechmaker: to small groups of party members burnishing their case for advancement, at an outdoor rally in the rough and tumble of a campaign, in the bear pit of the nation's parliaments, to a sceptical community group or business organisation, to a town hall full of supporters expecting the highest form of oratory, or in the cynical confines of the National Press Club in Canberra.

But a speech is more than a political tool or form of communication; its impact and importance can be far greater. A speech can define a moment in time, help to explain and give meaning to events as they turn, and serve as a signpost marking a decisive moment in the affairs of a nation. Political speeches can be the springboard to announce a new policy, launch a campaign or a new initiative, act as a rallying-call for action, summon a higher purpose, inspire a new movement for change, break a taboo or slay a sacred cow, chart a new course or bring a journey to an end, sound a warning bell for the future, remember the past, expound a philosophy, send forces into battle, celebrate a victory or mourn a defeat, or provide consolation and meaning in times of great despair. In these moments our attention often turns to our political leaders to speak for, and on behalf of, the nation by leading through their words.

A truly great speech quickens the pulse, electrifies an audience and binds that audience to the speaker's cause. Elevated eloquence can make a speech soar. Prose can become poetry. Words and sentences can linger in the air and dance in our minds long after a speech has ended. Pictures can be painted that are unforgettable. Arguments and ideas can transcend long held views and expose hidden truths or herald a change of view.

'Of all the talents bestowed upon men', Winston Churchill wrote in 1897, 'none is so precious as the gift of oratory. He who enjoys it wields a power more durable than that of a great king. He is an independent force in the world. Abandoned by his party, betrayed by his friends, stripped of his offices, whoever can command this power is still formidable'.

Unlike the conservative political forces, a progressive party like the Australian Labor Party places a premium on the importance of speeches as a way to educate, agitate and organise for change. Bob Hawke told me in an interview in July 2010 that 'Speeches by leaders of reformist governments, which is what Labor governments should be, need to be educative in making the electorate understand the need for change. That's the critical role, which I saw for speeches that I had to make'.

In an interview with Paul Keating in June 2010, he told me, 'All leaders of any substance have been leaders capable of telling a story. Storytelling is, of its essence, the conceptualisation of ideas. Without a schematic or framework, subjects and events appear in isolation and with no purpose'.

Kevin Rudd said in an interview with me in October 2010 that 'Speeches are of fundamental importance for providing vision, direction and action for the nation and for any reformist party seeking to lead the nation'. He said, 'The function of an effective speech is to make the complex comprehensible in defining the problem and defining the way forward in dealing with the problem. Secondly, for a reformist party in government, it is the mechanisms through which you connect your historical values of the party and the nation with the challenges of the day'.

Anybody can make a speech; few can make speeches that are truly great. So what makes a great speech? Above all, it must achieve its purpose: to persuade, to explain, to inspire, to challenge, to apologise, to acquit, to convict, and so on. It may be great if it helps to understand a turning point in time, if it advances an important argument or idea, or if it helps to shape an event or an evolving issue.

A speech may be great because it is enlivened by the use of literary devices. This could be the wordplay of arranging words and sentences in a particular way, utilising techniques such as: alliteration or assonance (using words that sound the same); anadiplosis (using a word from the previous sentence to begin a new sentence); anaphora or epiphora (repeating words at the beginning or end of a sentence); antithesis (contrasting words or ideas); parallelism (using similar sentences in succession); parenthesis (breaking into a sentence to make a new point); periphrasis (using more words than necessary); polyptoton (repeating words with similar meaning); repetition (re-using words or sentences); or tricolon (punctuating a sentence with three run-on statements).

Or it could be changing the meaning of the words and sentences to render sections of a speech particularly memorable, employing techniques such as: allusion (referring to something indirectly); anthypophora or erotema (asking and answering rhetorical questions); hyperbole (exaggeration); innuendo (to imply something indirectly); irony (an unusual meaning); metaphor (using one thing to describe another); oxymoron (words that contradict each other); or satire (to ridicule through sarcasm or irony).

It may be great because of the content of the speech, its sheer logic, its theme, its structure and flow, the marshalling of facts and figures, stories told or words quoted, the use of humour, questions asked for answered, a personal anecdote or a historical analogy, or a force of argument that builds to an obvious conclusion. Conversely, empty and banal rhetoric, devoid of substance or purpose, can be fatal for a political leader.

It may be great because of the memorable delivery or cadence: tempo, rhythm, tone, pitch. The presentation could make the speech a moment of great drama and theatre, or one of solemn reflection. A speech may be interpreted differently if it is read rather than heard; hearing a speech can often animate its words, whereas reading cannot. Indeed, the Roman orator Cicero believed that the success of a speech was inexorably linked to its delivery.

Or it may be the venue: a conference of Labor Party members at the Sydney Town Hall – so labelled by Graham Freudenberg as NSW Labor's 'secular cathedral' – or onboard a battleship being sent to war, or on the floor of the nation's parliaments and televised to the nation. The speaker needs to understand the outlook and expectations of the audience if their speech is to be effective.

Greatness may come because the occasion demands it: facing the threat of invasion, a memorial service, an election campaign launch. The occasion will often lend itself to a great speech. The pomp and pageantry of a United States presidential inauguration was the setting for the magisterial inaugural speeches of Abraham Lincoln, Franklin D Roosevelt and John F Kennedy. The challenges of war prompted Churchill's fighting wartime rhetoric. The historic march on Washington DC in 1963 was the event that backlit Martin Luther King Jr's 'I have a dream' speech.

Finally, it may be great because of the response it elicits from the audience. The Greek philosopher, Aristotle, believed that a speech must appeal to the audience via logos (reason and logic), pathos (emotion, empathy and understanding) and ethos (by the speaker's interaction with the audience and by their character). The audience who first hears the speech may not be the audience that appreciates its greatness. Lincoln's Gettysburg Address was not instantly famous. Instead, it attracted mixed reviews. Ben Chifley's 'the light on the hill' speech was immediately newsworthy, but not for its encapsulation of the essence of the Labor cause, but rather his attack on the mine workers' union.

But, ultimately, a great speech needs a blend of some, if not all, of these factors mentioned.

There is much to learn by studying the great speeches themselves. From earlier times: Pericles' funeral oration, 'fix your eyes upon the glory of Athens'; Socrates, knowing he was going to die, 'it is now time for me to depart'; Augustus declaring 'I found Rome a city of brick and left it a city of marble'; Jesus of Nazareth's fabled sermon on the mount.

In more modern times: Edmund Burke's speech to the electors of Bristol on the importance of the politician's 'judgement'; Patrick Henry's freedom-cry 'give me liberty or give me death'; Lincoln's Gettysburg address recalling 'a new nation, conceived in liberty, and dedicated to the proposition that all men are created equal' or his second inaugural address, pledging 'malice toward none, with charity for all'; the stirring rhetoric of the Irish orators Patrick Pearse arguing 'Ireland unfree will never be at peace' and Daniel O'Connell 'calling for justice to Ireland'.

The great challenges of recent decades: Franklin D Roosevelt's first inaugural address, 'the only thing we have to fear is fear itself' or his declaration of war against Japan in 1941, 'a day that will live in infamy'; Churchill's wartime defiance, 'we will never surrender' or his post-war warning that an 'iron curtain has descended across' Europe; Charles de Gaulle's 'the flame of French resistance must not and shall not die'; John F Kennedy's rhythmic and lyrical inaugural address, 'ask not what your country can do for you – ask what you can do for your country'; King's 'I have a dream' speech; Nelson Mandela's 'ideal for which I am prepared to die'; Robert F Kennedy's 'ripples of hope' speech from South Africa or his impromptu eulogy for King; Tony Blair's optimistic 'a new day has dawned, has it not?' and his lament years later that 'the visions are painted in the colours of the rainbow and the reality is sketched in duller tones of black and white and grey'; the moving funeral oration for Princess Diana, 'the most hunted person of the modern age', by her brother Earl Spencer; and Barack Obama's promise of 'hope' and 'change' and his belief that 'yes we can'.

Many of these great speeches may have drawn on the words and ideas of others. Ghostwriting is not new. George Washington had the assistance of

Thomas Jefferson, James Madison and Alexander Hamilton when drafting his farewell presidential address. Secretary of State designate, William Seward, assisted Lincoln with his first inaugural address. Since Judson Welliver was employed as a 'literary clerk' to United States President Warren Harding in 1921, the White House has used the services of a full-time speechwriter, or a team of speechwriters. In Australia, Prime Ministers such as John Curtin and Chifley were assisted with their speechwriting by advisers including Don Rodgers and Lloyd Ross. Freudenberg was the first person employed specifically as a speechwriter in Australian politics, first writing speeches for Labor leader Arthur Calwell in the 1960s.

Robert Menzies did not approve of politicians using speechwriters, believing that the words spoken by somebody who did not write them would not be authentic. 'I never employed a speechwriter myself', he said in a memoir, 'partly because I had an obstinate objection to having other people's words put into my mouth'. Reflecting this view, as William Safire notes in his political dictionary, the United States journalist Walter Lippman wrote in 1942:

> [N]o one can write an authentic speech for another man; it is impossible as writing his love letters for him or saying his prayers for him. When he speaks to the people, he and not someone else must speak. For it is much more important that he could be genuine, and it is infinitely more persuasive, than that he be bright, clever, ingenious, entertaining, eloquent, or even grammatical.

Indeed, it is for this reason that there is often friction in the speaker-speechwriter relationship. A point recognised by Jimmy Carter's speechwriter, Hendrik Hertzberg, in his book, *Politics*:

> The speechwriter's very existence is an affront to the politician, because it intimates that the politician is too lazy or stupid to decide for himself what it is he is going to say … The speechwriter is different from the other members of the court. The politician does not seem bigger or grander because he has a speechwriter. Having a speechwriter is apt to diminish the politician in the eyes of the public, because the one thing a leader cannot delegate is his inner essence, and if what the leader says is not a reflection and product of his inner essence, then what *is*? If someone else is writing the words he speaks, then what *do* those words express? By giving the politician *something* to say, the speechwriter suggests by implication that the politician has *nothing* to say. So a politician is generally a little resentful toward and ashamed of his speechwriter – not ashamed of the particular person who holds the job, simply of the fact that the job exists.

Despite the professional challenges faced by speechwriters, they are an indispensible part of any modern political operation. The speechwriter in modern politics is as essential as any other aide or assistant to a politician or party leader. The key reason modern politicians have sought the services of a professional writer to assist in the drafting of speeches is simply because they do not have the luxury to spend hours drafting their speeches. And why not employ a gifted wordsmith to give their speeches some additional gravitas?

Don Watson – who drafted speeches for Paul Keating – says, in an introduction to a collection of Keating's speeches:

> The speechwriter's task is to find the means by which politicians can touch the audience, move them, interest them, help them, help them understand, enrage them, engage them, please them. Speechwriters are value-adders; they take the raw material and cook it. They make a meal of it.

Hawke argues that speechmaking is an essential skill needed for effective political leadership. In an interview with Hawke for this book in July 2010, he said:

> When I was president of the ACTU (Australian Council of Trade Unions) I didn't have a speechwriter, but when I became prime minister and a member of parliament, I did. But it is absolutely essential when you are prime minister. I think one of the essential problems that Kevin Rudd had was that he tried to do much writing himself. When I was prime minister there were very few speeches that I wrote entirely myself.

Rudd could not be more different from Hawke in his approach to speech-writing. Interviewing Rudd in October 2010, he said:

> The first thing about political speechwriting is that it's got to be you. It has to have the character of authenticity about it. And it is for that reason that of all the speeches that I delivered (as prime minister), the vast bulk of those speeches were written by myself or substantially crafted by myself.

He acknowledged that this would be 'the complaint of anybody … who has worked for me as a speechwriter'. But he defended it as necessary: 'the reason is, for good or ill, it has to be consistent with my own values and my own understanding of the values of the party and that of the country, and my own intellectual framework for understanding current challenges'.

Speechwriters are important, but in the end, as Keating said in an interview for this book in June 2010:

> Speeches can only ever be the speech of the leader; that is, they reflect his or her sentiments for without they have no authenticity or authority. For instance, no speechwriter would have let John Howard deliver the republic speech, the Redfern Park speech or even the sentiments of the unknown solider speech. Craft can belong to speechwriters, but sentiment and substance only belongs to the owners of the speech: the leaders.

Some with a cynical disposition may look at this collection and assume that many of these uplifting and history-making words were not written by the person who spoke them. But this ignores the cardinal rule of speechwriting: whoever speaks the words, owns them. The task of a speechwriter is to amplify the thoughts, ideas and arguments of the speaker. It is a collaborative relationship – the writing is shared between the speaker and the writer – and in the final analysis, the speaker will usually approve the final draft and will say what they want to say.

For as long as there have been speeches, speechmakers and speechwriters, commentators have mourned the decline of the great political speech. Today the cry has become louder with critics pointing to the use of focus group and poll-tested words, the use of calculated political language, hackneyed clichés, predictable platitudes, phrases and slogans – all poisoning the modern political speech. Even a storied speechwriter like the late Ted Sorensen – who drafted speeches for John F Kennedy – became a critic, writing in his autobiography, *Counsellor: A Life at the Edge of History*:

> Kennedy's eloquence is deemed old-fashioned today. His style, say some, is too lofty in this hectic age of cynical sophistication. Today presidential themes and drafts are edited by committee. Stirring phrases have been replaced by sound bites and applause lines. Majestic understatement has lost out to hyperbole. Presidents announce but do not inspire. Politicians are obsessed with making the nightly news instead of making history.

While there is an element of truth in this, it also reflects the changing nature of politics and political communication – not least Kennedy's rare gifts and that of his speechwriter. Today, the traditional set-piece speech has to compete with 24-hour news, in multiple-media formats, prone to sensationalism, hyperbole and showbiz. Politicians struggle to engage an increasingly busy, cynical and disengaged citizenry. Speeches are not the only way to engage with voters. The tools available to a politician to communicate are also growing: short doorstop press conferences, longer press conferences, interviews on television and radio and in print, media releases or statements, blog posts and social networking forums such as Twitter and Facebook, advertising, telephone canvassing, direct letters and emails.

The long form political speech has always been changing. Parliament remains the preeminent setting for a political speech, but it too has changed, with the introduction of frequent radio broadcasts mid last century, to the televising of Question Time in the 1980s to the daily web-based broadcasting of today. Speeches to political rallies, town hall meetings, party conferences, via radio and television broadcasts, think tanks, business and community groups, as settings for speeches, have ebbed and flowed in popularity.

Politicians and political leaders need to be able to deliver speeches in a variety of settings which demand different styles of speechmaking: party conferences, political rallies, meetings of organisations, party branch meetings, schools, gala events and in Parliament. Not every speechmaker can deliver speeches in gatherings of equal excellence. Curtin is probably without peer in addressing a party conference. Chifley, HV 'Doc' Evatt and Arthur Calwell could keep outdoor audiences enthralled. Whitlam and Keating were great debaters in Parliament. Hawke is unmatched at a political rally or in an industrial tribunal, and could be brilliant on television and radio. But like all speakers, he did not excel in every environment. Hawke's passionate speaking style seemed out of place in the formalised and usually demure House of Representatives. When I asked Hawke in July 2010 about his parliamentary speeches, he said, revealingly:

> Well, the basic point I'd make Troy, is this: I didn't like Parliament or the Parliamentary process. I never ever liked the Parliamentary scene. It is a necessary part of the job, but in my experience as an advocate, I was used to a situation where the outcome depended upon the quality of your argument. For me, Parliament was just a charade. I just couldn't get excited about it because it didn't matter if you made a terrible speech or a good speech, the decisions were already made. In the government party room, the decision would be taken and it was just a charade to debate it in Parliament. So I never had a real love of, or commitment to, the Parliamentary debate process. And that may explain why I think I put more into speeches outside of the Parliament than inside.

As a form of communication, a speech is the oldest and is still among the most important. It offers an opportunity for a more considered, more thoughtful, more meaningful way to communicate political ideas. As Watson argued, a speech is 'a gesture towards order and respectability in a world which prizes spontaneity and tends towards chaos'. It also offers the best opportunity to connect up the varied threads of a political program and unify it into a compelling narrative which above all explains the leader and the party's purpose. A narrative is important because it helps to encapsulate into a story or a theme where that party or government wants to take the nation and why.

* * *

The purpose of this book is to bring together speeches which give voice to Labor's enduring values, philosophy, history and achievements, and also speeches which placed the party and its principal figures at the centre of historic events. The scope of the book is confined to 'great Labor speeches' – those delivered within the orbit of the Labor Party. In recent years there have been several collections of Australian speeches published, but none has focused exclusively on politics, in and outside of the Australian Parliament, nor have they focused on speeches within a Labor context. So this book is a canon of Labor speeches; an anthology of the words which form a rich tapestry of the party's history. They provide a prism through which to explore this history. Moreover, because of Labor's longevity, these speeches provide a window into the history of the nation, telling the story of Australia through the voices of those who sought to shape that story.

In this book, there are speeches that stir the imagination and inspire, such as Whitlam's declaration that 'It's time'; Hawke promising 'national reconciliation, national recovery, national reconstruction'; and Dorothy Tangney's hope that Australia could be 'a model for all other democracies to follow'. And history does not properly record that if Premier Joe Cahill failed to convince the NSW Labor Party conference in 1957 of the need for 'a great cultural centre', then there would not be a Sydney Opera House.

There are speeches appealing to humanity, such as Hawke's plea to end apartheid as the world cannot ignore 'the spirit of men and women yearning to be free'; Susan Ryan's defence of 'the principle of the equality of men and women'; and Don Dunstan's belief in immigration because of 'the strength that comes from diversity'.

There are speeches of sorrow and redemption such as Rudd's 'we say sorry' to Australia's Aboriginal people and Kim Beazley's hope that the Parliament could, for these Australians, 'render justice and restitution'.

There are speeches urging moderation and caution, such as Evatt's principled stand against the attempt to ban the Communist Party, arguing that 'no man should be deprived of civil rights' and TJ Ryan taking the fight up to Billy Hughes in the First World War, declaring, 'I am opposed to conscription'.

There are speeches that call for courage in the face of adversity such as Curtin telling Parliament that 'a great naval battle is proceeding' which threatened the invasion of Australia and Andrew Fisher declaring that Australia would support Britain 'to our last man and our last shilling'.

There are speeches that seek to mute the trumpet sound of war such as William Holman's opposition to the Boer War as 'the most iniquitous, most immoral war ever waged'; Calwell's stand against the Vietnam War, 'on the side of sanity and in the cause of humanity'; and Simon Crean on the deck of naval ship departing for Iraq and telling the troops, 'I don't believe that you should be going'.

There are speeches which keep faith with Labor's purpose and philosophy such as the discovery that Chris Watson spoke of Labor's purpose as 'a light upon a mountain', 40 years before Chifley's famed 'light on the hill' speech; Whitlam's trust in 'human improvement and human progress'; and Keating's belief in Labor as 'the people who can dream the big dreams and do the big things'.

There are speeches attacking the forces of conservatism such as Bob Carr's description of the battle on the waterfront as 'a day that will live in industrial infamy'; Keating's 'cracker night' metaphor to describe his political opponents; and Hughes' description of Alfred Deakin as having 'abandoned the finer resources of political assassination and resorted to the bludgeon of the cannibal'.

There are speeches given in moments of high drama and emotion like Whitlam's 'nothing will save the Governor-General' speech following his dismissal or those during the 1950s' split when John Cain urged his colleagues not 'to thrust a dagger into a Labor government'.

And there are speeches which celebrate and mourn the party's fallen such as Nicholas McKenna's belief that 'to know Chifley was to love him', Frank Forde's eulogy for Curtin where he said that 'the captain has been stricken in sight of the shore' and Curtin's description of Watson as 'one of the most eminent of the band of prominent Labor men'.

This book is structured into seven sections: 'Reconciling Australia'; 'Reform, Progress and the Future'; 'The Campaign Trail'; 'History, Tradition and Ideology'; 'War and Conflict'; 'Australia and the World'; and 'Victory, Defeat, Love and Loss'. Each speech is prefaced with an introduction, seeking to place the speech and the speaker into its historical context, recalling its immediate impact, arguing why it mattered, explaining how it helped to shape history and why it deserves to be remembered. Some of the speeches are presented in full, but most have been edited to conserve space. Editing is denoted by ellipses […]. Sources are provided at the conclusion of the speech.

The focus is on the Labor Party and not the broader labour movement. The selection of speeches reflects those that seek to enlarge our vision of the future and, in Lincoln's words, reflect 'the better angels of our nature'. Yes, there are references to thorny issues such as White Australia, but no specific speech extolling its virtues. The selection reflects most of the mainstream policy and political issues: economics, social policy, workplace relations, immigration and multiculturalism, Aboriginal reconciliation, the environment, inequality, the arts and foreign policy. There are speeches delivered at party conferences, at campaign launches, in Parliament, overseas, at town halls and on battleships and battlefields. There is a disproportionate focus on party leaders, reflecting the undeniable reality that in most cases it is party leaders who are given the opportunity to speak on major issues, commanding an audience and attention that no other party figure regularly does. It is the leader who gives the policy speech. It is the leader who is the focus of media attention. It is the leader who sits at the table adjacent to the dispatch box in the House of Representatives. While there are many fine speeches by party members delivered regularly at party branch meetings and at party conferences, it is doubtful that it can be demonstrated they have shaped history. Unfortunately, there are not enough female voices in this book. This is a disappointing but also unavoidable problem, given that few women held prominent leadership positions within the party or held a large number of seats in Parliament until the 1980s. Nevertheless, there are speeches given by Labor's first female parliamentarian, first female minister and first Prime Minister. The focus is on speeches with national political currency, rather than those given by State political figures. However, where a State political figure has made a national contribution, they are represented, such as Ryan, Dunstan and Carr. The time-span reflects the life of the Labor Party – the oldest speech in the book was given in 1891; the most recent in 2011.

Researching, finding and reading literally hundreds of speeches, reaching back more than a century, has been a thrilling and rewarding process. The process of then selecting, re-typing, editing the speeches and also writing the introductions to the speeches, has been arduous and lengthy. This selection of speeches has been informed by extensive research and consultation with leading political scientists, historians, politicians, journalists and commentators, but ultimately reflects my own preferences. Some speeches presented in this book are well known, others less so. Some have been reproduced many times, others less frequently. Several have been unearthed from the archives and deserve a new audience. Naturally, some will disagree with my choices.

* * *

This book is aimed at spotlighting moments in Labor's history, and the nation's history, providing a window into Labor's soul, iterating its purpose, reflecting its vicissitudes and showcasing its achievements through the power of political speech. This anthology is a testament to the power of political speech to make and to shape history and its use as an instrument to achieve what politics is all about: leadership. Stretched end to end like a piano accordion, the speeches in this volume show a remarkable level of continuity in the language used to articulate Labor's vision over time and, indeed, fidelity with Labor's enduring values. The most successful speeches are those given by individuals with a strong anchor of philosophy, values and purpose to power their vision for the nation. It is why the speeches within these pages serve not only as signposts in our history, but, more importantly, provide inspiration to those dedicated to the continuing cause of Labor.

It is also why those who believe in the power of political speech, who are inspired, moved and motivated by great speeches, need to defend them. Most speeches today fail to excite and inspire, let alone persuade or interest an audience beyond even the mildest reflex. There are many reasons for this: policy convergence, the risk-adverse nature of modern politics, the lack of really transformative ideas, the media's often trivial reporting of politics and the lack of leadership displayed by our politicians. But above all, most political speeches fail because of their blandness and their propensity towards spin. There is a need to guard against speeches that are nothing but exercises is vacuous obscurantism, whose words and sentences are polluted with empty rhetoric, stripping away any meaning, argument or purpose. Barack Obama's campaign slogan 'Yes we can' and his inauguration rally-cry 'Be the change' are rare examples of short and simple slogans that can be immensely powerful and chime with his larger political messaging. Moreover, they can crystallise the key argument and purpose of a speech in just a few words. (Capturing the essence of a speech in a single line is also a method adopted to title speeches in this book.) But the more common careful, calibrated, pragmatic one-line sound-bites, absent any eloquent and stirring language, or any kind of coherent theme or purpose, and seemingly more attuned to political strategy and tactics, are inevitably dull and pedestrian. These tricks of the trade, harvested from focus groups and polling, serve only to decouple language from meaning. More importantly, they serve no real purpose beyond a headline, at best.

As Churchill once said, 'Words are the only things that last forever'. This book argues that speeches matter and illustrates this belief with examples from history – some well known, some not so much, others excavated from the archives and presented afresh for a contemporary audience. Its purpose is to provide a prism through which to explore the history of the Labor Party and its contribution to Australia. But most of all, the aim of the book is to provide encouragement and inspiration for those who – with faith, hope and courage – continue to serve Labor's cause and to inspire the next generation of true believers.

Under a sunny sky at Wattie Creek, Gough Whitlam bent down and scooped up a handful of red dirt and poured it into Aboriginal elder Vincent Lingiari's hands symbolising the historic transfer of land into traditional ownership.
Source: Newspix

PART 1

Reconciling Australia

GOUGH WHITLAM

'I put into your hands this piece of earth itself'

Gough Whitlam pours the earth into Vincent Lingiari's hands at Wattie Creek

At Wattie Creek, as the sun radiated its warmth from above, Prime Minister Gough Whitlam and Gurindji chief Vincent Lingiari stood together on the red earth under a clear blue sky. Whitlam bent down and scooped up a handful of dirt and then poured it into Lingiari's hand, symbolising the transfer of that land into traditional ownership.

The Wave Hill cattle station in the Northern Territory had been the scene of a protracted pay dispute and disagreements over native title. It was a dispute between the owners of the station and the traditional inhabitants of the land, the Gurindji people, who had established a settlement at Wattie Creek. Eventually, a settlement between the station and the traditional owner was reached.

Whitlam travelled to Wattie Creek to hand over the Crown lease to most of the traditional lands held by the Gurindji people. *The Sydney Morning Herald* reported that a crowd of around 350 people were in attendance, including three former Ministers for Aboriginal Affairs, the then minister, Les Johnson, and the shadow minister, Bob Ellicott.

Whitlam spoke of the Gurindji's 'shared struggle' and 'fight for justice', acknowledged the need 'to redress the injustice and oppression' and pledged 'this act of restitution'. This speech was simple and eloquent in its brevity and poignancy.

Whitlam recalled in his memoir, *The Whitlam Government*, that it was HC 'Nugget' Coombs who suggested Whitlam pour earth through Lingiari's hands. In response to Whitlam's speech and gesture, Lingiari responded, 'We are all mates now'.

'I put into your hands this piece of earth itself'

Wattie Creek, 16 August 1975

Vincent Lingiari and men and women of the Gurindji people.

On this great day, I, Prime Minister of Australia, speak to you on behalf of the Australian people – all those who honour and love this land we live in.

For them I want to say to you:

First, that we congratulate you and those who shared your struggle, on the victory you have achieved nine years after you walked off Wave Hill Station in protest.

I want to acknowledge that we Australians have still much to do to redress the injustice and oppression that has for so long been the lot of black Australians.

I want to promise you that this act of restitution which we perform today will not stand alone – your fight was not for yourselves alone and we are determined that Aboriginal Australians everywhere will be helped by it.

I want to promise that, through their government, the people of Australia will help you in your plans to use this land fruitfully for the Gurindji.

And I want to give back to you formally in Aboriginal and Australian law ownership of this land of your fathers.

Vincent Lingiari, I solemnly hand to you these deeds as proof, in Australian law, that these lands belong to the Gurindji people and I put into your hands part of the earth itself as a sign that this land will be the possession of you and your children forever.

Source: The Whitlam Institute.

PAUL KEATING

'It begins, I think, with that act of recognition'

Paul Keating's landmark speech calling for reconciliation at Redfern Park

The High Court's 1992 Mabo decision asserted that common law recognised indigenous native title where there was a continuous association with the land, overturning the concept of *terra nullius*.

In a nationally televised address on 15 November 1993, Prime Minister Paul Keating outlined the government's legislative response. He spoke of the 'oldest continuous civilisation on earth', their culture and history, and the inherent connection that indigenous people have to the land.

It was the fulfilment of the task that Keating set for himself in this speech a year earlier at Redfern, where he promised to lay 'the basis of a new relationship between indigenous and non-Aboriginal Australians'. Redfern, on the outskirts of Sydney's CBD, is a place of entrenched indigenous disadvantage. Speaking to a predominantly indigenous audience of around 2000 people, Keating outlined his vision of reconciliation. No Australian Prime Minister had ever spoken like this before. Keating acknowledged past wrongs as a way of accepting responsibility for working together to end these injustices.

While media reports of the speech noted its positive reception among indigenous Australians, there was extensive reporting on Keating's acknowledgement of blame for past wrongs. The headline in *The Sydney Morning Herald* said: 'Keating blames racism for Aboriginal suffering'. But a few days later the *Herald* praised the speech for its courage. 'What Mr Keating had to say', it reported, 'should hearten Aborigines and encourage all Australians to face up to their past and to share their future more justly'.

'It begins, I think, with that act of recognition'

Redfern Park, 10 December 1992

Ladies and gentlemen,

I am very pleased to be here today at the launch of Australia's celebration of the 1993 International Year of the World's Indigenous People. It will be a year of great significance for Australia.

It comes at a time when we have committed ourselves to succeeding in the test which so far we have always failed. Because, in truth, we cannot confidently say that we have succeeded as we would like to have succeeded if we have not managed to extend opportunity and care, dignity and hope to the indigenous people of Australia – the Aboriginal and Torres Strait Island people.

This is a fundamental test of our social goals and our national will: our ability to say to ourselves and the rest of the world that Australia is a first rate social democracy, that we are what we should be – truly the land of the fair go and the better chance.

There is no more basic test of how seriously we mean these things. It is a test of our self-knowledge. Of how well we know the land we live in. How well we know our history. How well we recognise the fact that, complex as our contemporary identity is, it cannot be separated from Aboriginal Australia. How well we know what Aboriginal Australians know about Australia.

Redfern is a good place to contemplate these things. Just a mile or two from the place where the first European settlers landed, in too many ways it tells us that their failure to bring much more than devastation and demoralisation to Aboriginal Australia continues to be our failure.

More I think than most Australians recognise, the plight of Aboriginal Australians affects us all. In Redfern it might be tempting to think that the reality Aboriginal Australians face is somehow contained here, and that the rest of us are insulated from it. But of course, while all the dilemmas may exist here, they are far from contained. We know the same dilemmas and more are faced all over Australia.

That is perhaps the point of this Year of the World's Indigenous People: to bring the dispossessed out of the shadows, to recognise that they are part of us, and that we cannot give indigenous Australians up without giving up many of our own most deeply held values, much of our own identity – and our own humanity.

Nowhere in the world, I would venture, is the message more stark than it is in Australia. We simply cannot sweep injustice aside. Even if our own conscience allowed us to, I am sure, that in due course, the world and the people of our region would not. There should be no mistake about this – our success in resolving these issues will have a significant bearing on our standing in the world.

However intractable the problems seem, we cannot resign ourselves to failure – any more than we can hide behind the contemporary version of Social Darwinism which says that to reach back for the poor and dispossessed is to risk being dragged down. That seems to me not only morally indefensible, but bad history.

We non-Aboriginal Australians should perhaps remind ourselves that Australia once reached out for us. Didn't Australia provide opportunity and care for the dispossessed Irish? The poor of Britain? The refugees from war and famine and persecution in the countries of Europe and Asia?

Isn't it reasonable to say that if we can build a prosperous and remarkably harmonious multicultural society in Australia, surely we can find just solutions to the problems which beset the first Australians – the people to whom the most injustice has been done?

And, as I say, the starting point might be to recognise that the problem starts with us non-Aboriginal Australians. It begins, I think, with that act of recognition. Recognition that it was we who did the dispossessing. We took the traditional lands and smashed the traditional way of life. We brought the diseases. The alcohol. We committed the murders. We took the children from their mothers. We practised discrimination and exclusion. It was our ignorance and our prejudice. And our failure to imagine these things being done to us.

With some noble exceptions, we failed to make the most basic human response and enter into their hearts and minds. We failed to ask – how would I feel if this were done to me? As a consequence, we failed to see that what we were doing degraded all of us …

Down the years, there has been no shortage of guilt, but it has not produced the responses we need. Guilt is not a very constructive emotion. I think what we need to do is open our hearts a bit. All of us.

Perhaps when we recognise what we have in common we will see the things which must be done – the practical things … If we improve the living conditions in one town, they will improve in another. And another. If we raise the standard of health by twenty per cent one year, it will be raised more the next. If we open one door others will follow. When we see improvement, when we see more dignity, more confidence, more happiness – we will know we are going to win. We need these practical building blocks of change.

The Mabo judgement should be seen as one of these. By doing away with the bizarre conceit that this continent had no owners prior to the settlement of Europeans, Mabo establishes a fundamental truth and lays the basis for justice. It will be much easier to work from that basis than has ever been the case in the past. For that reason alone we should ignore the isolated outbreaks of hysteria and hostility of the past few months.

Mabo is an historic decision – we can make it an historic turning point, the basis of a new relationship between indigenous and non-Aboriginal Australians. The message should be that there is nothing to fear or to lose in the recognition of historical truth, or the extension of social justice, or the deepening of Australian social democracy to include indigenous Australians. There is everything to gain.

Even the unhappy past speaks for this. Where Aboriginal Australians have been included in the life of Australia they have made remarkable contributions. Economic contributions, particularly in the pastoral and agricultural industry. They are there in the frontier and exploration history of Australia. They are there in the wars. In sport to an extraordinary degree. In literature and art and music.

In all these things they have shaped our knowledge of this continent and of ourselves. They have shaped our identity. They are there in the Australian legend. We should never forget – they have helped build this nation …

It seems to me that if we can imagine the injustice we can imagine its opposite. And we can have justice. I say that for two reasons: I say it because I believe that the great things about Australian social democracy reflect a fundamental belief in justice.

And I say it because in so many other areas we have proved our capacity over the years to go on extending the realms of participation, opportunity and care.

Just as Australians living in the relatively narrow and insular Australia of the 1960s imagined a culturally diverse, worldly and open Australia, and in a generation turned the idea into reality, so we can turn the goals of reconciliation into reality.

There are very good signs that the process has begun … this generation of Australians is better informed about Aboriginal culture and achievement, and about the injustice that has been done, than any generation before … I think we are beginning to see how much we owe the indigenous Australians and how much we have lost by living so apart …

There is one thing today we cannot imagine. We cannot imagine that the descendants of people whose genius and resilience maintained a culture here through fifty thousand years or more, through cataclysmic changes to the climate and environment, and who then survived two centuries of dispossession and abuse, will be denied their place in the modern Australian nation.

We cannot imagine that. We cannot imagine that we will fail. And with the spirit that is here today I am confident that we won't. I am confident that we will succeed in this decade.

Source: <www.keating.org.au>.

Paul Keating, just a year into his prime ministership, delivers his landmark speech on the importance of reconciliation to a predominantly indigenous audience at Redfern Park in 1992. No Prime Minister had ever spoken about this issue so eloquently or so movingly as Keating did on this day.
Source: Fairfax

PAUL KEATING

'An opportunity to right an historic wrong'

Paul Keating announces to the nation the legislative repsonse to the High Court's Mabo judgement

In response to the High Court's historic *Mabo* decision, which recognised native title in common law, the Keating Government set out to provide a legislative framework to give practical expression to the decision in Commonwealth law.

After months of negotiation and the longest Senate debate in the history of the Parliament, Prime Minister Paul Keating was able to negotiate and secure the passage of legislation which fulfilled this objective. It was a response that won widespread support from many indigenous Australians, key farming groups and all of the States, except Western Australia.

In this nationally televised address, Keating outlined the *Mabo* judgment and the legislative response of his government. He spoke movingly of indigenous culture and history. Recognising that 'this generation cannot be held responsible for the cruelty of previous generations', he called for a 'fair go' for indigenous Australians. 'To ignore Mabo', he said, 'would be the final cruelty, and we would be held responsible – by the world and by future generations of Australians'.

Writing in *The Sydney Morning Herald*, Geoff Kitney praised the 'strong logic in the arguments' used and in 'the simple, direct explanation of why Mabo is important and why a national response to it is essential'.

'An opportunity to right an historic wrong'

Broadcast to the Nation, Canberra 15 November 1993

When the High Court of Australia handed down the Mabo judgement last year, it set our generation of Australians a great challenge.

The Court's decision was unquestionably just.

It rejected a lie and acknowledged a truth.

The lie was terra nullius – the convenient fiction that Australia had been a land of no one.

The truth was native title – the fact that the land had once belonged to Aboriginal and Torres Strait Islander Australians and that in some places a legal right to it had survived the 200 years of European settlement.

So here was an issue the country could not ignore – either legally, or morally.

There was another form of title that had to become part of the way we manage land in Australia.

We owe it to Aboriginal Australians, to all Australians, we owe it to our fair and democratic traditions and to future generations of Australians – to recognise this native title.

Tonight we are within reach of an enlightened, practical response to Mabo

This week, I will be proposing legislation to Parliament which meets both the spirit of the High Court's decision and Australia's responsibilities and needs.

The Bill will necessarily be complex, but this evening I want to cut through the complexity to some of its simple principles.

First we need to get the background straight.

Over tens of thousands of years Aboriginal people had developed a complex culture built on a profound attachment to the land.

The land nourished them spiritually as well as materially. In the landscape and the life upon it they saw evidence of the epoch of creation.

Down through the generations they passed on laws, customs, traditions and ceremonies reflecting an obligation to care for the land which went to the heart of their society.

Yet this most remarkable fact about Australia – this oldest continuous civilisation on earth – has until now been denied by Australian law.

The first European settlers declared that the land had belonged to no-one and the indigenous Australians were shunted aside, often with appalling brutality.

Much of the despair and degradation, conflict and disease, and many of the problems which Aboriginal Australians face today are a consequence of this dispossession.

We have no need – nor any use – for guilt. This generation cannot be held responsible for the cruelty of previous generations.

But to ignore Mabo would be the final cruelty, and we would be held responsible – by the world and by future generations of Australians …

There is much in Australian history of which we can be tremendously proud – for here in Australia we have created a modern, tolerant, free, prosperous and democratic society.

But we must understand that Australia's success has had a price – and surely the highest price has been paid by Aboriginal and Torres Strait Islander Australians.

They often paid with their lives; with their rights, their dignity and happiness; with their land.

When the connection to the land was broken, their society and economy was devastated.

But the connection was not broken everywhere – and it is a testament to the tenacity and resilience of Aboriginal Australians that so much of the culture - so much of the Aboriginal story – has been passed on through generations down to this day.

In 1982, Eddie Mabo and four others began action seeking a legal declaration of their traditional land rights in the Murray islands of the Torres Strait.

Ten years later on 3 June 1992, the High Court decided that his people were entitled as against the whole of the world to possession – and I emphasise 'possession' – occupation, use and enjoyment of these lands.

Thus the High Court of Australia recognised native title – and Aboriginal custom and tradition as a source of Australian common law.

The Court accepted that native title existed where two fundamental conditions were met:

- that their connection with the land had been maintained, unbroken down through the years
- and that this title had not been overturned by any action of a government to use the land or to give it to somebody else.

It is probably only where there is so-called vacant Crown Land, and in remote areas where traditional Aboriginal life has not been disrupted, that native title exists.

Nevertheless, the High Court's decision posed many questions …

From the outset the Government recognised that these uncertainties needed to be faced: the Court had made its decision but there was not the body of administration and law to give effect to it.

From late last year the Government has been developing a framework for such a law and discussing the principles on which it would be based – the first of these principles being justice for indigenous Australians.

What sort of country would we be – how could we claim respect for the law – if, after the highest court in the land has recognised native title, we deny it?

How could we say that we stand for a fair go if we were to wipe away a title to land which has lasted through thousands of years of occupation of the continent and 200 years of European settlement?

How could we explain it to Aboriginal Australians? How could we explain it to the world?

To deny the High Court decision, to deny native title in Australian common law would deny justice: for it would deny indigenous Australians rights to land enjoyed by other Australians.

And the result could only be antagonism – courtroom battles and uncertainty in the community and in industry.

There is no decent or practical option but to recognise the High Court decision and make it work.

Which brings me to the second of our objectives.

We must maintain a system of land management in Australia which provides clear and predictable rules; security and certainty for people who hold land; and a capacity for dealings in land to proceed effectively.

So it must be an efficient system of land management, but it must also be fair.

The legislation which we will introduce this week will accomplish these objectives.

It will enable us to determine who has native title, where, and the rights involved.

It will give Aboriginal people holding native title the right to negotiate about actions affecting their land – a right, but not a veto.

It will permit governments to step in and decide, in the final analysis, whether an important economic project should proceed.

It will have the Commonwealth government play its proper role in setting clear rules and standards for dealings which affect native title, but leave land management to State and Territory governments if they accept the national standards.

It will set up a system of courts and tribunals, in effect as an umpire on matters of native title.

It will, to the extent practicable, preserve native title from extinguishment, and where it is extinguished, ensure just compensation, and it will provide security, so that no one who owns a home, a farm, a mine, a tourist operation – no one – need have concern about their tenure.

No one group will get all they want from this legislation – not Aboriginal people, not industry, not governments.

But the national interest will be served, and only the Commonwealth legislation is capable of serving it ...

There is only one way to provide certainty – and that is with a single, uniform, national approach, a fair and predictable set of rules which everyone can work with.

This is not just my view, it is the view of seven out of our eight States and Territories, all of whom believe this legislation can work.

With the challenge of Mabo effectively met – with native title efficiently brought within our land management system, we can move on.

We can move on to see Mabo as a tremendous opportunity it is.

An opportunity to right an historic wrong.

An opportunity to transcend the history of dispossession.

An opportunity to restore the age-old link between Aboriginal land and culture.

An opportunity to heal a source of bitterness.

An opportunity to recognise Aboriginal culture as a defining element of our nationhood and culture.

And to make clear that this Australia, this modern, free and tolerant Australia can be a secure and bountiful place for all – including the first Australians.

Source: Author's personal files.

As NSW Premier, Bob Carr delivered the first apology from a head of government to the stolen generations of Aboriginal Australians. In this speech he recognised that for there to be true reconciliation 'there must be an acknowledgement of a great wrong'. It would take another decade for a national government to deliver an apology.
Source: Australian Labor Party (NSW Branch)

BOB CARR

'The right to belong'

Bob Carr delivers the first government apology to the stolen generations

NSW Premier Bob Carr was the first head of government in Australia to apologise to Aboriginal Australians for past wrongs, including the forced separation of children from their families.

In this speech, following a formal motion supporting reconciliation, he referred to the 'systematic annihilation of Aboriginal communities' and recognised that 'if there is to be reconciliation with justice, there must be an acknowledgement of a great wrong'.

Carr emphasised the need for true and lasting reconciliation to come from Aboriginal and non-Aboriginal Australians from all walks of life and from all parts of New South Wales. He called this 'a thousand points of light that contradict the negativism and hostility that comes from some'. He concluded by recognising that everybody has 'the right to belong to Australia with full dignity, worth, equality and justice'.

Other State parliaments would follow, including those with conservative governments. Nationally, Prime Minister John Howard was unmoved by the bipartisan generosity and humanity all over Australia. It would not be until 2008 that a national government would also apologise and, in so doing, set the basis for lasting reconciliation.

'The right to belong'

NSW Legislative Assembly, Sydney 14 November 1996

In his landmark oration, the inaugural Vincent Lingiari Lecture in Darwin on 22 August, the Governor-General of Australia, Sir William Deane, called upon the parliaments of Australia to affirm their support for true national reconciliation by passing formal resolutions expressing that support … It is altogether fitting that the Parliament of New South Wales should be among the first to respond. The senior Australian Parliament should always give leadership on great national issues.

It is important too that we recognise not only that the dispossession of Aboriginal people began here in 1788 but that this Parliament enacted laws which carried on the systematic annihilation of Aboriginal communities …

The basis of the current divisive debate originated in the false and ignorant assertion that Aboriginal Australians are a privileged group. That laughable claim can be quickly dismissed. The fact is they are the most underprivileged group in Australian society. Recognition of the true facts, the hard realities, is essential to reconciliation …

If there is to be reconciliation with justice, there must be an acknowledgment of a great wrong – something beyond the havoc wrought by the impact of our civilisation upon a people who had nurtured this continent for more than 50,000 years before 1788; something beyond the history of dispossession, disease, and disruption and the relegation of Aboriginal people to mere fringe dwellers in their own land.

I refer to the fundamental denial of Aboriginal identity – the pervasive assumption that Aboriginal culture, customs, languages, beliefs and traditions were worthless. That denial permeated policies and laws passed by this Parliament over more than a century. It was the ultimate dispossession: to rob a people of the value of their identity. There could be no greater wrong than that. For two-thirds of this century that denial was enshrined in the Australian Constitution. Section 127 of the Constitution stated:

> In reckoning the numbers of the people of the Commonwealth, or of a State or other part of the Commonwealth, Aboriginal natives shall not be counted.

It was the constitutional counterpart of the legal concept of terra nullius. The Constitution said that the Aborigines were not to be counted, and the law said that they did not inhabit the land. As the High Court ruled in its Mabo judgment, that was 'a travesty of fact and a fallacy of law'. True it is that this section was dropped after the 1967 referendum, together with the provision which prevented the Federal Parliament making laws relating to Aborigines. But attitudes based on the idea that Aborigines did not count as Australians persist. They remain a barrier against reconciliation. It is part of our job to challenge those attitudes wherever they exist.

The denial of Aboriginal worth and Aboriginal values found its ultimate expression in the destruction of Aboriginal families. That course was pursued as a matter of ill-conceived government policy in this State and in the rest of Australia for much of this century. That treatment resulted in generations of Aboriginal children being removed from their mothers and fathers, brothers and sisters, and communities. Even as late as December 1965, this Parliament passed an adoption Act which allowed Aboriginal children to be taken from their natural families without parental consent. Like most legislation of that kind, going back to the notorious Aborigines Protection Bill of 1915, it received bipartisan support.

Honourable members will know that the Human Rights and Equal Opportunity Commission is completing its national inquiry into the separation of Aboriginal and Torres Strait Islander children from their families. My government has assisted that inquiry by making a very full and frank submission … The submission brings together for the first time the laws, procedures and regulations by which Aboriginal children were separated from their families and communities, and were systematically stripped of their family and community identity. It is an unflinchingly honest account of policies that resulted in thousands of families being separated for no reason other than that they were Aborigines.

They are the stolen children of lost generations – and it was all done in the name of the State and in the name of this Parliament. That is why I reaffirm in this place, formally and solemnly as Premier on behalf of the government and people of New South Wales, our apology to the Aboriginal people. I invite the House to join with me in that apology.

In doing so, I acknowledge with deep regret Parliament's own role in endorsing the policies and actions of successive governments which devastated Aboriginal communities and inflicted, and continue to inflict, grief and suffering upon Aboriginal families and communities. I extend this apology as an essential step in the process of reconciliation …

Whatever we do in this Parliament, reconciliation will come through the people themselves, Aboriginal and non-Aboriginal Australians. There is, I believe, growing support for reconciliation all over New South Wales – a thousand points of light that contradict the negativism and hostility that comes from some. Ordinary men and women of all ages, of different ethnic backgrounds and of many occupations are coming to realise that there needs to be understanding and acceptance of the past before we can shape a better future …

The study of the past, not only of the past 200 years but our increasing knowledge and respect for the Aboriginal achievement over 50 millennia, teaches us important lessons. What stands out for me from this history is the persistence, perseverance, and resilience of the Aboriginal people – a brave and hardy people …

We should be under no illusions. If Australia continues to allow Aboriginal people to suffer the world's highest infant mortality and one of the world's lowest life expectancies, if Australia back-tracks on the Mabo legislation, if Australia side-tracks the recommendations of the Royal Commission into Aboriginal Deaths in Custody, we will find ourselves as a nation before the International Court of Justice …

The claim that the Aboriginal people make on Australia is no more and no less than the claim that we Australians of the fifth or first generation make for ourselves. That claim is the right to belong to Australia with full dignity, worth, equality and justice. I repeat that there can be no true reconciliation without justice.

Source: NSW Legislative Assembly Debates (Hansard).

KIM BEAZLEY

'To render justice and restitution'

Kim Beazley's response to the Bringing Them Home report

On 27 May 1997, the *Bringing Them Home* report, detailing the forced separation of Aboriginal children from their families, was tabled in the Commonwealth Parliament. Prime Minister John Howard expressed his personal sorrow but refused to apologise for past wrongs.

During Question Time the next day, Labor leader Kim Beazley moved a motion of apology and reconciliation. As Beazley spoke to the motion, Howard 'shooed from the chamber his backbenchers', *The Sydney Morning Howard* reported. The only government member to speak on the motion was Peter Reith. Debate lasted 31 minutes. The motion was lost 83-46.

Beazley spoke movingly with great emotion and feeling about the need for reconciliation and an acknowledgement of past wrongs.

Via correspondence with Beazley in Washington DC in mid-2010, he said, 'Without doubt it is the experiences of our indigenous population since European settlement which constitute the most singular blight on our national conscience'. He praised Kevin Rudd's historic apology in 2008 as 'without doubt the finest statement by the Rudd Government'.

Beazley acknowledged that he 'briefly broke down in making' the speech. He said, 'part of that was a product of missing out on sleep reading Ron Wilson's report. The premier reason was the content of the report itself. No-one reading it could fail to be moved by its content, written though it was with the cool judgement of a first-rate judicial professional'. He said, 'the stories it detailed would break anyone's heart'.

It was Beazley at his best, demonstrating empathy and leadership at a time when the Prime Minister of the day had failed to do so.

'To render justice and restitution'

The House of Representatives, Canberra 28 May 1997

I move … that:

(a) recalling the Australian people's overwhelming decision in the 1967 referendum to confer upon the Commonwealth Parliament responsibility for enhancement of the rights and well being of Aboriginal and Torres Strait Islander people;

(b) reaffirming the abhorrence of racism shared by the Australian people and their Federal and State governments;

(c) reaffirming Australia's recognition of the Universal Declaration of Human Rights, the International Convention on the Prevention and Punishment of the Crime of Genocide and the International Convention on the Prevention of All Forms of Racial Discrimination;

(d) recalling the Parliament's commitment in October 1996 to the principles of racial tolerance; and

(e) recognising the profound economic and social disadvantage suffered by Aboriginal and Torres Strait Islander people –

This House:

(1) affirms that the tabling of *Bringing Them Home*, the Report of the National Inquiry into the Separation of Aboriginal and Torres Strait Islander Children from their Families, presents the nation with an unprecedented historical opportunity to render justice and restitution to Indigenous Australians, for the good of all Australians;

(2) acknowledges the immense trauma inflicted upon the Aboriginal and Torres Strait Islander peoples of Australia as a result of the separation of Aboriginal and Torres Strait Islander children from their families under past government policies in place from before the time of Federation until the early 1900s;

(3) affirms that the racially discriminatory policies and their continuing consequences are a matter of national shame;

(4) affirms that current future and Federal and State governments are responsible for assisting Aboriginal and Torres Strait Islander people to rectify the ongoing effects of those policies;

(5) affirms its commitment to a just and proper settlement of the grievances of people adversely affected by those policies; and

on behalf of the nation –

(6) unreservedly apologises to Aboriginal and Torres Strait Islander Australians for the separation policies;

(7) calls upon Federal and State governments to establish, in consultation with Aboriginal and Torres Islander community, appropriate processes to provide compensation and restitution, including assistance for the reunification of families and counselling services;

(8) calls on the Federal Government and State governments to establish appropriate education programs to enhance community awareness of the history and continuing consequences of past practices and policies of racial discrimination; and

(9) calls upon the Federal Government to declare a National Day in recognition and remembrance of the great suffering which flowed from the separation policies, and to affirm our nation's commitment to justice for Indigenous Australians, today and for the future.

The motion which I read to the House earlier on is a motion which is a direct response to the issues made in the *Bringing Them Home* report …

The speech that I want to make here today is not about apportioning blame in politics. I do not want to do that, nor to claim that there is some special position in relation to the Australian Labor Party that applies to us and not to other people …

As I read through that report, the materials contained within it refer to operations that occurred when the Labor Party was in office. For those things that we are responsible for, I apologise, as Leader of the Australian Labor Party.

This is a terrible, terrible record. This record does not deal with the experience of Aboriginals in their good-hearted homes with kindly foster parents … Many very decent people took up that fostering status, and they did so without maliciousness and with the very best intentions. This report is not really about them …

It does refer to them of course in the context of the extent to which those people nevertheless, without knowing it, were implicated in a deculturalisation of a race, with all the loss of identity that flowed from that and the extraordinary difficulties that they confronted. However, what the report does detail is very different experiences, experiences of viciousness of extraordinary dimensions – experience of sexual assault, of physical assault, of overt pressured propagandisation.

This is not a matter that we can sweep under this table. This is not a matter that we can stand aside from. This is not a matter about which I direct blame at this government. It is not a matter about which I would believe that I am in any moral position to do so, and that is not what my intention is here today.

My intention is to try to provide this parliament with an opportunity that the Western Australian parliament, under Richard Court – of all people – and the South Australian parliament, under John Olsen, took without any blush, without any concern for their reputations and without any worry about what might be the legal implications of what they said. They decided that they would stand in their parliaments and apologise; they would stand in their parliaments and make a statement about what their intentions were. This is what we believed that we would have an opportunity to discuss here today. We have not.

I raised a question earlier on: the question of compensation for the situation in which the Aboriginal people of this country found themselves. The question of compensation is a question which governments consider repeatedly. They consider it in relation to people who have committed acts, either whilst in government or in private organisations, without any maliciousness at all ... Why should not the Aboriginal people of this nation be accorded equality? ...

I was going to read some of these cases, but I cannot. I was up pretty late going through it – and this would have been a better speech if I had not ...

The easy way is to allow a motion to proceed to make the first step of restitution: that is the apology ... The second part ... is for the Commonwealth to engage the states in a conversation as to how they will handle it. The third part ... is an opportunity not to do the compensation on budget, but to draw down from it from time to time. The fourth part ... is to get a formula in place, as suggested at length in this report, whereby, for various types of problems, people's situations are assessed and dealt with. That is the easy way.

The hard way is this: ignore it and let those compensation cases roll through the court with every piece of disturbance in race relations in this country that follows as, one after another, the courts compensate Aboriginal people for the wrongs done them. That is the hard way; it is the divisive way in this community.

I urge the Prime Minister (John Howard) to seize this opportunity now and to take the easy way for all of us, and to reach a conclusion on this that will ensure that this parliament performs its responsibilities for an apology, and that this parliament performs its responsibilities for restitution.

It is a situation that lies in his hands and cries out for leadership – he must provide it.

Source: Commonwealth of Australia Parliamentary Debates (Hansard).

KEVIN RUDD

'We say sorry'

Kevin Rudd's historic apology to Australia's indigenous peoples

In this historic speech, Prime Minister Kevin Rudd delivered a formal apology to Australia's indigenous peoples.

In Opposition, Rudd committed himself to delivering an apology if he became Prime Minister. But when he came to office in 2007, Rudd said in an interview for this book that he was advised by 'the political smart class around town' that to deliver an apology 'was very dangerous'. If he persisted, he was told 'don't overdo it' and 'get it done quickly and 'get it over with'. By 'political smart class', Rudd says he was referring to Labor figures in government and in the party organisation. Rudd says he had 'no idea whatsoever what its political impact would be – none – positive or negative'. But he did think 'it would be, on balance, negative'.

'When I sat down to write the speech', Rudd said in an October 2010 interview, 'I had serious writers block'. None of the ideas suggested by staff and others 'captured my imagination'. It was a visit with a member of the Stolen Generation, Nanna Fejo, which helped Rudd 'achieve the empathy' needed to write the speech. Rudd said that he was still writing at 3 am on the morning of the speech. Although up again at 7 am to continue writing, he was still dictating the conclusion of the speech, only minutes before he was due to speak.

The speech took place on the first parliamentary sitting day of the new government. The galleries of the House of Representatives were full. On the lawns of Parliament House, and countless other public areas around the nation, millions were watching. Members of the Stolen Generations were seated in the chamber. Also present were former Prime Ministers Gough Whitlam, Malcolm Fraser, Bob Hawke and Paul Keating. John Howard was absent, along with several other coalition Members of Parliament. Rudd says Howard's absence was 'sad'.

For most Australians, as Keating said, it was 'a day of open hearts'. Whitlam said the speech was 'greatly conceived, greatly phrased and greatly delivered'. It was Rudd's finest moment as Prime Minister.

'We say sorry'

The House of Representatives, Canberra 13 February 2008

I move:

That today we honour the indigenous peoples of this land, the oldest continuing cultures in human history.

We reflect on their past mistreatment.

We reflect in particular on the mistreatment of those who were Stolen Generations – this blemished chapter in our nation's history.

The time has now come for the nation to turn a new page in Australia's history by righting the wrongs of the past and so moving forward with confidence to the future.

We apologise for the laws and policies of successive parliaments and governments that have inflicted profound grief, suffering and loss on these our fellow Australians.

We apologise especially for the removal of Aboriginal and Torres Strait Islander children from their families, their communities and their country.

For the pain, suffering and hurt of these Stolen Generations, their descendants and for their families left behind, we say sorry.

To the mothers and the fathers, the brothers and the sisters, for the breaking up of families and communities, we say sorry.

And for the indignity and degradation thus inflicted on a proud people and a proud culture, we say sorry.

We the Parliament of Australia respectfully request that this apology be received in the spirit in which it is offered as part of the healing of the nation.

For the future we take heart; resolving that this new page in the history of our great continent can now be written.

We today take this first step by acknowledging the past and laying claim to a future that embraces all Australians.

A future where this Parliament resolves that the injustices of the past must never, never happen again.

A future where we harness the determination of all Australians, indigenous and non-indigenous, to close the gap that lies between us in life expectancy, educational achievement and economic opportunity.

A future where we embrace the possibility of new solutions to enduring problems where old approaches have failed.

A future based on mutual respect, mutual resolve and mutual responsibility.

A future where all Australians, whatever their origins, are truly equal partners, with equal opportunities and with an equal stake in shaping the next chapter in the history of this great country, Australia.

There comes a time in the history of nations when their peoples must become fully reconciled to their past if they are to go forward with confidence to embrace their future. Our nation, Australia, has reached such a time.

And that is why the parliament is today here assembled: to deal with this unfinished business of the nation, to remove a great stain from the nation's soul and, in a true spirit of reconciliation, to open a new chapter in the history of this great land, Australia.

Last year I made a commitment to the Australian people that if we formed the next government of the Commonwealth we would in parliament say sorry to the Stolen Generations. Today I honour that commitment …

Some have asked, 'Why apologise?' Let me begin to answer by telling the parliament just a little of one person's story – an elegant, eloquent and wonderful woman in her 80s, full of life, full of funny stories, despite what has happened in her life's journey …

Nungala Fejo, as she prefers to be called, was born in the late 1920s. She remembers her earliest childhood days living with her family and her community in a bush camp just outside Tennant Creek … sometime around 1932, when she was about four, she remembers the coming of the welfare men. Her family had feared that day and had dug holes in the creek bank where the children could run and hide … The kids were found; they ran for their mothers, screaming, but they could not get away. They were herded and piled onto the back of the truck. Tears flowing, her mum tried clinging to the sides of the truck as her children were taken away to the Bungalow in Alice, all in the name of protection.

A few years later, government policy changed. Now the children would be handed over to the missions to be cared for by the churches … She and her sister were sent to a Methodist mission on Goulburn Island and then Croker Island. Her Catholic brother was sent to work at a cattle station and her cousin to a Catholic mission … She stayed at the mission until after the war, when she was allowed to leave for a prearranged job as a domestic in Darwin. She was 16. Nanna Fejo never saw her mum again …

The stockman had found her again decades later, this time himself to say, 'Sorry'. And remarkably, extraordinarily, she had forgiven him.

Nanna Fejo's is just one story. There are thousands, tens of thousands of them …

The hurt, the humiliation, the degradation and the sheer brutality of the act of physically separating a mother from her children is a deep assault on our senses and on our most elemental humanity.

These stories cry out to be heard; they cry out for an apology. Instead, from the nation's parliament there has been a stony and stubborn and deafening silence for more than a decade … But, as of today, the time for denial, the time for delay, has at last come to an end … Decency, human decency, universal human decency, demands that the nation now steps forward to right a historical wrong …

Let the parliament reflect for a moment on the following facts: that, between 1910 and 1970, between 10 and 30 per cent of indigenous children were forcibly taken from their mothers and fathers. That, as a result, up to 50,000 children were forcibly taken from their families. That this was the product of the deliberate, calculated policies of the state as reflected in the explicit powers given to them under statute …

But we must acknowledge these facts if we are to deal once and for all with the argument that the policy of generic forced separation was somehow well motivated, justified by its historical context and, as a result, unworthy of any apology today.

Then we come to the argument of intergenerational responsibility, also used by some to argue against giving an apology today. But let us remember the fact that the forced removal of Aboriginal children was happening as late as the early 1970s …

There is a further reason for an apology as well: it is that reconciliation is in fact an expression of a core value of our nation — and that value is a fair go for all …

As has been said of settler societies elsewhere, we are the bearers of many blessings from our ancestors and therefore we must also be the bearer of their burdens as well …

This is not, as some would argue, a black-armband view of history; it is just the truth: the cold, confronting, uncomfortable truth … And until we fully confront that truth, there will always be a shadow hanging over us and our future as a fully united and fully reconciled people.

It is time to reconcile. It is time to recognise the injustices of the past. It is time to say sorry. It is time to move forward together.

To the Stolen Generations, I say the following: as Prime Minister of Australia, I am sorry. On behalf of the Government of Australia, I am sorry. On behalf of the Parliament of Australia, I am sorry.

And I offer you this apology without qualification. We apologise for the hurt, the pain and suffering we, the parliament, have caused you by the laws that previous parliaments have enacted. We apologise for the indignity, the degradation and the humiliation these laws embodied. We offer this apology to the mothers, the fathers, the brothers, the sisters, the families and the communities whose lives were ripped apart by the actions of successive governments under successive parliaments …

I know that, in offering this apology on behalf of the government and the parliament, there is nothing I can say today that can take away the pain you have suffered personally. Whatever words I speak today, I cannot undo that …

I say to non-indigenous Australians listening today who may not fully understand why what we are doing is so important, I ask those non-indigenous Australians to imagine for a moment if this had happened to you …

Today's apology, however inadequate, is aimed at righting past wrongs. It is also aimed at building a bridge between indigenous and non-indigenous Australians – a bridge based on a real respect rather than a thinly veiled contempt.

Our challenge for the future is now to cross that bridge and, in so doing, embrace a new partnership between indigenous and non-indigenous Australians … the core of this partnership for the future is to closing the gap between indigenous and non-indigenous Australians on life expectancy, educational achievement and employment opportunities …

The nation is calling on us, the politicians, to move beyond our infantile bickering, our point-scoring and our mindlessly partisan politics and elevate at least this one core area of national responsibility to a rare position beyond the partisan divide. Surely this is the spirit, the unfulfilled spirit, of the 1967 referendum …

Today the parliament has come together to right a great wrong. We have come together to deal with the past so that we might fully embrace the future. And we have had sufficient audacity of faith to advance a pathway to that future, with arms extended rather than with fists still clenched.

So let us seize the day. Let it not become a moment of mere sentimental reflection. Let us take it with both hands and allow this day, this day of national reconciliation, to become one of those rare moments in which we might just be able to transform the way in which the nation thinks about itself, whereby the injustice administered to these Stolen Generations in the name of these, our parliaments, causes all of us to reappraise, at the deepest level of our beliefs, the real possibility of reconciliation writ large …

So let us turn this page together: indigenous and non-indigenous Australians, government and opposition, Commonwealth and State, and write this new chapter in our nation's story together. First Australians, First Fleeters, and those who first took the Oath of Allegiance just a few weeks ago. Let's grasp this opportunity to craft a new future for this great land: Australia.

Source: Commonwealth of Australia Parliamentary Debates (Hansard).

Outside the Redfern Community Centre in Sydney, Australians watch Kevin Rudd deliver the historic apology speech to the stolen generations of Aboriginal Australians which laid the basis for genuine reconciliation.

Source: National Library of Australia

PART 2

Reform, Progress and the Future

JOHN (CHRIS) WATSON

'For the benefit of the whole of the people of Australia'

Labor's first leader, Chris Watson, outlines the policies
of the first national Labor Government

Soon after being sworn in as Australia's youngest Prime Minister at age 37, John (Chris) Watson addressed the Parliament on 'the intentions of the government'.

In this speech, Watson outlines a range of policy measures that his government would seek to legislate. They reflected the aims and ideals of the party since the 1890s, but refined in more recent times under Watson's leadership of the parliamentary party. He addresses a range of issues from industrial relations to social policy and foreign policy. Many would be fulfilled under future governments, as Watson's government was to be short-lived. The speech was 'received with loud cheers', *The Sydney Morning Herald* reported.

Although out of office within months, Watson continued to give voice to the vision and values of the early Labor Party. At the Melbourne Trades Hall in September 1904, *The Age* reported that Watson said the party 'had engendered in the minds of the people the belief that something could be done, through legitimate and peaceful methods, to alter their position for the better, and to improve the prospects for those who would come after us'. He said that Labor's policies 'tend in the direction of socialism' but urged moderation and gradualism in Labor's methods. Speaking to a large gathering at the School of Arts in North Sydney in April 1906, Watson said Labor stood for practical socialism, subscribed to the collective 'school of economics' as it was 'more humane', and 'offered a doctrine of hope to the people', *The Daily Telegraph* reported.

This is the first major speech by a Labor Prime Minister outlining the vision of a reforming and progressive Labor government.

'For the benefit of the whole of the people of Australia'

The view we take is that we should submit a practical program – a list of measures which we have a reasonable expectation of passing during the time at our disposal …

For immediate work we propose to resume the discussion upon the Conciliation and Arbitration Bill at the point at which it was dropped by the last administration a few weeks back. We are in agreement with the members of the last administration so far as the general principle involved in the measure is concerned; that is, we believe in a measure providing for compulsory arbitration, as distinguished from any substitute put forward in either State or federal politics for voluntary arbitration …

We propose to bring within the scope of the Bill, first, the railway servants of the States, and, secondly, all other servants of the Commonwealth or of the States who are engaged in industrial enterprises carried on by those governments …

Another proposal is to introduce, as the first measure in the Senate, a Federal Capital Sites Bill … I believe that a settlement of the question will tend to encourage the growth of a larger and broader national feeling than that which has hitherto existed in regard to federal politics … We should first, I think, adopt a definite design, which would leave room for no mistake that could be foreseen by human prescience, and which would permit eventually of grand and noble edifices being erected, which would do credit to, and be worthy of Australia …

Another measure which we intend to introduce is the Trade Marks Bill … I have always regarded the federalisation of trades marks as a necessary corollary of the patent law, and I think that under federal administration such legislation should involve very little extra expense …

The next Bill with which we propose to deal is that relative to the appointment of a High Commissioner in London … such an officer would be appointed to voice in a distinct way the feelings and aspirations of Australians before the great nations of the world, and particularly in connection with our relations to the British Government …

Another measure with which we propose to ask the Parliament to deal is a Bill relating to Papua … we have to do our utmost from a humanitarian standpoint for those who are now in Papua … until the Parliament passes some measure sanctioning a governmental organisation for Papua, it will be impossible to secure adequate development of the territory.

… we propose introducing a Postal Bill to correct minor defects in the Postal Rates Act, and to deal with postal matters generally …

Another Bill which we intend to introduce is one to provide for a survey of the Western Australian railway. I am sure that our friends from Western Australia will be gratified to hear that …

Another measure with which we hope to deal next session is that relating to federal quarantine … this is largely a professional and departmental matter, and does not involve any political question …

I think it is desirable, as a matter of policy, to indicate to the House that the government have made up their minds to ask for the grant of a large sum, apart from the ordinary military estimates, for expenditure on warlike material. The impression has got abroad in the past that the Labor Party are opposed to any adequate provision being made for defence … there are some items of expenditure with which I think we might dispense for one or two years, whilst we are making special provision for warlike material …

We admit there are huge difficulties in the way of the establishment of a Commonwealth system of old-age pensions, but difficulties are created only to be surmounted, and we think that in this case they can be overcome …

We also propose during next session to take steps in regard to the tobacco monopoly. It is known to us that the importation, manufacture, and distribution of tobacco throughout Australia today is, practically speaking, in the control of one combine … there must be a certain degree of competition …

We intend to introduce, also during next session, a Banking Bill, dealing particularly with the note issue, and containing certainly a section on the lines of the Canadian provision, that insists upon 40 per cent of the cash reserves of the banks being held in government notes. With regard to this proposal, I may say it is well known that our party is in favour of a Commonwealth Bank of deposit and issue …

I have attempted to outline, so far as has been practicable today, what the immediate proposals of the government are … after having given pledges to the people … I say we have a right to expect support …

I am concerned only with putting before the House, in a clear, distinct, and unmistakable way, the proposals we have to submit to the Parliament, and to express the opinion that, in our belief, at any rate, they will be for the benefit of the whole of the people of Australia. …

Source: Commonwealth of Australia Parliamentary Debates (Hansard).

Dorothy Tangney on her election to the Senate in 1943. Tangney was the first woman elected to the Senate and the Labor Party's first female federal parliamentarian. In this speech, Tangney praised the Curtin government's war effort and spoke passionately about the need for social and economic justice in peacetime. Source: John Curtin Prime Ministerial Library

DOROTHY TANGNEY

'A model for all other democracies to follow'

Labor's first female parliamentarian delivers her first speech at a time of war

In 1943, Dorothy Tangney became the first woman elected to the Senate and also Labor's first female federal parliamentarian.

It had taken 43 years for Labor to preselect a winning female candidate. Yet, placed fourth on Labor's ticket, it is unlikely that Tangney would have won without John Curtin's landslide victory.

When Tangney was sworn in, *The West Australian* reported that she spoke 'in a firm, clear tone' and pointlessly mentioned that she was wearing 'a deep blue frock with short puffed sleeves and a gored skirt. Her suede shoes were in a matching blue and she was hatless, her curly fair hair parted at the side in a short shingle'.

Moving the address in reply to the Governor-General's speech the next day, Tangney praised the Curtin Government's wartime leadership, the contribution of men and women on the home front, and those serving in the defence of Australia. Tangney spoke passionately about the need for the peace not to be 'lost' and urged her colleagues to 'build up a democracy on the very best basis that Australia can provide' so it is 'a model for all other democracies to follow'. Tangney recognised 'the great honour in being the first woman to be elected to the Senate' but also that 'it is not as a woman that I have been elected to this chamber. It is as a citizen of the Commonwealth; and I take my place here with the full privileges and rights of all honourable senators'.

It remains an important speech, not only because it was delivered by Labor's first female federal parliamentarian, but for the breadth of vision that it conveys.

'A model for all other democracies to follow'

The Senate, Canberra 24 September 1943

I realise the great honour which has been done to me in affording me the opportunity to move this Address-in-Reply. I also realise my great honour in being the first woman to be elected to the Senate. But it is not as a woman that I have been elected to this chamber. It is as a citizen of the Commonwealth; and I take my place here with the full privileges and rights of all honourable senators, and, what is still more important, with the full responsibilities which such a high office entails …

I pay tribute, first, to the wonderful achievements of our men and women in the fighting forces who in every sphere of action have so gallantly upheld the prestige of Australia. I also pay tribute to the remarkable achievements of our Allies … The work which has been done by our Allies and the men and women of our forces has been backed up no less by the vast army of industrial workers, both men and women, who, in the past four years, have worked night and day so loyally and well to turn out the sinews of war in order that the best human material we have available shall, with the best possible equipment, bring closer the day of victory.

Particularly, I pay tribute to the women in industry who, for the first time, have been called upon to take their places in fields hitherto the prerogatives of men, especially those engaged in the engineering industry who have turned night into day, and have pursued a way of life completely foreign to anything they had known before … I hope that when the day of peace comes what has been so willingly surrendered by our workers in industry will not be forgotten, and that the maximum of what they have voluntarily given up in the war effort will be the minimum upon which our new industrial standards will be based.

I do not forget the men and women on the land who with every great inconvenience have toiled from daylight to dark in order that we and the members of our fighting forces shall be fed, and our food commitments to our Allies, particularly Great Britain, shall be met …

I pay tribute to the Curtin Government which was called to office at a time of crisis unprecedented in the history of the nation. Under conditions never before paralleled in this country, and with a minority in both Houses, it was still able to call the nation to a total war effort and to coordinate the various forces necessary for the success of that effort …

Because of the measures that were taken we are now … free from danger of foreign aggression; but we are not free from the responsibilities which lie up on all of us to bring to the oppressed peoples of the world the same measure of freedom and democracy as we enjoy, and we must not rest from our labours until that happy state of affairs is instituted …

We must also remember that the government which was recently elected by the people of Australia has a two-fold duty to perform. First and foremost is the winning of the war, the giving of the maximum possible assistance to our Allies so that peace may be won. But there is also a very heavy responsibility upon the government to see that the peace shall not be lost.

All of us know what happened after the last war; that it was a war to end all wars, and would make this country fit for heroes to live in, but instead of Australia being made fit for heroes to live in, it became a land for paupers to die in. We must be certain that a similar state of affairs shall not follow in the wake of this war.

Therefore, I put it to the Senate that one of the chief functions of the government is to work towards a policy to ensure that, once our national safety is assured, the fate of those on the home front will be safeguarded, and we shall build up a democracy on the very best basis that Australia can provide.

The last Parliament laid down the foundation of a plan of social services. Social security is the right of every Australian; and I trust that on the foundation already laid we shall be able to build a much stronger edifice which, no matter how fierce the winds of reaction may blow against it, will be able to endure.

Thus we shall make this country what it should be, a model for all other democracies to follow. In order to do this we must observe fully the Atlantic Charter. Every citizen has at least two rights – freedom from fear and freedom from want …

In any scheme of reconstruction … we must give, first, social security to all … we must have federal control of education … to carry out a policy which will give to every Australian citizen the benefits which only education can confer … we have at present a system of pensions which, to my mind, are very inadequate … it is the duty of this Parliament to provide that men or women who have given a lifetime of service to the nation shall be given, when they reach pensionable age … their share of the national dividend which they have helped by their labour to create over the years … I do not think that the introduction of a system that would assure the best medical attention to all would destroy initiative, or discourage anything that the doctors at present do or could do … our present housing conditions are causing a great deal of discomfort but even of hardship to many members of the community …

In any scheme of social service we must be certain that these reforms are introduced, and that our health and education systems and our housing facilities give to the worker, and indeed to every other member of the community, what he has a right to expect. I use the word 'worker' in the broad sense. In Australia, after all, we are all workers …

… the great task which confronts this Parliament is the same task which confronts the people of Australia – that is, to bring this war to a just and honourable conclusion. To this task we must bend all our energies. The way will not be easy, because there is a great deal to be done before not only the Japanese, but also the Germans, are beaten back to the confines of their own lands. When this has been accomplished, we must proceed with the plans which have already been partly put into operation, so that we may give to every man, woman and child in this community the social security which is their birthright …

Source: Commonwealth of Australia Parliamentary Debates (Hansard).

ARTHUR CALWELL

'We cannot afford to fail'

The post-war immigration program, forever changing the nation, is announced

In the 1943 election campaign, Prime Minister John Curtin proposed a doubling of the population to ensure the 'development and protection' of Australia. He believed that it was vital for economic growth and to provide security from the threat of invasion. His successor, Ben Chifley, understood the need for skills to minimise capacity constraints as the economy expanded. He also saw it as part of Labor's universal mandate to help those displaced persons from war-torn Europe. 'We owe something to humanity', Chifley said in 1949.

As Minister for Immigration, Arthur Calwell's speech on 2 August 1945 was an announcement of official government policy. He spoke of the need to 'hold' Australia against future invasion and 'for the fullest expansion of our economy'.

The program was largely directed at British ex-service personnel, their dependants and those from selected countries in Europe. Although it is a nuanced speech, which spoke of the challenges and of the opportunities of a large-scale immigration program, some of the language is jarring. Calwell makes it clear that the 'newcomers' must be 'assimilated'. Yet, he also makes it clear that the government would not tolerate 'campaigns ... on racial and religious grounds by persons who have ulterior motives'.

Although Calwell was a staunch believer in a White Australia, he did believe in 'security for all and a genuine equality of opportunity for all', as he wrote in his book, *Labor's Role in Modern Society*.

Via correspondence in mid-2010, Calwell's daughter, Mary, expressed the family's view that not enough recognition has been paid to Calwell for leadership in ushering in Australia's visionary post-war migration program.

Indeed, few decisions have so profoundly changed the social fabric and shaped the economic prosperity of Australia, for the better.

'We cannot afford to fail'

The House of Representatives, Canberra 2 August 1945

If Australians have learned one lesson from the Pacific war now moving to a successful conclusion, it is surely that we cannot continue to hold our island continent for ourselves and our descendants unless we greatly increase our numbers.

We are but 7,000,000 people and we hold 3,000,000 square miles of this earth's surface. Our coastline extends for 12,000 miles and our density of population is only 2.5 persons per square mile. Much of our land is situated within a rain belt of less than 10 inches per annum and this area is, therefore, largely uninhabitable.

In those parts more favourably situated, much development and settlement have yet to be undertaken. Our need to undertake it is urgent and imperative if we are to survive. While the world yearns for peace and abhors war, no one can guarantee that there will be no more war. A third world war is not impossible, and after a period of fitful peace, humanity may be face to face again with the horrors of another period of total war.

It would be prudent for us, therefore, not to ignore the possibility of a further formidable challenge within the next quarter of a century to our right to hold this land. We may have only those next 25 years in which to make the best possible use of our second chance to survive.

Our first requirement is additional population. We need it for reasons of defence and for the fullest expansion of our economy …

Immigration is, at best, only the counterpart of the most important phase of population building: natural increase. Any immigration policy, therefore, must be intimately related to those phases of government policy that are directed towards stimulating the birth-rate and lowering the infant mortality rate in Australia itself …

On the other side of the picture, the department (Department of Immigration) will approach its problem from the basis that it is economically unsound to bring migrants to the country until there is continuous employment for them, and secondly, proper housing and other social amenities to help them to fit themselves quickly into the Australian way of life …

People who talk glibly about bringing millions of people to Australia in relatively short periods have no conception of either the physical or the economic factors that operate in an expanding population … In view of the alarming fall in the birth-rate, and the decline of the average Australian family from six children in 1875 to three children in 1925, and then to slightly over two children at present, our immediate problems will be to hold our population figures with some migration …

Australia wants, and will welcome, new healthy citizens who are determined to become good Australian citizens by adoption. …

Any immigration plan can succeed only if it has behind it the support and the goodwill of the Australian people …

Three matters of major importance have to be dealt with before any organised plan of large-scale immigration is possible. The first of these is the demobilisation, rehabilitation and re-employment of the men and women in the Australian fighting services … The second is the overtaking of the lag in national housing and the provision of additional houses to meet the demands of an increasing population. The third is the provision of adequate shipping to bring new citizens to Australia under reasonably comfortable circumstances …

For the foregoing reasons, we intend to embark on an adequate publicity campaign in Britain and in other centres of potential immigration on the European continent, designed to explain to the people there our anxiety to receive them on the one hand, and the causes of the delays that are inevitable on the other …

… negotiations have carried on for some time between the United Kingdom government and the Commonwealth government for the conclusion of two agreements.

The first of these is to cover free passages to Australia for British ex-service men and women and their dependants, or the dependants of such British personnel as elect to be demobilised in Australia. The second covers assisted passages to civilians in the United Kingdom who are not eligible under the free passage scheme …

Pending the resumption of large-scale adult migration, the government will take every available opportunity to facilitate the entry into Australia of accepted children from other countries. The government has already approved in principle a plan to bring to Australia, in the first three years after the war, 50,000 orphans from Britain and other countries that have been devastated by the war …

Another field of possible migration, that is economically self-contained, is provided in the approach to manufacturers in Britain and other overseas countries to remove their centre of production, or a part of it, to Australia, bringing not only plant and markets, but their personnel and their families as well. …

The Australian people must help newcomers to become assimilated. We have been too prone in the past to ostracise those of alien birth and then blame them for segregating themselves and forming foreign communities. It is we, not they, who are generally responsible for this condition of affairs …

Unfortunately, campaigns are fostered in this country from time to time on racial and religious grounds by persons who have ulterior motives to serve. The activities of such people cannot be too strongly condemned. They are anti-Australian and anti-Christian, and make not for national unity and national wellbeing but for the creation of discord and bitterness that is harmful to Australia at home and abroad …

In conclusion, I assure the House that we are approaching the problems associated with immigration with a full realisation of their importance and their difficulties, but with a recognition that this question is something essential to our national welfare …

The accomplishment of our immigration policy will require the support of every political party in the House and of every public organisation in the community. We cannot afford to fail. There is so much dependent on the success of our population policy that failure will spell national disaster.

Source: Commonwealth of Australia Parliamentary Debates (Hansard).

HERBERT VERE 'DOC' EVATT

'No man should be deprived of civil rights'

In the shining moment of his career, Doc Evatt makes the case
against banning the Communist Party of Australia

The Menzies Government's *Communist Party Dissolution Act* sought to break up the Communist Party in Australia (CPA) and punish its supporters. Introduced in April 1950, it targeted Australians for their beliefs, not their actions. Private property could be confiscated and jobs taken away. It was an affront to freedom of expression and association.

It was seen by some as a tactic to wedge the Labor Party because, if the party opposed the legislation, then it could be accused of being a CPA sympathiser or having links with the CPA. Although Labor and some unions were infiltrated by communists, and possibly even Labor leader HV 'Doc' Evatt's office and department, the threat to national security was not clearly established.

Although feelings inside the Labor Party were mixed, Evatt led a trade union sponsored High Court challenge against the laws and won. The Court said the Act reached beyond the government's powers.

Menzies' Government held a referendum in September 1951, seeking constitutional change to uphold the Act. Evatt led the campaign for the 'no' case, arguing that the laws breached individual freedom and liberty. The referendum was narrowly defeated.

In this speech, delivered after the Act had been declared invalid but before the referendum had taken place, Evatt argued the law adopted 'totalitarian methods in order to defeat the totalitarian doctrine of communism'.

The then deputy Labor leader, Arthur Calwell, recalled in his memoir, *Be Just and Fear Not*, that Evatt's 'two greatest attributes were his compassion for humanity and his sense of justice'.

In this speech, Evatt is passionate and principled, employs powerful language and stirring rhetoric, uses his knowledge of the law and his ability as an advocate to demolish the Menzies Government's proposals.

'No man should be deprived of civil rights'

The House of Representatives, Canberra 10 July 1951

… This is a Bill of great significance and importance … it represents a direct frontal attack on all the established principles of British justice. It goes much further than the legislation which was recently held by the High Court of Australia to be unconstitutional. I think I can establish that this is one of the most dangerous measures that has ever been submitted to the legislature of an English-speaking people.

I do not think that a Bill of this character would receive a moment's consideration from the mother of parliaments, the British parliament, for in that parliament traditions of political liberty and established justice are always recognised and are, indeed, all powerful …

It applies equally to the United States of America. In that country, proposals such as this, despite the deep hostility of Americans to communism, have never been brought forward. The American constitution would probably prevent the acceptance of a Bill of this character. The American constitution is based fundamentally on a belief in justice …

I shall sum up the attitude of the Australian Labor Party on this subject. In the first place it is stated excellently in two basic declarations of the Labor conferences of 1948 and 1951. The first of those two declarations reads as follows:

> Conference reaffirms its repudiation of the methods and principles of the Communist Party and the decisions of previous conferences that between the Communist Party and the Labor Party there is such basic hostility and differences that no communist can be a member of the Labor Party. No communist auxiliary or subsidiary can be associated with the Labor Party in any activity and no Labor Party Branch or member can cooperate with the Communist Party.
>
> Conference further declares that the policy and the actions of the Communist Party demonstrates that the party's methods and objects aim at the destruction of the democratic way of life of the Australian people and the establishment in its place of a totalitarian form of government which would destroy our existing democratic institutions and the personal liberty of the Australian people.

Then the conference made the following declaration:

> The Australian Labor Party expresses its adherence to the basic freedoms of the right of association and the right of expression, which are fundamental principles associated with the Australian democratic way of life. We therefore

declare that any proposal for the banning of a political party because of hostility and objection to its platform and beliefs, no matter how repugnant such may be, is a negation of democratic principles and should be rejected. Conference stresses that freedom of expression enables the community to determine the soundness or otherwise of political philosophies and reject such views as are inimical to the people's interests.

Secondly, I point out that from the point of view of the Australian labour movement, it is a fundamental proposition that any person who attempts to endanger in any way the internal security or defence of the country can be, and should be, dealt with under the criminal laws that are in force.

Thirdly, I think that it is clear from a careful examination of the High Court's judgement that the judges declared that this Parliament, and all governments, have full powers under the constitution, without any amendment of it being necessary, to deal with offences of every kind of a treasonable, seditious or subversive character ...

Fourthly, if the existing criminal law needs strengthening in these respects the Labor Party will support amendments to it.

Fifthly, no justification exists for abandonment of the recognised principles of British justice, through the introduction of alien measures that are characteristic, not of a democracy, but of a police state.

Finally, the present proposal, which is designed to effect a permanent amendment of the constitution, will introduce into the constitution wide powers, indeed blanket powers, that will lead inevitably to the partial overthrow of the basis of the constitution and will injure the safeguards of justice contained in that document. There is not the slightest doubt that this amendment could be used at some future date to divide, weaken or even destroy the political and industrial labour movements of Australia ...

The tragedy is that this measure is being put forward by a government, part of which at least calls itself liberal. But the Bill authorises action which is the very antithesis of liberalism. None of the great liberals of Britain would consider such a measure for one moment. Even today no party in the House of Commons, and I do not believe a single member, would endorse such a proposal. Liberalism stands for the proceedings of justice and the due processes of law ... it is a sad and tragic thing that a Liberal Government should sponsor such a measure in this century ... This Bill bears no semblance of liberalism. It is extreme reactionary conservatism. Indeed, it is more than that. It is totalitarianism. It is fascist in spirit and a definite step towards the police State ...

I say that the prime minister is using communism as a bogy to delude the people … What it is doing now, it is doing for political purposes in an attempt to deceive the people …

If an individual be guilty of a crime against his country, including the crime of conspiracy, we say that he should be prosecuted. The government … wants to proceed against certain individuals because they hold particular political ideas, either alone or in common with others. We say that mere ideas or beliefs do not enter the picture, and that what matters is what a man does or attempts to do. We say that no man should be convicted, or deprived of civil rights merely because he holds certain beliefs … it is not the beliefs but the crime that matters …

In this great democracy the people are being asked to adopt totalitarian methods in order to defeat the totalitarian doctrine of communism. For those reasons we shall urge the people of Australia to reject these proposals. We believe that they are retrograde. The government, apparently, believes that it can establish a dictatorship over ideas …

To support an alteration of the constitution as we are now asked to do would be to become a party to tyranny and injustice. The Australian people should therefore be asked to reject the measure and to refuse to put a fascist and totalitarian blot on their constitution.

Source: Commonwealth of Australia Parliamentary Debates (Hansard).

JOE CAHILL

'A great cultural centre'

The indefatigable old-school NSW Labor Premier, Joe Cahill, delivers
the speech that ensures Sydney gets its Opera House

The Sydney Opera House would not exist if it were not for the vision and determination of NSW Labor Premier, Joe Cahill.

Encouraged by Eugene Goossens, the conductor of the Sydney Symphony Orchestra, Cahill backed the call for an opera house and argued that it would help 'to develop and mould a better, more enlightened community', he said in 1954. The next year, the government announced that Bennelong Point would be the location. An international design completion was won by Danish architect Jøern Utzon in 1957.

But Cahill still needed to convince his party that they should fund a building that traditional Labor voters did not often frequent. In May 1957, after a long and heated debate, a motion in the parliamentary party caucus supporting the opera house passed by just 24-17 votes. Some were agitating for another debate in June. Cahill decided that the party conference that year would have the final say.

The Daily Telegraph reported that the conference had already given Cahill a 'beating' on several contentious policy issues. The election of the party's executive had been fiercely contested. Party members were calling for 'homes before the Opera House'. A conference resolution opposing the project would have almost certainly spelt its demise. The pragmatic course of action may have been to sink the project. But this underestimated the vision and tenacity of Joe Cahill. He saw an opportunity to win support for the project at the conference once and for all, despte some opposition.

When Cahill addressed the conference on the Saturday evening he focused on the cost of the project, saying it 'would make not even a perceptible ripple on our financial ocean'. He argued that Labor 'can ignore the arts and the sciences', but 'that is not the Labor way of doing things'. He made the case for 'a great cultural centre'. Cahill, who had never seen an opera, a ballet or a symphony, won them over and the conference supported a motion to fund 'homes as well as Opera Houses'. Cahill's speech had won over his party.

It was Cahill who ensured that Sydney received a building of stunning architectural design befitting the magnificent harbour that it overlooks. However, Cahill would die of a heart attack in 1959 and never see it completed.

'A great cultural centre'

Sydney Town Hall, Sydney 15 June 1957

Two years have slipped away since the last Annual Conference of the NSW ALP and in that long interval many things have happened and many changes have been wrought …

We have carried on with our appointed task and we have never deviated from that line of duty which must always be followed by the accredited representatives of the Australian labour movement …

Our greatest advertisement today is the major things we have accomplished … the 40-hour week, greatly liberalised compensation for injured workers, more generous industrial pensions, superannuation benefits, long service leave, annual holidays and all those other enactments of your Labor Government in NSW.

None can indefinitely gloss over the achievements of the State Labor Government in the wide field of education … cover up the fact that we have done more in the direction of providing new hospitals and additional beds for patients than any other Australian State; ignore our achievements in providing adequate electrical power for city and country …

It is not really necessary that I should tell you what we have done for the primary producer in a thousand different ways; that we have given an entirely new deal to local government, extending its activities and widening its powers; that we have given unprecedented aid to the cooperative movement; that social welfare has become one of our major concerns; and that we have completed hundreds of great new works – dams and bridges, hospitals and schools, power stations and swimming pools.

Of course you know these things. But I want you to ponder upon the very happy position in which the worker in NSW finds himself today …

'Homes before opera' is a cry that was raised recently – and quite legitimately. Which brings me to a subject which has merited considerable discussion – the question of building a State Opera House.

I would not like to think that this proposition is a fiercely controversial one, particularly in our movement, which, ever since it first came into existence, has done so much to advance cultural progress …

A government can … ignore the arts and the sciences and, as a consequence, have more money to spend on more plebeian things. But that is not the Labor way of doing things. It is not a way that ensures national progress.

An opera house is a proposition from very long ago and there is no doubt that there is a very considerable section of Labor people which favours a great cultural centre devoted to the musical arts, drama, ballet and associated entertainment.

If we start nothing we complete nothing.

The proposed opera house will, it is suggested, be financed by public subscription and special lotteries at a cost annually which, when considered in true perspective, is infinitesimal.

Actually, the cost to the government in the first year will be no more than £100,000 – almost one-twentieth of one per cent of the State's overall expenditure in the current year (£177,800,00). Or putting it another way, one two-thousandth part of our annual expenditure. It would make not even a perceptible ripple on our financial ocean.

What more convincing evidence could one have in support of an opera house than those record queues of just ordinary people who recently braved bitterly cold weather for long hours to purchase, at relatively high prices, the right to see a top-class ballet …

Concluding, I would like to say that, not withstanding a deplorable tendency by a section of the press and other incorrigible 'knockers', the institution of responsible Parliamentary government was never so well rooted in the opinions and feelings of the people of this state as now …

It would be a tragedy if what began in the minds of our pioneers and founders as a noble ideal, an enduring vision giving courage, determination and foresight for the future should, now or ever, end up in the hands as a corpse under the knives of assassins whose approach to economic, social, political, national or international problems is thoughtless, selfish or irresponsible.

The future, as always, is a closed book. The only thing we know about it is its uncertainty, and in these circumstances, if we can meet the challenge of today and tomorrow with the courage, determination, foresight and application to duty of our Labor forebears, we shall not fail in the trust and responsibility which have been imposed in us, the accredited and elected representatives of the people …

Source: Australian Labor Party (NSW Branch) Papers, State Library of NSW.

GOUGH WHITLAM

'The way of the reformer is hard in Australia'

An ascendant Gough Whitlam outlines the challenges for modern Labor

In his landmark Ben Chifley Memorial Lecture, then Labor backbencher Gough Whitlam argued that the constitution had 'handicapped' Labor governments from implementing its policy objectives.

He said that Labor's prospects for being a reformist government were being stymied by the shackles imposed by the constitution. 'Labor', he said, 'is in the unfortunate position of being unable to carry out its basic philosophies when in office'. Examining the provision of health, tertiary and school education, housing and urban development, Whitlam argued for a greater, more interventionist, Commonwealth role.

These still developing, yet visionary, ideas had an electrifying effect in the Labor Party. Whitlam adviser, Richard Hall, said in his unpublished biography of Whitlam that 'there had been nothing quite like it in Labor history before, except perhaps very distantly at the 1921 conference'. 'Whitlam', Hall said, 'laid out his foundations for a reforming Labor government'.

Critical to his thinking about Labor's future policies within the context of the constitution was Whitlam's membership of the Constitutional Review Committee established as a Joint Parliamentary Committee by the Menzies Government in 1956.

Whitlam's lecture was widely reported in the media at the time. It was seen as putting the case for wider powers for the national government and as the ideas of a young and visionary politician.

This speech would lead to some important changes to Labor's policies at future party conferences.

The 1957 speech was sponsored by the ALP Club at The University of Melbourne, who published and printed it, and sold it for one shilling.

The lecture marked the arrival a 41-year-old rising political star, who had been in Parliament just four years. Moreover, it provided the foundation for his creative, progressive and reformist government, still 15 years away.

'The way of the reformer is hard in Australia'

The University of Melbourne, Melbourne, 19 July 1957

What part is the Labor Party to play in Australian politics? The party's humanitarian objectives have met with considerable success. They are accepted by its political opponents. The widowed and fatherless, the veteran and superannuated may still be poor, but they are no longer destitute. Society accepts the challenge of unemployment.

Some of the more venerable Liberals tell us from their counting houses that the Labor Party should henceforth accept the capitalist basis of society. They say that the Liberals and Labor should be like the Republicans and Democrats in the United States or the Conservatives and Liberals in Canada, who have been described as being like two bottles, exactly identical in capacity, bearing different labels — and both empty ...

The Federal Parliament enjoys under the Constitution ample opportunities for redistributing income among Australians and carrying out other superficial and palliative reforms ...

It seems, however, that the party has, in the last three years, reaffirmed the socialist faith which it espoused in the days of the Chifley governments. It desires to remould society and the economy, not merely to redistribute wealth among Australians where they are but to guide investment towards the development of the country as a whole, to rationalise and modernise industry and community services so as to provide all Australians with more value for their incomes.

Thus Labor has repudiated the North American and Western European roles which its rivals would impose upon it and continues the same role as its sister parties in the United Kingdom and New Zealand. Much of the frustration, and even demoralisation, in Labor ranks in recent years flows from the fact that the Australian Labor Party, unlike the British and New Zealand parties, is unable to perform, and therefore finds it useless to promise, its basic policies. It has been handicapped, as they were not, by a Constitution framed in such a way as to make it difficult to carry out Labor objectives and interpreted in such a way as to make it impossible to carry them out.

The Constitution ... defines the subjects upon which the Parliament can legislate. These subjects are limited, firstly, by the horizon of those who framed the Constitution and, secondly, by their willingness to deprive the State Parliaments of existing powers. Since State Parliaments had not concerned themselves with economic policy at the time of Federation and had passed very little social or industrial legislation, it is not surprising that such subjects are not listed among the Commonwealth's powers in the Constitution …

The second reason for the Commonwealth's powers being so limited was that the founding fathers, being members of the State Parliaments, were loathe to see any more diminution in their status than was inevitable in the interests of common defence, common nationality and the exigencies of commerce.

Now, however, it has become generally recognised in Australia, as elsewhere, that governments have a responsibility for the general state of the economy, for the level of employment, for the stability of the value of the currency, and for the rate and balance of economic development …

The Chifley government was competent and determined to carry out the party's policies. It was, however, unable to nationalise the banks and, since the words in the Constitution dealing with insurance were the same as those dealing with banking, it would have been unable to nationalise insurance. It was unable to achieve a public monopoly of interstate airlines and, since the expressed constitutional powers over sea navigation are no wider than the implicit powers over air navigation, it would have been unable to secure a public monopoly of interstate shipping. It was unable to institute the National Health Scheme. It had to content itself with a makeshift arrangement with the States over housing …

Labor is in the unfortunate position of being unable to carry out its basic philosophies when in office and of being unable to advocate its policies at an election without the heavy proviso that a referendum will be carried to permit these policies being carried out …

The Labor Party's objective is 'the socialisation of industry, production, distribution and exchange to the extent necessary to eliminate exploitation and other anti-social features in those fields'. One of the methods advocated is 'nationalisation of banking, credit and insurance, monopolies, shipping, public health, radio services and sugar refining'. It is impossible at present for the Commonwealth or the States to pass legislation carrying out any of these policies …

While it is virtually impossible for Australian governments, State or Federal, individually or collectively, to eliminate exploitation and other anti-social features in industry by socialisation, it is to a great extent impossible for them to do so by legislative guidance of other kinds …

Since the 1946 referendum, it is hard to think of any constitutional limitation on the Commonwealth's power to provide social services in cash. There are, however, very great limitations on its ability to provide social services in kind. At the time when the Constitution was formulated, the State governments spent nothing on housing, next to nothing on health, and very little on education … Since they are activities which affect all Australians alike, there would seem to be no reason why they should not be co-ordinated, planned and financed on a national basis …

Although the word 'health' nowhere appears in the Constitution, it is clearly a subject in which research should be carried out, costs borne and co-ordination achieved on a national basis …

… the Commonwealth has played no part in conducting and coordinating tertiary education in Australia … The best chance, however, of securing more money from the Commonwealth for education is to give the Commonwealth more responsibility in coordinating standards and allocating expenditures …

The biggest headache and heartache to individuals since the war, particularly to those raising families, has been the provision of housing of reasonable quality at a reasonable price … The Commonwealth has sufficient power over banking and insurance … to see that adequate finance is made available for this purpose. The Commonwealth has also made large sums available for the purchase and construction of war service homes and for the construction of Housing Commission or Housing Trust dwellings …

If Australians expect a more effective exercise of those functions which governments have assumed since Federation … if they want a concerted effort to improve our housing, health and educational standards, they will have to make it possible for the Commonwealth Parliament to perform these tasks …

It is regrettable but true that the Labor objective of a unitary and decentralized system in Australia runs up against strong vested interests in the Labor Party itself. The Australian Labor Party is actually a confederation of six State Labor parties … State Labor governments have not done much in recent years to temper the winds of capitalism to the shorn lambs but have been able to give some of the modified raptures of capitalism to their most loyal followers … many Labor MLAs fail to realise that the further development of Labor objectives requires more national planning, regional administration and less domination by the large coastal cities where the State Parliaments and big businesses have their headquarters …

What steps should be taken to enlarge the powers of the national Parliament and to redistribute the powers of the States? First, we should always support a referendum to grant to the Commonwealth Parliament the legislative power which it does not have, especially economic or social powers such as marketing, credit and investment, housing, health and education …

Many Labor supporters in the past have taken the dog in the manger attitude that a power should be denied to the Commonwealth Parliament when there is a conservative government in office for fear that the power in the immediate future will be used to Labor's disadvantage. Such an attitude is a short-sighted one; it shows a lack of both confidence and principle … The Liberals are not greatly worried if the people's elected representatives are unable to redeem their electoral promises to lead the people into the promised land or to the light on the hill.

State Labor governments could do much to set up stronger provincial or regional or local administrations within their own borders … The greatest role, however, in achieving Labor's objectives must always be with a Federal Labor government …

A Labor government should recreate the Inter-State Commission … a Labor government should make more use of our anti-trust laws … A Labor government should make more use of the external affairs power to extend its legislative competence, in particular by implementing conventions and treaties … A Labor government should institute arrangements with the States … to acquire failing industries or compete with monopolies where it cannot itself directly enter into such a business activity… It should make positive offers to the States to accept a reference of their powers over railways, hospitals, universities and housing … Hand in hand with uniform laws and principles throughout the continent should go the decentralisation of administration … The Commonwealth should consciously take the lead in establishing regional administrative centres for its postal, taxation, social services, repatriation, military, customs, employment, migration, health and electoral activities.…

A Federal Circuit Court, equal in status to the Supreme Courts of the States, could deal with matters arising under the Bankruptcy Act and under the Matrimonial Act which, it is to be hoped, will soon become law … It could become a Commercial Court dealing with Bills of Exchange, Copyrights, Patents and Trade Marks … It would also be desirable to have the Court hear appeals in administrative matters, eg, under the Taxation, National Health, Customs, Excise, Repatriation, Public Service, Courts Martial, Lands Acquisition, Audit and Electoral Acts …

The way of the reformer is hard in Australia. Our parliaments work within a constitutional framework which enshrines Liberal policy and bans Labor policy. Labor has to persuade the electorate to take two steps before it can implement its reforms: first to elect a Labor government, then to alter the Constitution. …

I have analysed many of the difficulties of government in Australia which are encountered by Labor governments … I have suggested a few reforms … The main challenge is to awaken the Australian public to the very serious obstacles our Constitution places in the way of efficient and responsible government …

Source: The Whitlam Institute.

DON DUNSTAN

'The strength which comes from diversity'

*Don Dunstan urges a non-discriminatory immigration
policy and the end of White Australia*

Don Dunstan was a leading campaigner for Australia to adopt a non-discriminatory immigration policy.

The Labor Party's 1963 Federal Conference established a committee to consider the party's immigration policy. Dunstan was a member of the committee. It 'unanimously' recommended to the party's 1965 Conference that the 'Maintenance of White Australia' be removed from Labor's policy platform and instead the party support a 'vigorous and expanding immigration program administered with sympathy, understanding and tolerance'.

The adoption of the report was moved by Dunstan, who was South Australia's Attorney-General at the time, and seconded by party leader Arthur Calwell. Calwell had administered the White Australia policy as a Minister in the Chifley Government and privately still supported it. Dunstan recalled in 1993 that Calwell seconded the motion 'with ashes in his mouth'.

It was a landmark decision: the abolition of a founding principle of the party. It demonstrated the party's capacity to renew and reform itself, consistent with changing community attitudes. Dunstan was an important voice in urging the party towards this position. Dunstan's handwritten notes on his copy of the report of the so-called Immigration Review Committee provide clues to his speech, which has been lost to history. He wrote: 'to ensure an adequate settlement of migrants without reference to race, colour or creed'.

This speech, which attracted considerable media attention, was made to the Victorian Association for Immigration Reform a few years after the policy change. At the time, Dunstan was Opposition Leader in South Australia.

He urges Australians to see the economic and social benefits of a non-discriminatory immigration program and not to 'fear freedom and diversity', but understand that 'for our society to develop successfully it needs the strength which comes from diversity and from the mixture of cultures and peoples which can make us effectively cosmopolitan'.

'The strength which comes from diversity'

Melbourne, 16 December 1968

... Already this year I gave a talk in Melbourne about people's attitudes to racial differences in this country, and ... said that I believed that the attitude of many Australians to people who had a different pigmentation of skin from their own, was as stupid as it was un-Christian.

These words of mine were taken from context and much misquoted, but there ensured a debate in the Federal House (of Representatives) which gave rise to a statement from the Minister for Immigration and he said, 'The purpose of Australia's immigration policy is to maintain the homogeneity of the Australian people. I feel sure that the people of Australia would not wish this government to aim at creating a multiracial society and the policy of the government certainly does not'.

What are the overriding assumptions in a belief that a homogenous or rather a homogenised people is the basis for a satisfactory developing Australian society? I believe that the assumptions are the same as those which have constantly led Australians to fear freedom and diversity.

I believe that for our society to develop successfully it needs the strength which comes from diversity and from the mixture of cultures and peoples which can make us effectively cosmopolitan. The Australia of today is very different from the Australia of 20 years ago. That is a very trite remark, but I believe for the purpose of the immigration program, as shown, has its value to Australian society, not merely in providing additional members of the workforce but of integrating people with different ideas, different backgrounds, different styles of living, eating, singing, dancing and what have you.

From what was our Australian mode of life before the program began, Australia was not only able to absorb the European migrants with their very different background, but the quality of life of Australian citizens has been immeasurably improved by what they brought us.

I believe that Australian society could be further improved by the addition of people who could bring to us the best we could gain from the Indians, Chinese, Japanese, Malays, West Indians and Pacific Islanders.

Nobody in Australia would seriously suggest that there is no considerable value in the cultures of these countries, but the barrier is the fear by some Australian people of incorporating into our society people with a discernibly different skin pigmentation ... We are still, in too many areas of life in Australia, institutionalising the fears and inhibitions of the ignorant and the frightened, and it is more than time that we grew up …

In order to maintain our projected rate of growth industrially, and to maintain a steady increase in the workforce which cannot be provided from the rate of natural increase in Australia, even were we to be considerably more fecund than we are, we must have more migrants …

At the present rate there is no sign that the social tensions which do arise in other countries from coloured migration will occur here. Although the Australian people are prejudiced through fear and ignorance, against people with different coloured skin, I feel their prejudice can be dispelled when they come to know people from the background they had previously derided.

The fears and distrust are only reinforced and increased when housing, employment and sexual competition creates a feeling of distrust against people who are discernibly different …

If, by means of bilateral agreements with the non-European countries prepared to provide migrants we can arrange a balanced intake of non-Europeans each year, and I see no reason why these agreements could not be made, then we can have a migration program which does not produce adverse results and would be useful to and inestimably enhance Australia.

Source: The Don Dunstan Foundation.

Don Dunstan was one of the Labor Party's leading advocates for the abolition of the White Australia policy from the party's platform. He moved the critical motion that struck this founding policy from the party's platform at the federal conference in 1965. In this photo, he is campaigning as South Australia's progressive and pioneering Premier. Dunstan played a significant role in helping to shape the party's national direction in the 1960s and 1970s.
Source: Dunstan Collection, Flinders University

GOUGH WHITLAM

'All men and women should be equal in making
the law as they are before the law'

*A joint sitting of the Parliament passes far-reaching
progressive legislation, ending Senate obstruction*

Despite passing more laws in three years than in all the years combined since Federation, the Whitlam Government still faced significant obstruction to the passage of its legislation in the Senate.

After just 18 months, Prime Minister Gough Whitlam decided to force a double-dissolution election on six Bills that had not been passed by the Senate: to reduce the variable quota between electorates, providing for the election of Territory senators, that the formula for Territory senators not be determined by population, the creation of Medibank (the forerunner to Medicare), Medibank administration, and a controlling body for petroleum and mining resource exploration and development.

When the government was returned at the 1974 election, it held a joint sitting of both the House and Senate, provided for under section 57 of the Constitution to break deadlocks. It was the first and only time a joint sitting had been held, even though there were double-dissolution elections in 1914 and 1951. The joint sitting took place over two days and was broadcast on television – the first time Parliament was televised.

In this speech, Whitlam proposes legislation to provide for 'one vote, one value' in elections. He said that it 'affirms the government's belief that every person's vote is of equal value no matter where that person lives. It affirms our belief that all men and women should be equal in making the law as they are before the law'.

Thirty years later, Whitlam reflected that his 'longest campaign has been for equal representation'.

Whitlam's opening speech to the joint sitting recalls not only the passage of landmark legislation during the Whitlam years, but also the conviction, courage and determination of a leader prepared to risk losing government to secure the passage of important progressive legislation.

Other Bills were introduced and debated by relevant Ministers, including Bill Hayden, who introduced the Bills establishing Australia's universal health scheme.

'All men and women should be equal in making the law as they are before the law'

The House of Representatives, Canberra 6 August 1974

This is an historic and unprecedented, sobering occasion

We are witnessing for the first time a joint sitting of the House of Representatives and the Senate of Australia. It is the first time that the members of both Houses have sat together as a single legislative body. It is the first time that the proceedings of Parliament, of either House, have been televised to the nation.

I welcome the opportunity thus provided for the Australian people to see the workings of their Parliament at close hand, to consider the Bills now before us and to reflect on the reasons why this extraordinary Joint sitting of Parliament has come about, for momentous as the sitting is, the reasons for it are not a matter for pride.

It has come about because of the repeated refusal of the Senate to pass legislation which has been approved by the House of Representatives, the people's House, the House where alone governments are made and unmade.

It has come about because despite two successive election victories by the Australian Labor Party, despite the clear endorsement by the Australian people at the elections only two weeks ago of the party's policies and of the specific measures now before us, the Senate and the opposition are still resolved to obstruct the government's program and to frustrate the will of the people …

Let it be understood that this joint sitting is a last resort, a means provided by the constitution to enable the popular will – the democratic process – ultimately to prevail over the tactics of blind obstruction

The constitution provides that if the Senate in certain circumstances twice rejects Bills passed by the House of Representatives, the governor-general may dissolve the Parliament and new elections may be held. That is what happened last April and May

The constitution further provides that if, after a double dissolution and fresh elections, the Senate still obstructs such a Bill a joint sitting of both Houses may be held to consider it. That is what is happening now

Even the sitting itself, an event clearly envisaged and provided for by the constitution, has been subject of a desperate last minute, last ditch legal challenge by our opponents.

Now, at last, at long last after sustained stonewalling and filibustering the Parliament can proceed to enact these essential parts of the government's legislative program

Before dealing with them however, I want to speak as gravely as I can of the implications of this long process of obstruction. The repeated rejection of this Bill is part of a pattern of obstruction adopted by the opposition since the Australian Labor Government came to power. It has been rightly described by Sir Robert Menzies as a falsification of popular democracy. Writing in 1968, Sir Robert said:

> It would be a falsification of democracy if on any matter of government policy approved by the House of Representatives, possibly by a large majority, the Senate representing the States and not the people could reverse the decision.

Mr chairman, we have seen in the history of this Bill one example of such a falsification

It is fitting that the first Bill to come before this first Joint sitting of the Australian Parliament should be designed to strengthen the equality of popular democracy in Australia.

The essential purpose of this Bill is a simple one. It is to enshrine the principle of one vote, one value. It will establish equality of representation as the paramount objective when electoral boundaries are drawn …

Specifically, the Bill provides that in any electorate the number of voters shall be not more than 10 per cent above or below the average number of voters in all the electorates of the State concerned. At present, a variation of 20 per cent is permitted … We shall be ensuring that the number of voters in each electorate is much closer than it is now to the ideal of equality. We shall thus be removing from the electoral law much of the scope now afforded for malapportionment and gerrymandering of electorates …

Throughout Australia, and even within particular States, some people's votes are worth 50 per cent more than others – in fact, up to 90 per cent more than others. That is unjust. It is a denial of the very essence of democracy and a travesty of the electoral process …

Our proposals are the culmination of a long campaign of debate and action inside and outside the Parliament. When we moved the proposals as amendments to Electoral Bills in 1961, 1965 and 1968 Liberal and Country Party members defeated them. When Senator (Nicholas) McKenna in 1964 and Senator (Lionel) Murphy in 1968 and the honourable member for Grayndler, the father of the Parliament, Mr (Fred) Daly in 1971 introduced the proposals in private members' Bills, the Liberal and Country Party Ministers would not allow a vote to be taken upon them.

Finally, in May this year, the government submitted a referendum to the Australian people seeking to have the principle of electoral equality entrenched in the constitution. We sought then to introduce equality on the basis of electorates of equal population. The constitution always has provided that the number of electorates in the several States shall be in proportion to their populations.

The present Bill, of necessity, relies on a different test of equality – the number of voters in each electorate. The Leader of the Opposition (Billy Snedden) has supported that principle. He did so when he opposed our referendum. On 5 May, the right honourable gentleman, in a considered press statement objecting to the principle of equal population electorates, stated:

> If the so-called democratic elections referendum was passed it would allow electorates to be based not on the number of voters but on the number of people. This represents a fundamental departure from the principle of one vote one value – the only right and proper principle on which to base electoral redistributions. Australia's electoral system must be based on the underlying principle that the voter has an equal say compared to any of his fellow voters.

He may now have the grace to acknowledge that our legislation will promote precisely that principle.

I shall deal briefly with two other aspects of our legislation

The variation of 20 per cent from the quota, which we intend to reduce, has been provided in the Commonwealth Electoral Act since Federation.

In 1965, however, the then government amended the Act to oblige the electoral commissioners to depart from the quota of electors to a much greater extent than before. What had been a reasonable discretion allowed to the commissioners became a direction to them to do what is neither reasonable nor democratic. They were obliged to consider a whole host of factors which gave undue weighting to remote or sparsely populated electorates. Yet these electorates are all much less extensive than they were before the expansion of the Parliament in 1949 and telecommunications and transport connections with them and within them have immeasurably improved.

In our legislation we propose to remove many of these factors from the list of considerations to which the commissioners must pay regard … The proposal in the Bill is, we believe, a fair and just proposition. It leaves the Commissioners with a very reasonable degree of discretion. We also propose to allow for more frequent redistributions …

We believe the purpose of this Bill to be a clear and honourable one … it affirms the government's belief that every person's vote is of equal value no matter where that person lives. It affirms our belief that all men and women should be equal in making the law as they are before the law. It gives to those who sit in this Parliament at this historic joint sitting of this Parliament the opportunity to stand up and be counted, to say whether they believe in these democratic principles and, above all, in the supreme principle of one vote one value.

For its content and its implications, for its real value and its symbolic importance, for its contribution to the cause of democracy in a world where democracy seems daily more frail, I commend this Bill to honourable senators and members.

Source: The Whitlam Institute

GOUGH WHITLAM

'To redress past injustice and build a more just and tolerant future'

*Gough Whitlam calls for tolerance and justice at the
proclamation of the Racial Discrimination Act 1975*

When Gough Whitlam became Prime Minister, he was determined to lead a government that presented 'a clean face to the world in racial matters', he wrote in his memoir, *The Whitlam Government*.

Among the many achievements in this area was the liberalisation of Australia's citizenship and immigration laws, expanding services for migrants, excluding racially selected sporting teams from Australia, introducing portable benefit rights for pensioners and setting up ethnic radio stations in Melbourne and Sydney.

The 'greatest reform in combating racial discrimination', Whitlam said, was the ratification of the International Convention on the Elimination of All Forms of Racial Discrimination.

The *Racial Discrimination Bill*, enabling ratification of the Convention, was agreed to by Parliament on 4 June 1975. The legislation made racial discrimination unlawful, provided formal machinery for hearing and resolving complaints, established a Community Relations Council and provided legal remedies against discrimination.

Whitlam spoke at a small ceremony in Canberra to mark the proclamation of the Act. Whitlam's first Minister for Immigration, Al Grassby, who had lost his seat at the 1974 election, was appointed as Commissioner for Community Relations.

In his memoir, Whitlam described the date of this speech as 'a historic benchmark in the history of Australia'. 'For the first time', he said, 'the nation solemnly affirmed its opposition to all forms of racial discrimination'.

On the 20th anniversary of the legislation, Prime Minister Paul Keating recalled that it was 'ground-breaking legislation' which reminds us 'that tolerance and justice are things we live by and goals to which we aspire'.

'To redress past injustice and build a more just and tolerant future'

The Department of the Attorney-General, Canberra 31 October 1975

The struggle to give equal rights to migrants, Aborigines and other ethnic or racial groups does not end with formal citizenship or the grant of the franchise. That is the beginning.

In Australia we are still working to eliminate racial discrimination from our laws … The long-term and continuing need is to entrench new attitudes of tolerance and understanding in the hearts and minds of the people.

It is for that reason that we have passed the *Racial Discrimination Act* – a historic measure, symbolic of the aims and philosophy of the Australian Government, and a further stage in the struggle for human rights by minorities everywhere.

Let it not be forgotten that Australia is a multi-racial society – a remarkably diverse and successful one. A quarter of our workforce was born overseas. More than three million people have come to us from sixty different countries and locations around the world during the past quarter-century of mass migration. We all know the changes they have brought to our great cities … Australia has a unique opportunity to show the world what one of the youngest of all nations can do in promoting peace, tolerance and unity among all sections of the people.

It is of course extraordinarily difficult to define racial discrimination and outlaw it by legislative means. Social attitudes and mental habits do not readily lend themselves to codification and statutory prohibitions. Nevertheless, I believe that our new law achieves the best possible result …

Unlike the United States, we have no bill of rights … There is a need to spell out in an enduring form the founding principles of our civilisation, and in particular the principle that all Australians, whatever their colour, race or creed, are equal before the law and have the same basic rights and opportunities. If our Bill lacks the rhetorical grandeur of the American documents, it will have, I trust, the same compelling and lasting force.

I hope it will not be thought that by enacting this law we imply any low opinion of the tolerance and good nature of' Australians. We are, on the whole, an exceptionally generous and understanding people. When we look at the history of our immigration program and compare our record with that of any other multi-racial society, it is remarkable how smooth and harmonious this great experiment has been.

True, we have far to go in restoring the rights of the Aboriginal people, and no government has done more than mine to redress their long history of injustice. But for all that, and without complacency of any kind, we can fairly claim that the Australian people are among the most tolerant and decent in the world.

The purpose of the *Racial Discrimination Act* is not so much to correct present abuses – though certainly it will do so where necessary – but to set standards for the future, and build a climate of maturity, of goodwill, of co-operation and understanding at all levels of society.

The Act defines a number of fields in which racial discrimination will be outlawed and equality of opportunity upheld by law – in access to places and public facilities, in land and housing, in the provision of goods and services, in the rights to your trade unions, in employment, and in advertising.

We also establish the office of Commissioner of Community Relations – an officer whose task it will be to enforce and uphold the principles of the Act and promote friendship and understanding between all ethnic groups. There is no one more fitted for this task than Al Grassby – a great Australian, an outstanding former Minister in the government, and a firm friend and counsellor to migrants everywhere …

The main sufferers in Australian society – the main victims of social deprivation and restricted opportunity – have been the oldest Australians on the one hand and the newest Australians on the other. We stand in their debt. By this Act we shall be doing our best to redress past injustice and build a more just and tolerant future.

Source: The Whitlam Institute.

BILL HAYDEN

'We cannot achieve social reform unless we competently manage the economy'

Bill Hayden repositions the Labor Party in the post-Whitlam years and provides the foundations for government

'Australia's got the future. Hayden's got the team', said the slogan behind the speakers' podium at Labor's 1979 National Conference. At the time, Labor was well ahead in the polls and Opposition Leader Bill Hayden was more popular than Prime Minister Malcolm Fraser.

In his speech, Hayden sought to move beyond the Whitlam years. Labor, he said, had 'disappointed and disillusioned many Australians by some of our actions'. But having lost several elections, Hayden said, Labor 'had paid for our mistakes'. 'Now', he said, 'it's Malcolm Fraser's turn'.

He sought to reclaim Australian patriotism, promising to restore 'national pride' during a time of division and poor national leadership. He harked back to John Curtin and Ben Chifley, associating himself with these 'plain men'. He promised 'reconciliation', 'reconstruction' and 'renewal'.

In what Laurie Oakes reported as 'the most effective theme', Hayden said 'now is not the time for the visionary reform programs of earlier years'. He said 'the scope for reform will have to be won by hard work, by discipline, and by a commonsense approach to policy'.

He said demonstrating 'responsible economic management' would be essential in regaining government. He said 'we cannot achieve social reform unless we competently manage the economy'.

The speech was cathartic for the party, still enamoured with Whitlam. Via correspondence with Hayden in early 2010, he recalled that he frequently argued that Labor needed to effectively advocate its economic credentials if it was win future elections and secure lasting social reform.

'We cannot achieve social reform unless we competently manage the economy'

Space Theatre, Adelaide 18 July 1979

I count it as a great privilege to deliver this speech, to this conference, at this time.

More than ever before, our country and our fellow Australians are looking for constructive and just national leadership. We in the Labor Party can provide that inspiration and that hope.

What we have to kindle is the unity of reconciliation. What we have to deliver is the substance of reconstruction and renewal.

I have said many times during these recent difficult years – more often in the last 18 months – that there is nothing wrong with Australia, nothing wrong with its people. What is wrong – all that is wrong – are the policies of Malcolm Fraser, and those who feed off them.

If we get rid of Fraser and his administration, we get rid of his policies. If we get rid of his policies, we get rid of much of the despair and the distress, and the rank bloody injustice that are now so much a part of society.

Then, and only then, under a national Labor government, can Australia begin the regeneration that will bring equality and national pride to this country, and dignity and fair play to all its people. The task is before us.

As you know, this is my first National Conference as national leader. It's our first National Conference since the electoral disaster of 1977. A disaster for us as a party certainly – no one can deny that – but a greater disaster for our nation's unity and welfare, and for its future …

That is why I now say, confidently, that this also is our last National Conference before Labor is returned to national office next year. It is our job – at this conference, and in the months ahead – to ensure we keep this promise, to the people. It's a promise we must keep. Australia can't afford, cannot take, any more of Mr Fraser and what he's doing to this country. The burden is too great.

There are two further points I want to make about that 1977 election result, and what happened two years earlier. I do so with no sense of seeking to overdo the public confessional thing – or believing that self laceration in the public square is in any way revitalising. But the points must be made finally – and then buried with the past.

First – I know, and you know, that as a government we disappointed and disillusioned many Australians by some or our actions, our individual excesses, in the period 1972 to 1975. But I also know that our mistakes were honest mistakes – and that they did not even begin to cast a shadow on the many reforms and programs we introduced – and the fairer and more equal society we brought about during three years of office.

Second – we were twice brought to account for those mistakes by the Australian people. 1977 ruled off the ledger. We paid for our mistakes, and we paid in full – and now it's Malcolm Fraser's turn. At the elections next year, Fraser will have to settle his account. The Labor Party, and the Australian people, must ensure he is charged in full measure …

For us as a party, there are no short cuts … no sitting on our hands thinking Malcolm Fraser will do it all for us; no sliding into the quicksand of believing all we have to do is recapture the euphoria of reform that swept us into office seven years ago.

That, quite candidly, just isn't going to happen. Too much has changed, both in Australia and overseas, to imagine we can wind back the clock to heady circumstances of the early 1970s. The economic and political climate that incubated the Whitlam years of reform have simply gone …

That doesn't mean the Labor Party must also be different in the sense of abandoning ideals or principles – far from it. The needs and wellbeing of all the people in our country are the reasons we exist as a party. They are the basis of all our policies, and they are the factors that give continuity and relevance to the Labor movement. They are what this conference is all about. But we will not find our future in the past.

Much and all as we may regret it, now is not the time for the visionary reform programs of the earlier years. This is the period of the hard slog; and the scope for reform will have to be won by hard work, discipline, and by a commonsense approach to policy. There is frankly, no easier way, and we can't fool ourselves, or the people, by thinking that there is.

Within this new and different climate, there are, I believe certain fundamentals that must be acknowledged if we are to fully regain the people's confidence to win the right to conduct the nation's affairs.

First, and above all else, we must demonstrate beyond doubt that we are competent economic managers. That competence – and the public's recognition of it – is the absolute essential underpinning of everything we want to do. Without it – without an unqualified commitment to pursue responsible economic management – then we might just as well pack our bags and give the game away …

I'm not talking about responsible economic management as an end in itself. I'm talking about responsible economic management guided by a sure sense of social and economic justice, and providing the means for successful social reform. I repeat – in the climate of today, we cannot achieve social reform unless we competently manage the economy …

The six major theses which I see as making up a basic election strategy … are: the economy, which of course includes unemployment; the related issue of taxation; the family; industrial relations; energy and petrol pricing; and Fraserism and its consequences. It's in this broad context that my Federal colleagues and I have been developing detailed proposals within our existing policies for much of the past year and a half …

One of the tragedies of contemporary Australian politics is the absence of any similar patriotic response from the Australian people to their national leadership. It is widely felt among Australians that national leadership has failed, that the bloody self-serving and self-seeking politicians have made an unholy mess of things … The intense feeling the Australian people have for their country has not been matched by qualities of national leadership.

To put it frankly, the people have not been given any reason to feel proud of their national government and this has reacted adversely on national pride. One of the tasks of the next Labor Government is to restore national pride and this can only be done by providing honest, creative and stable government.

There is no doubt in my mind that there is a great desire among the Australian people for national renewal and the restoration of national dignity. They are searching for the sort of revival and renewal that plain men, but visionary men, like (John) Curtin, (Ben) Chifley and (John) Dedman brought to Labor's great plan for national reconstruction after World War Two. They know they won't get any such renaissance of national identity from the barren doctrines of Fraserism, with its spiritual and emotional meanness and its intellectual poverty.

Only the Australian Labor Party has the traditions, the intimate links with every facet of the Australian experience, and the great range of talents, to fill this void in the Australian consciousness. We are the only party whose history spans the full course of the Australian Commonwealth. We are the only party with the fierce commitment to a national Australia – and the intellectual respectability needed to spark such revival.

With such credentials – and in such a climate as exists today – only the Australian Labor Party can restore the credibility of national politics and the faith of the Australian people in the integrity of their national government.

… We are on the way back to government; great challenges and great opportunities face us. I offer you no magic formula, no easy way into office.

But we do have the team, the policies and the commitment to Australia. And I have no fear of the people's judgement, whether it is next year or next month.

Source: Laurie Oakes, Labor's 1979 Conference Report.

Bill Hayden was the critical bridge between the Whitlam and the Hawke-led Labor Party. His 1979 national conference speech was cathartic for the party. He understood that economic policy was vital to securing lasting social reform. His reform of the Labor Party organisation and his policy development provided the basis for Bob Hawke's 1983 election victory.
Source: Australian Labor Party (Queensland Branch)

BOB HAWKE

'Australia's gravest economic crisis in fifty years'

*Bob Hawke addresses the National Economic Summit
Conference on Australia's economic challenges*

The first major act of Bob Hawke's government was to stage a National Economic Summit Conference.

An election promise, the Summit gathered government, business, unions and welfare groups to discuss the state of the economy and to attempt to agree on common goals and actions. Over 100 participants gathered in the House of Representatives chamber. It was to serve as a framework for consensus politics and as a catalyst for major economic reform. A communiqué was issued at the conclusion of the Summit which agreed on the scale of the economic challenges and outlined a policy approach to deal with these.

In an interview with Hawke in December 2011, he iterated that the Summit was the vital springboard for his government's economic reform agenda. It also heralded a new way of communicating and educating the electorate about economic policy. 'We educated the electorate', Hawke said. 'The Australian electorate at the time was probably the most economically literate electorate in any democracy in the world.'

Hawke's opening speech to the Summit was his first major speech as Prime Minister. With a heady mix of excitement, challenge and optimism, Hawke said that the summit was 'historic not only in the sense that nothing of this scale and scope has been attempted before, but as an event of genuine and seminal importance in the life and history of Australia'.

Paul Kelly, writing in *The Sydney Morning Herald*, called it 'a new form of government'. Peter Bowers, also in *The Sydney Morning Herald*, said that Hawke's speech left 'the chamber steaming in consensus like a cow paddock after a rain shower'.

Graham Freudenberg, who drafted Hawke's and NSW Premier Neville Wran's Summit speeches, said in his memoir that 'the summit was the apotheosis of his philosophy and advocacy' and it 'set an ineffaceable stamp upon his government'.

'Australia's gravest economic
crisis in fifty years'

The House of Representatives, Canberra 11 April 1983

On behalf of the Australian government, I have the greatest pleasure in welcoming all participants and observers to this historic National Economic Summit Conference ...

We meet here today as the representatives of the Australian people, in a time of Australia's gravest economic crisis in fifty years ... They have imposed a high trust upon us. We must try our very best not to let them down ...

The results we seek – and these must be regarded as only a minimum measure of our success – should be:

- first, a heightened appreciation of the need to work constructively together to meet the great challenges now confronting our country; and

- second, an increased likelihood of all participants tailoring their expectations and claims upon the community's resources to the capacities of the economy, and the urgent need for a reduction in unemployment and a restoration of growth to an economy now in deep recession ...

This conference itself is part of the process of bringing Australia together. Behind the concept of the conference lies my long-held belief – a belief I am convinced is now shared by the overwhelming majority of the Australian people – that Australia can no longer afford to go down the path of confrontation and fragmentation which has embittered and disfigured so many aspects of the national life, for much of the past decade ...

And I deeply believe that this conference has a part to play, not only in the urgent and immediate task of achieving national economic recovery, but in laying foundations for the whole future of this great country of ours ...

So, in a double sense, this is an historic conference – historic not only in the sense that nothing of this scale and scope has been attempted before, but as an event of genuine and seminal importance in the life and history of Australia.

Let me say very firmly, that when I speak of consensus on Australia's economic and social problems which I hope will emerge from this conference, I am not settling – and none of us should be prepared to settle – for the lowest common denominator, the barest minimum of agreement on an approach to a solution of the current crisis.

If genuine consensus is to emerge, it must mean an understanding on the part of all sections of the Australian community, of the constraints they will be called upon to accept and the contribution they will be called upon to make to the process of national reconciliation, national recovery and national reconstruction.

It will mean a recognition and acceptance of restraint by all sections of the community. It must mean a recognition – a sense of realism of what can be achieved in the near future. We must understand that there are no miracle cures, no overnight solutions. It calls for a sustained, concerted national effort. This conference is only a beginning.

Specifically, the tasks this conference should set itself are:

- to secure broad agreement on the role of an incomes and prices policy, in efforts to promote employment and to achieve recovery and growth, and to ensure that the benefits of recovery are not lost in another round of the wages-prices spiral;
- to devise machinery for achieving the necessary restraint, including methods of wage fixation, influencing non-wage incomes, and price surveillance;
- to secure a better and wider understanding of the broad economic framework, within which we have to operate;
- to seek broad agreement on the relationship between a successful prices and incomes policy and the implementation of policies on industrial relations, job creation and training, taxation, social security, health, education, and the other major community services;
- to examine the competitiveness and efficiency of the Australian economy; and
- finally, to reach agreement on arrangements and machinery to monitor and continue the work of this conference, especially in regard to continuing the process of consultation and cooperation between government, business and unions, initiated by this conference itself.

And of course, I must repeat what I made very clear during the recent election campaign … The governments of Australia, and in particular, the national government, cannot escape and do not wish to escape their primary and fundamental responsibility for the economic and social policies of this nation. But effective policy cannot be made in a vacuum. Decisions that are going to achieve our great national objectives cannot be made in isolation from the economic and social realities.

And the purpose of this conference is to expose us all, including those with direct responsibility for government decision-making, to those realities – the realities of the current situation and the realities of what must be done if there is to be a resolution of Australia's present crisis …

So often in our affairs the emphasis has been put upon the competing struggle between wage and salary earners and business, and residually, welfare recipients. I believe we must come to put the emphasis upon the fact that they all have a common goal and therefore a common interest. They all seek the same thing – the maintenance, and through time, an improvement, of their standards of living.

The indispensable condition for the achievement of this common legitimate goal is real economic growth – an increase in the per capita output of goods and services … The very essence of our mutual task now is to work together to recreate those conditions in which the achievement of that legitimate, common, goal is possible …

During the recent campaign, I frequently drew the parallel between the supreme crisis of the early 1940s and the present crisis. Of course, the two are very different in nature and scale. Survival itself was at stake in 1942. But in one sense, the present crisis is more complex, and at least as challenging, to our resourcefulness as a people …

But now as then – every bit as much as in 1942 – the essential requirement for victory remains the same – the united effort of a united people working together to achieve agreed goals and common objectives.

More than forty years ago, one of the very greatest of all Australians stood in this place in this historic chamber to give this message to the people of Australia. On that occasion, 16 December 1941, John Curtin said:

> Our Australian mode of life, our conditions, our seasons, all that go to make up the natural conditions of living, make us better equipped (for the purpose of meeting this crisis) than are the peoples of many other countries … the qualitative capacity of our population compensates in large measure for the shortage of our numbers … I, like each of you, have seen this country at work, engaged in pleasure, and experiencing adversity; I have seen it face good times and evil times, but I have never known a time in which the inherent quality of Australia has to be used so unstintingly as at this hour.

My fellow Australians, I do not pretend to compare the scale of the crisis which John Curtin steered this nation to triumph with our task today. But I do believe that the essential elements which Curtin defined as the key to victory are as relevant in 1983 as they were in 1941 …

If we at this conference dedicate ourselves to provide leadership to this great people, I have absolute confidence that they will respond with a united effort and a renewed determination to beat this crisis and to build an even better future for this great nation, Australia.

Source: The Bob Hawke Prime Ministerial Library.

SUSAN RYAN

'The principle of the equality of men and women'

Susan Ryan introduces the historic Sex Discrimination Bill

Susan Ryan, a trailblazer for women in politics, had long argued for women to have opportunities to live and work, free from discrimination.

In pursuit of greater equality for women, in opposition, Senator Ryan had moved a private member's Bill in 1981, laying the groundwork for many of the concepts in the 1983 Sex Discrimination Bill. The Fraser government had failed to do anything substantive for women; a 1979 cabinet proposal to introduce anti-discrimination legislation, put forward by ministers Peter Durack and Bob Ellicott, was rejected.

Labor sought to eliminate discrimination 'on the ground of sex, marital status or pregnancy' in employment, education, accommodation, property and the activities of clubs and the administration of Commonwealth laws and programs. It prohibited sexual harassment in the workplace and provided for 'recognition and acceptance within the community of the principle of the equality of men and women'. It also enabled ratification of the UN Convention on the Elimination of All Forms of Discrimination Against Women, signed by the Fraser government in 1980. The Human Rights Commission would be the principal body to put the measures into effect and the position of Sex Discrimination Commissioner would be established.

Previously, women could find themselves forced to leave employment because of marriage or pregnancy, unable to obtain housing loans without a male guarantor, lacking access to some trades training courses and post-graduate education, and often denied superannuation.

In this speech, incorporated into Hansard, Ryan said that the purpose of the Bill was to enshrine 'the principle of the equality of men and women'.

The Bill passed with the support of the Australian Democrats. In her memoir, Ryan said that the *Sex Discrimination Act 1984* was 'probably the most useful thing I've done in my life'. In 1986, the bookend to this legislation, the *Affirmative Action (Equal Opportunities in Employment) Act* was passed, which sought to end more 'structural discrimination in the labour market', Ryan said.

'The principle of the equality of men and women'

The Senate, Canberra 2 June 1983

I am delighted that I am able to move the introduction of a major piece of legislation on a matter which so deeply affects the rights of women and men.

The objects of the Bill are to give effect to certain provisions of the UN Convention on the Elimination of All Forms of Discrimination Against Women which the government plans to ratify in the near future; to eliminate discrimination on the ground of sex, marital status or pregnancy in the areas of employment, education, accommodation, the provision of goods, facilities and services, the disposal of land, the activities of clubs and the administration of Commonwealth laws and programs, and discrimination involving sexual harassment in the workplace and in educational institutions; and to promote recognition and acceptance within the community of the principle of the equality of men and women ...

The statistics give clear evidence of deeply embedded structural inequalities in our society: unemployment rates amongst women (11.2 per cent in February 1983), particularly young women (29.7 per cent), remain considerably higher than amongst men (9.9 per cent and 24.7 per cent) ...

Nearly two-thirds of women are employed in only three occupational groupings: clerical; sales and services; sport and recreation. Even within occupations where women predominate they are seldom found in key decision-making positions ...

36 per cent of employed women work part-time ... 78.4 per cent of part-time workers are women.

Only 5 per cent of all apprentices are female; if hairdressing apprentices are excluded, young women comprise less than 2 per cent of apprentices.

Average weekly full-time earnings for Australian women were 76.4 per cent of male earnings in 1981. Female average weekly earnings at December 1982 (latest available) were $283.30. The corresponding male rate was $352.10.

This Bill offers an opportunity to combat some of these inequalities ...

The Bill will cover both direct and indirect discrimination on the ground of sex, marital status or pregnancy. Direct discrimination occurs when there is a specifically directed policy or action which treats one group less favourably than another. Indirect discrimination occurs when a policy or practice which on the face of it appears to be neutral or non-discriminatory, by its operations results in discrimination against one particular group of persons …

Commonwealth and State experience has shown that most discrimination occurs in the area of employment. The Bill makes unlawful discrimination against applicants for jobs and employees generally and also against persons who are commission agents or contract workers …

With regard to education, it will be unlawful for an educational authority to discriminate on the grounds of sex, marital status or pregnancy against a person applying for admission as a student or against a student. Single sex educational institutions are exempted from the legislation.

The Bill also makes unlawful discrimination in the provision of goods and services, including services relating to banking, insurance and the provision of loans, credit or finance, and services of the kind provided by government authorities or local government bodies.

The Bill makes it unlawful for a club, the committee of management of a club or a committee member to discriminate on the ground of sex, marital status or pregnancy in relation to members or applicants for membership …

The Bill specifically makes unlawful discrimination involving sexual harassment in employment by employers or by co-workers and in education by members of staff. The Commonwealth is the first jurisdiction to introduce such provisions …

Administration of the Bill is vested in the Human Rights Commission. The functions of the Commission will include holding inquiries into and making determinations on complaints; hearing applications for exemption from the Act; undertaking research and educational programs; and examination of existing and proposed legislation to ensure its consistency with the provisions of this Act.

The Bill establishes a Sex Discrimination Commissioner who is required to investigate and conciliate complaints of discrimination …

The introduction of this Bill represents the initial step towards the fulfilment of the Government's major election commitment to women …

I commend the Bill to the Senate.

Source: Commonwealth of Australia Parliamentary Debates (Hansard).

BOB HAWKE

'A triumph of compassion over prejudice'

Bob Hawke defends Australia's immigration policy against attacks by the Liberal and National parties

The post-war immigration program was one of the key reasons Bob Hawke joined the Labor Party in 1947. 'I was passionately convinced of the economic and humanitarian correctness of this policy', he wrote in his memoirs. Successive governments supported a strong immigration program and a policy of multiculturalism underpinned by social justice. But in the 1980s these policies were questioned by the Liberal and National parties.

In 1984, Liberal leader Andrew Peacock called for more 'balance in the migration intake'. In 1990, Peacock's misrepresentation of Japanese investment in a high-tech city of the future – the so-called Multi-Function Polis – led journalist Paul Kelly to declare he was not fit to be Prime Minister. In 1988, John Howard called for Asian immigration to be 'slowed down a little'.

Howard's remarks led to spirited debate in Parliament. In this speech, Hawke recognises the unity underpinning the migration program through successive governments. It was a policy which expressed a 'triumph of compassion over prejudice, of reason over fear, and of statesmanship over politics'. Offering a window into his personal beliefs, Hawke speaks of his 'belief in the brotherhood of man', which was taught to him by his father, a Congregational minister.

In an interview with Hawke in mid-2010, he said, 'even though I ceased to be a formal orthodox believer, the logic of the proposition was irrefutable. ... We have a moral obligation in trying to uplift the least privileged'.

The motion supporting Australia's immigration policy was carried 81 votes to 53. Three of Howard's Liberal Party colleagues crossed the floor to vote with the government, including former Immigration Minister, Ian Macphee, and a future Immigration Minister, Phillip Ruddock. In the Senate, Peter Baume, crossed the floor to vote with the government.

Michelle Grattan and Ross Peake, writing in *The Age*, said Howard had 'suffered great political damage' as a result of the immigration debate.

'A triumph of compassion over prejudice'

The House of Representatives, Canberra 25 August 1988

I move that this House –

(1) acknowledges the historic action of the Holt Government, with bipartisan support from the Australian Labor Party, in initiating the dismantling of the White Australia Policy;

(2) recognises that since 1973, successive Labor and Liberal/National Party Governments have, with bipartisan support, pursued a racially non-discriminatory immigration policy to the overwhelming national, and international, benefit of Australia; and

(3) gives its unambiguous and unqualified commitment to the principle that, whatever criteria are applied by Australian Governments in exercising their sovereign right to determine the composition of the immigration intake, race or ethnic origin shall never, explicitly or implicitly, be among them.

One of the great and rare distinctions of Australian political leadership in the last generation has been its bipartisan rejection of race as a factor in immigration policy. This has been a triumph of compassion over prejudice, of reason over fear, and of statesmanship over politics.

Twenty-two years ago my party, the Australian Labor Party, disowned its own historic white Australia policy, and the government led by Harold Holt, to its everlasting credit and honour, abolished the white Australia policy and began to dismantle the administrative machinery of discrimination.

This motion is before this House today because that great and rare distinction has been put in jeopardy by the Leader of the Opposition (John Howard) – the inheritor of the role, but not the mantle, of Holt, Gorton, McMahon and Malcolm Fraser. I say this most sincerely to the Leader of the Opposition: this motion has not been brought forward in any attempt to drive him into the ground. It is not, because if he would retract his position then, as far as this side of the House is concerned, what has happened would be regarded as an aberration and would be forgotten. We would be pleased and proud to re-embrace once again an unqualified bipartisanship on this important issue.

Let us look at the statements of the Leader of the Opposition. On 1 August, in regard to Asian immigration, he said:

I do believe that if in the eyes of some in the community it – Asian immigration – is too great, it would be in our immediate term interest and supportive of social cohesion if it were slowed down a little, so that the capacity of the community to absorb was greater.

On 12 August the Leader of the National Party of Australia (Ian Sinclair) said that the figures showed that there were too many Asians coming into the country. On 9 August Senator (John) Stone said:

Asian immigration has to be slowed. It is no use dancing around the bushes.

On 15 August, he also said that it will require a reduction in the excessively high proportion of immigrants from Asia. Those statements remain unretracted. The position of the Leader of the Opposition on 17 August was as follows:

I do not intend to alter one inch the stand that I have taken . . . I do not intend to alter my position on this issue.

The paragraph shuffling in the party meeting last Monday has not changed anything. If, according to the Leader of the Opposition, in the eyes of some in the community Asian immigration is too great, he believes it would be in our immediate term interest and supportive of social cohesion if it were slowed down a little … That has broken the tradition. It has broken the practice of the past and the Leader of the Opposition knows it, his colleagues know it, every commentator in the community knows it and, significantly, every Asian leader knows it.

He has not only broken the traditions of his predecessors but also unfortunately he has broken his own strongly asserted position in this House. Almost four years ago to this very day, on 23 August 1984, the Leader of the Opposition spoke on this issue and he pleaded eloquently for bipartisanship. On 23 August 1984 he advised that just two weeks previously he had successfully moved, with an overwhelming majority of the New South Wales convention of the Liberal Party, a motion on this issue. The Hansard shows that, speaking of that motion, he said:

It recalled amongst other things, that past coalition government policies were built upon a non-discriminatory approach to immigration and a level of intake and a pace of change. During that debate, which was reported fairly extensively by the media, I expressly rejected the proposition that the Liberal Party should take a stand against Asian immigration. I supported the policies of the former coalition government which were humanitarian and liberal in the true sense of the word. We were prepared to take, with the Labor Party's generous support, people from war-torn parts of South East Asia.

Importantly he said:

We were prepared to persuade people around Australia to accept that policy.

… But now, rather than leading, rather than – in his own words – persuading people around Australia to accept the principled and the unqualified position of his predecessors against any suggestion or possibility of discrimination, and instead of accepting that responsibility of leadership, he has unfortunately become the follower of the lowest common denominator.

Let me make it clear – and I want the Leader of the Opposition to know this – I do not accuse him of racism or of being a racist. In a sense, sadly, I make the more serious charge, I make the more damning indictment, of cynical opportunism, in a cynical grab for votes. His polling shows that there is this prejudice in the community and he has unleashed within his coalition and within the wider community the most malevolent, the most hurtful, the most damaging and the most uncohesive forces. Far from 'one Australia' he has guaranteed a divided Australia …

Let me make it crystal clear that we in the Government repudiate the Opposition's position. We repudiate it on moral grounds and we repudiate it on grounds of this nation's economic self-interest. This is one of those occasions when moral and economic interest coincide.

Let me deal briefly with the moral issue … If there is one fundamental aspect of the Christian position, it is the belief and faith in the fatherhood of God. There is one thing which follows as a matter of logic and faith from that position; that is the belief in the brotherhood of man. Any suggestion of antagonism or discrimination on the grounds of race repudiates and is repugnant to that fundamental position. Let me say, for those who do not in any formal sense embrace the Christian position but who are driven by the compulsion of compassionate humanism, that belief in the brotherhood of man is just as fundamental …

If the Leader of the Opposition doubts that his remarks have had any adverse impact on these people I say to him: talk to these kids in their schools; talk to those who have received hate letters in the mail over the last three weeks; talk to the people whose homes and cars have been attacked; talk to those who have been forced to read disgusting graffiti about themselves; and talk to those proud Asian Australians who have been here for many generations and who now feel they are seen as some sort of threat to the social cohesion of the country of which they are proud …

Following the period when we were in economic recession at the beginning of the 1980s, we have turned increasingly to seek enmeshment of the Australian economy in that of the world's most dynamic and economically fastest growing region. It is clear that to do anything to turn our backs on or to prejudice our relations with that region would be against the economic interests of this country.

It is critical that we keep in mind the extent of Australia's economic ties with Asia. Five out of the top ten export markets of this country are in Asia. Half of our national annual exports are now sold to Asian countries ... Japan is our largest export market. Our exports to China and Hong Kong have leapt by over 300 per cent in the last years. In the area of foreign investment, which we know is critical to this country, Asian investment in the Australian economy is worth around $35 billion ... Asia is critical to the future of our fastest growing industry, tourism. One in four of our international tourists now comes from Asia ...

This motion provides the opportunity for repudiation and retraction. The motion asserts that this Parliament of the Commonwealth of Australia, speaking on behalf of the people of Australia, repudiates explicitly, and by any implicit process of paragraph shuffling, the concept or suggestion that discrimination against any race has or will have any place in the immigration policies or the domestic policies of this great Australian nation.

Source: Commonwealth of Australia Parliamentary Debates (Hansard).

PAUL KEATING

'Our Head of State should be one of us'

*Paul Keating announces to the Parliament his government's
vision for an Australian republic*

Paul Keating advanced the idea of an Australian republic more than any other political leader.

In his 1993 election policy speech, Keating promised to establish a Republic Advisory Committee to advise the government on ways to progress a republic. This speech is the government's response to the report of that Committee chaired by Malcolm Turnbull.

A republic was not merely symbolic; it was how Australia 'could embody and represent our values and traditions, our experience and contemporary aspirations, our cultural diversity and social complexity', Keating wrote in his book, *Engagement: Australia Faces the Asia-Pacific.*

In this 30-minute evening address broadcast live on national television, Keating made the case for an Australian republic and outlined the government's minimalist model, hoping to maximise support. Keating said at the outset that 'each and every Australian should be able to aspire to be our head of state'. He returned to that theme at the conclusion: 'We share a continent. We share a past, a present and a future. And our head of state should be one of us'.

There was 'thunderous applause', reported *The Sydney Morning Herald*, from the galleries and the backbenches at the conclusion of Keating's speech.

Opposition Leader John Howard committed the coalition parties to holding a constitutional convention to debate the republic issue if they won office. Following the Keating Government's defeat in 1996, Howard held the convention in early 1998. A compromise set of proposals was agreed on and put to the people on 6 November 1999, and not supported.

An Australian republic remains part of Labor's platform, but lacks a champion like Keating.

'Our Head of State should be one of us'

The House of Representatives, Canberra 7 June 1995

It is the government's view that Australia's Head of State should be an Australian and that Australia should become a republic by the year 2001 ...

Honourable members will recall that to fulfil an undertaking given during the last election campaign, on April 28 ,1993, the government established a Republic Advisory Committee to prepare an options paper which would describe the minimum constitutional changes necessary to create a federal republic of Australia ...

In the eighteen months which have passed since the release of the report, the idea of an Australian republic has come to occupy a central place in our national political debate: not only in this Parliament but within the political parties, in major representative and community bodies, in schools and universities, communities at large and, I daresay, around countless Australian dinner tables.

In the process many Australians have come to favour a republic. Just as many, perhaps, now believe it is inevitable.

Many may regret the prospect of change and be unsure about the means by which it can be achieved, but recognise that sooner or later we must have an Australian as our Head of State. That one small step would make Australia a republic.

Governments can wait for opinion to force their hand, or they can lead. They can wait for the world to change and respond as necessity demands, or they can see the way the world is going and point the way.

We are approaching the 21st century and the centenary of our nationhood ... The fact is that if the plans for our nationhood were being drawn up now, by this generation of Australians and not those of a century ago, it is beyond question that we would make our Head of State an Australian ...

This is not because our generation lacks respect for the British monarchy, or the British people, or our British heritage, or the British institutions we have made our own, or our long friendship with the British in peace and war. On the contrary, Australians everywhere respect them, as they respect the Queen. But they are not Australian ...

The people of modern Australia are drawn from virtually every country in the world. It is no reflection on the loyalty of a great many of them to say that the British monarchy is a remote and inadequate symbol of their affections for Australia ...

It is not a radical undertaking that we propose.

In proposing that our Head of State should be an Australian we are proposing nothing more than the obvious. Our Head of State should embody and represent Australia's values and traditions, Australia's experience and aspirations. We need not apologise for the nationalism in these sentiments, but in truth they contain as much commonsense as patriotism.

This is a point worth making: this republican initiative is not an exercise in jingoism; it is not accompanied by the beat of drums – or chests. It asserts nothing more than our unique identity. It expresses nothing more than our desire to have a Head of State who is truly one of us …

At present, under the Constitution, Australia's Head of State is the Queen and her 'heirs and successors in the sovereignty of the United Kingdom'. Anyone reading the Australian Constitution who is unfamiliar with the practical realities of Australian government would assume that the role of the monarch was central.

In fact, the involvement of the British monarch in Australia's affairs is now very limited. The Queen's role as Head of State is in most respects carried out by the Governor-General. Of the responsibilities the Queen retains, the most notable is her appointment of the Governor-General which, by convention, she does on the advice of the prime minister.

We are not quite alone among the countries of the world in having as our Head of State someone who is not one of our own citizens, but we are in a very small minority – and a majority of the countries in the Commonwealth of Nations are republics with their own Head of State … The Queen of Australia is also Queen of the United Kingdom and 14 other countries in the United Nations.

Notwithstanding that the Queen is Australia's Head of State and fulfils that duty conscientiously, when she travels overseas she represents only the United Kingdom. Her visits abroad often tend to promote British trade and British interests – they do not promote Australia's trade and interests. This is, of course, right and proper for the Head of State of the United Kingdom. But it is not right for Australia …

Each and every Australian should be able to aspire to be our Head of State. Every Australian should know that the office will always be filled by a citizen of high standing who has made an outstanding contribution to Australia and who, in making it, has enlarged our view of what it is to be Australian.

In these and other ways, the creation of an Australian republic can actually deliver a heightened sense of unity, it can enliven our national spirit and, in our own minds and those of our neighbours, answer beyond doubt the perennial question of Australian identity – the question of who we are and what we stand for.

The answer is not what having a foreign Head of State suggests. We are not a political or cultural appendage to another country's past. We are simply and unambiguously Australian. If only by a small degree an Australian republic fulfilled these ideals it would be worth it …

We therefore intend to ask the Australian people if they want an Australian republic with an Australian Head of State.

The change we propose has very limited implications for the design of Australia's democracy. It is the so-called 'minimalist' option. All the essential Constitutional principles and practices, which have worked, well and evolved constructively over the last hundred years will remain in place …

There has been considerable debate in the community about how the Head of State should be chosen … The debate is principally between those who support popular election and those who favour election by the Parliament.

The desire for a popular election stems from the democratic sentiment which all Australians – including all of us in this place – share. However, the Government has come to the view that if a new Australian Head of State were to be elected by popular mandate, he or she would inherit a basis of power that would prove to be fundamentally at odds with our Westminster-style system of government. It should be recognised that a Head of State, whose powers derived from a general election, would be the only person in the political system so elected …

I think there is a consensus that the Head of State should be, in some sense, 'above politics'. With this the Government agrees. The Head of State should be an eminent Australian, a widely respected figure who can represent the nation as a whole …

We therefore propose, as the Republic Advisory Committee suggested, that the Head of State be elected by a two-thirds majority vote in a joint sitting of both Houses of the Commonwealth Parliament on the nomination of the Prime Minister and the Cabinet …

A two-thirds majority vote of both Houses would require bi-partisan support and ensure that the Head of State had the blessing of all the major parties …

The Government believes that, taken together – the authority and source of the Head of State's powers coming from the Parliament, removal by the same means as appointment, and the capacity to censure – these elements provide effective counterweights to the substantial authority vested in the Head of State through the reserve powers …

The Government puts forward these proposals to provide a basis for considered public discussion. The Australian Constitution cannot be changed in any way without a referendum, and to succeed at a referendum a proposed change must win the agreement of a majority of voters in a majority of States and a majority of voters overall.

The Government proposes to put the question of a republic to the Australian people some time in 1998 or 1999. Acceptance at the referendum will mean that Australia can be a republic by the year of the centenary of Federation, 2001. Before the referendum, there will be extensive consultation with the people of Australia …

The detail of the changes we propose may at first glance obscure the meaning of them. The meaning is simple and, we believe, irresistible – as simple and irresistible as the idea of a Commonwealth of Australia was to the Australians of a century ago.

The meaning then was a nation united in common cause for the common good. A nation which gave expression to the lives we lead together on this continent, the experience and hopes we share as Australians.

The meaning now is still a product of that founding sentiment – it is that we are all Australians. We share a continent. We share a past, a present and a future. And our Head of State should be one of us.

Source: <www.keating.org.au>

PAUL KEATING

'When the government changes, the country changes'

Paul Keating, on the eve of the 1996 election, warns the Australian people about the dangers of a Howard Government

Paul Keating's address to the National Press Club in the final week of the 1996 election campaign was his last major speech as Prime Minister.

When I interviewed Keating in June 2010, the speech still invoked a mix of regret and remorse along with pride and satisfaction but, above all, disappointment – not for him, but for the nation. As Keating thumbed through the speech and read passages aloud, he said, it 'was very much about the new order'. It 'said more about Australian public life and where we've come to than anything else'. The speech recalled his government's achievements and revisited its philosophy.

For Keating, the significance of the speech was the 'warning' that it offered voters about a Howard Government. He read aloud the passage on industrial relations, which accurately predicted an unravelling of the government's policies. 'The country can't say that it wasn't told', Keating said. 'The point is that countries make mistakes and they get things wrong.'

Keating's speech came at the end of a spirited election campaign. He declared that Australia 'has changed inexorably and for the better'. He spoke of a 'social democracy' being the goal of public policy. He connected the various elements of his 'big picture' agenda: native title and reconciliation, the republic, the drive into Asia, economic growth and jobs, the arts and a vibrant multicultural Australia.

It was also a speech that coined a political cliché: 'when the government changes, the country changes'. And so it did.

The speech is a reminder of a reformist Labor government with a progressive and uplifting vision for the nation, led by a bold leader with an ambition for Australia's future that remains unequalled.

'When the government changes,
the country changes'

National Press Club, Canberra 29 February 1996

I've always believed that there's been a position of importance between the government and the media, and I'd like to think that over the years I've been able to work with the Press Gallery and the media, to talk about Australia – to tell people about the need for changes, to tell them why, to try and describe the sort of country we want – and I think that together we've been able to see something larger and to work towards it …

The story of all these years since, is that Australia has changed inexorably and for the better – it's changed at the hands of a conscientious government. It's changed at the hands of a government that was determined to give the country an even break. It was determined not to treat the public cynically – not to hand them mush – as coalitions had handed them for years and years and years, and that the hollow men of the Liberal Party should take their proper places in the parliament on the opposition side. I think the media rose to that challenge, and I think that the reporting through the 80s and 90s of economic change – the need for it – the calibrations of the changes, the shifts in social policy, the need for a cohesive society, the sense of some social democracy emerging as an object of national policy – all of these things …

The government built a market economy and grafted on to it an equitable social policy – the likes of which Australia had never seen – and the compact together is now unique in the western world. It's given us quite phenomenally high rates of economic growth, spectacular rates of employment growth and low inflation. It's given us a complete change in our industrial culture. That compact has with the Australian community, come by way of the wages Accord – the good sense in setting wages and conditions. That compact has come in trying to build a better country …

… the Australia today compared to a decade or so ago is almost unimaginably different. It's an interesting, vibrant, lively, competitive, outward-looking country. It's confident, it's exciting. It's got a future which I think has no parallel for us … what nation has been given an inheritance like we have? 18 million of us, a continent of our own, a border with no-one – and the chance to actually live in a beautiful country, rather than one simply spoiled by the careless commitment of industrial resources.

And on top of that, living in the fastest growing part of the world – in the region of the world where there's an economic revolution taking place without precedence in history. An economic revolution that will make the industrial revolution look like a Sunday afternoon picnic – 2.5 billion people, economies growing at 8 per cent to 10 per cent a year, and we're right in the middle of it – and we're out there, competitive and ready to embrace it.

But we know that you have to go there together, we have to go there as a united country. We have to declare that we are unique. We have to be assertive about ourselves, and that confidence and assertion can only come with confidence in who we are and what we are …

All countries need a break in their history. The great break for us was the post-war migration program. It made us more diverse, more interesting, more vibrant and gave us more critical mass. I think the next break was the market economy's social graft which Labor has put into place, because then we've got the best of all worlds – vitality, diversity, strength, critical mass, and a good economy with the right bases to it, and a cohesive social fabric that makes every Australian feel as though they matter and that they are important …

This selection puts all that to test. Did we build a new standard? Have we created a change? Or are we going to slide back into the old comfort station of someone who says he feels relaxed and comfortable about the past, the present and the future? Do we just nod gently off, back to sleep again, like we did in the Rip van Winkle years of Menzies and his successive governments? Or will the new standard of energy, of drive, of ministers actually running the policy, of accountability, of truth – will all these things be simply a remnant of a decade of change – which then finishes or closes were a coalition government to be elected? Because I think this is what the election is boiling down to.

The Coalition have laid out no philosophic basis for their election. At Mr Howard's policy speech there was no philosophy, there was no structure, there was no thoughtfulness – just a grab-bag of promises driven by a polling agency and an advertising agency. In other words, he thinks that if he puts a few baubles in the right places on the basis of rote and rotation – that it's his turn, the fact that he's just stuck around so long – government will just fall into his lap.

I believe there's always got to be a road-map for Australia, there's always got to be philosophy, there's always got to be belief, and there's always got to be passion. Because if the ministers and the prime minister are not passionate, they don't believe, and they haven't that thing which is not at any place in the Liberal campaign manual – imagination – Australia would have remained just a modest country with very modest prospects …

Ask John Howard why he says he'll keep Medicare – he says: 'Oh, because I think Australians have come to believe in it, and we think we can do some other things in private health'. Not one dollar of his commitments went to public health – not one dollar … Only money kicked upstairs for private hospitals and specialists – as always, as always. Always run by the lowest common denominator of the Liberal Party …

Take industrial relations – they're running their cheap little ads on radio over the weekend. Well, isn't it nice to go into an election where both parties agree on Medicare, both parties agree on industrial relations, both parties agree on the environment – authorised by A Robb for the Liberal Party. Now why would they authorise a cynical thing like that? Because they want to pretend that they'll keep Medicare and a decent industrial relations system, and support for the environment.

On industrial relations they're saying this: if you join the workforce and you change jobs you lose the Award protections. 1.4 million Australians do this every year … So in other words they'll have no industrial protections, they'll have no right to collectively bargain. They'll have to make their contract in secret – the only people to have common knowledge of the contract will be each individual person and their prospective employer. There'll be no Industrial Relations Commission vetting it, to see that it meets the no disadvantage test, because that would not be there – and Mr Howard has made clear the Arbitration Commission – the AIRC would not have a role. So there's no umpire. He's got a thing called the Employment Advocate, but it's got no powers – and if a young person or a person joining the workforce for the first time went to the Employment Advocate – of course they wouldn't get the job. So they'd just degrade the system …

He believes in families, but he doesn't believe in the thing that most sustains families outside of the unity of the family itself – and that's of course a wage or a salary … he will not support a decent wage increase …

Then he talks about the environment. They've opposed the external affairs power which was central to the Gordon below Franklin, the World Heritage area, which we've used in a number of places. They have opposed all the declarations over the years – Shoalwater Bay, Shelbourne Bay, Jervis Bay – and yet they expect the Australian community to gullibly swallow that Mr Howard's a born-again environmentalist …

The fact of the matter is that John Howard has gone through this election campaign believing in none of those things …

We will not have a government which believes in these things, because the opposition is not a social democratic party – it's a deeply conservative party.

And John Howard correctly has described himself as the most conservative leader the Liberal Party's ever had, and that's why these policies are the way they are.

The other thing about it is, you can't have a little bit of them … In other words, when you've got them, you're stuck with them – and there's no turning it out until another election. And then will the fire keep burning? Will the fire go out? Will the drive be lost? I think it will …

Mr Howard says – the subliminal message is, 'it's time for a change', to which we say: 'a change to what Mr Howard?' He says: 'oh, we want to change, we want to change, but we think that Labor's got it pretty right on Medicare, the environment and IR – we're even advertising the fact we have similar policies. We want to change to look just like you. We want a change of government, so we can be just like you'. To which I say: 'well, if that's what the Australian people want, why wouldn't they take the architects of the policy, the authors of the policy – the believers who put the structure into place? Why would they go to the photocopiers?'

So I'll finish on these two points. We should never start the new century on the back foot. We shouldn't elect to office a prime minister who will not lead us into that century – understanding its future, having enough imagination to grasp it, and the leadership and the courage to actually go and do it – to actually make it work. We shouldn't do that. Because, were that to happen we would be giving up the opportunity of our history – the most strongest growing part of the world, the most exciting time, and us never more able to participate in it.

When the government changes, the country changes … what we've built in these years is I think so valuable – to change it and to lose it, is just a straight appalling loss for Australia.

So, this election is going to boil down to two things – philosophy and competence. Whether each of the parties has a philosophy for government and is competent? Whether it can actually do the job? Whether it can cut the mustard of the hard policy and the discipline and the accountability and the calibration, and the belief in it all and the truth of it all? Or whether we're going to go back really, to the dismal old days of the 70s – with a group of ministers who just can't make it all work, can't bring the public with them – and where we slide back into that morass of uncompetitiveness, and where we look backwards and not forwards? …

The main issue of the election is whether the real government of Australia – not the pretend one, the real one, with the real policies, the real beliefs, the real imagination goes on to continue driving and guiding this country and believe in this country – or whether we have a group of people who think the only reason they can get into office, is to buy their way back with money they don't have.

I don't think it's come to this, and I don't think the Australian public will either.

Source: Editor's personal files

KIM BEAZLEY

'Demonising the reputation of those who work on our waterfront'

Kim Beazley defends the rights of unionised workers on the waterfront

The 1998 confrontation on the waterfront ignited a battle of class warfare and joined the twin wings of labour movement – industrial and political – into a battle fought on the docks, in the media, on the floor of the nation's parliaments and in the nation's courtrooms.

The result was a reformed waterfront, but the Maritime Union of Australia was not defeated and the right of workers to bargain collectively was upheld.

The waterfront dispute began in earnest on 7 April 1998 when Patricks locked out their workforce. The next day, Workplace Relations Minister Peter Reith announced measures to reform workplace practices, including funding for redundancy payments to unionised workers. Patricks planned to replace the workforce with non-union labour trained in Dubai. Security guards took control of the waterfront while wearing balaclavas, carrying mace, with dogs on chains at their side.

'The actions of this government', Labor leader Kim Beazley said in Parliament, 'are to target a particular union and seek to destroy the lawful rights of the workers to organise'. Beazley said it reflected 'a centuries-old hatred of organised labour ... [it] is a debate that has been around for a hundred years'.

Beazley, via correspondence in mid-2010, said that 'You can draw a line through the motivations of the then government behind this legislation to the WorkChoices legislation of almost a decade later'. He said 'this was a partisan political attack resisted by a broader community than Labor's partisan supporters. Many workers are heartland Liberal supporters, including many trade unionists'.

'Demonising the reputation of those who work on our waterfront'

The House of Representatives, Canberra 8 April 1998

These stevedoring bills have nothing whatsoever to do with waterfront reform. The actions of this government have nothing whatsoever to do with waterfront reform. The actions of this government are to target a particular union and seek to destroy the lawful rights of the workers to organise, the lawful rights of all Australians to be represented by people whom they choose, the lawful rights of Australians to work once they have made a choice as to how they should be represented …

Reflect on this: these workers have been sacked, not made redundant under the normal provisions of redundancies. Redundancies occur when a worker is surplus to requirements. There are no workers here who are surplus to requirements. Their sacking has not been based on any information provided to them that they are surplus to requirements. They have been sacked in order to be replaced by another work force. It has nothing to do with competition on the waterfront …

The legislation is endorsing a process of unlawfully sacking Australian workers for one reason and one reason only, and that is that they happen to be members of a union. If the Minister for Workplace Relations and Small Business (Peter Reith) does not believe that, within the framework of his own Workplace Relations Act, his Act is unlawful, let me quote from subdivision C of his Act, 'Unlawful termination of employment by employer'. Subsection 170CK(2), states:

> … an employer must not terminate an employee's employment for any one or more of the following reasons:

and it goes through the reasons. The second reason states:

> (b) trade union membership or participation in trade union activities outside working hours or, with the employer's consent, during working hours.

You may not be sacked if your interest in life is going to be advanced by being a member of a trade union – not redundant workers but unionists sacked in order to destroy a union for the political benefit of the Liberal Party, not for productivity on the waterfront. Furthermore, there are more unlawful elements of this particular action. I cite the employer's duty in relation to the award under which those sacked workers are now employed. I go through the employer's duty to notify under the award. It states:

> Where an employer has made a definite decision to introduce major changes in production, program, organisation, structure or technology that are likely to have significant effects on employees, the employer shall notify the employees who may be affected by the proposed changes and the union or unions.

The second part of it, defining that first clause, states:

> Significant effects include termination of employment.

So they have breached the award. Because there are a very large number of members of our work force who work under awards, all Australians know that awards give them protection. The processes in those awards are the processes that guarantee their security …

It does not matter whether or not you feel any particular sympathy for members of the Maritime Union – this government has worked very hard at demonising the reputation of those who work on our waterfront – but all Australians will feel sympathy this Easter for the 1,400 families who do not know what will happen to their breadwinner as a result of the actions which are undertaken here …

In order to justify therefore a set of unlawful acts on the part of those employees, this government has entered into a conspiracy with them to seek a confrontational solution and has now entered into a conspiracy to attempt to establish an ex post facto justification for this particular unlawful act as far as Patricks is concerned.

These sackings have never been about waterfront reform; the activities of Patricks have never been about waterfront reform. The management of Patricks have displayed a mendaciousness; they have displayed a conspiratorial bent. They have not dealt honestly and straightforwardly with their work force, and they have been aided and abetted in that regard by this government for months and months now …

What happened when we confronted this situation when we got into office? We had an overmanned waterfront – 10,000 stevedores – left in place by the Fraser-Howard government of the late 1970s and early 1980s. We had a wretched practice as far as movement of two-thirds of our exports was concerned. The Labor government put in place reforms and the number working on the waterfront came down from 10,000 to just over 3,000. These were redundancies, not sackings. Furthermore, they were voluntary redundancies. They were workers surplus to requirements … In that process agreements were entered into between the parties on the waterfront, which have produced, by the minister's own admission, world's best practice outcomes – all achieved through a process of negotiation …

110

This is a government which desires confrontation for various purposes. Firstly, they have a visceral hatred of organised labour. It is a centuries old hatred of organised labour. In many ways, the debate that we are having here is a debate that has been around for a hundred years as far as Australian history is concerned. There has always been a complete unwillingness by our political opponents to accept the fact that if as an individual you approach an employer and expect to bargain on an equal basis you cannot …

What we see here is a government energised to unfairness, a government energised to produce an outcome to deprive Australians of jobs … This has been a consistent pattern of conspiracy to do down ordinary Australians – a persistent pattern of misleading and duplicity by this government …

The ordinary worker in Australia has choice, the ordinary worker in Australia values their freedom and the ordinary worker in Australia has an opportunity to collectively bargain and negotiate with their employer if they so choose. That has been a right that Australians have valued for the best part of this century. It is a right that they have sought and it is a right of which they have now been deprived.

Source: Commonwealth of Australia Parliamentary Debates (Hansard).

BOB CARR

'A day that will live in industrial infamy'

Bob Carr describes the attack on waterfront workers as 'an act of industrial vandalism'

In the NSW Parliament, Bob Carr characterised the waterfront battle instigated by Patricks as 'a day that will live in industrial infamy', drawing on the words of Franklin D Roosevelt in the aftermath of the Japanese attack on Pearl Harbour in 1941.

'It is an attack on Australian unionism', Carr said, 'funded by the Australian taxpayer'. He labelled it an 'act of industrial vandalism' with the sole aim 'not about reform' but 'about driving unions out of the Australian work-force'.

Carr's speech was delivered as an answer to a question from a government backbencher during Question Time. Almost every sentence of Carr's speech was met with boisterous interjections from the Opposition.

As Carr argued, it was also a defining event for the Howard Government, forever characterising it as a divisive, ruthless and confrontational government. As Carr recalled in his book *Thoughtlines*, 'vivid in most Australians minds' were the images of 'the dogs on chains, the brawny men in balaclavas, the distressed little girls, the smiles of John Howard and Peter Reith after the mass sackings'.

'A day that will live in industrial infamy'

NSW Legislative Assembly, Sydney 8 April 1998

The naked truth is that 1,400 Australians have been sacked because they belong to a trade union. The naked truth about what happened in the dead of night on 7 April 1998, a day that will live in industrial infamy, is that 1,400 were sacked because they belonged to a trade union.

Let this be clear: by this action the Howard-Reith Government has declared to the world that in Australia union membership is a sackable offence.

Patricks stevedoring may have provided the guard dogs and the security group to lock out its work force in the dead of night, it may have organised the mercenaries to replace them, but the guiding hand in all of this is the Howard Government. And more than that – the Howard Government is supporting Patricks with taxpayers' money to the tune of $250 million. It is an attack on Australian unionism funded by the Australian taxpayer …

Again I emphasise that the 1,400 workers who have been sacked have committed one offence and one offence only: they are members of the Maritime Union of Australia. They are members of a trade union. They and their union have not been on strike. They and their union have not refused to negotiate. They and their union have not rejected the workplace agreements legislation. They have never rejected waterfront reform. They have not broken any law.

Indeed, as we can demonstrate to the House – and will in debate later this afternoon – the process of reform, particularly in the Port of Sydney, has achieved a substantial increase in efficiency and productivity. That process, which was put in train by the Hawke and Keating governments, was well on track to achieve further gains, especially for our hard-pressed primary producers, until this act of industrial vandalism threatened unprecedented disruption.

What they have done is simply to exercise their lawful rights as Australians: the lawful right of all workers to organise; the lawful right to choose who shall represent them in the workplace. The price they have paid for the exercise of their lawful right, a right fought for and embedded in the fabric of Australian democracy for a century, is the sack …

Today's legislation in the Federal Parliament states, 'The Minister may authorise payments that are directly or indirectly in connection with the reform or restructuring of the stevedoring industry'. But these sackings are not about reform, they are not about restructuring: they are about driving unions out of the Australian work force.

Source: NSW Legislative Assembly Debates (Hansard).

MARK LATHAM

'The ladder of opportunity'

Reflecting strong Labor values and promoting an ambitious policy agenda, Mark Latham makes the case for a Labor government

Mark Latham was a freshly minted Labor leader when he arrived to address the ALP National Conference in January 2004.

Around 800 delegates sat in cascaded seating, watching a video montage of the new leader's background. The INXS song 'New Sensation' heralded Latham's arrival and he descended the stairs, through the crowd, and took his place on the stage, under the banner 'Mark Latham and Labor – Opportunity for All'.

Latham gave an uplifting and inspiring speech. He championed the idea of the 'ladder of opportunity', which he spoke of when he first became Labor leader. He wanted to expand opportunity and reward 'ambition and aspiration'. He spoke of a big policy agenda – education, health, workplace relations, environment, foreign policy, immigration – and of 'a big country' that was 'big in size, big in spirit, big in character'.

Writing in his diary, Latham said, 'Nervous all morning ... the speech rolled out my Third Way themes: a positive party, opportunity matched by responsibility, responsive and flexible service delivery, rebuilding social capital, opening up our democracy, and economic policies based on competition, incentive and budget savings'.

Steve Lewis, writing in *The Australian*, described it as 'a defining election pitch' aimed at 'establishing clear battlelines' for the election.

Note: Some may disagree with my decision to include this, or any, speech by Latham in a book of great Labor speeches. But this speech earned a warm reception at the time. It reflects strong Labor values and promotes many good Labor policies. It refreshed Labor's traditional values for the modern era. It recalls much of the 'third way' policy project advocated by Bill Clinton and Tony Blair, but it is authentically Australian, authentically Labor and authentically Latham.

'The ladder of opportunity'

Sydney Convention and Exhibition Centre, Sydney 29 January 2004

When I became the Leader of our great party two months ago I said that I wanted to be positive. I said that I didn't believe in opposition for opposition's sake …

I've always believed in the Labor Party as the great positive force in Australian politics:

The Party that gave us Medibank and then Medicare.

The Party that expanded the education system and dared to dream of opportunity for all.

The Party that built the modern Australian economy and made us internationally competitive.

The Party that made us relevant in Asia and proudly told the rest of the world that we believe in Aboriginal reconciliation.

And we believe in Australian independence – an Australian Republic …

You ask me the big difference in Australian politics? The Howard Government campaigns on fear. We campaign on opportunity. I want to talk to you about the future, not the past. About hope, not fear …

Delegates, the Australia I believe in is a big country. Big in size, big in spirit, big in character. And that's our task: to be bigger than the Howard Government.

Big enough to invest in the education and health care of our children.

Big enough to provide public housing for the poor and care for the aged and disabled.

Big enough to protect the environment and ratify the Kyoto Protocol.

Big enough to protect our great natural assets – to save the Murray Darling and the Great Barrier Reef.

Big enough to care for our regions and – once and for all – stop the full sale of Telstra …

Big enough to help the working poor and put some decency back into the industrial relations system. The Tories say it's a sin to represent working people. I say it's a virtue. Like you, I'm proud of where I come from. I'm proud to be Labor.

That's why my government will abolish AWAs and restore the role of the Industrial Relations Commission. I don't believe in a dog-eat-dog industrial relations system. I want cooperation and productivity in Australian workplaces.

And as we work together as a nation, we need a better balance between work and family ... That's why a Labor Government will introduce Paid Maternity Leave and improve the rights of working parents.

Delegates, I see Australia as a big country but also a prosperous country. Labor built the modern Australian economy and we should always be proud of that achievement. Competition and productivity are Labor words. They don't belong to the Tories. They belong to us ...

We are a prosperous nation but surely, delegates, we can make better use of our prosperity ... That's what I want for Australia: prosperity with a purpose – all Australians climbing the ladder of opportunity ...

I believe in ambition and aspiration. I believe in the powerful combination of hard work, good family and the civilising role of government services. I say that economic aspiration is good and social mobility is even better – all Australians climbing the ladder of opportunity.

The problem is that the Howard Government has been taking out the rungs. I want to put them back in.

More rungs in early childhood development: child care and preschool places, qualified teachers in our child care system, and a national reading program for our children. That's the first rung on the ladder of opportunity.

The next is school education ... I want every school in this country to be a high-achieving school – good teachers, parents and students working together. That's why Labor will introduce a needs-based funding system: all schools – government and non-government – reaching a strong national standard for resources and results ...

The third rung on the ladder of opportunity is post-secondary education. When they leave high school, I don't want any young Australian to have to pause for a moment about whether or not they can afford a higher education ... The best way to increase our productivity and economic growth is through investment in education ...

The health care of our nation – it's the fourth rung on the ladder of opportunity. Medicare is a universal system of health care. It can never be means tested. It can never be a two-tiered system. If it's not universal, it's not Medicare ...

Reward for effort – it's another rung on the ladder of opportunity. I want more incentive, more reward for the hard workers in our society ... We need to make the tax system fairer and put some incentive back into the Australian economy.

There are other rungs on the ladder of opportunity: home ownership, aged care, regional employment ...

MARK LATHAM: 'THE LADDER OF OPPORTUNITY'

Our services will provide new opportunities for people, but they must also demand responsibility in return. We can provide all the services in the world, but unless people are willing to work hard and respond the right way, we won't get the results we need for Australia. Responsibility from all, opportunity for all: that's what I call a good society …

Delegates, a strong community requires more than high incomes and government services. It needs strong, healthy relationships between people … We need to rebuild community and work with the voluntary sector. This is why I have decided to appoint Lindsay Tanner as the Shadow Minister for Community Relationships, in addition to his existing responsibilities …

In government, delegates, we will invest more in basic services and invest more in the Australian community. But for every dollar we invest, we have to cut a dollar from the existing budget. That's our approach for the next campaign: better services, fully paid for …

Delegates, protecting Australia's national security is the first and final responsibility of an Australian Government … Our policy has three pillars: our membership of the United Nations; our alliance with the United States; and comprehensive engagement with Asia. But delegates, Labor's three pillars rest on a rock. And the rock is an independent, self-reliant Australia. When I have to make a decision on Australia's national security, I'll only ask one question: what is in Australia's national interest? …

And delegates I give you this pledge: a Labor Government will never send young Australians to war in search of weapons that don't exist, for a purpose that's not true …

We need to make our country more self-reliant in the war against terror. Because, delegates, the Howard Government has been neglecting the home front … That's why we need a Coastguard – to keep Australia safe from the people smugglers, the gun runners and the drug merchants … I also want a Department of Homeland Security – a single Commonwealth agency to do the practical work with the States and Territories on national security …

Delegates, modern politics is broken and we need to fix it … After years of broken promises and broken programs, they no longer trust the political system … So I commit myself here today to this great national purpose: reinventing and revitalising our democracy, opening up greater public participation, cleaning out the excesses of the political system, governing for the people, not the powerful …

In the lead up to this Conference, I've had lots of advice … Some people said, 'whatever you do, don't mention asylum seekers. It's not popular'. Well, I believe in our policy. I'm proud of our asylum seeker policy and I'm going to talk about it. Not because it's popular. But because it's right … I believe in strong border protection, but I also believe in the fair treatment of refugees …

So, delegates, in every way, there's a big challenge ahead of us as we enter the campaign for 2004. Let's keep up our new momentum at this conference. Let's show the renewed determination of our party and our movement – to work together, to give Australia a government as big as the party we serve.

As big as the country we love – an Australian Labor Government.

Source: Editor's personal files.

KEVIN RUDD

'The single greatest threat to our economic security in a generation'

*Kevin Rudd outlines the government's response to
the emerging Global Financial Crisis*

The worst global economic downturn since the 1930s saw the financial system go into meltdown, trade flows seize up, confidence plummet and advanced economies contract.

The government's response was to act quickly to stabilise the financial system by guaranteeing bank deposits and stimulate the economy. This included large-scale infrastructure investment, energy efficiency measures for homes and social housing.

Although there was criticism over implementation of some measures, Australia largely weathered the economic storm and emerged comparatively stronger than other nations.

In this speech, delivered a day after the announcement of the government's first major stimulus package, Prime Minister Kevin Rudd analysed the origins of the crisis and outlined the response.

Rudd began with a quote from John F Kennedy, which he had used in his reply to the Howard Government's last budget in May 2007. (Kennedy himself had borrowed it from Franklin D Roosevelt a generation earlier.)

Rudd labelled the Global Financial Crisis as 'the single greatest threat to our economic security in a generation'. He attacked 'extreme capitalism' and the 'obscene failures in corporate governance' fuelled by the 'twin evils' of 'greed' and 'fear'.

He said the G20 group of world economies (including Australia), rather than the smaller G8, would be a more effective forum for global economic cooperation. His address to the United Nations in September 2008 had argued for the G20 to lead global economic cooperation, which it eventually did. Few world leaders were so quickly cognisant of the economic calamity about to happen or the response needed to deal with it.

In January 2010, *The Australian* named Rudd as their 'Australian of the Year', praising his 'adept handling of the economy during the GFC and its aftermath'.

'The single greatest threat to our economic security in a generation'

National Press Club, Canberra 15 October 2008

Last year, in my formal reply to the last Budget of the Howard Government, I referred to a great remark from a great American President, John F Kennedy. Speaking at a time of unprecedented American prosperity, President Kennedy said:

> the time to fix the (leaky) roof is when the sun is shining.

And I said back then the sun was shining on Australia. Back then, because of an unprecedented global economic boom, the sun had been shining on Australia for the better part of a decade. But all that began to change, a little more than three months later, with the beginning of what we now have come to call the Global Financial Crisis.

What began as a patch of bad weather in America has now become a cyclone that has threatened to engulf the world. It has smashed its way across the globe. It has swept aside financial institutions that had survived a combination of World Wars and world depressions across the centuries …

These are testing times. But my message to the nation today is that while these winds of ill-fortune have battered institutions and shattered confidence across the world, the Australian financial system remains strong. Our economy remains strong. And the government has set a national course of action to see Australia through this international crisis.

Ladies and gentlemen. We are being tested. Of that there is no doubt. But our country and our economy will prevail. In part, because in the time the government has been in office, we have been planning ahead – preparing for the worsening of the storm …

I know that many Australians are deeply concerned about the future. Make no mistake – this is the single greatest threat to our economic security in a generation. And it's the most significant upheaval in the global financial system in our lifetime.

That is why the government has acted decisively with the $10.4 billion Economic Security Strategy: to do everything possible to keep our economy growing; to do everything possible to create new Australians jobs; to do everything possible to build new Australian homes; to do everything possible to help those in greatest need; to do everything possible to prepare for the future.

In the last few weeks the global financial crisis has moved into a new and dangerous stage. Its origins go back to the beginning of this decade, with the collapse of the dot com boom. US authorities responded with aggressive cuts in interest rates. That opened up an era of cheap debt that was accompanied by increasing financial complexity and a greater appetite for risk. Financial products – from basic sub-prime home loans to complex financial derivatives – were built on the shallow foundations of a cheap debt economy.

Loans were advanced to millions of people, especially in the United States, with no realistic prospect of them ever being repaid. And those loans were financed through complex financial products that were understood by neither investors nor regulators. The balkanisation of risk, the attenuation of risk sought the impossible dream of the elimination of risk and responsibility – so that ultimately nobody believed they carried risk and responsibility.

And through it all, the ratings agencies blessed these products as safe investments – ratings agencies that have yet to face their own day of reckoning – and the products they sanctioned continued to proliferate.

Credit default swaps also played an important role in the excessive underwriting of high-risk mortgages. The ability and willingness of providers of credit default swaps to offer cheap insurance against counter-party risk exaggerated the credit worthiness of the assets and the counter-parties that backed them to the final investors.

This mix of cheap credit and cheap insurance ultimately resulted in these sub-prime assets being sold all over the world to investors, from both large scale financial institutions to small scale investors like councils, corporations, charities, churches and even ordinary households.

They had no chance of understanding what they were investing in, until crunch-time came late last year, when the absurdity and the obscenity of the leverage contained in these investments finally began to erupt.

By then, it was clear things had gone badly wrong. And it was then that the financial crisis erupted. Because when analysts went looking to find which institutions had exposure to those sub-prime loans, those exposures weren't transparent and couldn't be easily found.

There was no clarity about who held which investments, nor what those investments really contained. Clouds of suspicion began to gather over one financial institution after another. As those clouds began to gather, lending began to dry up. And what had begun as the sub-prime lending crisis slowly morphed into a global crisis of confidence.

The causes were complex: failures in transparency; failures in lending standards; failures in prudential standards; failures in risk-management;

failures in corporate governance – in fact, obscene failures in corporate governance which rewarded greed without any regard to the integrity of the financial system.

And these failures weren't limited just to businesses on the margins of the financial system. They happened in our major global financial institutions, the Wall Street investment banks that were pillars of the global financial system.

And that is where we've arrived in recent weeks, as markets have lost confidence even in leading global financial institutions and in the international financial system itself …

What we have seen is the comprehensive failure of extreme capitalism – extreme capitalism which now turns to government to prevent systemic failure. The institutions of government that extreme capitalism spent decades deriding.

So what is to be done? The collapse of this house of cards has had devastating consequences both for financial markets and for the real economy … But Australia is in a stronger position than comparable nations. We have four of the world's 20 AA rated banks … The regulation and supervision of Australian financial institutions leads the world … These are important national institutional strengths at a time of global systemic weakness …

It is clear that the global economic impacts of this crisis will be profound. The boom that saw the strongest period of global economic growth in thirty years is over. The IMF is now forecasting the slowest growth in advanced economies for over a quarter of a century …

That is why the government has taken decisive, early action to support our economy and our financial system …

First, we have acted to maintain liquidity in financial markets.

Second, we have guaranteed bank funding …

Third, we have guaranteed bank deposits …

Fourth, we have acted to protect financial institutions from speculators and short selling …

Fifth, we have acted to support competition and liquidity in the mortgage market …

Sixth, we have acted to reform the regulation of credit in Australia.

And seven, the government has been active all year in the Financial Stability Forum, the IMF and the G20 in forging consensus for consistent regulatory responses to the global financial crisis across all major economies.

The Economic Security Strategy the Government announced yesterday was decisive action, responsible action and early action – In extraordinary and dangerous economic times. The Economic Security Strategy was made possible by the $22 billion surplus we built in the May Budget as a buffer for the future ...

The Strategy contains five key measures:

- $4.8 billion for an immediate down payment on long term pension reform;
- $3.9 billion in support payments for low and middle income families;
- A $1.5 billion investment to help first home buyers purchase a home;
- $187 million to create 56,000 new training places in 2008-09;
- An acceleration in the implementation of the Government's three nation building funds to bring forward the commencement of investment in nation building projects to 2009 ...

As we contemplate the impact of this financial crisis on real economies, real people and real lives, it must also galvanise us to act in the future so that we never allow greed and lax regulation to put us in this position again.

I addressed this matter in my recent speech to the UN General Assembly, which among other things, called for reforms to the Basel capital adequacy requirements. One of the points in that speech related to executive remuneration. At that time, I said that financial institutions needed to have clear incentives to promote responsible behaviour rather than unrestrained greed ...

To put it simply – when markets fail, governments must act. We know that from history. As a government and as a nation we must respond to the twin evils which are at the root of this malaise – greed and fear. Fear is the first of these demons which we must see off. Dealing with the greed which has caused the fear will come after that.

We're not a people who panic. As Australians, we take the good and the bad in our stride. And we go forward. And we intend to join with other nations to re-build the architecture of the global economy, so this global financial crisis is not repeated in the future. This will be tough. But I have absolute confidence that the nation will make it through – together.

Source: Editor's personal files

PART 3

The Campaign Trail

ANDREW FISHER

'To try and awaken the patriotism of Australians'

*Andrew Fisher delivers his famous Gympie speech – the
first modern election campaign policy speech*

As the 1910 election approached, people clamoured for Labor's program. Labor leader Andrew Fisher urged them to wait until a major speech at Gympie. 'Wait for Gympie!' became the catch-cry.

This speech crystallises the core of Labor's platform for the coming election. It reflected the aspiration of Labor to be a party of national government with a broad agenda.

A crowd of 2000 people filled Gympie's Olympia Theatre. For three hours, Fisher outlined policies on: workplace relations, pensions, defence, a transcontinental railway, a national currency, development of the Northern Territory, a federal capital, an agricultural research bureau, a tax on unimproved land values, and support for the sugar industry.

There were frequent cheers and applause from the audience. The newspaper coverage was extensive. Fisher's plea to 'wait for Gympie', *The Age* reported, 'did not overrate the importance of the proposals he made'.

Although long and detailed, the speech energised Labor's supporters. It was published by the party as 'Mr Fisher's Policy Speech'. It is likely that this speech inaugurated the tradition of policy speeches given by party leaders at election time.

At the next election, Labor won 50 per cent of the vote. It was the first time any party had won a majority of seats in both the House and the Senate.

When Fisher delivered Labor's 1913 policy speech in Maryborough to a crowd of 3000 supporters, following a civic reception with brass band and a torchlight procession the night before, he could claim that he had delivered on its promises. But at the 1913 election, Fisher's government was defeated by one seat.

He would return to office in 1914 – his third and final term as Prime Minister, before resigning to take up the post of High Commissioner in London.

'To try and awaken the
patriotism of Australians'

Olympia Theatre, Gympie 30 March 1909

I had no difficulty in selecting Gympie for this address, because, 16 years ago, the electors did me the honour to send me to the State Parliament, and gave me my first opportunity in public life. Eight years ago, when I thought it well to become a candidate for Wide Bay in the Federal Parliament, the electors of Gympie endorsed my candidature by a large majority. I feel, therefore, I am amongst friends …

Just look at the increase in trade during those periods. The imports and exports from 1893 increased £102,286,000 to £204,268,000 in 1908. I mention these figures to show that a country that is making progress in that way is a country that, if well governed, will see to it that every person honestly able and willing to work should be able to earn sufficient to enable him to keep his wife and family in comfort …

The Commonwealth Parliament has power to deal with customs and excise, it has power to put on a protective tariff it has, rightly or wrongly, settled on a policy of protection for Australia, and I think it is the intention of the people that that policy should continue …

I am going to ask you tonight, and the people of Australia, to give the Federal Parliament equal powers with the states to ensure it giving effect to industrial laws, and to ensure that when a judgment is given by the court in favour of employees it will have the same enforcing powers as that given by parliament in favour of employers …

Another matter of importance is that of old-age pensions … I am here to say that every act that this government can do to ensure carrying out the principles of the Invalid and Old-age Pensions Act will be done. Whatever financial embarrassment we may meet with that will be carried out to the letter. Once inaugurated, we shall be able, in the not far distant future, perhaps, to give effect not only to the old-age pensions, but to the invalid pensions as well …

The industrial life of Australia is dependent on its coastal and overseas trade … In the possible absence of the imperial squadron this vast trade would be exposed to attack, which could easily be effected by cruisers from beyond the range of guns at the forts. We feel that there is a deeper obligation than even the protection of property … we propose, in addition to the three destroyers we have already ordered … inaugurating a much larger policy in the near future, if Parliament and the people endorse it … Australia is an integral portion of the British Empire and any naval force must therefore be a portion of the sea power of the British nation …

This is not a policy of hysteria, such as we have had lately, but a policy that would begin in earnest, and continue in earnest, and would entirely depend upon the patriotism of the country and the spirit of our youth and manhood to defend their country … My aim has always been to try and awaken the patriotism of Australians. I hope that the call of the sea may be heard more and more in the future by our young men …

We propose now that we shall have compulsory military training, beginning with boys in school after 10 years and ending at 20 years … We associate with this scheme the establishment of a gun factory, a small arms factory, and ammunition factories. We think these things are absolutely inseparable from proper defence.

As regards the iron industry – nationalisation is the policy of the Labor Party. It is necessary for defence and other purposes …

We feel that we should have a High Commissioner in London and a Bill will be introduced next session to give effect to that desire …

Another matter I wish to refer to is the Northern Territory. That Territory is larger than France, Germany, Belgium, Switzerland, and Italy put together, and I feel that is the duty of the national Parliament of Australia to take over that vast tract … and, by doing so, find some means of settling and protecting it …

In regard to the Federal capital site, I see no reason to alter the view that the government of the Commonwealth should have its own house and its own country; and, for that reason, we will proceed with the building of the Federal capital as soon as the proper place for it has been ascertained.

I feel that while the matter of the transcontinental railways is in the future … I shall be pleased if the survey of the West Australian line is of such a character as will enable parliament to come to the conclusion that the line should be constructed …

We want an Agricultural Bill to provide for a bureau for the investigation of agricultural matters and the dissemination of information in regard to these matters …

Other Bills to be brought forward are the Norfolk Island Acceptance Bill, Bills of Exchange, Marine Insurance, Bankruptcy, Electoral Amendment, Public Service Amendment, Navigation, Seamen's Compensation, Customs Act Amendment, and I have no doubt some other Bills will be discovered to be necessary.

I now want to say to you that it will be necessary to raise revenue for the services I have indicated. I propose to submit to you a proposition for a Commonwealth Note issue for Australia ... how much better it would be if we had a paper issue on the same principle for the whole of the Commonwealth. People on each side of the border would not have to pay exchange ...

We propose to submit to parliament a Bill to provide for the taxation of unimproved land values ... It is a fair tax, a reasonable tax, and a necessary tax, if Australian lands are to be developed ... We think that land should not be a private monopoly in this country so long as people are desirous of using it ...

My last reference is to the sugar industry. We have made a success of the white-labour policy. Nearly all our sugar is now produced by white labour and we have largely helped to populate 500 miles of the north coast of Queensland by people of our own race; and by that means we have helped to defend that part of the Commonwealth. It is worth the money for that alone ...

I hope that justice will be done to the federal finances whoever is to carry on the government of the country.

Source: National Library of Australia.

JAMES SCULLIN

'Parliament has vindicated itself as the guardian of the people's rights'

*Jim Scullin lashes the Bruce Government as it falls, ahead
of Labor winning the subsequent election*

In 1926, the Bruce Government proposed a referendum to expand the Commonwealth's reach over industrial relations, but it failed to win support.

In a stunning policy back-flip, in 1929 Prime Minister Stanley Melbourne Bruce proposed that the Commonwealth transfer its industrial relations powers to the States, except for those governing the maritime industry and the federal public service.

After one of the longest debates in the Parliament's history, on 10 September 1929, Bruce moved to guillotine debate.

Labor leader Jim Scullin's speeches on 10 September and later on 12 September 1929, notwithstanding the substantial role of former Nationalist leader Billy Hughes and others, were important moments in the fall of the Bruce Government.

Analysing Scullin's speeches, *The Canberra Times* reported that he 'is the very fire itself'. Scullin ramped up the debate and skewered the foppish, well-heeled, spats-wearing Bruce and his government, arguing that the Tories had betrayed the foundation on which it was elected. Scullin, returning to Parliament after a serious illness, accused Bruce of an 'abuse of power'. Quoting the government's policy at the previous election and several public statements, Scullin destroyed Bruce with his own words.

With debate adjourned by Bruce on 10 and 11 September, following the defeat of the government when the House was in Committee (including by several serving or former Nationalist Party members organised by Hughes), the House resumed on 12 September and Bruce announced that an election had been agreed to by the Governor-General.

Scullin said 'Parliament has vindicated itself as the guardian of the people's rights'.

The subsequent election landslide to Labor saw the party achieve its best result since 1914 and Bruce became the first Prime Minister to lose his seat in Parliament.

'Parliament has vindicated itself as the guardian of the people's rights'

The House of Representatives, Canberra 10-12 September 1929

10 September 1929

… This Bill has not been discussed in the country to the slightest degree. It has not been even hinted at as far as the people of Australia are concerned, and now there is not to be a proper open discussion of it in this Parliament. What is the reason for the attempt of the government to bludgeon this class of legislation through the House? …

One has only to read the comments that have appeared in the press of this country to perceive that the methods adopted by the government are bringing this Parliament into contempt …

When the second reading debate of a drastic measure such as this, which is to undo what has been accomplished during 25 years, is put through in 60 hours, and 46 of those hours form part of a continuous sitting, honourable members of this parliament have no proper opportunity to discuss it. Yet now we have the declaration that this is an urgent measure, and we are asked to finish to the end of clause 6 by 11 o'clock tonight …

This proposal is an abuse of the power which the government possesses … The amendment places before honourable members a clear-cut issue; we have to decide whether or not the electors are to control this parliament. At nine successive elections the principle of federal arbitration has been affirmed by the people, and this Bill is an endeavour to flout their expressed will …

Why did the first federal parliament unanimously resolve in favour of the exercise of the industrial power of the Commonwealth, amongst the supporters of the proposal being many of those who had helped to frame the constitution? Yet, at this late hour, the prime minister – who has not given sufficient study to our constitutional history or to industrial matters – presumes to lecture the committee as to what was contemplated by the framers of the constitution.

The right honourable gentleman has declared that the Bill is of paramount importance. If it is, surely it is fair to consult the people before we pass it. Do we believe in democracy or in oligarchy? That is the issue before us. The prime minister, when claiming that he has a mandate from the people, said that he had told the electors that the government proposed to take any steps necessary to establish industrial peace. This Bill, he says, is the fulfilment of that undertaking; this is one of the steps he was authorised by the people to take. It is not a step at all; it is a somersault.

His reasoning in regard to the mandate was extraordinary. He said that when he went before the electors in 1925 he did not tell them that he intended to ask for increased power in regard to industrial matters, and that in 1928 he merely asked for a general power to bring about industrial peace. But in 1925 and 1928 he indicated clearly to the electors that he proposed to bring about industrial peace by strengthening the Commonwealth industrial laws, and not by running away from the principle of federal arbitration as this Bill proposes. He argued that the people had given to the government a general power to do anything it thought necessary to achieve industrial peace.

The right honourable gentleman utters many vague statements and cryptic phrases, but this is the first occasion on which I have heard that when a party addresses the electors in general terms and asks for general powers, it gets from them a mandate to go backwards or forwards to continue arbitration or abolish it. How can the mandate that the government got from the people be a mandate for federal arbitration, or no federal arbitration, as the government may think fit? A mandate that can be stretched at will, that can be made black today and white tomorrow, is no mandate at all …

The government talks about a mandate from the country. I have before me a little book, edited by Sir Neville Howse, campaign director of the Nationalist Party at the last election. In it there is the declaration that the policy of the Nationalist Party was to continue arbitration … This book contains the policy on which the government went to the country, and it says nothing about the abolition of arbitration. The policy speech of the prime minister certainly contains no reference to the abolition of arbitration …

Now, in the twinkling of an eye, the prime minister has changed his attitude; and the bulk of his supporters have also changed theirs. I am reminded of a part of a day that I spent in a military drill-yard, where I saw a sergeant drilling raw recruits. The sergeant said to the squad, 'Quick march!'. The squad marched 50 yards, and were then ordered, 'Halt, right about face, quick march!'. They march. The prime minister says 'Halt, right about face, quick march!'. They march back. Honourable members behind the government are the political awkward squad.

This measure is not being decided upon its merits. I agree with the right honourable member for North Sydney (Billy Hughes) that if honourable members on that side were free to carry out the pledges that they gave to their electors, there would not be even six of them supporting the prime minister. There should be some honour between this parliament and the people who established it. There should be some honesty among honourable members. They should openly and frankly carry out as near as possible the promises that they made to their electors; who, undoubtedly, were convinced at the last elections, that this government and this opposition were both pledged to maintain arbitration …

By this measure the Government is not only destroying federal arbitration, but also undermining the very foundation of this Parliament, and the democratic principle upon which it has been built; because it should be, and is, broad-based upon the will of the people of Australia.

12 September 1929

… This Parliament is but 10 months old. The right honourable gentleman has accepted a grave responsibility in advising the governor-general to dissolve it, and His Excellency a grave responsibility in accepting that advice …

It could have obeyed the mandate it received from the people ten months ago to proceed with the federal arbitration system and make it effective. Had that pledge to the electors not been broken, parliament would not have insisted upon the government going again before its masters. Parliament has vindicated itself as the guardian of the people's rights. It has told the government that, notwithstanding its majority, it cannot flout the will of the people, and that irrespective of the consequences to any party it must go back to the electors and get a new mandate, or abandon the measure which was introduced in defiance of the will of the people …

I make no complaint for having to face a general election. The Labor Party is prepared to meet the government forces at the polls, and to abide by the judgement of the people.

Source: Commonwealth of Australia Parliamentary Debates (Hansard).

JOHN CURTIN

'Victory in war, victory for the peace'

John Curtin, battling the storm of war, makes the case for sticking with Labor

As a Labor speaker, John Curtin is probably without peer. He could energise audiences with the fiery power of his rhetoric and convince even the greatest sceptic with the compelling force of his arguments. If the occasion demanded solemnity, he could speak with deep feeling and sensitivity. The Clerk of the House of Representatives, Frank Green, thought Curtin to be the Parliament's greatest orator. His biographer, Lloyd Ross, believed that only Winston Churchill was his equal as a speaker.

In this fighting speech, Curtin presents Labor's policy for the 1943 federal election – an election that saw Labor achieve is greatest ever victory in federal politics.

Curtin recalls how the government ascended to power and reviews the prosecution of the war, presents Labor's plans for domestic policy and for the planning of the peace, and promises 'victory in war, victory for the peace'. Curtin, ever the political fighter, was unafraid to assail his opponents mercilessly over their handling of the war, even while that war was still going on. Curtin insisted that he had no plans to implement Labor's quixotic socialist objective, describing it during the campaign as a 'dead tiger'. He said, 'we have not socialised Australia, and we do not intend to do it just because we are at war'.

The two-hour speech was broadcast around Australia and to soldiers abroad, via a 'hook-up of about 100 national and commercial broadcasting stations', *The Age* reported.

Curtin 'complained of nervousness several times before making his policy speech', said *The Sydney Morning Herald*, and his acceler-ated delivery meant that he finished 'three minutes before scheduled time'.

The usually conservative *Herald* urged voters to support Curtin's government, arguing, 'we could not choose a better leader today'.

'Victory in war, victory for the peace'

Broadcast, Canberra 26 July 1943

Men and women of Australia,

As head of the government which for 20 months has had the solemn duty and grave responsibility of maintaining intact our country, I give you an account of the government's trusteeship.

The circumstances in which the Labor government took office in October 1941 were unprecedented. Two Prime Ministers had failed to control the Parliament and the parties comprising the then government had split into bitter factions, with place and position tussling against duty and principles in the deeds and words of senior ministers.

The Labor government had to devote itself with unflagging industry, and often with heart-breaking pains, to reshaping the country's war machine in all its components because of the certainty of which it never lost sight but of which a former war-time Prime Minister (Robert Menzies) had said in a speech in London in March, 1941, could not happen – war with Japan.

In two months, with so much to do, so much to set right, the Labor government faced war in the Pacific – the inevitability of which had governed all its actions in that pitifully short period. The nation looked to Labor, and it did not look in vain. In the words of *The Age* newspaper, 'it is a matter for gratitude that in virile, statesmanlike form, national leadership is being provided'.

The inheritance the Labor government accepted from its predecessors was a heavy burden. Blind to the dangers in the Pacific, the Menzies and Fadden Governments had left Australia very much unprepared. Australia's resources were spread over many far-flung battle fronts. The men of the three services fought with fine efficiency and made conspicuous contributions, but at home the then government had left the country almost undefended. Australia was a sector as menaced, and as helpless, as the Philippines.

The essentials for defence in the hands of the commanders, as the result of the previous government's policy, were so sadly inadequate that only a limited disposition of forces could be made. But the Labor government rejected that concept. In association with the commanders, it developed a plan to prevent this great country from being doomed …

The Labor government took prompt and effective measures to develop Australia's maximum effort. Before the outbreak of war with Japan, the Labor government secured the return to Australian waters of Australian warships;

the Citizen Forces were called-up for full-time duty; VDC personnel were enlisted for full-time duty; and within four months its establishment was increased to 80,000. The 6th and 7th divisions and later the 9th division of the AIF returned to Australia in accordance with the recommendation of the government's military advisers ...

As a result of (The Department of) Labour's re-organisation of manpower and womanpower, 1,172,000 are now in the fighting forces or war production, compared with 554,000 when the Fadden government left office ...

When the Labor government took over, there were six government munitions factories and 76 annexes. Today there are 43 government factories and 180 annexes. They employ 79,000 persons as against 37,000 when the Fadden government was in office ...

The creation by the Labor government of the Allied Supply Council was a master stroke which has been hailed repeatedly by our Allies. Australia is the quartermaster of the entire South-west Pacific Area ...

Social security has received the government's close consideration ... the Labor government twice increased the rate paid to invalid and old-age pensioners and the added annual cost, including cost of living adjustments ... Blind pensioners were assisted and ... A scheme of vocational training for invalid pensioners was introduced. A grant for pensioners' funeral benefits was made. Pensions were extended to cover aborigines.

The Labor government has always had prominently in its policy the betterment of the status of women. One decision in conformity with this policy was an increase in the rate of the maternity allowance, the abolition of the means test and special provision for payments to the mother before and after the child's birth. Widows' pensions enabled the Labor government to go further in enhancing the position of women ... Steps were taken to liberalise the payment of child endowment and money provided for creches for children of women war workers ...

The Labor government has given the widest consideration to the pay, conditions and general welfare of the fighting forces. It increased rates of pay on two occasions, and also widened the scope of payment to include many sections not formerly covered ...

One of the landmarks in the Labor government's administration was the Repatriation Bill ... The paramount problem ever before service men and women is re-establishment in civil life ... the government pledges itself to ensure that every man and woman of the forces who, on discharge, is in need of employment, will be provided with reasonable opportunities for such employment ...

This government's policy of full development of resources, full employment of manpower and full provision for social security is a basis not only for Australian reconstruction but for a stable and peaceful commonwealth of all nations. It means prosperity at once for us and for others. In banishing want, we shall have gone far to free the world from fear …

Another important aspect of the Labor government's national welfare plans is health and medical services. Work has been proceeding continuously on the formulation of a comprehensive health scheme …

As the war proceeded Australia took an increasingly active part in international relationships. The Labor government was able to have Pacific War Councils established in London and Washington; to obtain entree of an Australian representative on the British War Cabinet and to ensure making certain Australia's voice was heard …

The nature, extent and balance of Australia's part in winning final victory is due for review …

The Navy will be maintained at the strength necessary for the existing ships plus approved additions to the strength, together with all administrative and ancillary services.

The Army will be maintained at the strength necessary for providing for an Army Corps for offensive operations in accordance with the plans of the Commander-in-Chief, South-west Pacific Area; and adequate forces for the defence of Australia and New Guinea and for relief of units outside the mainland …

The Air Force will be maintained at the strength authorised under the program of the maximum strength required for the defence of Australia against invasion to the extent to which aircraft can be provided …

That, then, is the history of the threat which the UAP and the Country Party allowed to hang over Australia; the record of what the Labor government has achieved; the undertaking of what the Labor government will work and strive for in the future …

In war and for the peace you cannot risk a non-Labor government taking office. What a government it would be! … Who would be the leader of leaders? Would it be Mr Fadden or Mr Menzies or Mr Hughes or Mr Cameron or Mr Abbott or Mr Spender? Would the war effort come first with them? Or would they, as Mr Hughes said in his broadcast last April, go on 'intriguing for months'? …

The Australian Labor Party has no association or affiliation with any other party or faction nor with any 'isms', whatever their origin, which may be put forward …

I give you the Labor government's policy in a phrase – victory in war, victory for the peace. On that we stand inflexible, for a lost peace would be marked by horrors of starvation, unemployment, misery and hardship no less grievous than the devastation of war …

Our country has now withstood the direst trials; it has lived through its darkest hour; it is now confronting the dawn of a victorious and a better day. The Labor government has done its duty. Australia stands at this election one of the free countries in the world. For that we have toiled and striven. And we know that the time has come when a preserved Australia can once again advance.

Source: The John Curtin Prime Ministerial Library.

With a rarely surpassed eloquence grounded in logic and reason coupled with oratorical flourish, John Curtin could transfix an audience like nobody else during his time. He would raise and lower his voice. He would punch the air with his hands and sweep them from side to side as he pivoted to look at one section of the audience or another. He would button and unbutton his jacket. After a major speech, Curtin would be drained of energy, often for days. In this photo he is addressing a wartime rally in Sydney in 1942.

Source: Fairfax

BEN CHIFLEY

'To win the peace for the greater happiness and prosperity of all'

Ben Chifley reviews Labor's record and outlines his vision for post-war reconstruction

Ben Chifley's voice was coarse, rough and unpolished. 'The bad speaking voice he had', Chifley's press secretary, Don Rodgers, recalled in an oral history, 'was a legacy of his early open-air campaigning days when he spoke at street corners and from hotel balconies'. Frank Green, the Clerk of the House of Representatives, said Chifley 'was not an impressive speaker in the House'. Yet, this was part of his appeal: his matter of fact and plain speaking style reflected his personality.

The 1946 election campaign was the first federal election after the war had ended and Chifley's first as Prime Minister. It was also the first election contested by the Liberal Party of Australia, led by former Prime Minister, Robert Menzies.

Mindful of the British people who had failed to return Winston Churchill's Tory government in July 1945, seemingly ignoring Churchill's wartime leadership, Chifley spoke at great length not only about the prosecution of the war, but also about post-war reconstruction.

The policy speech was broadcast from Canberra and lasted just under one hour.

In typical Chifley style, particularly when broadcasting, it was hardly a stirring performance. But when he spoke, he did, as LF Crisp noted in his biography of Chifley, convey 'his warmth, sincerity, strength and magnetism'.

Chifley's government was returned by the voters. The election result was a vindication of both Curtin and Chifley's stewardship of the war and their post-war reconstruction plans. While a few seats were lost at the election, including that of Deputy Prime Minister Frank Forde, it was the first time that Labor had won back-to-back elections.

It would be Labor's only success at the federal polls for 26 years – until Gough Whitlam's 1972 election victory.

'To win the peace for the greater happiness and prosperity of all'

Broadcast, Canberra 2 September 1946

Fellow citizens,

This is the first peace-time general election since 1937. Three years ago, the Labor Party's policy was given by the late Mr John Curtin, whose untimely death is still being mourned by every Australian who recognised his great wartime leadership and who appreciated his unselfish devotion to duty. His work, and that of the party he led, for Australia in war must continue into the peace. To that, I pledge my whole party.

Australia is about to enter upon the greatest era in her history. This country of ours has come through two world wars and weathered the miseries and hardships of a depression, all in the space of a little over 30 years. Although it seems to be a paradox, the fact is that participation in wars has hastened Australian development and expansion. Forward steps have been taken in record time that would have occupied much longer in what were regarded as normal times.

Today, Australia has become the great bastion of the British-speaking race south of the Equator. Strategically and economically, our country has assumed a position in the Pacific on behalf of the British Commonwealth of nations of such importance that development and responsibility go hand in hand.

It is my purpose to show that, since the Labor Party assumed the duties of government in the crisis of 1941, Australia has been successfully led through a war effort that won world-wide admiration, on to victory, and then for the past twelve months through a transition period that has been passed with greater ease than any in the United Nations.

It is also my purpose to show that the record of achievement in national leadership – contrasted with the demonstrated ineptness of the opposition parties when the test of crisis found them wanting – justifies the people in entrusting to the Labor Party the government of Australia in the great years that lie ahead …

With the coming peace, wartime controls have been lifted widely and the National Security Act will expire on 31 December 1946. Measures to maintain a stabilised economy will be effected by legislation in Parliament. It is to the maintenance of that economic balance – in which lies the true welfare of all our people – that the Labor government is pledged, and, upon the policies to ensure that maintenance, the government takes its stand at this general election.

It has been the privilege of the Labor government to direct the policy of the Australian war effort during the greatest crisis in the Commonwealth's history. Victory was achieved, thanks to the gallantry of the Australian and Allied forces, the ability of the High Command, the aid from Britain and the United States, and the efforts of the Australian people ...

Australia is now in the stage of transition from the interim post-war commitments to the determination of the ultimate strength and organisation of the forces for the future defence of the Commonwealth ...

The important lesson learned from Australia's experience in the Pacific war is that this country is no longer a peaceful outpost, isolated by distance from war's destructiveness. Australia is vulnerable to attack and each year brings developments in the science of warfare that lessen still further our chance of living unmolested.

The way to assure Australia of the protection of a virile aerial defence force – the front-line fighting force in modern war – is to maintain an industrial organisation capable of producing most modern aircraft from our own resources and capable of rapid expansion in the event of a threat. That is the Labor government's policy ...

The Australian nation's interests and influence in the peace should not be less than they were in the war, and the foreign policy the government is developing has the purpose of giving full expression to those interests ... Australia's relations with Britain today are, therefore, firmly based on the hard realities of world politics, with Australia not only giving practical expression to her rights but also assuming and effectively carrying out the heavy responsibilities that belong to her new status ... to act as a guardian of British interests in the Pacific area ... the ANZAC Pact of 1944 with New Zealand was another manifestation of this recognition of regional obligation ...

The government places its record of demobilisation and reestablishment before the Australian people with confidence ...

Sixty thousand former service men and women, provided with living allowances, have to date commenced free professional vocational training ... Over £1,500,000 have already been advanced in special rural loans and another £1,000,000 at similar low interest rates in business and professional loans ...

Ample funds have been made available by the Labor government to give effect to the War Service Homes Act ...

The Banking Act 1945 provides for the control of the banking system in Australia ... the government's banking legislation has been designed to adapt the banking system to present-day conditions and to provide the Commonwealth Bank, as Australia's central bank, with adequate powers to serve the national interest ...

Australia has expanded tremendously her productive capacity. We now stand on the threshold of a wondrous commercial industrial age. We have expanded our industrial capacity, developed our industrial skill, broadened the scope and vision of our industrial management, and fostered and stabilised our internal economy ... I ask all Australians to play their part, both for the economic and defensive welfare of the nation, to increase productivity ...

Despite the multiple cares of the government involved in a war threatening the very existence of Australia as a nation, the government never lost faith in ultimate victory. The best evidence of this is furnished by the Labor government's great extension of social services and health benefits since it took office in October, 1941. The government has proceeded in firm adherence to the belief that there should be freedom from want for all our people ...

The policy presented to the people by the Labor government for the general elections to be held on 28 September 1946 is linked with three important questions upon which the electors are asked to vote by referendum. The government asks you to vote 'yes' to all three questions so that the Commonwealth parliament will be able to legislate as follows:

- To provide social services on the widest possible scale;
- To provide for the organised marketing of primary products;
- To deal with terms and conditions of employment in industry ...

I have given you the record of the Labor government in the last five years. It is really the story of Australia, of a young country exalted to nationhood in the testing fire of war by its people's own magnificent efforts ...

Were the late John Curtin alive today he would give praise to the Australian people who, in 1943, endorsed all that the Labor government had done and planned to do for Australia. Today, in 1946, the Labor government asks the people for further confirmation of its policies for the advancement and development of our country. Imbued with political honesty, the government makes no extravagant promises and has a full realisation of the responsibilities of government.

Your alternative is a hotch-potch of two policies, presented separately by the Liberal Party and the Country Party. These two parties could not work together even in the compelling atmosphere of war and split asunder in October 1941. They still remain apart; opposing each other in many electorates, and speaking with different voices on major policy issues. They are torn by personal jealousies and petty hostilities.

These parties, that once paraded a policy of 'sound finance', now attempt to corrupt the people and threaten our national economy with promises that will not stand examination and, indeed, that amount to unbridled election bribery on a scale that cannot possibly be paid …

I urge the people to unite in a stirring effort to retain the Labor government. You, the people, trusted Labor – when all others had failed – to save the country in the face of the enemy. You, the people, can trust Labor to win the peace for the greater happiness and prosperity of all men, women and children in our fair land and for the secured welfare of those generations to come.

Source: AW Stargardt, Things Worth Fighting For: Speeches by Joseph Benedict Chifley, *Melbourne University Press, Melbourne, 1952.*

Ben Chifley was not known as a particularly inspiring or dynamic speaker.
A legacy of open-air campaigning and speaking from the back of flat-bed trucks
and hotel balconies left him with a rough speaking voice. But his plain-speaking
style endeared him to the party and to the voters. He told party members in
1951, 'You have to be quite clear about what you believe in, whether popular
or unpopular, and you have to fight for it.'
Source: Australian Labor Party

GOUGH WHITLAM

'It's time'

Gough Whitlam delivers the landmark 'It's Time' election policy speech

With the words, 'Men and Women of Australia', Gough Whitlam presented Labor's policy speech for the 1972 election at the Blacktown Civic Centre. The opening words were borrowed from John Curtin, who used them regularly, including in his 1943 election policy speech. The ideas, themes and language were closely related to Whitlam's equally visionary 1969 policy speech.

It was a night-time speech broadcast to the nation on television and radio. The venue was overflowing with Labor supporters resplendent in orange and black 'It's Time' t-shirts, badges and sashes. Posters, banners and balloons decorated the hall. The audience included sporting and entertainment celebrities, party and union leaders, shadow ministers and party members. Around 1500 people packed into a venue designed to fit 1000. The energy and enthusiasm of the crowd were palpable.

After an introduction by ALP National President Tom Burns, Whitlam walked onto the stage to applause and cheers. Whitlam said: 'There are moments in history when the whole fate and future of nations can be decided by a single decision. For Australia, this is such a time ... It's time for a new government – a Labor government'. Whitlam's purpose was 'to promote equality, to involve the people of Australia in the decision-making processes of our land, and to liberate the talents and uplift the horizons of the Australian people'.

Not wanting to take anything for granted, in his reading version of the speech, Whitlam struck out 'we are coming into government after 23 years of opposition'.

The editorial of *The Sydney Morning Herald* said it was a 'strong and confident speech, offering many good and imaginative ideas'.

After 23 years in the political wilderness, this speech would catapult Labor to victory.

'It's time'

Blacktown Civic Centre, Blacktown 13 November 1972

Men and Women of Australia!

The decision we will make for our country on 2 December is a choice between the past and the future, between the habits and fears of the past, and the demands and opportunities of the future. There are moments in history when the whole fate and future of nations can be decided by a single decision. For Australia, this is such a time.

It's time for a new team, a new program, a new drive for equality of opportunities: it's time to create new opportunities for Australians, time for a new vision of what we can achieve in this generation for our nation and the region in which we live. It's time for a new government – a Labor government …

We have a new chance for our nation. We can recreate this nation. We have a new chance for our region. We can help recreate this region.

The war of intervention in Vietnam is ending. The great powers are rethinking and remoulding their relationships and their obligations. Australia cannot stand still at such a time. We cannot afford to limp along with men whose attitudes are rooted in the slogans of the 1950s – the slogans of fear and hate. If we made such a mistake, we would make Australia a backwater in our region and a back number in history. The Australian Labor Party – vindicated as we have been on all the great issues of the past – stands ready to take Australia forward to her rightful, proud, secure and independent place in the future of our region.

And we are determined that the Australian people shall be restored to their rightful place in their own country – as participants and partners in government, as the owners and keepers of the national estate and the nation's resources, as fair and equal sharers in the wealth and opportunities that this nation should offer in abundance to all its people. We will put Australians back into the business of running Australia and owning Australia. We will revive in this nation the spirit of national cooperation and national self-respect, mutual respect between government and people.

In 24 hours, Mr (William) McMahon will present to you a series of proposals purporting to be the Liberal Party program. But it is not what he will say in 24 hours that counts; it is what could have been done in the past 23 years, what has happened in the last 20 months on which the Liberals must be judged. It is the Liberal Party which asks you to take a leap in the dark – the Liberal Party which dispossessed the elected Prime Minister in mid-term, the Liberal Party which has produced half-baked, un-costed proposals in its death-bed repentance. It is the Liberal Party whose election proposals are those which it has denounced and derided for 23 years.

By contrast, the Australian Labor Party offers the Australian people the most carefully developed and consistent program ever placed before them. I am proud of our program. I am proud of our team. I am proud to be the leader of this team.

Our program has three great aims. They are:

- to promote equality;
- to involve the people of Australia in the decision-making processes of our land; and
- to liberate the talents and uplift the horizons of the Australian people.

We want to give a new life and a new meaning in this new nation to the touchstone of modern democracy – to liberty, equality, fraternity.

We propose a new charter for the children of Australia. The real answer to the modern malaise of juvenile crime, drugs and vandalism is not repression and moralising. The answer is to involve the creative energies of our children and our youth in a creative, concerned community.

We will make pre-school education available to every Australian child. We do this not just because we believe that all Australian children should have the opportunities now available only to children in Canberra, but because pre-school education is the most important single weapon in promoting equality and in overcoming social, economic and language inequalities.

Under a Labor government, Commonwealth spending on schools and teacher training will be the fastest expanding sector of Budget expenditure. This must be done, not just because the basic resource of this nation is the skills of its people, but because education is the key to equality of opportunity …

We will abolish fees at universities and colleges of advanced education. We believe that a student's merit rather than a parent's wealth should decide who should benefit from the community's vast financial commitment to tertiary education …

We intend to raise the basic pension rate to 25 per cent of average weekly earnings …

We will establish a universal health insurance system – not just because the Liberal system is grossly inadequate and inefficient, but because we reject a system by which the more one earns the less one pays …

We will establish a National Compensation Scheme to reduce the hardships imposed by one of the great factors for inequality in society – inequality of luck.

We will involve the national government in a massive effort to rebuild our existing cities and to build new ones … It's not just because 85 per cent of our people live in cities and towns, but because in modern Australia social inequality is fixed upon families by the place in which they are forced to live even more than by what they are able to earn.

We will make a massive attack on the problem of land and housing costs. The land is the basic property of the Australian people. It is the people's land, and we will fight for the right of all Australian people to have access to it at fair prices …

We will exert our powers against prices. We will establish a Prices Justification Tribunal not only because inflation will be the major economic problem facing Australia over the next three years but because industrial cooperation and good-will is being undermined by the conviction among employees that the price for labour alone is subject to regulation and restraint …

We will change the emphasis in immigration from government recruiting to family reunion and to retaining the migrants already here. The important thing is to stop the drift away from Australia …

We will issue national development bonds through an expanded Australian Industry Development Corporation – not just because we are determined to reverse the trend towards foreign control of Australian resources, but because we want ordinary Australians to play their part in buying Australia back.

We will abolish conscription forthwith. It must be done not just because a volunteer army means a better army, but because we profoundly believe that it is intolerable that a free nation at peace and under no threat should cull by lottery the best of its youth to provide defence on the cheap.

We will legislate to give aborigines land rights – not just because their case is beyond argument, but because all of us as Australians are diminished while the aborigines are denied their rightful place in this nation. …

The key to financing Labor's program must be strong and continuing economic growth based on sound national planning and national cooperation between government, employers and employees …

I have tried tonight to give you in the broad and in some detail a program for Australia under a Labor government, a picture of what I believe Australia can become over the next three years …

Before this campaign is out, I shall have completed twenty years as a Member of Parliament. The basic foundations of this speech lie in my very first speeches in the Parliament, because I have never wavered from my fundamental belief that until the national government became involved in great matters like schools and cities, this nation would never fulfil its real capabilities.

For thirteen years now I have had the honour to fill the second highest and then the highest place my party can bestow. Throughout that time I have striven to make the policies of the Australian Labor Party, its machinery, its membership, more and more representative of the whole Australian people and more and more responsive to the needs and hopes of the whole Australian people …

We of the Labor Party have used these crucial last years in opposition to prepare ourselves for the great business of moving our nation ahead, to uniting our people in a common co-operative endeavour and to making the democratic system work once more …

But the best team, the best policies, the best advisers are not enough. I need your help. I need the help of the Australian people; and given that, I do not for a moment believe that we should set limits on what we can achieve, together, for our country, our people, our future.

Source: The Whitlam Institute.

'Let's put this state in better shape', NSW Labor leader Neville Wran delivers Labor's 1976 election policy speech at the Blacktown Civic Centre. Wran would win government just months after the electoral drubbing of the Whitlam government and would show Labor how to win elections and how to govern in the modern era. Source: Australian Labor Party (NSW Branch)

NEVILLE WRAN

'Sound, stable, responsible and honest government'

In Labor's darkest hour, Neville Wrans shows Labor how to win and how to govern for the modern era

Neville Wran's NSW election victory in May 1976 was a turning point for the Labor Party. Coming only months after the electoral defeat of the Whitlam Government, Wran showed Labor how to win and, later, how to govern for the modern era.

At a time when many thought Labor was a spent force, out of the blue came Wran to lead Labor back to power in the nation's oldest and largest state. Wran's election victory had national implications. His model of government: a popular and dynamic leader attuned to the modern-media age, leading a government of moderate, yet progressive reform, with sound economic management, would be the model of Labor governments for the next 30 years. As Bob Hawke said in his *Memoirs*, 'The Labor Party as a whole owed a great debt to Wran; after the devastation of 1975 he was able to show with his 1976 victory in NSW that Labor was still alive and capable of governing. The longevity of his government, his professionalism and style, were an important stepping stone for the Hawke Labor government'.

Wran delivered his campaign policy speech at the Blacktown Civic Centre, where Gough Whitlam had opened Labor's federal campaign in 1972. With the slogan 'Let's Put this State in Better Shape', the central element of Labor's campaign was Wran's empathy and leadership style. Wran promised 'sound, stable, responsible' government and moderate reform. He focused on bread and butter State political issues. It was a model of government inspired by Labor Premier Bill McKell, who led Labor to power in NSW in 1941. It is also a speech that boldly outlines major reforms and unashamedly promotes Labor values.

Wran would go on to lead a government of significant achievement and become one of the country's most popular and successful political leaders, winning back-to-back 'Wranslide' election wins in 1978 and 1981 and chalking up electoral accolades not matched before or since. After ten years in government, he retired in 1986, undefeated and still ahead in the opinion polls.

'Sound, stable, responsible and honest government'

Blacktown Civic Centre 12 April 1976

On 1 May, the people of NSW have the chance to restore our State to its proper place of leadership in Australia.

A Labor government will get down to the real business of our State, the real priorities.

Let's get an effective public transport system.

Let's get fares down.

Let's reduce the crippling loss on the State railways.

Let's get prices down – the basic necessities like milk and bread.

Let's put the consumer first.

Let's stop the rates spiral.

Let's get land and housing costs down.

Let's have at least truly free school – government and non-government alike.

Let's fight to keep Medibank safe.

Let's make sure that every migrant who chooses to live in this State can enjoy all the opportunities of real equality for himself and all his family.

Let's end discrimination against women, against migrants, against Aborigines.

Let's get a system of law where all citizens are truly equal before the law.

Let's create a State where all of the unequalled natural beauties of NSW and the unparalleled heritage of our history are preserved for all time – for the lasting benefit of all the people of NSW and all the people of Australia.

These are the aims, these are the goals I set before you tonight, the aims, goals and ideals of a Labor government in NSW – a program to put NSW first over the next three years.

For 11 years under (Robert) Askin and (Eric) Willis, then under (Tom) Lewis and Willis, now under Willis, NSW – Australia's richest State, Australia's largest State, Australia's premier State, has fallen further and further behind – in the quality of life for its citizens, the quality of the services and the taxpayer pays for, and above all in the quality of public administration, the integrity, decency and openness of our public affairs.

NSW once led Australia and Australia always looked to NSW for leadership. Now, NSW leads Australia only in the level of its taxes and the size of its public debt, in its rate of inflation and its level of unemployment.

The people of NSW can do better.

Labor will do better.

Labor will put our State in better shape to provide all citizens – the men, women and children of its great cities, in its country towns, the people on the land – with a better return for the wealth they produce for this State and for this nation.

Labor will put our State in better shape to deal with the deep economic problems which all Australian governments now share and must all tackle – together …

Let me say without equivocation: a NSW Labor government will cooperate fully with any elected government in Canberra – for the protection of the people of NSW and for the promotion of the interests of NSW …

But we will not be bullied into accepting measures against the interests of NSW for which Canberra has no mandate. We will insist that the federal government fulfils its undertakings with this State.

We will not permit the destruction of Medibank …

We will not allow the federal government to tear up agreements with this State for the new growth centres …

We will resist the reintroduction of fees for universities and colleges of advanced education …

We will not accept the dismantling of the Australian Schools Commission …

This is not a time for new or extravagant promises. The people of NSW are too intelligent for that. They know the state of the nation and the condition in which 11 years of Askin, Lewis and Willis has left this State …

The big question for Sir Eric Willis is not 'Where is the money coming from?', but 'Where has the money gone?'

The immediate task for the NSW Labor government will be to strike a genuine balance between the taxes you pay and the services you pay for – in short, to get full value for your money …

Let Sir Eric Willis answer this: during the last three years federal grants to NSW – outright grants and special grants increased at the highest rate in the history of Federation, yet the huge increases available to the State were never fully reflected in the benefits to the people of this State. Where did all that money go? …

The continuing task for NSW financial arrangements is to restore a proper balance between finances and functions, between taxes levied and services provided, between the money you pay and the return you get.

In NSW the overwhelming imbalance and the heaviest burden caused by government mismanagement is in the field of public transport …

Liberal policies have driven people away from public transport. Only improved services – fast, safe, clean, comfortable trains, buses and ferries – can bring the people back to public transport …

We have already announced … the most responsible and comprehensive transport policy yet produced by any party … It has been thoroughly researched, expertly analysed and closely costed. It is designed to drag our transport system out of the 19th century and into the last quarter of the 20th century …

The waste in public transport and the deterioration of the public transport system adds to the burden of the private motorist. A modern effective public transport system is needed if the private car owner is to get better value for his heavy personal investment. Let's not forget that the two big investments, the two big financial burdens carried by most Australians are the car and the home.

We are determined to implement policies to help ease these enormous private burdens.

For young people seeking to build or buy a home it takes longer and costs more to get a home in NSW than in any other State …

We shall place emphasis on the building of homes – to increase the housing stock of this state.

That means more jobs, more homes, and less pressure on rents …

For all home owners in NSW, rates have become a burden out of all balance with services which local government is able to provide.

Local council rates are too high … unless local councils and ratepayers do receive direct federal assistance, the State must take its own initiatives to help ratepayers.

NSW has too many local government bodies … there must be sensible amalgamations to reduce the number of municipal and shire councils after adequate consultation …

The established principle of Australian democracy is that elections must reflect the views of all qualified electors. In Australian elections, this is secured by the compulsory voting principle. This long-recognised principle will henceforth apply to local government elections.

We are determined to enhance the role of local government in the planning and preservation of this environment.

In environmental matters our basic objective is to make sure that the people of the area immediately concerned, and all concerned citizens of NSW, can have their say in the decisions which affect the environment before the final and irreversible decision is made.

We want to involve the people in these decision-making processes …

Sydney has the dirtiest air, the dirtiest rivers and the dirtiest beaches of any capital city of Australia.

We will ensure that our natural resources – air, water and land – are kept clean for the use and enjoyment of the people of NSW …

I have spoken of the two great costs to the taxpayer and the private individual – transport and homes. A third great cost lies in the provision of public and private health services.

It is absolutely essential that in 1976 that NSW should have a government committed wholeheartedly to the protection of Medibank. Anything less than wholehearted commitment will inevitably mean the destruction of Medibank …

A NSW Labor government will take all steps necessary to reopen outpatients' departments at public hospitals and will take urgent action to establish community health and welfare centres …

This miserable story has been repeated in the field of education …

A Labor government will ensure full employment for all qualified teachers with a view to reducing class sizes, increasing remedial teachers, providing specialist teachers for migrants – adults and children …

Labor's entire approach to education is based on the idea of the inalienable right of every child, of each human being, to develop their full potential as individuals …

It is the family in NSW which has been hit worst by the pricing policies of the present State government. It failed to protect the consumer …

Consumer organisations will be given complete access to the Prices Tribunal …

We will … prevent deceptive packaging.

We will require manufacturers and suppliers to open date stamp all packaged foods.

We will insist that ingredients on all packaged and pre-prepared foods be listed …

The shortcomings of the Liberal government come down to a fundamental failure in human relations, a deep-seated failure to understand the real hopes and needs and aspirations of the people, the ordinary citizens.

Nowhere is this more evident than in the field of industrial relations where the NSW government, as the State's largest employer, has direct and inescapable responsibility …

We will ensure that public servants, teachers and police officers have access to the Industrial Commission ... legislate to provide full portability of long service leave ... remove the anomalies in the Workers Compensation Act which have resulted in absurdly high premiums for no commensurate benefit to either employer or employee ...

Our party recognises that it is a basic human right that no individual or group in the community should be discriminated against or excluded from the fullest participation in the social, economic and cultural life of the community or from the fullest share of all of the opportunities the community offers.

Laws or practices which discriminate against women or migrants or Aborigines will be ended. We will re-introduce legislation to prohibit discrimination on the grounds of sex or marital status in such fields as employment, superannuation and borrowing ...

NSW cannot be said to enjoy full democracy until the whole Parliament is truly democratic and truly representative. In this election, we seek a mandate to put to the people a proposal for the democratic election of members of the Legislative Council ...

Our sole commitment – open and complete – is to all the people of NSW, wherever they live, whatever their status. The task is to get the priorities right; and the great priority is the real welfare and real interests of the ordinary man, woman and children of this State and to that priority we of the Labor Party pledge ourselves without qualification.

In the specific proposals I have outlined tonight there is nothing that is beyond the reach of NSW, given sound, stable, responsible and honest government ...

Why should NSW, once the leading state of Australia, still the wealthiest state in Australia and certainly the highest taxed State in Australia, ever lag behind in the standards of government services, in the equality of life, in the opportunities open to all citizens. We can do much better ...

My vision for NSW is that the old pioneer State will once again be the real pioneer, the pioneer in providing a decent and dignified life for every citizen, the pioneer in progress and prosperity for all the people of NSW and the people of Australia.

Tonight, once again, I dedicate myself and the Australian Labor Party to that noble task and to that splendid vision.

Source: Neville Wran Papers, NSW State Archives.

BOB HAWKE

'National reconciliation, national recovery, national reconstruction'

Bob Hawke presents his policies and plans to the nation to defeat Fraserism

The policies for the Hawke Government were spelt out in the 1983 election policy speech. The venue was the Sydney Opera House. Supporters filled the Opera Theatre and 1000 more spilled out onto the Opera House steps.

The centrepiece of Bob Hawke's appeal was to promise consensus. In the 1970s he had been the great industrial relations advocate, peace-broker and conciliator. Now, as Labor leader he was pledging to 'bring Australia together', promising industrial harmony and to repair and reconstruct the economy. Hawke's aim was 'national reconciliation, national recovery, national reconstruction'. The words 'recovery and reconstruction' were agreed on to frame Bill Hayden's campaign. Hawke, who displaced Hayden as Labor's leader, added 'reconciliation' as the final theme. Watched by his father, wife and daughters in the audience, Hawke led a blistering attack on the Fraser Government and said the election was 'a fight for the future of Australia, for the true heart and soul of Australia'.

Peter Bowers, writing in *The Sydney Morning Herald*, noted that Hawke was consciously 'subdued', a kind of 'quiet persuader' – a far cry from the dynamic and passionate Hawke people had come to know. Hawke spoke so slowly that he ran well over the allotted television time and ended up skipping paragraphs and pages of the speech.

In mid-2010, Hawke said in an interview for this book, 'I think I may have been relatively subdued. I didn't want to appear cocky. I just wanted to really mobilise the party to go out and work as hard as they could to achieve the best result that we could'. Nevertheless, Hawke said, he 'had a quiet confidence that we were going to win'.

Hawke would lead Labor to its greatest election victory since 1943.

'National reconciliation, national recovery, national reconstruction'

The Sydney Opera House, Sydney 16 February 1983

My fellow Australians, today we set out together on a task much greater than winning an election. The task is to win the future for Australia and all Australians.

The real fight – the fight for Australia – is not just between competing parties or competing policies – important as they are. Much less is it a contest between personalities.

There are tremendous issues involved in this historic election on the fifth of March – first and foremost, the right of all Australians to a job; and whether the disastrous economic policies, the political opportunism and the divisive leadership which together have produced Australia's present catastrophic unemployment are to be changed.

For the sake of the one million and more Australians who face unemployment unless there is a change, those policies must be changed, and will be changed – by the Australian Labor government after 5 March.

But above all, this is a fight for the future of Australia, for the true heart and soul of Australia.

For we are asking, on the fifth of March, for a decision from the Australian people which will declare to the world that the politics of division, the politics of confrontation – the deliberate setting of Australian against Australian – which have debased the national leadership and disfigured the national life for so long, have no part in the true Australian way.

And the first pledge I now make, a commitment which embraces every other undertaking, is that everything we do as a government will have the one great goal – to reunite this great community of ours, to bring out the best we are truly capable of, together, as a nation, and bring Australia together to win our way through the crisis into which the policies of the past and the men of the past have plunged our country …

My fellow Australians, let me from the very beginning of this campaign and to the end of this campaign, sound a note of caution and realism. We offer no miracles. We offer no overnight solutions for the immediate problems we face or the deep-seated problems we must face together.

I believe the Australian people have had enough of election promises made only to be broken. I offer no fistful of dollars to be snatched back after the election. What I do offer is a program to produce growth and expansion in the economy, achievable goals for the rebuilding and reconstruction of this nation …

The new path for Australia after the fifth of March 1983 will be national reconciliation, national recovery, national reconstruction.

For let there be no mistake – there can be no economic recovery, there cannot be a beginning towards recovery, until there is a national effort towards national reconciliation. And that effort must begin with the national leadership and the national government …

That is why we undertake, immediately on assuming office, to convene a national economic summit conference, fully representative of Australian industry, the Australian workforce and the Australian people through their elected governments …

Its purpose is to create a climate for common understanding of the scale and scope of Australia's present crisis, to explore the policy options, and to ensure that the relevant parties, governments, business and the unions – clearly appreciate the role that each of them will have to play in pulling the country out of its present economic mess …

As a result of the months of painstaking consultation, discussion and work, we, the representatives of the incoming Labor government, have reached an historic accord with the trade union movement which will form the basis for a firm, genuine and workable prices and incomes policy for this nation.

The whole thrust of our policy is to attack the twin evils of unemployment and inflation together – to get growth back into the economy while ensuring that Australian living standards no longer continue to be eroded by inflation …

In short, in this hour of Australia's worst economic crisis for fifty years, we shall ask all sections of the Australian community to show the common restraint and share the common burden for the common national purpose …

The aim of the incoming Labor government is to restore growth to the Australian economy … increased growth will be restored by:

- building desperately needed public capital works and services;
- tax reductions for low and middle income earners;
- widening of opportunities for borrowing by business, farmers, and homebuyers;
- and providing support for private sector investment …

Until this crisis is overcome there will be no reduction of existing protection levels. We recognise the current crisis facing many industries where import competition is threatening their very survival. We will immediately review the need for additional short-term assistance in selected industries to provide a necessary breathing space until steady growth is restored …

The learning gap between Australia and the rest of the world is widening … If all Australian children are to enjoy equal education opportunities, the funding of all schools, government and non-government, must be based on fairness and need …

Together with the unemployed, the main victims of Fraserism are those who depend for their income on social welfare payments – the aged, the handicapped, the invalid, the bereaved, the single parents. It is unforgivable that after seven years of Fraserism a million and a half people on social security are admitted by the government itself to be living in poverty …

We are committed to raising over a three-year period the basic pension rate …

The Labor government will return to the basic principle of the right of all Australians to health services according to their medical needs. Labor's new Medicare program involves simply the replacement of the present crippling health-fund contributions by an income-related levy of one per cent of taxable income …

Environmental issues have become more prominent in this campaign than in any previous election, through the bitter and diverse controversy over the proposed Gordon-below-Franklin dam, the building of which will irreversibly damage a key part of Australia's and the world's natural and cultural heritage. A Labor government will use all the powers at our disposal to ensure that the dam is not proceeded with, but at the same time ensure that Tasmania is not economically disadvantaged in any way …

Labor believes that one of the most important tasks in Australia today is to restore values to Australian politics … and one of the most fundamental tasks of all in this respect is to think again about some of the values built into the Constitution under which we have as a nation lived and worked for over 80 years …

Our most immediate constitutional reform priority is the achievement of fixed term four-year parliaments … Labor will also establish an independent, public and permanent Electoral Commission to oversee the whole electoral process. We will seek the support of Parliament for the public funding of election campaigns, the disclosure of donations to political parties and for the regulation of unfair political advertising.

Labor has a comprehensive program of law reform, based on the principles of equal access to the law, the protection and promotion of fundamental rights and liberties, and the speedier and more sensitive reaction of the law to social change …

Labor has a comprehensive women's affairs policy, developed in recognition of the fact that Australian women do not yet experience total equality with men, or enjoy full participation in all aspects of our society …

Another area of unresolved conflict involves the Aboriginal people of this country – the first Australians. As a group, they continue to experience the worst conditions – the worst health, housing, employment, education, and the greatest poverty and despair. While this situation persists, we can never truly bring this country together.

Central to this question is the issue of land rights. A Labor government will not hesitate to use, where necessary, the constitutional powers of the Commonwealth to provide for Aboriginal people to own the land which has for years been set aside for them …

Even in times of an economic crisis of such proportions as the present, the defence and security needs of Australia must remain paramount … We will maintain Australian's commitment to the ANZUS Treaty …

We will seek even closer relations with our ASEAN neighbours and in particular, seek to widen trade opportunities in this region …

My fellow Australians,

I said at the outset that this election was not a contest between personalities. And let me emphasise that I now come before you as the leader of a team – a team of men and women with a quality, experience, dedication and vigour which makes me deeply proud to lead them.

But your choice on the fifth of March goes even deeper. It is nothing less than a judgement about the very nature of Australia – the kind of Australia you want for yourselves and the children of Australia. And ultimately this transcends even the question of economic crisis.

For there is no way Australia can surmount this crisis if we allow our country to slide deeper and deeper into the national divisiveness which has marked most of the past decade. The need for national reconciliation, the need for Australians to be brought together and to work together, is something I have held as fundamental throughout my public career …

Just forty years ago this year, in a time of Australia's gravest crisis, when our very existence as a nation was at stake, the people of Australia gave their overwhelming support to take Australia through to final victory. John Curtin led Australia through the crisis to triumph, by bringing Australia together.

In very different times, in a very different kind of crisis, the task and the challenge remain the same – to bring Australians together in a united effort until victory is won.

Source: The Bob Hawke Prime Ministerial Library.

Bob Hawke, after delivering Labor's election campaign speech at the Sydney Opera House, as thousands of supporters spill over the steps on the edge of Sydney's majestic harbour. A few weeks later, Hawke would lead Labor to one of its greatest ever victories in federal politics.
Source: Fairfax

PAUL KEATING

'The most important election in memory'

Paul Keating makes his pitch for an unprecedented fifth term for Labor

Paul Keating returned home to his electorate, in Sydney's south-west, to deliver Labor's 1993 election policy speech. Using Bankstown as a reference point, Keating presented a narrative of the vast changes that Australia had experienced during the 1980s and used this story to frame the future purpose and vision of the Labor government.

He said that the election boiled down to a referendum on Opposition Leader Dr John Hewson's 'radical right-wing proposals', which he branded as 'hostile to fundamental Australian beliefs and Australian institutions'. He contrasted these with Labor's strengths, providing stability, certainty, protection: Medicare, education, industrial harmony, social justice. But above all Labor did not stand for a 'miserable 15 per cent tax on virtually everything you buy', he said.

Keating stood in front of a cobalt blue curtain designed by Baz Luhrmann and looked out to an audience of hundreds of cheering Labor faithful, including Neville Wran, Gough Whitlam and Bob Hawke.

His delivery was at first uneven. Parts were inaudible. He was nervous. But as the speech went on and the response from the crowd boosted him, Keating relaxed and delivered a fine policy speech that was well received by the media for its content and composition.

Days later, at a dinner for Keating's staff at a restaurant in Sydney, he spoke about the campaign in the context of Labor tradition. 'It's only ever been about the Labor Party', he said. 'The other bastards have never had any ideas. It's always the same miserable stuff that they've always been on. We are the entrepreneurs of political life and we are the people who can dream the big dreams and do the big things.'

'The most important election in memory'

Let there be no mistake. This is the most important election in memory.

Today we stand against radical right-wing proposals which are hostile to fundamental Australian beliefs and Australian institutions and all that we have achieved in recent years.

Not new proposals, but old ones. Proposals which have been tried in other countries and which in every case have failed – at great social and economic cost. Dr Hewson says these other countries did not try hard enough. He is nothing if not zealous.

In this election there is Dr Hewson – Dr Hewson and Tim Fischer – or there is Labor.

I ask every Australian to think about this: when you wake up on March 14, whoever has won the election, there will still be unemployment. There will still be problems to solve.

If Labor is re-elected there will also be an Accord between the unions and the government, guaranteeing industrial peace, low inflation, and a continuation of that spirit of cooperation.

There will still be Medicare, guaranteeing quality health care to all Australians regardless of age or circumstance.

There will still be equity and access in education.

There will still be a social safety net providing care for the aged, the sick, the less well-off and the unemployed.

There will still be social policies expressly designed to manage the change we are going through, to alleviate the hardship and minimise the social damage.

And there will be every reason to believe that we will continue to succeed in our ambition to become a great trading nation, a great Australian social democracy, a proud and independent country, united and cohesive – and able to deliver to all our people living standards and a way of life unequalled in the world.

And there will be no GST. No miserable 15 per cent tax on virtually everything you buy.

But if the Coalition is elected, within six months there will be no Accord – instead discord – no universal health system, no safety net.

And there will be a GST.

There will be much less equity and access in education.

Workers will lose the protection of awards and be forced back to negotiate individual contracts with their employers or take the sack.

Everyone will be paying a 15 per cent tax on virtually everything they buy.

And you can be absolutely sure, not one new job will have been created by these measures.

This is why this is the most important election in memory.

There really never has been a clearer choice: between the Australian traditions of fairness and equity, and the economic and social jungle of Reaganism and Thatcherism which other countries have just abandoned.

Fairness and equity have served Australia well, and never better than in this difficult period of change.

We believe in change. To meet the national necessity, we instigated it. But we believe it should be managed: we believe it should be moderated by supportive social policies. We think it should be calm.

Recognising that all change should have a social purpose, we take account of the social consequences.

I lived here in Bankstown for forty years. This suburb of Sydney had all the best qualities of an Australian community. It still has. It is a microcosm of modern urban, multicultural Australia. Now, as then, it draws its strength from the people, and the people draw their strength from Bankstown.

Perhaps because Bankstown was such a strong community, there was a certain fearlessness about it, a great sense of security, a sense of self-sufficiency. One of the home-truths I picked up was that the world owes no one a living …

I think I began to understand towards the end of the 70s – it was then I began to form what was, for me at least, a new idea about Australia …

I became convinced that Australia could be more than a quarry and a farm; that we could find a place in the front rank of trading nations. This of course was contrary to the prevailing wisdom.

Yet in the early 1980s it very rapidly became apparent that the idea was not an option, but an absolute necessity. We no longer had any choice.

The story since then has been a remarkable one. The Australian people are bringing into being a new Australia. An Australia which has more than doubled exports in nine years. An Australia which has tripled exports of manufactures and services …

These things have happened with remarkable speed.

And so have these things: we have the lowest inflation in thirty years. The highest productivity in thirty years. The lowest number of industrial disputes in thirty years. We are far more competitive than we have ever been.

What is more, we have a population with a proven capacity for change, and a proven willingness to meet the challenges Australia faces.

But in the face of this success, our opponents talk incessantly of failure. Where there is hope they counsel despair. To sell their plan, they think it is necessary to talk Australia down – to extinguish people's faith.

My counsel is hope. These days it is more than hope – it is belief. Belief in what the 90s holds for us all. I've always said that I wanted to be around for the 90s – to see it all come true, to be part of the transformation.

Our opponents say they have a plan. The word plan is forever on their lips. Their pollsters demand it. But they have the wrong plan.

Labor has more than a plan – we have a whole national change – a sea-change, born of national necessity, happening now. A change sustained by faith in Australians.

A change not shaped by a computer model or a textbook, but bedded in reality and commonsense.

A change that does not break the mould of Australian society, but reshapes it by drawing on its strengths.

One that does not look back to the values of Thatcher's Britain or Reagan's America but forward to the next century …

In an era of change the watchwords of good government should be care, support, cooperation. We must take the people with us. That is a Labor article of faith.

We also recognise that on the way to our great social goals there have been problems as well as successes, and we recognise our responsibility for them. As prime minister, I recognise my responsibility for them. Governments in Australia in the eighties were not always as prudent or wise as they should have been.

Nor were all companies: in the newly deregulated economy, a lot of their behaviour was not in the best interests of Australia. The excesses of the 80s must not reappear in the 90s. The last thing we need now is a return to the 80s philosophy of 'greed is good' and that the only useful interest is self-interest …

Unemployment is the greatest problem we face. It is the problem of the era. It is, overwhelmingly, the principal concern of the government.

We have managed to achieve more economic growth than most other comparable countries. We have had four consecutive quarters of growth.

But it has not yet begun to create enough jobs. And we're not helped by a sluggish international economy.

What then is the answer? What is Labor's jobs strategy for the 1990s? Over the next three years, Labor will place the emphasis where it has to be. On business and on incentives to invest. Labor's jobs strategy is designed to assist recovery in business …

There is the other lesson I learned growing up in Bankstown. In hard times you stick together. When you're confronted with a challenge, unity is strength.

Every time Australians cooperate, every time they form a partnership, every time they agree on a common goal, every time they combine their ideas and their energy, they make Australia stronger.

If one word describes Labor's policy for Australia, it is 'cooperation'.

Our policy must never be to undo the ties that bind us but rather to strengthen them as we did with the Accord between government and the unions last week …

We recognise that child care is essential if women are to take a job, undertake training or study or look for work …

We recognise and appreciate the important role played by women who choose to stay at home while their children are growing up …

Medicare is another concrete expression of the quality of our society and of Labor's commitment to it … A measure of our care for one another …

In education, we will continue to pursue the goals of access and equity … In doing this we meet the challenge of the new economic order. Education is our great comparative advantage. We must keep it and build on it …

As our success depends on the bonds between us, it depends on the strength of our culture. Labor guarantees support for those great Australian institutions which preserve the nation's heritage, encourage ideas, disseminate information and strengthen national cohesion …

The government has long spoken of the need to address the historic and continuing injustice done to Australia's indigenous people … Any government that I lead will be determined to complete the process of reconciliation Labor has begun, and at last return to the indigenous people of Australia the dignity, social justice, health, opportunity and living standards to which all Australians are entitled …

It has been Labor's consistent theme that our success as a nation depends on our ability to harness all our resources, human as well material. It depends on having faith in our institutions and confidence in ourselves and in each other …

It is perhaps in part because Australians are growing in confidence that more and more of them are questioning whether it is appropriate for Australia to have as its head of state the monarch of another country …

Early in the speech I said that this community was remarkable for being so strong and so cohesive … Bankstown has drawn on its people, it has drawn on its community spirit, it has drawn on its sense of justice and fairness – on those traditions common to all Australians – to make the transformation from one world to another…

To my mind, it is because Australians know these things and for so long now have practiced them that Australia is a great country, and a country with great prospects. It is because we have the wisdom both to succeed in the world and to live together in Australia. And in the end I think that is at the heart of our pride, and why we love Australia.

And why we must make sure that the ties that bind us are never broken.

Source: Editor's personal files.

KEVIN RUDD

'A choice between the future and the past'

Kevin Rudd delivers Labor's winning election campaign policy speech

Kevin Rudd's campaign launch and policy speech was the first of only two formal set-piece speeches that Rudd gave during the 2007 campaign. The other was to the National Press Club in the final week.

Rudd's policy speech was a careful distillation of the key themes of his leadership and his pitch for government over the previous year. Informed by party research, and with many contributions from those working on the campaign, the final text was worked on and polished by Rudd almost up until the point of delivery.

Rudd spoke to an enthusiastic audience of Labor supporters, which included Labor's three living former Prime Ministers: Gough Whitlam, Bob Hawke and Paul Keating.

Rudd focused on the choice the Australian people faced at the election: 'between the future and the past' and about 'the new challenges that we face in the future'. He zeroed-in on the most critical vote winning policy: the Howard government's unfair and extreme workplace relations laws. He outlined Labor's policies to assist 'working families' and on education, health, climate change, infrastructure and broadband. Rudd attacked the Howard government's economic management and declared, unequivocally, 'I have no intention today of repeating Mr Howard's irresponsible spending spree'. Rudd was prepared to let Howard outspend him in the campaign. 'Today', Rudd said, 'I am saying loud and clear that this sort of reckless spending must stop'. It was a bold and audacious move to demonstrate Rudd's 'economic conservative' credentials – and the audience lapped it up.

In an interview with Rudd in October 2010, he said that he represented 'the reformist tradition' in the Labor Party and tried to reflect this, and his own personal political values, in the speech.

'A choice between the future and the past'

Brisbane Convention Centre, Brisbane 14 November 2007

On November 24, Australians will face a stark choice: a choice between the future and the past.

Today, the case I put before the Australian people is that if we are to secure the future for our families, for our communities and for our nation – the government of Australia must now change.

After 11 years, Mr Howard has lost touch with working families. He has become so used to being in office that he no longer understands what fairness actually means. After 11 years Mr Howard has become stuck in the past.

He simply doesn't understand the new challenges that we face in the future:

- the challenges of climate change and water;
- the challenges of the digital economy;
- the challenge of the rise of China and India;
- the challenge to fix our hospitals, once and for all; and
- above all, the challenge to transform our education system.

Mr Howard has no plans for the future because he's not going to be there to deal with the challenges of the future. It's official – Mr Howard's retiring. And we all know that Mr Howard's chosen replacement, Mr Costello, wants to take WorkChoices even further.

The way forward for Australia is to elect a new Prime Minister and a new government with fresh ideas to meet the challenges of the future.

A new Prime Minister and a new government who understand and respect the values upon which our nation has been built: values of decency, values of fairness, values of respect.

A new Prime Minister and a new government who believe that the great Australian value of a fair go for all has a future – and not just a past ...

Australians are a decent people – but Mr Howard's WorkChoices laws are not decent laws ... WorkChoices embodies so much of the differences between the values of our party and those of our opponents.

We believe in rewarding hard work, achievement and success. We believe in protecting those who can't stand up for themselves. We believe in a decent safety net and a decent standard of living for all working families. We believe in helping those who fall on hard times ... WorkChoices is an assault on all these values ...

That's why on November 24 we must say no to Mr Howard's WorkChoices laws. If elected, we will abolish WorkChoices. If elected, we will abolish AWAs. And if elected, we will ensure flexibility and fairness at work …

Mr Howard's government has lost touch with working families … Mr Howard says 'working families in Australia have never been better off'. Mr Costello says there is no housing affordability crisis. Mr Brough says there is no childcare affordability crisis. How out of touch can you get?

For Labor, fairness is in our DNA. We understand that working families are under financial pressure and they need every bit of help we can offer.

That's why we have also put forward a national housing affordability strategy – so that we can keep alive the great Australian dream of one day owning your own home.

We have put forward policies to help with the family budget.

We will increase the Childcare Tax Rebate to 50 per cent.

We will introduce a 50 per cent Education Tax Refund.

We will extend dental care to teenagers through the Medicare system.

We will establish a Petrol Price Commissioner and a national inquiry into grocery prices to make sure working families aren't ripped off.

None of these represent a silver bullet. But they do offer practical help to working families under financial pressure …

Friends, Australia needs new leadership with fresh ideas for the future.

With barely a week to go of this election campaign, Mr Howard's government has put forward no new ideas for the future. It has run out ideas. It has run out of energy. And it has run out of time.

I am offering new leadership with a plan for the future – Mr Howard is offering no leadership, other than a plan to retire and handover to Peter Costello …

And whatever amount of money Mr Howard may yet throw at these long standing challenges over the next ten days, it is just not going to be real. The truth is – it's all just too late to be believable.

Remarkably as interest rates rose yet again last week, we now find Mr Howard running up the white flag on inflation and running up a huge bill in a desperate bid to get re-elected. A bill he is happy to leave for us all to pay – once he heads off into retirement.

Monday's feeding frenzy of expenditure would actually make inflationary pressures worse. Mr Howard spent nearly $10 billion on Monday – trying to buy his way out of political trouble.

And he did so little more than an hour after the Reserve Bank of Australia issued its monetary policy statement warning of rising inflationary pressures. How irresponsible can you get? ...

I have no intention today of repeating Mr Howard's irresponsible spending spree.

Unlike Mr Howard, I will heed the warnings of the Reserve Bank. Unlike Mr Howard, I will not place in jeopardy households already struggling with mortgages. Unlike Mr Howard, I don't stand before you with a bag full of irresponsible promises that could put upward pressure on inflation.

Today I am saying loud and clear that this sort of reckless spending must stop.

I am determined that any commitments I make are first and foremost economically responsible. That's why the commitments I announce today will cost less than one quarter of those Mr Howard announced on Monday ...

On hospitals, we have put forward a national plan to end the buck-passing between Canberra and the States ...

Mr Howard has spent a decade in denial on the critical challenge of climate change. Even now, Mr Howard still opposes Kyoto. I make this commitment – if we are elected, I will immediately ratify Kyoto.

Mr Howard has opposed carbon targets and emissions trading. If elected, I will implement a 60 per cent carbon target and establish Australia's first national emissions trading scheme.

Mr Howard has opposed boosting the renewable energy target. If elected, I will implement a renewable energy target of 20 per cent by 2020 ...

Mr Costello has said the national government has no role in urban water – I fundamentally disagree. Climate change has made urban and rural water supplies a matter of national significance and therefore a matter of national responsibility. That's why if elected we will establish a National Desalination and Urban Water Recycling Fund ...

For 11 years Mr Howard's government has failed to provide leadership in developing our nation's infrastructure. If elected, I will provide that leadership. I will establish Infrastructure Australia – to tackle the nation's infrastructure bottlenecks.

I will establish a Building Australia Fund. And as one of our first nation-building investments, in partnership with the private sector, we will build a state of the art, fibre optic to the node, National Broadband Network ...

Nation building requires vision. And the cornerstone of my vision for Australia's future is an education revolution ...

I believe education is the engine room of equity. The engine room of opportunity. And the engine room of the economy ... My vision for Australia is to build the best education system in the world – so that we produce the most innovative, the most skilled and the best trained workforce in the world.

The sad reality is that over the last decade Australia has been falling behind – falling behind in early childhood education, in trades training and in our national funding for universities ...

That's why we announced in chapter one of our education revolution that we will provide 15 hours a week for 40 weeks a year in pre-literacy and pre-numeracy play-based learning for every four year old in the country.

In chapter two we announced we will introduce a 50 per cent Education Tax Refund to enable parents to claim a refund for their investment in the modern tools and resources of their children's education.

In chapter three we announced we will tackle the chronic shortage of maths and science teachers by halving HECS for those disciplines at university, and we'll halve it again for those graduates who go on to teach maths and science in our schools.

In chapter four we announced we will introduce comprehensive Asian language education across the school system to equip the next generation of Australians with the languages of the major economies of the future.

In chapter five we announced we will build state of the art Trades Training Centres for each of Australia's 2,650 secondary schools.

Today I announce three further chapters in Labor's education revolution ...

Over the next four years, a Federal Labor government will fund an additional 450,000 training places across Australia ...

We will connect Australia's more than 9,000 primary and secondary schools to our National Broadband Network – at speeds of up to 100 megabits per second ...

Labor will undertake a ground-breaking reform by providing every Australian secondary school student in years nine to 12 with access to their own computer at school ...

Universities are critical to the education revolution that Australia so urgently needs ... an incoming Labor government will double the number of national undergraduate scholarships to a total of 88,000 by 2012.

I also announce today that if elected an incoming Labor government will double the number of post graduate scholarships to nearly 10,000 students across Australia by 2012.

And if elected we will create for the first time in Australia 1000 high-value mid-career research fellowships, valued at $140,000 each, to help reverse the brain drain. This will help retain Australia's most talented academics at home …

Friends, it's good to be back in Brisbane today where I began this election campaign a month ago. It's especially good to be back home with Therese and the kids. And for the record Therese, I haven't forgotten that today's our 26th wedding anniversary.

Friends, if we are elected in ten days time, I want to be a Prime Minister for all Australians.

A Prime Minister for Indigenous Australia.

A Prime Minister for rural Australia, where so many of our fellow Australians are going through such tough times with the drought.

A Prime Minister for our regions that stretch so far beyond our magnificent cities.

If elected, I also want to ensure that Australia once again has its own voice in the affairs of the world … And on Iraq, the time has come to implement an exit strategy for our combat forces – forces who are needed much closer to home …

I approach this election with a passionate commitment to Australia's future. The values I bring to leadership are the values instilled in me by my family. They are also the values that are intrinsic to this great party …

I believe that as a community we have a responsibility when one of us falls down, we must help to lift them back up. That's what decency and fairness is all about.

Another thing I have learnt is the absolute value of hard work. Of not being wasteful. And the importance of planning for the future …

I stand before you today as a candidate for the prime ministership of Australia. I am proud of the plan we have put forward for Australia's future …

The nation now needs new leadership for the future … And today, I stand before you ready to deliver that new leadership for Australia's future.

Source: Editor's personal files.

PART 4

History, Tradition and Ideology

GEORGE BLACK

'To make and unmake social conditions'

One of Labor's first parliamentarians, George Black,
explains Labor's role in its formative years

In mid-1891, the Labor Party burst into existence as a parliamentary party, with the election of 35 candidates to the NSW Parliament. No Labor Party had achieved such success, so soon, anywhere else in the world.

Over the next three years, representatives of organised labour were elected to parliaments in Queensland (four in 1892), Victoria (10 in 1892), South Australia (eight in 1893) and Tasmania (one in 1894). But even if these numbers are combined, they do not match the success in NSW. It makes NSW the birthplace of the Labor Party as a parliamentary and political force.

It also marked the beginning of a new type of parliamentary party: with a platform and objectives, solidarity and a pledge, and a caucus organising model. However, unity took time to fully manifest; Labor's representatives would soon split. In 1894, only four members were re-elected under the Labor banner; 25 chose to stand as independent Labor candidates.

One of Labor's first parliamentarians, George Black, said in a landmark speech shortly after being elected that the party's goal was 'to make and unmake social conditions'. 'The men we represent', Black said, are 'those who labour with either hand or head, with either mind or muscle'. For these men, Labor sought 'a little more of the world's pleasure, leisure and treasure'.

Labor would position itself as a party that would support governments which sponsored legislation that advanced Labor's objectives. Over time Labor would aspire to leading a government in its own right.

The Sydney Morning Herald's reporting of this speech noted Black 'spoke with great moderation' and called the strategy of 'support in return for concessions' one of 'imprudent frankness'. The other guardian of conservative virtue, *The Argus*, feared that a 'class' party would lead to 'strife in the land'.

Labor would continue to build in NSW, winning majority government in 1910.

'To make and unmake social conditions'

NSW Legislative Assembly, Sydney 16 July 1891

... We have been told by the premier that he is not aware of the existence of the Labor Party. But if he be not aware of its existence he is remarkably alive to its influence, and he has just as much as Hon Members on the other side thrown out baits for our support. We may swallow the baits from one side or the other; but we do it advisedly. We do it knowing that they are baits, and we do it for our own purposes – not that we want to give support to Sir Henry Parkes because he is Sir Henry Parkes, or because he is a free-trader; or to Mr Dibbs because he is Mr Dibbs, or because he is a protectionist; but simply for our own purposes.

The Hon Member for Argyle has told the House one of the reasons that have brought the Labor Party into existence – the strike. That is, I am bound to admit one reason; but a still more patent reason is the Payment of Members' Act. Had not payment of members existed, I venture to say that not one labour representative who now sits here could have sat here ...

As my Hon friend, the member for The Namoi, has pointed out, this debate originally started on the proviso that it was not to border or touch in any way on the fiscal question. In spite of that, however, the fiscal question has been introduced, and it affords us an opportunity for saying what I said here last night at a late hour: that we, who represent the Labor Party, have given our pledge not in any way to vote with any regard to the fiscal question. We do this irrespective of beliefs held by some of us, that there are certain virtues in free-trade and protection, because those who have returned us have chosen to think what I think with them: that there is no health in either protection or free-trade for any man who has to labour with either his hands or his head.

The men we represent are the wage-earners – those who labour with either hand, with either mind or muscle – and if we declared for either policy for protection or free-trade, we should be false to our constituents ...

Protection means, if it means anything, an increase of internal production. And free-trade means, if it means anything, an increase of commerce, an increase of exchange with other countries. But neither policy means a greater share, or a fairer share of the wealth which is either created or imported to the hands who make the wealth. Neither policy means a greater opportunity for access to the sources of wealth.

If that be so, and I submit it is logically correct, then it is evident that the Labor Party, and those who returned the Labor Party, hold only sensible positions when they say that they have come into this House neither to support free-trade nor protection, but to support that ministry that will give them what they want.

We have only one ministry to deal with at the present time – we can only have one ministry to deal with at a time. That ministry has offered us not all that we want, but perhaps a great deal more than we might have fairly expected. The question for us to consider is not only have they offered us enough, but are they likely to keep their promises? We expect something more than promises. Too long have the people of this country been gulled by promises made on the hustings or in governor's speeches. We have been returned to this House, sir, to see that such promises are not only made, but kept. We intend to fulfil that duty.

The motto of the labour party in this House is 'support in return for concessions'. If you give us concessions, then our votes will circulate on the government benches, and if you do not give us concessions then we shall withdraw our votes from circulation there. That is the position we hold …

We have not come into this House, then, to make or unmake ministries. We have come into this House to make and unmake social conditions, but we have not come in for the purpose of vengeance. We have not come to avenge ourselves on certain individuals, no matter how much we may dislike those individuals. We have come into this House prepared to know nothing of what has been done in previous parliaments. We have come into this House with a clean record, with a clean sheet. We have come into this House, only to know what is done in the House while we are in it. With what has been done before we have no connection nor interest; and it strikes me that if every other member came into this House under the same conditions there would be a great deal more business done …

We want legislation. We do not want mud-throwing. We have come into this House to secure some measure of very much-needed legislation, and therefore we have no desire to rake up the past …

The question for us to consider is, how much useful legislation can we do before the House rises at Christmas time? … We want to get as much out of the Hon gentleman who sits at the head of the government benches as possible; and if we cannot get very much from him, we will put some one in his place from who we can get more. It is just as well that the House should understand that from the beginning. We have come here for that purpose, and we do not want to make any secret of it. In a House that may follow this, as I have said, we will stand probably in a different position, and may in a future day occupy other seats. At present we sit here. We sit in a neutral position. We know exactly what we have got to face. We know exactly what we have got to fight for.

We have got to fight misrepresentation, in the press of the country especially. Ever since the Labor Party has come into existence it has been consistently blackguarded by a certain section of the press. We have been alluded to by one paper as 'good creatures' and as 'rag-tag and bob-tail', as if they expected to see us coming into the House wearing moleskins, and carrying picks and shovels on our shoulders.

We have come here to show that we have just as much intelligence as other members, no matter on which side of the House they sit; that we have just as much good taste, and just as much determination to carry on the business …

Our purpose here is to do work, to do honest and intelligent work, to do it if possible without offending anybody; but if it be necessary to give a display of our power, to give it – because we have not come here to mince matters – we have been sent here by … people who have been somewhat accustomed to be minced, if I may be allowed to use the phrase …

It is hardly necessary for me to indicate how we shall vote after what I have said. I have only to say that we do not vote as we intend to vote out of any love for the premier, or out of any dislike to the opposition; but because we do not see that we are to get anything by waiting, because we believe that there is nothing to be said or done on behalf of either free trade or protection that will benefit us; that in neither system is there any health for those whom we represent.

What we want for those whom we represent is, as someone said the other day, a little more of the world's pleasure, leisure and treasure. We have come here to endeavour to obtain that. We can only obtain it in one way, that is by holding the balance of power in this House; and by holding it in accordance with the motto I have already mentioned, 'Support in return for concessions', we believe we can obtain much. In future we hope to obtain a great deal more.

Source: NSW Legislative Assembly Debates (Hansard).

JAMES MCGOWEN

'We are the representatives of the masses of the workers'

The first NSW Labor Premier gives a thoughtful
speech on the purpose of the Labor Party

Throughout the 1880s and early 1890s, the fiscal question was the galvanising issue in NSW politics. Henry Parkes and George Reid were the key free traders. The protectionists coalesced around George Dibbs, Edmund Barton and William Lyne.

Labor supported those who offered the most concessions. In 1891, the government led by Dibbs, was beset by a fiscal crisis; it had no money. The government proposed to increase taxes on imports. Reid, opposed to the government, suggested a referendum to allow people to have their say. It fell to Labor to decide the matter. Leading Labor figure, Jim McGowen, proposed a plebiscite. But when McGowen's motion failed, the Labor caucus decided to support Reid's referendum plan. But when the vote came, the divisions within Labor on free trade and protection manifested themselves: two-thirds went for Reid, one-third for Dibbs. McGowen, a protectionist, followed the principle of caucus solidarity and voted for Reid's motion.

Labor would reform under McGowen's leadership. The protectionists rebranded themselves as progressives and eventually petered out. The free traders became the main non-Labor force.

In this speech, McGowen makes the case for a plebiscite. He illuminates the early thinking of Labor's founders and the purpose of the party. Labor's mission was to represent 'the masses of the workers' and did so favouring the ballot box over revolutionary methods, he said. 'I was not elected as a protectionist or as a free trader, but as what is called a labour man.'

Party historian and speechwriter Graham Freudenberg says this speech 'breathes the character of the man' and demonstrated 'the true purpose of the Labor Party'.

'We are the representatives of the masses of the workers'

NSW Legislative Assembly, Sydney 10 December 1891

I rise … as a representative of that much maligned party, on whose shoulders the whole responsibility of the present position is said to rest, and on whose shoulders the vote is taken. Rightly or wrongly we are representatives of the masses of the workers, who, for the first time in the history, not only of this colony, but I believe of the whole world, sent in any large number of men to represent their class straight from the workshops to the Legislative Assembly.

I unhesitatingly and advisedly use the word class, because I desire to say something about what has been said about our class representation. Having had no previous experience in the political world, we banded ourselves together in a compact body, and whether we have done right or wrong, while this House remains in existence we know that we shall have to suffer the consequences of that wrong, or reap the plaudits of those who sent us here if we do the right thing.

Ever since I have been 18 years of age, in this, which is almost my native country, I have been fighting in the rank and file of the protectionists, and I do not think that there are very many older protectionists on the right hand of Mr Speaker than your humble servant has been in the rank and file of the workers. But I have found in the constituency I have to represent that whenever the election of a member of Parliament came on, we, the working men, were fighting one another tooth and nail on this party line which separated the two parties in the House.

No doubt Hon Members are fully aware that when the last struggle took place by the workers of NSW against the encroachments of their rights, as they thought, by the employers, and that when there was likely to be some disturbance in our civil world, when one or two enthusiastic representatives or advocates, of the cause of the workers, rose and almost said to the men, 'Why do you, the people, two-thirds of the community, put up with the action of your representatives in Parliament, when the whole world are turned loose on you, the very people whom you support to maintain law and order'.

Then when some of those people almost spoke in a revolutionary style, those of us, working in some prominent places in our labour unions, blamed them just as much as the civilised world, and the papers did.

Then it was said to us, 'Why do you not come together and exercise your manhood suffrage, and send direct into our legislative halls men who, from the very exigencies of their lifetime, will be best able to give expression to the views and aspirations with which we are all imbued' ...

We did so, but, before doing it, we called the attention of the press and the people to the fact that we were divided by this line that has come into our party politics; that were men who would stand together loyally and honestly in the cause by which we earned our daily bread, but that we were fighting like bitter foes in this faction fight which was not of our seeking, that has been brought into our political world against our wish, and very often to our detriment.

We found that we had many times to choose the lesser of two evils, and the lesser of those evils were men who were necessarily somewhat prejudiced against the aspirations of the masses of the people. Well, the press, the people, our own leading organisations, advised us in this way, 'If this one question divides you, and prevents you from standing shoulder to shoulder in the exercise of your manhood suffrage, why do you not drop it out of sight?' We did so, and we had the assistance of both free-traders and protectionists ...

I hope that, whatever course we are compelled to take in this Parliament, the only thing we brought with us we will take out unsullied – our reputation. We formulated a platform on which we could all combine. We presented that to the workers of NSW, and they stuck loyally to us. We are under no compliment to either side of the House, because for every seat we contested, free-traders and protectionists alike sought election.

We found ourselves, as I have said, political novices. We met in caucus, and we decided as man to man by pledging our names that we would abide by the decision of the majority, no matter what was the result ...

We entered this House with a strong desire to support the government then in power, because we contented, and justly so according to our election, that we had nothing to do with party strife, that we were desirous of forcing on legislation in the interests, not only of the class we represented – which, as I have previously said, is an important consideration in the community of any civilised country – but also in the interests of the whole community.

We remained in our position from the time the House opened until it was closed, and having to give our vote on the very first resolution which meant the downfall or the upholding of a certain ministry, we voted for the ministry of Sir Henry Parkes ...

We supported the government in spite of what was said about us. We gave them our support consistently until it came to a question in which we were deeply interested. In seeking the suffrages of the workers, we asked them to vote for us because we believed in certain principles, and whether it pleased or displeased the representatives of the people in this House, we tried in a respectful manner to express our belief in those principles, and to advocate them, and then that government threw us over …

We have in our ranks men who have been strong and staunch fighters for the whole of their lifetime, either in the cause of free trade or in the cause of protection. When 18 years of age, I espoused the cause of protection, not in the interests of revenue, but in the interests of the workers, in order that the resources of the colony might be developed, and native industries fostered; but I unhesitatingly say that, when I was elected, I was not elected as a protectionist or as a free trader, but as what is called a labour man …

I said to the electors, 'I am more loyal to the cause of labour than I am to the cause of protection, and, if you think me worthy, I will enter the Legislative Assembly without considering my self as belonging to any fiscal party'. That was the compact into which I entered with the Labor Party, and I will prove my loyalty to my party in the event of a certain thing not being carried, and by my vote I will show what a protectionist will do when put upon his word of honour.

Having two different political elements in our party, we decided – and some of us proclaimed it in our published addresses to the electors – that the fiscal question should be referred to the people … It was to satisfy the desires of our own party, and in the interests of the whole community, that we proposed that motion for a plebiscite … If Hon Members are honest in their desire to legislate in the interests of a majority of the community they will admit that the best way to ascertain the wishes of that majority upon all questions of such magnitude as that of free trade and protection, will be by means of a plebiscite …

It is said that we cannot carry on the government of the country unless you have a good opposition … Why not let a majority of the people's representatives choose the government and remove it as soon as it is found that it does not come up to their expectations? If you do that you will have government for the people, by the people, and of the people. I consider that in no way can this fiscal question be more satisfactorily settled in the interests of the country than by a motion that will directly ascertain their wishes …

Source: NSW Legislative Assembly Debates (Hansard).

JOHN (CHRIS) WATSON

'The spirit of humanity'

Chris Watson rejects socialism and says Labor stands for the 'the spirit of humanity'

John (Chris) Watson's speeches are rarely, if ever, quoted these days. Indeed, many are lost to history. Some survive; others await excavation from dusty archives and rediscovered in old newspapers.

In the early 1900s, Watson frequently addressed large gatherings on the case for Labor around Australia. The myriad of social and progressive groups and societies would often host Watson as their guest speaker. Halls would fill with thousands of people who would come to hear Watson speak, usually as a form of evening entertainment and intellectual stimulation. He always expressed his passionate conviction in the cause of Labor and of his high hopes for what a Labor government could achieve.

In this speech, delivered in the House of Representatives, a week after the Watson government came to power, the new Prime Minister expounds further on the aims and objectives of the first national Labor government. He refers to his own personal philosophy and that of the Labor Party. He rejects the 'socialist' label. Instead, he says, Labor stands for 'the spirit of humanity; the spirit of those who care for the poor and the lowly; of those who are prepared to make an effort to interfere with the iron law of wages, and with the cold-blooded calculation of the ordinary political economist'. He aligns himself with the 'spirit' of May Day, saying his approach was 'of those who will leave no stone unturned, and no experiment untried, in their efforts to benefit humanity'.

'The spirit of humanity'

The House of Representatives, Melbourne 26 May 1904

At this hour it is not my intention to say much on the general tone of the debate on the programme I submitted a week ago.

I regret that so much time has been taken up with a discussion on what, after all, is only an abstract matter, because I would have preferred much, if we had been able, to have a clear fight on the issue whether this government is to retain office – if that issue is intended to be raised – or whether we are to get on to the work of the country, and, by accomplishing something, justify our existence as a parliament.

I think that the complaint of the honourable member for Bass – that we have been sitting here for about three months, and yet have nothing to show for our work – is justified. It is about time that, with the help of one side or the other, we buckled to, and gave some result to the country. With regard to the line of attack which has generally been followed … not on the program of immediate work presented by us, but rather on the question of whether our methods of organisation are justified; whether we are acting with propriety in insisting on a man doing in our party as he is required to do in every party – that is, to sink his minor convictions when a crisis arrives in order that the matters which he holds to be of larger importance should be given effect to.

That principle obtains in every party in a State … It is only the sheerest hypocrisy on the part of the honourable members on the other side to talk about the rules of the Labor Party and their organisation, when they know, every one of them, that they must give way to party discipline if they are to accomplish anything under the system of responsible government that obtains in every British community.

It is an absolute essential that we must give way here and there if we are to accomplish anything – and I say that honourable members, knowing that, were only speaking for party purposes when they complained of the methods of the Labor Party. We have followed their example. It is true that our members exhibit a degree of loyalty perhaps greater than that exhibited by members of some other parties …

I come now to the remarks of the honourable member for Werriwa. I was pained to think that an honourable and learned member, to whom I have always given credit for at least fighting fairly, if always hitting hard, should have descended to an attack of the description in which he engaged …

I felt it deeply that it should be suggested that any of us sympathized with free love, or the breaking down of the marriage institution. It was a most shameful thing, in my view, for the honourable and learned member, who know us so well, and knows the labour movement so well, to cast an imputation of that character upon us. He knows very well that no such sympathy is entertained by any man in our party …

I, for one, say that, although I may believe that a socialistic writer is sound on the economic side of the question, I am not necessarily bound to follow him into every aspect of social life, and to subscribe to his theories thereon …

But what did I say to those who waited upon me? I ask the attention of the honourable and learned member. This is what I said –

> I have to thank you for the kindly expressions conveyed to my colleagues and myself upon our assumption of office, and to say that so far as the general spirit behind the May Day movement is concerned, we are heartily in sympathy with it. What is that spirit?

… It is the spirit of humanity; the spirit of those who care for the poor and lowly; of those who are prepared to make an effort to interfere with the iron law of wages, and with the cold-blooded calculation of the ordinary political economist. That is the spirit which I recognise as being behind the May Day movement. It is not in any way circumscribed by any mere declaration of this or that plank of a platform, but is the motive of those who will leave no stone unturned, and no experiment untried, in their efforts to benefit humanity. That is the spirit with which we are heartily in sympathy, and I can challenge any honourable member to say that he is against it.

Source: Commonwealth of Australia Parliamentary Debates (Hansard).

In 1904, Chris Watson became the Labor Party's first Prime Minister. In this photo, he is pictured speaking in the Victorian Parliament, then home to The House of Representatives. He advocated policies 'For the benefit of the whole of the people of Australia' and spoke of Labor's mission as 'A light upon a mountain'. On his death in 1941, John Curtin described him as 'One of the most eminent of the band of prominent Labor men'.
Source: Australian Labor Party

JOHN (CHRIS) WATSON

'A light upon a mountain'

Labor's first leader invokes powerful imagery to illustrate
Labor's vision – half a century before Ben Chifley

Is it possible that Labor's first leader, John (Chris) Watson described Labor's cause as 'a light upon a mountain', half a century before Ben Chifley spoke of 'the light on the hill'?

In September 1904, Watson addressed a large meeting convened by the Social Democratic League at the Queen's Hall on Bourke Street in Melbourne.

According to a letter from a young woman, which can be found in Watson's personal papers, he spoke of Labor's cause as 'a light upon a mountain'.*

Watson said 'the object of the Labor Party' was 'progressive legislation'. He advocated using 'the machinery of government to protect the weak against the strong, that wrongs may be righted, and that evils may be eradicated from the body politic'. Watson said 'any person of humanitarian instinct', would be on the side of Labor.

But to secure progressive legislation, 'the only possible method was an alliance'. Watson advocated an alliance with like-minded parliamentarians such as Isaac Isaacs, HB Higgins and Charles Kingston. 'It is not proposed in this alliance to merge the Labor Party into any other party ... we would work together for certain definite objects', he said.

While caucus had previously agreed to align with the Deakin-led Liberals on some matters and Watson would 'support' a Deakin government that did not include George Reid, the party organisation always resisted an alliance or coalition. In July 1905, the federal conference directed the caucus not to enter into any alliance.

At the Social Democratic League, *The Age* said Watson gave 'a spirited address' and 'was received with cheers'. It was a 'statesman-like deliverance', said *The Advertiser*. *The Argus* said that a 'majority' in the audience 'cheered his points'.

The speech highlights the early struggles of the party working to see its ideals come to fruition and shows that the language used to communicate these ideals has long endured.

---

*   A survey of contemporary newspapers does not, unfortunately, confirm that Watson used this phrase. However, at the end of his speech, Watson engaged in a question and answer session with the audience, and it is likely that he uttered the phrase at that point in the evening. The letter highlights the phrase 'a light upon a mountain' in quotation marks, suggesting it is a direct quote taken from Watson's speech. [Letter from Kathleen Charles to JC Watson, 27 September 1904. MS 451/1/83.]

'A light upon a mountain'

Queen's Hall, Melbourne 25 September 1904

I was very glad to accept the invitation of the Social Democratic Federation (sic) to make a few remarks here this evening, more especially as it seemed necessary that something should be said, particularly to those who have been with the Labor Party in the past, in reference to this new departure which has just been taken.

In the first place, let me say that I have no harsh word to say to those who think differently from the great majority of the Parliamentary Labor Party on the question of the alliance. Each man and woman is entitled to come to his or her own opinion, and therefore I have no complaint if some people choose to look at this matter from another standpoint.

But you all know how, in each of the states, it has often been possible – sometimes principally though alliances – to pass some measures that have worked for the public good. It has to be remembered that the object of the Labor Party is, not to get men into Parliament or to keep certain men on the Treasury benches.

The party has always aimed at getting certain legislation carried into effect at the earliest possible moment. In most of the parliaments of Australia, the Labor Party has been a third party. If we were to have got anything done at all, the only possible method was by an alliance, whether tacit or expressed, with one or other of the older and more numerous parties …

On the other hand, we have everywhere the enthusiast who is prepared to die fighting rather than accept any compromise. I do not wish to under-value the enthusiastic and the quixotic man. The success of every movement depends on the enthusiast. But we should consider the immediate welfare of the great mass of the people.

If following the course of the enthusiast means that we are to wait an indefinite period for any reform, then it is a short-sighted policy, and we should rather take that which offers at the moment, as long as it is practicable.

In federal politics recently we have had some short-sighted ministries and some frequent and kaleidoscopic changes … But those changes to which I referred have affected the other parties, and there has been a gathering of the clans of reaction, and at the head of the gathering Mr Reid, who has issued a direct challenge to the Labor Party. Mr Reid has announced himself as an opponent of everything which the Labor Party stands for. He says that it is his mission to devote the rest of his life to killing everything in the nature of socialism.

I am not going to argue as to what socialism is, or what it hopes to achieve. That is an argument for another occasion. But I say there is no question as to which side any person of humanitarian instinct should be on this occasion. They should be on the side of those who would use the machinery of government to protect the weak against the strong, that wrongs may be righted, and that evils may be eradicated from the body politic.

Mr Reid has behind him the forces that work for monopoly, all the forces that are determined to exploit the public for their own benefit, and all the timid-hearted, who are afraid to step out of the rut in which they find themselves.

I am free to admit that the fight is going to be no child's play. It will require the assistance of every man and woman who believes that the doctrine of the individualist is a doctrine of hopelessness, and must eventually land the people in the mire of despair. The gloves are off, and it is as well that it should be recognised …

We should try and remember the Biblical injunction, 'Let him that is without sin cast the first stone'. If a man is in agreement with me on general principles I am justified in overlooking some defects of character. None of us are perfect. It is because of the weakness of human nature that there is a necessity for the Labor Party. We have had near us in the House men who gave our ministry reasonable support, men who were generally in harmony with us as to underlying principles of government. In a fight of this description, I am willing to accept the assistance of any man, inside or outside, who is against the common enemy …

But I say that if there is a man who for any reason has kept away from our party, but who has voted with us, it would, for this election at least, be suicidal for the organisation to shoot a man who is prepared to go eight-tenths of the way with them, while they allowed to escape unscathed the man who is against us on all points …

These men are willing to help us to carry through a certain proportion of our program because they believe in it. They are prepared to work against the domination of Mr Reid and his party, because they recognise that the domination of that party would work injury to the best interests of Australia.

It is not proposed in this alliance to merge the Labor Party into any other party, nor will the Labor Party swallow the smaller party to which it is allied. We work together for certain definite objects. The Labor Party will not abate one iota in its attempt to secure the whole program of the party …

The question is, are we to say that men who have accomplished much for democracy, and much for the principles for which the Labor Party have been fighting, are to meet with nothing but hostility? Are we to reject such men as Kingston, Higgins and Isaacs? ….

We want a strong combination to withstand this hostility and do it effectively so that when the battle is over there will be nothing left of the enemy. To do that we require the assistance of every man and woman who believes in progressive legislation.

Source: The Argus, 26 September 1904.

MS 451/1/83

334 Flinders Lane, Melbourne.

Sept. 27th. 1904

Confidential

Mr. J. C. Watson M.H.R.

Parliament House.

Melbourne.

Dear Sir,

I did not think any discourtesy was implied in your overlooking my note of some days back; I am not so heedless of the nature of the work you have in hand, as to expect that small personal requests should come uppermost in your mind.

I was glad to hear you put the case for the Liberal-Labor Alliance on Sunday night, and glad also that the Labor Party in Parliament are taking up an unequivocal stand; truly in that they are as "a light upon a mountain", bright, and exalted above the murky tide of Yes-Noisms upon which so many politicians are tossed at present.

If this has been diffuse and rather wearying I ask your forgiveness for it; my ideas of things are still in the crude stage I have no doubt; all I can bring to the cause I love best is one small vote, and one small Australian whom I hope to train to be a worthy citizen some day; perhaps in the latter result my own shortcomings may be more than counterbalanced.

I remain, Dear Sir,

Faithfully yours,

Kathleen Charles.

WILLIAM HOLMAN

'The State as the great instrument for good'

In the famous debate on socialism, one of Labor's greatest
orators, William Holman, defines Labor's philosophy

In April 1906, Australia's most famous public debate was held at Sydney's Centenary Hall.

Labor's brilliant orator, and future Premier, William Holman, debated the former Prime Minister and Premier, the elderly George Reid. The topic was 'The Principles of Socialism as Defined in the Objective of the Platform of the Labour Party'.

Tickets were sixpence each and sold out in advance. Over two nights, 2,000 people watched what was billed as a 'unique contest' and an 'oratorical duel' between two towering political figures. The Lord Mayor served as moderator. The debate considered workplace practices, monopolies and trusts, nationalisation of land and industry.

Holman was a moderate in the Labor Party. He argued Labor was socialist in so far as it described what *he* believed Labor's objective to be. Labor governed 'in the interests of all humanity', he said. Labor was dedicated to 'democracy' and advocated 'the equality of all men – their rights of life, liberty and happiness'. On the final night, Holman argued that Labor's socialism promised that 'all men shall be free, all men shall be equal, and no man shall make them afraid'. He defined in practical terms what Labor aimed to achieve. He did not rely on theoretical doctrines, notions of revolutionary struggle or state control.

Bede Nairn, writing in the *Australian Dictionary of Biography*, concluded that, although Reid did not fare badly, Holman 'sparkled' and 'excelled'.

The debates were reported as an event of national significance. The *Telegraph* said that 'socialism is a live political platform which must command transcendent importance at the coming federal elections'.

After the debate, a pamphlet providing a full record of proceedings was produced and sold by the party and unions, costing sixpence.

'The State as the great instrument for good'

Centenary Hall, Sydney 2-3 April 1906

2 April 1906

My Lord Mayor, ladies, and gentleman, I have a very long course to run in the opening half-hour which is allotted to me this evening, and I shall make no apology for eschewing all empty compliment and all unnecessary introduction. I hope, therefore, you will permit me to say, once and for all, that I fully recognise the distinction which I am enjoying tonight in meeting upon an equal platform a gentleman of the standing of Mr GH Reid, the late prime minister of the Commonwealth and the acknowledged leader of the anti-Socialist movement throughout the whole continent. I recognise no less the unique opportunity which I enjoy of presenting the views of our own movement before an audience like this – a gathering so large and representative in its character ... it is my desire as briefly as I can to put before you, in this opening speech, some coherent statement of the doctrine of that party, some description of the goal towards which we believe ourselves, and civilisation at large to be marching.

I do not propose to take up time by discussing our personal characteristics, and I do not think that Mr Reid will waste your time tonight with that. He has on various occasions admitted that, taken as a whole, the Labor Party may be regarded as a good deal more than half-civilised, and the other day the *Daily Telegraph* admitted in the handsomest fashion that we were a good deal more than half-Christian – some of us wholly so; and I do not propose to attempt to refute the assertions, either that we are barbaric on the one hand or anti-religious on the other, I am concerned wholly with the question of our goal, and I take it that this debate will proceed upon this understanding that we are, on the whole, a party of upright but mistaken men; that the Labor Party is a party honourable in intent, but erroneous in idea, and the question before us tonight is whether or not the ideals which the Labor Party profess are actually mistakes or not. That is the question.

The ideals of the Labor Party were recently presented to the world some fourteen months ago in the form of the celebrated objective, of which, I take it for granted, every occupant of this hall has heard, an objective which has given rise to so much criticism and so much debate throughout Australia. With your permission, I will open the debate by reading the objective, which is an attempt, possibly a feeble one, but still an attempt to put into plain and unmistakable English the ideal to which the members of the Labor Party are attached. The objective, which was adopted in January, 1905, reads thus:

> The civilisation of an Australian sentiment based upon the maintenance of racial purity, and the development in Australia of an enlightened and self-reliant community.

That is the first half of the objective. I do not suppose Mr Reid will take much exception to that.

> The securing of the full results of their industry to all producers by the collective ownership of monopolies, and the extension of the industrial and economic functions of the State and municipality.

That is the second half of our objective. There I say, is our declaration of the principles upon which we stand or fall. If that is Socialism – and I admit that it is – then we are Socialists. So far as that is Socialism, so far we are Socialists. If Socialism means that, and only that, then we adopt the entire doctrine. If Socialism means more than that as some have asserted, then we have nothing to do with it. We are not responsible in any way for any doctrines which go outside the four corners of the objective which we ourselves have published to the world.

There are two points about the second clause of this objective to which I wish to draw your attention. The first is this – that while the collective ownership of monopolies is indicated as our end, that is not the ultimate end, but merely the means to a further end, that further end being 'the securing of the full results of their industry to all producers'. We take that as the ethical basis of the labour movement that the 'full results of their industry ought to be secured to all producers'. We lay that down and say that the only practical method by which that can be achieved is 'by the collective ownership of monopolies, and the extension of the industrial and economic functions of the State and municipality'. That is the first point upon which I wish to say a word.

The other is that when we assert that the collective ownership of monopolies is the practical means by which our ideal can be achieved, we assert that that is a means practical now, not 50 years ago, or 100 years ago; not in the middle of the 18th century, or during the feudal period, but today ...

We say that it is obvious to every observer, and it is admitted by every thinker and writer of any importance upon social questions, that the central feature of industry as it exists today, not merely in this country, but the whole world over, is the enormous introduction of machinery, the introduction of mechanical means, which have revolutionised the character of industrial processes ...

The effect on the worker has been, to a very large extent, to displace him, and make him a superfluous element in the mechanism of production …

Now on the capitalist it has had this effect. It has made the small capitalist succumb under the pressure of competition to the big one … Is it not a fact that not merely in the great firms which are devoted to production, but in those which are devoted to distribution, and to finance, the rule is everywhere the same – that the small man is being gradually eaten up by his larger competitor …

In every direction in which we turn our eyes we find the history is the same. The big factory and the combination of factories beat the little ones …

Now we trace the history of this thing out, and we find the inevitable result is that after a while here, in England, and in the United States, a few large competing firms, finding the struggle growing keener and fiercer with each succeeding year, refused to compete, and combined into what is known as a pool or trust, in order that they may escape the miseries which they have inflicted on their weaker competitors …

Twenty years ago, when I first began to interest myself in the study of Socialism, we used to be told by its opponents that competition was a divine institution – a law of nature – which the Socialist was impiously and foolishly seeking to set himself up against. Today we see that the capitalist, who twenty years ago was preaching competition to us, thinks so little of it himself that he seized every opportunity to be rid of it, and the industries of the world are not now run upon a basis of free competition, but are every year run more and more on the basis of national control. But this is national control for the benefit of a few stockholders, for the benefit of a few large proprietors, for the benefit of the Standard Oil Company, the Beef Trust of America, the Tobacco Trust out here, and the Shipping Ring on the Queensland coast …

The history of America warns us that once a Trust is established it has complete power – firstly, over its rivals, whom it can crush out by underselling; secondly, over those from whom it buys its raw material, whom it compels to take any price it wishes; thirdly, over the consumer whom it can bleed to any extent it desires by forcing up prices; and, fourthly, over its unhappy employees, who, having been brought up to one trade only and having been accustomed to one single industry, are then denied the opportunity of selling their powers in that industry, in the open market, because they find there is no possible buyer for their powers except the one employer who holds all the channels and all the avenues that that industry possesses.

Then what do we propose? We say under those circumstances the State must step in; the State must buy out the Trust; the State must take the control of such industry; and we say that only by the State doing that can economic freedom be achieved for the masses of the people …

3 April 1906

… The Labor Party does not, as it happens, consist wholly of convinced Socialists. If it did, our objective ought to be couched differently. I understand the Queensland Labor Party does almost wholly consist of Socialists. Their objective is couched differently. Our Party includes a vast number of men, many of whom do not profess themselves to be Socialists at all, and our objective is a statement of principles upon which the whole Party is united and agreed …

Now, ladies and gentlemen, I wish to ask you to follow me if you will while I very briefly recapitulate the main phases of this debate … I explained that we believed industry was drifting towards a condition of Trust formation in almost every branch, with the possible exception of agriculture …

I explained that whether we liked it or not we believed we were rapidly approaching an era when competition would end … We see one industry after another being organised, and being brought under central control, being run on a national scale , and this being done not for the benefit of society, but for the benefit of a few favoured individuals who hold the stock which gives them this unrighteous control over the lives and fortunes of their fellow-men.

I said that, and that has not been denied, Mr Reid says there are many industries which are not yet trustified. What kind of argument is that? Suppose you show that the plague is raging in West Sydney, is it anything to say that the majority so far have not succumbed and nothing need be done? I say 'No'. When the plague raged in West Sydney, what did we do? We took over the private property which had been allowed to become a plague spot and a menace to the people and made it public property for the benefit and protection of all. When we see a plague spot in our industrial life shall we do less? Then also we shall take over the plague spot and control it for the benefit of all.

Mr Reid says that cannot be done – that you cannot get the money to buy over the industries … I say the money can be raised. I say it has been done, and I say the money has been raised. I say the advantage of doing it is the advantage pointed out by Mr Reid. That then we know no one is sweated, that no one is there with an interest in making a profit, and grinding the last pennyworth of energy and vitality out of every unhappy human slave who comes under his control …

The remedy for all these things is to call in the public conscience, to call in the conscience of the State, to appeal to the collective humanity and the collective good feeling of the whole community, and to say to every man, 'This enterprise is public, and no one man or woman shall be degraded by working in this enterprise under unjust and dehumanising conditions'. That is my position …

I say this, and I agree with Mr Reid, that the interests of humanity are the ultimate aim of all statesmen. I say that after all I realise – no one more fully than myself – that the difference between Mr Reid and us is largely a difference of opinion as to the means. The end I freely recognise is the same with both of us. But a mistaken conception of the means may be more mischievous to the best interests of society than deliberate perversion and depravity as to the end …

We say we regard the State as the great instrument for good, as the great instrument for uplifting humanity; we regard the State not as some malign power hostile and foreign to ourselves, outside our control and no part of our organised existence, but we recognise in the State, we recognise in the government merely a committee to which is delegated the powers of the community, and whose duty is to use those powers not in the interests of a favoured class, but in the interest of all humanity.

We recognise democracy. We recognise the equality of all men – their rights to life, liberty and happiness. State Socialism involves no tyranny and no despotism of the kind that denies that, but we say only by an organisation upon the lines of the whole community can we hope to throw off the real tyranny of financial and capitalistic control, only by the power of the State can the workers hope to work out their emancipation from the bonds which private property is able to impose on them today, and only by State Socialism, such as we now advocate, can we initiate a genuine republic in Australia, where all men shall be free, all men shall be equal, and no man shall make them afraid.

Source: Editor's personal files.

ANDREW FISHER

'We are all socialists now'

*A triumphant Andrew Fisher ridicules his critics
and urges continued progressive reform*

When the delegates to Labor's Fourth Commonwealth Political Labour Conference gathered at the Trades Hall in Brisbane in July 1908, they were only months away from seeing Labor form its second national government. Present were the great Labor figures of the era: John (Chris) Watson, Frank Tudor, King O'Malley, Frank Anstey, William Holman, James McGowen, Mat Reid, David Bowman and William Guthrie Spence.

Among the many issues they debated were: defence, pensions, immigration, land policies, banking, education, tariff protection, industrial relations and monopolies. Conference forbade the parliamentary party from entering into future alliances and removed the right of the parliamentary leader to select a Labor ministry. By 22-2 votes, conference decided to name the party, officially, the 'Australian Labour Party'.

Labor MPs sat in every parliament in the nation. Important reforms had been achieved. Andrew Fisher, Labor's leader, told the delegates that so many were rallying to Labor's cause that 'we are all socialists now'. But Fisher was not a radical or revolutionary socialist. Indeed, as he and many others explained at the time, socialism, for them, was about 'opportunity', 'fairness' and 'social justice'. In other words, Labor was socialist, in so far as it described *his* view of what Labor stood for, or, as he said, what the 'originators' meant it to be.

Socialism was a catch-all phrase which was an albatross for Labor. Although not adopted as an objective until Labor's second decade, and always carefully defined, it left the party's objectives open to almost any interpretation. It was used by Labor's opponents to attack the party.

Providing an insight into his and Labor's belief in the democratic processes of parliament, he says, 'with universal suffrage and an educated democracy, we can do in Parliament for the workers what we could not accomplish by the universal strike'.

'We are all socialists now'

Trades Hall, Brisbane 7 July 1908

No honour that has been conferred on me during my public career has been greater than the one which you have seen fit to elect me to now, to preside over the deliberations of this important gathering of representatives of Labor from all parts of the Commonwealth …

I am pleased to see women delegates present. It is not the first inter-State conference at which they have been represented … The presence of women means good to our movement. We have reached that stage in our political development that women are of great help to us. The presence of women, here, too, shows that women are today taking an active part in economic questions, and we as a Labor Party can congratulate ourselves on giving them every facility and encouragement to do so …

… I trust that not another federal election will take place without their being a woman endorsed as a Labor candidate for the Senate … This suggestion might at the commencement be unpopular. But we as a party were the first to launch out to enfranchise women, and those who took in hand the great work of adult suffrage should not look unkindly on the nomination of women to Parliament …

Now as to socialism. I say with pleasure that in my 20 years of public life I have seen this question, from being tabooed, sneered at and scouted, brought to first place in public discussion. We find it is the question in the Church, Parliament, in the streets and newspapers, and all over the civilised world. No more sneers and scorn for socialism!

Everyone has this great question to consider. We are all socialists now, and indeed the only qualification you hear from anybody is probably that he is 'not an extreme socialist'. I do not think the ideas of the originators have altered one jot. I do not say, either, that the fundamental principles are better understood by a number of the people, but many have discovered the fact that it pays them to be socialists. It is wonderful the influence a movement has on some people – trading people, too – when they find they can make a profit by another name!

There are two distinct bodies in our movement – the propaganda teacher and the practical politician. The very name of politician, of course, puts the politician outside the sphere of the teacher. The propagandist does not care whether he has two, three, or more with him; the politician does his best for the mass of the people he is serving, otherwise he should not have his place in Parliament …

As an individual, I am favour of proceeding by the way of the law to help the workers. There are two ways open – the universal strike, and the other way of providing the necessary courts to see that the worker gets his just remuneration. I am for the latter. I believe that we have reached the stage in Australia, where, with universal suffrage and an educated democracy, we can do in parliament for the workers what we could not accomplish by the universal strike.

There is no need for us to give up principles for expediency. If we cannot defend our position we have no right to succeed. If our opponents can show us by argument that we are wrong we should retrace our footsteps and admit our error. But we have yet to meet the opponents who can do so.

We have been twenty years blazing the track, and whilst our opponents have condemned us for the path we have taken they have ended by trying to follow in our footsteps …

Source: National Library of Australia.

*Andrew Fisher was the greatest leader in the party's first five decades.
Prime Minister for three separate terms, he advocated the need for Labor to
adopt a broad range of policies and direct its appeal to
all Australians. His policy achievements were substantial and he remained
the leading Labor figure in the party until John Curtin's prime ministership.
Source: Australian Labor Party (Queensland Branch)*

BEN CHIFLEY

'The light on the hill'

Ben Chifley gives the most famous of all Labor speeches

The weather in Sydney was chilly – the temperature never rose above 17 degrees Celsius. On the corner of Dixon and Goulburn Streets, the historic Trades Hall building was abuzz, as delegates gathered for the annual conference of the NSW Labor Party. They were almost all men, wearing three-piece suits and hats.

Prime Minister Ben Chifley had flown in from Canberra to address the assembled delegates. Labor had steered the nation through the war and implemented a far-reaching program of economic reconstruction. But the delegates, like the electorate, were growing tired of the government. Continued rationing, miners threatening to strike, the proposed nationalisation of the banks, were just some of issues on their minds.

Nevertheless, when Chifley entered the auditorium, the 500 or so delegates rose to their feet and clapped and cheered enthusiastically. Party officials sat at tables on the stage at the narrow end of the rectangular shaped room. Others stood and milled around near the stage.

Chifley spoke about Australia's growth and of his government's achievements. To the miners union, he urged restraint and understanding. He spoke about the very purpose of Labor. In words that would ring for generations, Chifley said the party's 'great objective' was 'the light on the hill'. It was a phrase probably used by John (Chris) Watson almost half a century before. Chifley had also used the phrase many times before, including during debate on the Banking Bill on 11 November 1947. It is a phrase that has biblical roots. The Bible speaks of 'the light of the world' and 'send out thy light ... bring me until the holy hill'.

The media did not immediately recognise the importance of Chifley's speech. 'Chifley lashes at miners', screamed the front page of *The Sydney Morning Herald*. They ignored the phrase 'the light on the hill'. Nor did the party. A tribute book titled *The Light on the Hill* did not include the speech of the same name. A book of Chifley's speeches published in 1952 titled this speech 'The betterment of mankind – anywhere'.

For the party's true believers, the words in this speech are sacrosanct. They provide both inspiration and direction. 'The light on the hill' reflects a cause never completed and always ongoing: to bring social and economic justice, security and opportunity to all.

'The light on the hill'

Trades Hall, Sydney 12 June 1949

… When I spoke to you twelve months ago, I mentioned, amidst all the talk of world war, that I did not believe that another war was imminent. I repeat that today and say with complete confidence that the possibilities of war have receded still further than twelve months ago.

But I remind you that although the likelihood of physical conflict in the world today is less than twelve months ago, the great economic conflict in the world – the wants and needs of thousand and millions of people in the world – that problem has become, if anything, more acute than it was twelve months ago …

In Australia today you have what I have probably said before – the Golden Age. I am one who has had enormous faith in the potentialities of this country and, allied with that, an enormous faith in the intelligence and ability of the Australian people who work in the various industries …

The Commonwealth government has a program in coordination with the NSW government, of needed public works – not scenic roads or shifting sands – but schemes absolutely desirable for the potentialities of this country to be realised. That program of public works – schools, hospitals, hydro-electric schemes, conservation of water and a hundred and one other things – totals about £700 million.

It does not include the planned expansion by private industry … I make this challenge here this morning. No government in the history of Australia has ever given to private industry so much assistance and advice and help as has been given by the Commonwealth Labor government … No matter what may be said in the newspapers in regard to private enterprise, I do not think that at any time in the history of Australia have people in all sections of the community been given a greater helping hand than by this government …

A new problem is our embarkation on the policy of bringing to this country a great number of migrants … If this country is to go ahead, it must have labour to produce things … I ask the labour movement to help the government in making these people feel as much at home as possible. They have come from war-torn countries. The sufferings that many of them had to bear are almost impossible to believe …we owe a debt to humanity to do something for them …

I mention the shortage of basic materials … I only want to say, if representatives of the miners' organisations are here today, that I read that yesterday they made a decision to recommend a stop-work meeting. I say this to the miners: it is a complete ingratitude on their part if, as a result of any decision they make, they hold up the coal production of this country at a time when their fellow citizens – their fellow unionists – need the thing they can produce most urgently …

We have improved housing, we have improved transport and we have improved amenities. All these presented great problems that sometimes looked insurmountable … they said that if they had a coal industry tribunal that they were able to get to quite readily, to have their grievances dealt with, that would remove unrest and loss of time in the coalfields. That was done by the Commonwealth and State governments … I know that, in many mines in this country, the conditions under which miners worked were for many years intolerable. I know many grievances needed rectifying …

I say this to the miners, realising their desire to get improved conditions and improved facilities and amenities in the mines: both governments have done all they could, having regard to physical limitations. It has not been a matter of financial limitations in that respect. We ask them to show some return for what has been done and what it is proposed to do by producing to the limit of their capacity because it is necessary to the lives and convenience and comfort, not of the rich, but of their fellow workers in this community.

I have had the privilege of leading the Labor Party for nearly four years. They have not been easy times and it has not been an easy job. It is a man-killing job and would be impossible if it were not for the help of my colleagues and members of the movement. No Labor Minister or leader ever has an easy job. The urgency that rests behind the Labor movement, pushing it on to do things, to create new conditions, to reorganise the economy of the country, always means that the people who work within the Labor movement, people who lead, can never have an easy job. The job of the evangelist is never easy.

Because of the turn of fortune's wheel your Premier (James McGirr) and I have gained some prominence in the Labor movement. But the strength of the movement cannot come from us. We may make plans and pass legislation to help and direct the economy of the country. But the job of getting the things the people of the country want comes from the roots of the Labor movement – the people who support it.

When I sat at a Labor meeting in the country with only ten or fifteen men there, I found a man sitting beside me who had been working in the Labor movement for fifty-four years. I have no doubt that many of you have been doing the same, not hoping for any advantage of the movement, not hoping for any personal gain, but because you believe in a movement that has been built up to bring better conditions to the people. Therefore, the success of the Labor party at the next election depends entirely, as it has always done, on the people who work.

I try to think of the labour movement, not as putting an extra sixpence into somebody's pocket, or making somebody prime minister or premier, but as a movement bringing something better to the people, better standards of living, greater happiness to the mass of the people.

We have a great objective – the light on the hill – which we aim to reach by working for the betterment of mankind not only here but anywhere we may give a helping hand. If it were not for that, the labour movement would not be worth fighting for.

If the movement can make someone more comfortable, give to some father or mother a greater feeling of security for their children, a feeling that if a depression comes there will be work, that the government is striving hardest to do its best, then the labour movement will be completely justified.

It does not matter about persons like me who have our limitations. I only hope that the generosity, kindliness and friendliness shown to me by thousands of my colleagues in the labour movement will continue to be given to the movement and add zest to its work.

Source: AW Stargardt, Things Worth Fighting For: Speeches by Joseph Benedict Chifley, *Melbourne University Press, Melbourne, 1952.*

BEN CHIFLEY

'The things we fight for'

In his final speech, Ben Chifley invokes the Labor cause as the cause of his life.

This is Ben Chifley's final speech. He would die just three days later, in Canberra while politicians and their guests celebrated the Parliament's Jubilee anniversary at a gala ball. Chifley declined to attend.

Days earlier, when Chifley rose to speak at the NSW Labor Conference at the Trades Hall in Sydney, there was a feeling of mortality permeating the air. He had led Labor to two election defeats. His health had been deteriorating. He had survived a major heart attack months earlier. A few days before this speech, Chifley made sure his will was in order and visited the elderly Jim Scullin – the former Labor Prime Minister and mentor to John Curtin and himself.

Chifley speaks of his 'affection for the movement', how Labor 'stands for the masses of the people', and he says he would relinquish his seat in parliament if the party thought there was a more able candidate. There are tough and bitter words for those who had challenged his government and questioned the party's future. He addressed those 'who feel they can best serve their personal interest or political expediency by trying to get over as far as possible to the right without becoming opposed to the Labor Party'. Chifley said, 'You cannot afford to be in the middle of the road. You have to be quite clear about what you believe in, whether popular or unpopular, and you have to fight for it'. He said: 'If I think a thing is worth fighting for, no matter what the penalty is, I will fight for the right, and truth and justice will always prevail'.

The Sydney Morning Herald characterised the speech as the 'rancour of a disappointed politician'. But Chifley's biographers, LF Crisp and David Day, describe it as a final political testament from a fading political veteran.

'The things we fight for'

Trades Hall, Sydney 10 June 1951

I have attended some conferences before where we have had victory and some where we have had defeat.

I hope that the defeat at the last elections, following on from the defeat at the 1949 elections, had not discouraged members of the labour movement from fighting for what they think is right – whether it brings victory to the party or not.

The labour movement was not created with the objective of always thinking what is the most acceptable thing to so – whether this individual will win a seat or whether the movement will pander to some section of the community.

The labour movement was created by the pioneers, and its objectives have been preached by disciples of the labour movement over the years, to make decisions for the best for all the people. If, from time to time, the policy is not favoured by the majority of the people, there is no reason why the things we fight for should be put aside to curry favour with any section of the people.

I say to you that, in the period I have been leader, I have always believed that the movement has to make up its mind what is the right thing to do and, no matter what the daily press says or any section of the community might say, we must go on fighting. I hope the spirit which animated the people who began the labour movement goes on today. We have a very great responsibility to more than half the people of Australia, despite the slander and calumnies of the press against the party and individuals in the party …

We have difficulties within our movement. Some feel they can best serve their own personal interest or political expediency by trying to get over as far as possible to the right without becoming opposed to the Labor Party.

I say to those people, and those who are well over on the left (and sometimes you have to get the magic eye out to see which way some go): I know which way I go. We have had over the last five or six years so-called leftists, people who were not prepared to obey the main body of the trades' union movement and Labor men who wish to curry favour with some section of the labour movement.

Neither of these classes of people are good to the labour movement and those who are prepared to abide by the decisions made by your conference here and by decisions of the executive of the party in between conferences

– both State and federal. We have had examples in the past fifteen months, between the 1949 elections and the last elections, of people shifting their ground. No one has any admiration for people who shift their ground.

The 1949 elections were won by the Liberals by a policy of hysteria, by the successful propaganda of branding the Labour government as a government for communism or socialism. This socialist outcry had people frightened of the terrible things which were to happen. There was, of course, not an atom of truth in them …

I do not care what people say about me, so long as I feel I am fighting for the great masses of the people. Some people are in the movement provided they can keep clear of everything unpopular done by the labour movement. You cannot afford to be in the middle of the road. You have to be quite clear about what you believe in, whether popular or unpopular, and you have to fight for it …

I want to make reference to the industrial position. When I was prime minister, I spoke to the miners about local stoppages. I have always tried to make an appeal to the trade unions to meet the local industrial authorities before engaging in any industrial troubles and thereby dragging other unions into it. I have asked them to consult the Australian Council of Trade Unions or other interstate bodies.

The workers in this country, whether right or left, should realise that you must have unity. It is essential that there be a united front in the political movement and I hope to see, in the days ahead, the political movement solidified and unified. Members have to stand in like soldiers and fight for the labour movement as laid down in the policy of the party.

I do not think the miners gave the labour government a fair go while it was in office. I believe that the Labor government did more which will ultimately prove of greater benefit to the economy of this country …

I put it to the waterside workers that the labour movement did more for the watersiders than any other government. There is no doubt about it, the waterfront industry in this country was a disgrace to any civilised community. The Labor government produced legislation covering the Waterside Worker's Federation but I know you cannot cure serious ills in a year or two …

I want to touch on the present action of the Menzies government. The government hits trade unions and everything associated with them. Vested interests which stand behind the government want to see unions destroyed. I do not say that of all employers. But the majority of them do not want to see labour fully employed. They want to see a surplus of labour so they can hit trade unions and trade union officials.

The policy of the Menzies government is to produce 'tame cat' unions – not unions that will fight for the workers irrespective of the consequences. The government wants unions to discuss things and agree with it. It wants the officials in their pocket. No trade union in this country, whether the Australian Workers' Union or any other union, that goes out to fight for things they believe in, can do so without creating the complete enmity of the people representing the interests behind the Menzies government …

What this country needs is development of its resources. And that will be achieved only if every man gives of his best. And I say that any trade union which causes an ill-considered strike is doing a disservice to other trade unions …

Surely no person in this country of eight millions believes we can carry on successfully without fully populating a country of such vast resources. When you hear of the Commonwealth proposing to cut down developmental work – while such great resources are waiting to be developed in Queensland, New South Wales and other States – I say frankly that to talk about cutting down such works is ridiculous … There is no room for talking about cutting down great developmental works such as electricity supplies and water conservation. It is economic folly …

I hope that in the elections ahead we will see the candidates chosen early and see that the best possible candidates are selected. I do not want to cast any reflections on my colleagues, but there can be no question that the labour movement wants the strongest and ablest candidates that can be obtained.

It is of no use saying that, just because I have been a long time in the labour movement, I should get selection. The first consideration should be that the ideals and the objectives of the labour movement should be furthered. All personal considerations must always be set aside. If the executive thinks that Chifley has been in long enough and is no longer useful, it should tell him so …

After the long association I have had with the labour movement, knowing all its faults and its difficulties, and all things people do and say, I have such an affection for the movement that it overrides any other consideration.

I am not going to belong to this section or that section because it may give me consideration. You will find some sections who will deliberately campaign secretly or otherwise against the Labor Party but they will find in the years ahead that they have made a mistake.

You will find that we are, after all, the only political party in this country which stands for the masses … It stands for the masses of the people and does not worry about social standing …

I hope that the executive will get the man to fight the election in each electorate chosen early and will get the best possible men. Just because a person has been a labour man for forty years is not enough …

I can only hope that the sincerity which you have shown over the years in victory and defeat won't be lost; that you will be inspired by the same things which inspired the pioneers of this movement, and that you will not be frightened and made to get over to the 'right' because of the whispered word 'communist'.

I could not be called a 'young radical' but if I think a thing is worth fighting for, no matter what the penalty is, I will fight for the right, and truth and justice will prevail.

Source: AW Stargardt, Things Worth Fighting For: Speeches by Joseph Benedict Chifley, *Melbourne University Press, Melbourne, 1952.*

This iconic image shows Ben Chifley delivering the most famous of all Labor speeches at the Trades Hall in Sydney when he spoke of Labor's driving purpose as striving to reach 'the light on the hill'. Although few realised the significance of the remarks, the words have since become Labor's philosophical lodestar.

Source: Fairfax

JOHN CAIN

'To thrust a dagger into a Labor Government'

John Cain, beset by treachery and betrayal, sees his government fall during the 1950's Labor split

The 1950s Labor split had its genesis in the heightened fears of communism during the cold war, which was exploited by Prime Minister Robert Menzies, who had sought unsuccessfully to ban the Communist Party.

Inside Labor, there were concerns about communism too, especially with a growing proportion of Catholics in the party's ranks. There were questions about Labor leader HV 'Doc' Evatt's links with, and sympathies for, communists. Several of Evatt's staff were disloyal towards him and had Russian links. Industrial Groups were formed to combat the communists in trade unions. The Catholic Church pressured the party to adopt a hardline stance against communism and supported the Groups. Communist infiltration of sections of the Labor Party and the trade union movement was widespread. Fears were further increased over the defection of Vladimir Petrov, a Russian spy, just before the 1954 election and, later, the establishment of a Royal Commission into Espionage in Australia.

During this period, Evatt grew increasingly erratic and his actions largely instigated the split. In late 1954, Evatt accused the Victorian state executive of the party, controlled by Groupers, of disloyalty. Soon the party split in Victoria and Queensland. Seven Victorian federal Labor parliamentarians were expelled and formed a new party, eventually becoming the Democratic Labor Party (DLP).

When the Victorian state executive was replaced with a new executive, four ministers in John Cain's Victorian Labor government indicated their support for the old executive and were suspended and later expelled from the party.

In April 1955, as his government was collapsing, Cain appealed for unity in the parliamentary party. Rebel members had voted with the opposing parties on a procedural motion, seeking to bring down the government. Cain attacked his 'former colleagues' for having 'ratted' on the party. They had betrayed Labor's 'principles', he said. The rowdy debate went on well into the next morning. The death-knell

'To thrust a dagger into a Labor Government'

Victorian Legislative Assembly, Melbourne 19 April 1955

We have just listened to two speeches in support of this remarkable want-of-confidence motion which has been the subject of much negotiation between (Bill) Barry and (Henry) Bolte during the last three weeks …

My former Labor friends in the corner have run away from the traditional principles that have been developed by the Labor party during the last 40 years … My former colleagues were reared on the principles espoused by the party to which they previously belonged and which was responsible for their election to this Parliament.

However, they have now 'ratted' on that party and have joined forces with their life-long enemies in this country – the members of the Liberal party. They have aligned themselves with members of that party for the purpose of trying to preserve a little group in this State which is outside the labour movement.

The labour movement was born and reared during the struggles of the early days when men and movements had great difficulty in achieving their objectives to improve working conditions. During those early years Labourites were attacked by everybody. One thing which has always been insisted on in the labour movement is discipline, and members of the opposition have for some years past been doing likewise …

Everybody now knows – and this is admitted by my former colleagues – that the record of the government which I led is one of which we can be very proud. That government brought this State from bankruptcy to affluence; that fact is admitted by most people.

… the people will not let it be wrecked by any government consisting of members of the opposition, because they know – and they are good judges – that the record of the Liberal and Country party marks it for the most part as a party of incompetents. The public know that the Labor government has balanced the State's Budget. It put education and hospitalisation on a satisfactory basis and it did likewise in respect of land and soldier settlement …

I have spent over 30 years as a member of the Victorian Parliament – some persons will say that is too long. I have always attempted to be constructive. For twenty years, both in and out of season, I have led both the 'Rights' and the 'Lefts', but never before have I been accused of being associated with Communists or Communism. The only reason why I am attacked today is that opposition members were told that if they did submit a motion along the lines of that which is now before the chair, the guilty men in the Ministerial corner would be afforded some ice on which to slide; they would be given some justification for running away from their principles. If the opposition does not give them ice on which to slide, they are damned.

Before I depart from that portion of my speech, let me say that I shall accept the decision of the House, whatever it may be. I have never been a 'squealer' – and I never shall be one. If the government is defeated I shall go to the country, but I shall do so with a record of achievements and accomplishments that I shall submit to the electors of this State, and some people will have to talk for a long time to convince the public that I am not right …

The opposition parties are not particularly happy about the present alignment; they have not swallowed the pill easily. They are not well disposed toward some of the members who occupy the Ministerial corner benches; they never have been. They know, as I do, that there are some outside forces behind them … The Santamaria group …

The people who are now inducing members of the opposition to make speeches which would lead the people of Victoria to believe that our government is party to a Communist conspiracy …

In spite of all the abuse, criticisms and other types of attack levelled at it over the years, the labour movement has made a tremendous contribution to the welfare of this country … I can cast my mind back to the struggles the old Shearers' Union and the old Miners' Union went through. In those days men were sent to gaol because of union activity. We were unpopular, of course, but we decided to send representatives to the Parliaments of this country in order to fight our way up …

Whatever members of the government may think about certain matters we will go into the constituencies and fight a grand fight in spite of all the splits that may have occurred and the splinter groups that may have been formed. We will not be influenced by churches or by any other outside body … When I say that we will not be influenced by the churches, I mean that we will not allow church organisations outside the party to run our movement. They do not understand our aims and aspirations. As individual church members we welcome them to the party …

It has not been claimed during the course of this debate that the government should relinquish office because of administrative deficiencies. The sole reason advanced is that of 'outside influences'. This very move today is an attempt on the part of certain people in the community outside the Labor Party to dominate that party. …

I have had a long association with the labour movement and I hope it has been at least a decent and honourable association. Irrespective of what people may think of me politically, if I had to end my connection with this Parliament, I would be able to walk down the street, ready to face the whole world and knowing that I had attempted to do the right thing for the mass of the people. I have no regrets about the situation that has arisen, although I feel sorry for my party colleagues who must face their constituents …

When men accuse me, and my colleagues, of being associated with the Communist Party in this country, they are making accusations that are untrue, unjust and unfounded. The members of the present government know that they have acted in the right way. They are not afraid to go to the people as they have a record of achievement unexcelled in this country's history. It is extremely gratifying to realise that the proposal that the government should relinquish office is not based on any administrative short-comings. It springs from the fact that somebody thought fit to accuse decent men of dishonest practices. There is no body in this country capable of fighting international Communism more vigorously than the Labor Party which has been most active in that direction for the past 30 or 40 years …

I request the public to consider the present situation carefully and to try to understand it. They should ask themselves why the honourable member for Carlton and the Leader of the Liberal and Country party have come together in a combination of such strange bed-fellows. As all members know, the honourable member for Carlton has not in the past been very favourably regarded by a majority of members of the opposition. Therefore, it is strange that he should now find himself in the political position that he now occupies. He must accept full responsibility for the course he is taking. Just as the late John Beasley never lived down his action in putting a dagger into James Scullin, the honourable member for Carlton will never live down his decision to thrust a dagger into a Labor government in this State.

I leave the matter at this stage and I ask members on both sides of the House to think it over. Whatever may have been my political differences with other members, nobody will ever be able to say that I have not played the game, that I have not done what I have thought to be the right thing, or that I have not adopted honest principles in politics. They will not be able to say that I, in association with my colleagues, have not faithfully served this State during the last two and a half years. I have been a member of Parliament for a long time and I have learned that what my fellow men think of me is of great importance. No member on either side of this House is prepared tonight to rise and vilify me personally, because it is known that I have always endeavoured to serve the State efficiently and effectively.

I leave my destiny in the hands of the parliamentary institution, to the welfare of which I have been a subscriber for many years. I realise what it is worth, and I know its background and history. I am mindful of the reforms that have been fought for in this Parliament over a long period, and I appreciate the great advantages and privileges that all citizens enjoy under the existing system of parliamentary government. I have in this chamber on many occasions supported that system. This is a place to which it is possible for a person from any walk of life to be elected. It has sometimes been said to me that a certain member did not appear to have much to offer in the way of public service, but I have always pointed out that no person ever elected as a member of Parliament has not had some contribution to make to the wellbeing of the community …

I leave the fate of the government in the hands of honourable members, as it is for them to decide it. On account of the principles that I have always adopted I shall be able to say, irrespective of what may be the decision of the electors, that I have never squealed after the people have spoken. Their verdict will always be accepted by me.

Source: VIC Legislative Assembly Debates (Hansard).

JOE CAHILL

'It is time to unite, not to fight'

During the Labor turmoil of the 1950s, Joe Cahill urges the party to remain united, avoids a split and saves his government

A formal split over communist influence was avoided in the NSW party during the 1950s. Premier Joe Cahill, the party organisation and union leaders had worked together to avoid what had happened to their Victorian colleagues. An important factor was Cahill's relationship Cardinal Archbishop Norman Gilroy and Bishop James Carroll, who were not agitating for a split in NSW.

In early 1955, rallies and conferences supporting federal Labor leader HV 'Doc' Evatt and attacking the Groupers and the Catholic Church were held throughout NSW. The party could have split as the ruling Right faction struggled to maintain its authority and some within its ranks feared a growing Left faction with communist links. The Labor Left did have an extensive network of members closely linked to communists.

A series of unity talks steered the party through the dispute without a formal split. A State conference in August 1955 elected a pro-Evatt state president, but Groupers dominated the other positions elected. The threat of federal intervention and an inquiry into the state branch in 1956 led to further compromises, but eventually intervention was accepted and a new executive appointed. NSW Labor won re-election that same year.

Evatt and Cahill both spoke to the 1955 conference. Cahill's speech was important in avoiding a split. Cahill was not closely identified with any of the warring forces, but was backed by the Labor Right faction. Cahill appealed for unity. 'It is time to unite, not to fight', he said. He asked delegates to 'rededicate ourselves to the magnificent cause of Labor'.

'It is time to unite, not to fight'

Sydney Town Hall 14 August 1955

Fellow members of the Australian Labor Party. For as long as any one of us can remember it has been the custom for the Labor leader in the New South Wales Parliament to attend this historic annual conference.

Great power, and great responsibility rest in this conference. From it stems the authority, the prestige, of Labor in this State. That authority, that prestige, must be upheld and reinforced by the Labor Party in Parliament: and I stand before you today as leader of our Labor government, which has been in office in this State for fourteen consecutive years.

In that time, Labor has shown that it can gain and hold the confidence of the people of this State.

Today, our parliamentary party is as strong as ever it was. We have not slackened in our efforts; we have retained the confidence of the people and of the party for five terms of office …

Yours is a government which can stand firmly and proudly on its merits – ours has been a record of progress and prosperity. There is none here who could dispute that we have a magnificent record during the years we have been a government – a record which I claim is second to that of no other previous State administration …

It was inevitable that the enemies of Labor should neglect no effort to fan the flickering flames of unrest and disruption. You and I, most of us, who have worked and suffered in the hurly-burly of political strife, for long or short terms, have learned to 'take' such illegal punching 'on the glove'. Of course, the members of your government were concerned and did everything possible to prevent the spread of internal conflict to this State. That was our duty. We, as well as you yourselves, know what an internecine conflict – a mutually destructive war – can mean.

It could mean the trampling deep into the ground of all the good work accomplished by Labor during 15 fruitful years. It could mean the defeat of the Labor government – the annihilation of your representatives in the Legislative Assembly and, ultimately and inevitably, the loss of the present majority in the Legislative Council. You are only too well aware of what has happened in Victoria.

In that State Labor now appears fated to remain in political discord for so long as it continues unable to solve its own domestic problems. But I do consider – and I feel that I should say so before this parliament of Labor

– that the unity of your parliamentary representatives in this crisis has been a stabilising factor in this State; that this unity – although it must be taken for granted that there were divergent opinions – has prevented a deterioration of the position even if it has not altogether stilled the last convulsions of the regrettable tumult.

So, because of recent developments this conference assumes a much greater importance than normally. Political interest throughout Australia is concentrated on happenings within these walls during two eventful days. Our political opponents have an avid concern regarding what may develop and emerge. It is in our hands to rudely disappoint them. While the anti-Labor press pretends to deplore anything which might be injurious to Labor and prejudicial to its political future, it has, during the past few months, and right up to the present day, been using its every clever artifice and subterfuge to divide and annihilate us as an industrial and political force. Unfortunately, some of our own people have used it …

Our political opposites have one – and only one – chance of winning next year's New South Wales elections. That chance hinges upon what I believe is the improbability that they can get us, men and women who have a grave responsibility as the representatives of a million and a half workers, warring among ourselves like so many Kilkenny cats.

This is a time to unite, not to fight. To forget minor differences and frictions. And to rededicate ourselves to the magnificent cause of Labor. Our party has always been big enough and tolerant enough to compose any internal differences whatever they may have been. There have been occasions, unfortunately, when the restoration of party harmony has been delayed – with dire results …

These are important years in our national and social development. They are years in which we are shaping not only our own but the destinies of generations to come. They are years of enlightenment and evolution. Of major change and progress. In whatever is taking place Labor has its part to play. It is a major role, one of the very first importance. But how can we, as a party, stand up to these grave responsibilities and play our part, capably and well, unless we are a united party – a united force for the good of all the people?

It has always been in times of political stress and challenge that Labor has shown its greatest strength.

That strength has come from unity within the party – unity in the industrial field, unity in the political field – and unity as between these two very important components …

Nothing should ever be contemplated which might imperil any Labor government. A Labor government – which is representative of yourselves – is always your strong right arm. Because of an unfortunate train of events, our party today is under strong challenge from political opponents. Imagining that they have us on the run, they are preparing to make a major assault on the citadel of Labor next year. They can never win here while Labor presents a united front. Surely we can still adjust any differences amicably among ourselves …

My allegiance always has been and always will be to the Australian labour movement. I have persistently fought alien penetration into our movement and will continue to fight disruptors, whoever they may be. I have had a lifetime association with the unions and the political wing … So, I can look back along the road I have trodden, with its bumps and pitfalls, and feel satisfied that I have done a job to the utmost of my ability … never have I been disloyal to a principle or a fellow-member …

Today I demand that same loyalty I have given to party while I lead in this State – the loyalty that any leader should have until he ceases to be leader. And I shall always demand from my colleagues loyalty to the labour movement and its healthy principles.

My counsel is that you will consider the problems of the moment dispassionately and with that sanity of outlook which has characterised Labor in all its greatest years.

Source: Australian Labor Party (NSW Branch) Papers, State Library of NSW.

GOUGH WHITLAM

'The impotent are pure'

Gough Whitlam delivers a broadside against the Victorian Branch of the ALP and demands they modernise and reform

When Gough Whitlam became Labor leader in early 1967, the party was in need of significant organisational reform, especially in Victoria. At the previous election, the party in Victoria had recorded its lowest vote in more than half a century.

In a conversation with Whitlam in mid-2010, he confirmed that party reform was vital to Labor winning government in 1972 and that he would have resigned if he was unsuccessful.

On the Queen's Birthday long weekend in 1967, Whitlam spoke at party conferences in Melbourne, Adelaide and Sydney. This trilogy of speeches were the most controversial and probably the most important of his career. He used the 1965 report by party secretary Cyril Wyndham as the basis for reform. He wanted the party leadership to have a say in the party's chief decision-making forums, expand internal democracy, increase transparency, modernise the platform and break the stranglehold of the party's controlling apparatchiks.

Whitlam would not accept the ruling hegemonic leadership of the Victorian branch of the party who believed that the party's so-called principles were more important than parliamentary power.

The audience in Melbourne gave Whitlam a hostile reception. *The Sydney Morning Herald* reported that Whitlam was initially 'booed' and 'jeered' but, later, many warmed to his theme. Whitlam criticised the Victorian branch for its pathetic electoral performance. Whitlam told his Victorian colleagues that 'we construct a philosophy of failure, which finds in defeat a form of justification and a proof of the purity of our principles. Certainly, the impotent are pure. The party was not conceived in failure, brought forth in failure or consecrated in failure. Let us have none of this nonsense that defeat is in some way more moral than victory'.

The Bulletin praised Whitlam's 'guts' and 'bold gestures'. The speech enshrines Whitlam's belief in the Labor Party as a cause for power and that there is no incompatibility between seeking power and remaining true to the party's principles.

'The impotent are pure'

Victorian ALP State Conference, Melbourne 9 June 1967

In the seven years since I last addressed the Victorian conference, the Australian Labor Party has lost three national elections and a Senate election. Each defeat has been heavier than its predecessor. The last general election in November produced Labor's lowest vote since 1906. It was the worst result since Labor was able to form government in its own right. The Senate candidate in Victoria received less than one-third of the votes. Victoria no longer has a two-party system but a one and a half party system. It has become equipartisan. In Victorian State elections we have similarly suffered three defeats, indistinguishable one from the other in severity and complete-ness. In both national and State elections, Labor in Victoria has consistently achieved the lowest vote in Australia, and the lowest vote at any time since Australia became a nation.

Yet Victoria is not intrinsically an anti-Labor State. Several years earlier, in my first year in parliament, the 1953 conference was addressed by my predecessor, Dr Evatt, at a time of increasing success for the party. Victoria had voted against the 1951 referendum. The Flinders seat had been won for the first time since 1929. The party held six of the 10 positions in the Senate and 15 of the 33 seats in the House of Representatives. Mr (John) Cain, the greatest of Victorian State Leaders, was Premier; his government had 38 supporters among the 65 members of the Legislative Assembly and 16 among the 34 members of the Legislative Council.

These simple and obvious facts should need no re-statement. If any business enterprise found itself faced with such a record of continuous and consistent disasters, it would be plunging towards bankruptcy. Its directors would be involved in serious reappraisal of their approach; its shareholders would be demanding examination of the board's policy and personnel. We, by contrast, euphemise deep disasters as 'temporary setbacks'; the nearer Labor approaches electoral annihilation, the more fervently we proclaim its indestructibility. We juggle with percentages, distributions and voting systems to show how we shall, infallibly, at the present rate of progress, win office in 1998. Worse, we construct a philosophy of failure, which finds in defeat a form of justification and a proof of the purity of our principles. Certainly, the impotent are pure.

There is nothing more disloyal to the traditions of Labor than the new heresy that power is not important, or that the attainment of political power is not fundamental to our purposes. The men who formed the Labor Party in the 1890s knew all about power. They were not ashamed to seek it and they were not embarrassed when they won it. They recognised the limitations of industrial action. In that recognition lay the very genesis and genius of the party. A minority party, they used their power single-mindedly to win benefits for the people they represented; nor did they hesitate to form governments as soon as the opportunity arose. In the eyes of their conservative opponents, as indeed in the eyes of Lenin, they were a set of unprincipled men and opportunists. This party was not conceived in failure, brought forth by failure or consecrated to failure. In more recent times, I have yet to learn that John Curtin saved this nation by staying on the opposition benches, or that Chifley thought that 10 December 1949 was a glorious day in the annals of Labor. So let us have none of this nonsense that defeat is in some way more moral than victory.

This conference, comprising a greater percentage of union delegates than any on earth, must reflect any idea that constant defeat and permanent opposition do not matter, that the labour movement can be strong and effective industrially, while being weak and ineffectual politically. On the narrowest industrial view, this is patently false. There is not a union affiliated with the ALP which has not called for the removal of the penal clauses of the Arbitration Act; many of them have suffered severe and unfair penalties because of the operation of the clauses. Yet there is not the slightest chance of their being removed until Labor wins power in the national parliament. The great industrial advances of modern times, like the forty hour week, have resulted from enactments of Labor governments.

On the wider field, the economic and social policies which can enhance or destroy industrial gains are the responsibility of governments, and in particular of the national government. The national government alone determines and applies economic policies which can make wage advances worthwhile, or can render them meaningless by inflation. Its economic policies determine whether unions will be in a strong bargaining position under full employment, or weakened by the threat of unemployment. Its views at wage hearings will carry powerfully with the Arbitration Commission. Its attitude towards its employees will profoundly affect the conditions under which all other employees work.

Wages and conditions are no longer the chief determinants of real living standards. The health and housing of ourselves and our families, our children's education, represent the most important social capital this nation has to offer. These are the things which determine the quality of life. They are matters of particular concern to us as democratic socialists, because the things which governments provide are those that determine most whether the community enjoys a measure of true equality.

The quality of life and equality in life is what socialism is all about. In Australia, the means of raising the quality and securing equality lie in the hands of the national government. Are we as socialists to permit that power to rest, or rather sleep, indefinitely in the hands of parties whose philosophy is not quality and equality, but philistinism and favouritism? Is this what being 'true to our principles' really means? …

There is a third delusion which makes for political ineptness and inertia. That delusion is that political pressure can be successfully exerted irrespective of parliamentary success or failure. The theory reached its zenith in protests on Vietnam and in the view that we have no responsibility for what happens there, or how many Australians are killed there, as long as we have made as shrill and voluble a protest as possible. The problem is not so easily solved; our consciences should not be so easily salved. Propaganda alone will not save a single Australian life or shorten the war by a single day. Those ends will be achieved by governments prepared to take peace initiatives … our aim must be to replace that government …

In the weeks after I was elected Leader on 6 February, every trap and inducement was laid for me to concentrate on the two questions of when I would get out of Vietnam and when I would go into Victoria. I was intent on de-escalating these controversies until it would be possible for the party to have rational discussions and to make constructive decisions on these crucial external and internal issues in the proper place and atmosphere. In the last week, attempts have been made inside this State and outside it to give the impression that the party's Vietnam policy would be preserved only if the party's present executive in Victoria were preserved and that the party's Victorian Executive must be preserved to preserve the party's Vietnam policy.

For internal party reasons, the party's whole foreign affairs and defence policy was restricted by the time of the last federal election to the simple proposition that all Australian troops should be withdrawn from Vietnam. The federal conference, the federal executive and the federal caucus never determined the party's policy in such narrow and negative terms. We do not believe in unilateral withdrawal of troops whether by the Americans, by ourselves or by the North Vietnamese or by anybody else. These words were used by my predecessor, Mr Calwell, in a telecast on 23 February last year. They were taped for the federal executive in July. In August 1965, the federal conference was reviewing the party's foreign affairs and defence policy, including the platform that Australian forces should not be committed overseas except under a clear and public treaty. The Victorian delegates proposed an amendment that the party work to reverse any decision of a non-Labor government that did not accord with this policy. This amendment was defeated. Mere withdrawal is neither practical nor principled. The war would just go on.

The overriding objective in Vietnam must be to stop the war. There is no office-bearer of the party at any level who does not support and urge the view that the Australian government should be striving for an armistice and an amnesty in Vietnam. While I lead it, the ALP will strive for those objectives …

It is true that some parties can exist only as pressure groups. The communists support this view because they do not want to win parliamentary representation or power; the DLP supports it because it cannot win parliamentary representation or power. Neither our traditions nor our purpose permit us to adopt this role for ourselves. We are in business to serve and preserve democracy, parliamentary democracy. I did not seek and do not want the leadership of Australia's largest pressure group. I propose to follow the traditions of those of our leaders who have seen the role of our party as striving to achieve, and achieving, the national government of Australia. These are our ends.

What are the means by which they can be achieved? The means must lie within the party itself. We have not been defeated because of our policies or our candidates. We have been defeated because the people thought that our organisation did not apply our policies and because they thought our organisation itself did not trust our parliamentarians …

In 1964 the federal executive authorised Mr Wyndham 'to undertake a thorough and comprehensive review of all aspects of the party's present federal structure' … The initial and basic recommendation was that the federal conference should consist of direct representatives from federal electorates and federal trade unions …

After the 1963 defeat, the federal executive thought that the party's federal structure needed review. After the 1966 disaster, it thought it too hard …

Our present federal structure is not geared to win elections for the House of Representatives, where all the great initiatives and responsibilities now lie. Why should not those who have to work and pay for candidates in federal electorates have a direct share in selecting those candidates, in framing the policies and in organising the campaigns? Why, too, should unions not have the same direct representation and responsibility at federal conferences which they have at State conferences?

All organisations, including radical parties, have establishments which resist change; all have vested interests. All the arguments for and against a national organisation, with a national conference directly representing federal electorates and unions, boil down to this question – Is the party to be organised in this last third of the 20th century on modern national lines representative of the whole membership of the party, or is it to remain a committee or coterie composed chiefly of State branch officers, a significant proportion of who are paid servants of the party …

Our entire platform emphasises the primacy of the national government. We are committed to a whole series of constitutional amendments, each one of which would raise the authority of the national parliament at the expense of the State parliaments. In our organisation alone, we remain State-dominated, State-oriented and State-financed …

Our federal conference, grouped on State blocs, has an inbuilt divisive-ness which exaggerates and exacerbates every difference of opinion, attitude and principle within our ranks. The task becomes one not of reconciling differences of real opinion; it is one of reconciling State delegations. For any intelligent observer to forecast the result of a decision, it is not necessary to go through the relatively difficult task of counting 36 heads. He need only be able to count to six. In what sense can such a conference be said to represent the rank and file of the branches or of the unions?

Many who do not necessarily disagree in principle with the general proposal for a national and representative conference and organisation believe that the time is not opportune. It is of course never the right time to do something important. Some think that new leadership or a so-called new 'image' is sufficient. On that score, I have no illusions. If this view is meant to be complimentary to me, it is a compliment I refuse to accept. I wish to lead a mass party, as the Labor Party used to be proud to proclaim itself, not a one-man band …

With our present structure, perpetuating and promoting differences and prejudices, we are not doing and cannot do the proper thing for the people we represent … To those who ask 'Why', I reply 'Why not'. We cannot convincingly oppose the conservatism of our political opponents with a conservatism of our own; we cannot stand as the party of change when we fear change in our own structure. We cannot expect the people to trust us with the great decision-making processes of this nation, when we parade, by retaining an exclusive and unrepresentative party structure, our manifest distrust of our own rank and file with the decision-making processes of the party.

Since, however, your branch seems to be bound to the present organisation of the party, I must refer to the organisation of the branch itself … Thus it comes about that the present executive includes an influential handful of men who have flouted ALP policy on unity tickets in the spirit if not the letter of the rule, who have organised or led political strikes in defiance of the ACTU, which have disregarded and indeed repudiated ALP and ACTU policy on the manning of ships to Vietnam, who have organised demonstrations against the Trades Hall Council Executive in this very chamber. It is disgraceful that these men should be on an ALP executive which can appear to influence federal policies and selections.

This conference will exercise its right to elect its own executive; I will exercise my right to repudiate such men as I believe disloyal to the ALP, disruptive of its electoral prospects and destructive of all that the ALP stands for …

The party throughout Australia and especially in Victoria must get into the best shape to earn the public support which will take us into power in Australia and in Victoria … If Labor fails to win a majority in the House of Representatives elections in 1969, you in Victoria do not want to be responsible for that failure. If Labor does win a majority in the House of Representatives election in 1969, you in Victoria want to see that there is a strong Victorian contingent in the federal government.

Your conference may largely determine whether and how soon there will be another federal Labor government.

Source: The State Library of Victoria.

GOUGH WHITLAM

'Human improvement and human progress'

*Gough Whitlam, three months before the dismissal, reflects
on the struggle of leading a reformist government*

By early 1975, the Whitlam government was unravelling at a rapid
rate, despite substantial reforms in key policy areas that were unveiled
that year: family law, education, consumer affairs, racial discrimination laws, health, arts and honours, foreign policy.

The opposition, now led by Malcolm Fraser, was determined to
force an election, using 'whatever power is available to it', he said in
March 1975. Scandals involving Jim Cairns and Rex Connor and the
loss of the Bass by-election had damaged the government.

In this speech, drawing on his Chifley Memorial Lecture two
decades earlier, Whitlam reflects on his government's achievements
and future aims, but speaks with a sense of regret that politics and
the weakening economy have undermined his vision for reform. He
lamented that the progress of reform had been stymied by the forced
early election in 1974 and the unrelenting campaign by the coalition
to undermine his government's legitimacy. This was the focus of a
report in *The Sydney Morning Herald*, who covered the speech.

But the most important aspect of this speech is Whitlam's reflections on the nature of a 'reforming government'. He said that, while
the conservatives view an electoral mandate as merely a 'permission
to preside', Labor saw it as 'a command to perform'. Drawing a link
between 'the American and French revolutionaries of the Age of Reason
with the modern parties of social reform', Whitlam says, Labor's
approach champions 'the tradition of optimism about the possibility of human improvement and human progress through the means
of human reason'. Whitlam identifies the 'underlying philosophy' of
Labor as being that of 'positive equality'.

It is one of Whitlam's greatest speeches as it gives voice to Labor's
enduring values and approach to politics as they informed the government that he led.

'Human improvement and human progress'

The University of Melbourne, Melbourne 14 August 1975

As the fourth Chifley Memorial lecturer in 1957, I said:

> The way of the reformer is hard in Australia.

I intended neither pessimism nor prophecy, although one may concede that little has occurred in the intervening 18 years or the last two and a half years to lead to the belief that reform in Australia is altogether a primrose path. In my 1957 lecture I attempted to point up the difficulties confronting the Australian Labor Party in carrying out its policies under a federal system and in particular the impediments which the Australian Constitution placed in the way of achieving reform.

This was no exercise in negativism, in finding excuses. You will accept that that has never been my way. I was however concerned then by the way in which the Labor Party's failure to move on, to look ahead, to attempt to find new ways towards reform was short-changing the Australian people and short-changing the party itself ... The party became obsessed with the idea that rather than being about renewal for the future, its purpose was to return to a more comfortable past – not renovation but mere restoration. As a result, both the achievements of the past and the hopes for the future receded equally. The party stagnated and the platform was stultified ...

The chief purpose of my 1957 Chifley lecture was therefore to examine not just the barriers against Labor reform put up by the Constitution but the means by which these reforms could be achieved within the Constitution ... The themes foreshadowed in that lecture became the basis for the substantial rewriting of the Platform at subsequent Federal Conferences of the Australian Labor Party ... The policies thus developed provided the framework for the 1972 policy speech and to that extent, the framework for the programs of the Australian Labor government in the past two and a half years ...

It is easy enough to generalise about the need for reform. Reform, however, must be relevant to objectives which are both desirable in themselves and perceived to be desirable by the public. A reform party needs to convince a majority of the people that the reforms it proposes are desirable and a reform government has to keep them convinced.

Quite apart from overriding questions of economic management there are always going to be four special difficulties in that task. The first is the sheer problem of public perception of what has been done and why it is being done – the so-called communications problem ... Secondly, there is a law of diminishing returns in politics whereby a demand once met ceases to be an issue. Thirdly, there is frequently a long delay between implementing a reform and the delivery of its actual benefits. Fourthly, a great many reforms ... are expressly intended to benefit a minority in the community who, in general, are among the least articulate and least influential in the community; they are therefore the people least able to translate their grievances into political action or their gratitude into effective political support.

In a sense the party of reform in a democratic system carries a self-created handicap as a reforming government. In opposition, its essential task is to raise the public perception of the need for change, the need for reform. That is, its task is to raise expectations. The nature of politics, founded as it is on human nature itself, is that there will always tend to be a gap, a shortfall, between expectations aroused and expectations met.

A conservative government survives essentially by dampening expectations and subduing hopes. Conservatism is basically pessimistic; reformism is basically optimistic.

The great tradition which links the American and French revolutionaries of the Age of Reason with the modern parties of social reform is the tradition of optimism about the possibility of human improvement and human progress through the means of human reason. Yet inevitably there will be failures, and the higher expectations rise, the greater the likelihood of at least temporary failure to meet them.

Up to December 1972 the task of the Australian Labor Party was threefold: first to state the reforms we proposed, secondly to state the means by which we intended to achieve those reforms, thirdly to convince a majority of the electorate that those reforms were both achievable and desirable. We achieved office because we raised expectations and convinced a sufficient majority that those expectations could be met. Yet the specific reforms we proposed were related to general goals and had to be so related if they were to be seen and accepted as part of our general mandate to govern.

The meaning of the 'mandate' ... has been especially scrutinised in the past two and a half years because of the very great emphasis my own government has always placed on the fulfilment of the program set out in the policy speech of 1972 and confirmed in the policy speech of 1974 ... the debate about the meaning of the mandate has centred on the question of whether in 1972 and again in 1974 the Australian Labor Party was given only a general mandate to govern or a specific mandate to implement each part of its program.

Is the mandate merely general or is it specific? Is it a grant of permission to preside or a command to perform? Our opponents naturally interpret it in the weakest sense as a general and highly qualified mandate to govern – on their terms and indeed by their grace and favour. I interpret the mandate as being both general and specific – a general mandate to govern for the term for which we were elected and a specific mandate to implement the undertakings we made, within that term ...

The mandate as I interpret it is to move by specific programs toward the general goals and the general objectives accepted by the people at the elections.

What was that goal? I defined it in these words in the parliament on 5 March 1970:

> On this side we believe there is one clear goal that this national parliament should set for itself, which should define and motivate each specific action we take. It is the goal of equality. The true quality of our national life will be principally determined by the way in which and the rate at which we advance towards true equality. It is this that gives meaning to our posses-sion of prosperity. If I interpret the history of this country and the character of our countrymen and women correctly, it is this search which alone can give any worthwhile, enduring meaning to our fortuitous possession of this most fortunate, peaceful and privileged continent in this most turbulent and deprived region of the world.

I regard the thrust towards equality as the natural extension of the great thrust of the Chifley government which was towards security for all. There is no phrase more quoted than Chifley's 'light on the hill'. Very few remember what the metaphor meant. As Chifley used it, it was not just a fine phrase but a quite specific objective – it was security ...

To that I add the basic objective of promoting the basic goal of equality. As I see it, the two goals are inseparable. I have always put the search for equality in positive terms, that is, the promotion of equality, not the imposi-tion of equality ...

I state the underlying philosophy in this way: in modern communi-ties, even the wealthiest family cannot provide its members with the best education, with the best medical treatment, the best environment, unaided by the community. Increasingly, the basic services and opportunities which determine the real standard of life of a family or an individual can only be provided by the community and only to the extent to which the community is willing to provide them. Either the community provides them or they will not be provided at all. In the Australian context, this means that the community, through the national government, must finance them or they will not be financed at all.

Over the span of years the common factor which links the doctrine of security and the doctrine of equality is the insistence upon community responsibility for the promotion of these twin goals. This concept of equality – what I call positive equality – does not have as its goal equality of personal income. Its goal is greater equality of the services which the community provides. This approach not merely accepts the pluralistic nature of our system, with the private sector continuing to play the greater part in providing employment and growth; it positively requires private affluence to prevent public squalor.

The approach is based on this concept: increasingly a citizen's real standard of living, the health of himself and his family, his children's opportunity for education and self-improvement, his access to employment opportunities, his ability to enjoy the nation's resources for recreation and cultural activity, his ability to participate in the decisions and actions of the community, are determined not so much by his income but by the availability and accessibility of the services which the community alone can provide and ensure.

The quality of life depends less on the things which individuals obtain for themselves and can purchase for themselves from their personal incomes and depends more on the things which the community provides for all its members from the combined resources of the community.

What we aim at is the achievement of the classic liberal idea of the career open to the talents – equality of opportunity – in a vastly expanded form. Equality of opportunity is a splendid ideal; but to confine it to equality of job opportunities is not merely to restrict it, but to negate true equality of opportunity. The older, narrower ideal of equality of opportunity concentrated almost exclusively on education. The assumption was that the mere provision of free education would guarantee equality of opportunity. Even in a community as homogeneous and socially mobile as Australia this has proved not to be the case.

In modern communities, not least Australia, opportunities, social, economic and cultural opportunities are really determined by where a family lives, even more than by a family's income. So we have no preoccupation with equality of incomes. We are striving for an equality of environment in the total sense of those things which increasingly the community alone can provide – welfare, health, education, recreation, transport.

The general argument against this concept turns on the question of private incentive and individual initiative. This really gets to the heart of the philosophical differences between the Labor Party and its opponents. The argument that collective welfare destroys private incentive is a very old one indeed. It is the argument which has been used to resist every advance in social welfare, even the most basic ones, such as the provision of old-age pensions …

The argument is in fact based on a particular view about human nature and human motives. In the final analysis it predicates fear and greed as being the principal spurs to human action. It says in effect that if people know they are guaranteed an income in retirement they will be both lazy and improvident during their earning days; if people are not afraid of the price of sickness they will abuse and overuse the health services the community provides; if public schools are made as good as private schools then parents will not work so hard to earn the fees for their children's education; if the attempt is made to make underprivileged communities more decent places to live, people will lose the competitive urge …

A political program, particularly a program for a democratic election is of course not an essay in philosophy. Policies are not developed in a political or economic vacuum; still less are they implemented in a vacuum once the appeal to the electorate has been successful. The program as presented in 1972 had to be related to economic and political realities as we judged them to be in 1972 and as we assumed, to the best of our judgement, they would exist during the three years for which we sought and won a mandate. Carrying out the program has to be related to the political and economic realities as they exist.

In 1972, we made two important assumptions which seemed very reasonable at the time. One was political; the other was economic. Both proved partly wrong. The first, the political assumption was that if elected we would have a clear three years to fulfil the program. The second, the economic assumption was that domestic growth would be sufficiently restored and that the world economy would remain strong enough to permit an avowedly expansive and expensive program of social reform to be implemented without massive tax increases or without massive inflation …

It is hard to estimate and hard to exaggerate the damage done to the Australian political system and the Australian economy by the conduct of the majority in the Senate. From the beginning, that conduct has had one overriding objective – to deny the very legitimacy of the Labor government. But its real effect has been to cast doubt on the legitimacy of an elected government itself, to cast doubts on the legitimacy of the electoral and constitutional processes …

So for most of the period of our government we have had to live with an unprecedented political problem.

Equally, there has been the problem of world-wide economic difficulties … Although in 1972 the Australian economy was already showing the signs of the twin problems of inflation and unemployment, with a poor growth rate which was subsequently to become world wide, the great catastrophes about to fall on the international economy were not foreseen …

When my government was elected our aim was to finance our new programs from growth. But world-wide inflation and recession frustrated this objective. This is no mere self-justification. The whole industrialised world is currently going through the worst peacetime inflation on record and the deepest recession since the 1930's …

What is not widely recognised is that Australia has fared comparatively well among the industrialised countries during this period of economic turmoil. Our unemployment has been a great deal lower than that suffered by a number of industrialised countries; our loss of production has been less; and many industrialised countries have had much more severe inflation. Unlike most industrialised countries, we have moreover been entirely free of balance of payments problems …

Now is a time for consolidation, evaluation and planning for the future with an appropriate balance between welfare and economic responsibility. Policy must always reflect our concern for those in want; it must choose the most effective and efficient means to that end. We have striven to reform the overall structure of the Australian economy.

In our first year in office, before Australia was engulfed in the world-wide economic turmoil, we pushed ahead with the revaluation of the Australian currency and tariff reductions and removed a number of anachronistic subsidies and taxation concessions which operated to support less efficient industries. We replaced the aged Tariff Board machinery with the more up-to-date and broadly constituted Industries Assistance Commission. Trade Practices Legislation has been passed and a Trade Practices Commission established to protect the consumer and enhance competition. I have no doubt that, in the long run, the Australian economy will benefit greatly from these measures …

The abiding challenge for statesmanship in a democracy is to try to get the priorities right and to resolve the conflicting demands about priorities in the context of the desirable and the possible, the politically possible, the economically possible …

One only needs recall that one of the principal charges against (NSW Governor Lachlan) Macquarie, one of the principal items used to discredit him in the Bigge Report, was the building of the Obelisk which still stands in what is now Macquarie Place as the measure of distance from all places out of Sydney. It was charged against Macquarie that he had got his priorities wrong.

Those who govern Australia are still accused of trying to build monuments, when their real wish is to get Australia's priorities right, right for the present and right for generations ahead.

Source: The Whitlam Institute.

BOB HAWKE

'The cause of Labor and social democracy'

Bob Hawke recognises the importance of the Fabian influence in Labor polititcs

The Fabian influence in Labor politics has been substantial. Many Labor leaders have consciously sought inspiration from the Fabian tradition in centre-left politics. Founded more than a century ago as a progressive, reformist intellectual political association strongly linked to the British Labour Party and identifying with socialist and social democratic ideals, it favours gradual rather than revolutionary means to achieve these ends. It serves to foster debate and promote progressive ideas through publications, seminars and conferences. Its name is taken from the Roman General Quintus Fabius Maximus. Early British Fabians included Sidney and Beatrice Webb, HG Wells and George Bernard Shaw.

The most prominent and dedicated Fabian in Australian politics is Gough Whitlam, who said that Fabianism insists on the importance of new ideas in politics. Bob Hawke said that Whitlam was 'our own Fabius Maximus'.

In this speech, delivered in his second year as Prime Minister to the centenary dinner of the Australian Fabian Society, Hawke seeks to explain the philosophy of democratic socialism within the context of Labor politics, drawing on the Fabian tradition. He also seeks to mesh the principles of Fabianism with that of his own approach to politics, emphasising the importance of 'gradualness' and 'consensus'. In the 1970s, with the experience of the Whitlam government front of mind, Hawke had often spoken of the need for 'gradualness' in implementing a reform agenda.

As he notes, the Fabian Society's members are 'bound by no dogma or creed or fixed body of doctrine'. Its importance is 'in the methodology of Fabianism', Hawke says, 'the primacy given to facts, knowledge, proper research' before concerted political action. Further, Hawke says the 'greatest and most enduring source of the influence of Fabianism' is 'the application of our ideas and our ideals to practical purposes and achievable goals'.

'The cause of Labor and social democracy'

Australian Fabian Society, Melbourne 18 May 1984

For any Association or secular institution to reach its first century is note-worthy and, in our times, remarkable enough in itself. That alone would be sufficient reason for us to join together tonight in this celebration of the centenary of the Fabian Society, brought into formal existence in London a hundred years ago this month …

I invite you all to consider the wider and deeper significance of this achievement – because it goes far beyond the Fabian Society's mere survival in the technical and temporal sense …

For this was, and is, that most difficult things of all to maintain – a political association. It was founded as, and remains, a purely voluntary association of like-minded men and women, bound by no dogma or creed or fixed body of doctrine. Unable to offer its members inducement or rewards, or to impose discipline or enforce rules; an association based entirely on moral and intellectual ground, and by the very essence of its nature and purpose, having only the loosest structure and formal organisation …

That a society so conceived could survive in such a century – and survive with continuing vigour – is surely striking testimony to the enduring strength of the cause with which it has been so closely identified and to which it has contributed so much – the cause of social democracy.

I deliberately use the words 'the cause with which it is identified', because the Fabian Society did not and does not claim to be a cause in itself.

Rather, it was called into existence to represent and promote an idea and an ideal – and, most important – a method, an approach by which that idea could best be implemented and by which the ideals of social democracy could be given practical effect.

And almost from the beginning, its founders envisaged that the vehicle would be a labour party – long before the British Labour Party as such existed.

Sidney Webb – one of the founders of the Fabian Society and for so long its presiding genius described the process this way:

> From 1887, the Fabians looked to the formation of a strong and independent Labour Party. We did all we could to foster and assist, in succession, the Independent Labour Party, then the Labour Representation Committee and then the Labour Party … but we also set ourselves to detach the concept of socialism from such extraneous ideas as suddenness and simultaneity of change, violence and compulsion, and atheism or anti-clericalism … nor did we confine our propaganda to the slowly emerging labour party, or to those

who were prepared to call themselves socialists, or to the manual workers or to any particular class.

So, from the beginning, the society drew its strength from its vision of the future of Labor and the Labor Party. But beyond this fundamental strength, many factors have contributed to the strength and survival of the society.

First, we cannot ignore the personal element – that extraordinary galaxy of political, intellectual and literary talent which made up the firmament of Fabianism – The Webbs, Graham Wallas, George Bernard Shaw; then later Tom Mann, who helped introduce Fabianism to Australia; then later on again people like Bertrand Russell, GDH Cole, Harold Laski and RH Tawney.

Many may think that, in terms of this contribution to Fabian philosophy and social democratic thought, Tawney was the greatest of them all. Certainly his great work *Equality* stands as the definitive exposition of the true meaning of social democracy, both as an ideal and a practical program.

Another source of the Society's strength was what we may call the methodology of Fabianism – the primacy given to facts, knowledge, proper research and solid information as the basis for action – whether political, social or economic action. It was the recognition, as Beatrice Webb put it, that:

> Reform will not be brought about by shouting. What is needed is hard thinking.

And the third and greatest and most enduring source of the influence of Fabianism was the idea of practical relevance. And this is the very essence of Fabianism. It is the recognition that the commitment to democracy and democratic means is fundamental. It is in the recognition that this fundamental commitment imposes on social democrats obligations and restraints in terms of both means and ends.

It is in the recognition, as I myself put it in the *Resolution of Conflict* lectures – the Boyer Lectures, in 1979 – 'of the need for those who would advocate change to temper their fervour with a sense of gradualism'.

And it cannot be emphasised, too strongly or too often, that this approach is not a matter of mere pragmatism. It is equally a matter of principle. It is a principle which follows inexorably from our commitment to democracy. And it is a principle which lies at the very heart, not only of Fabianism, but social democracy throughout the world.

It is of course the classic concept of Fabianism – the inevitability of gradualness. And nothing is more widely misunderstood or more frequently misrepresented. It was never conceived as a justification for opportunism. It was, and is, a principle of necessity.

The principle was first and best propounded by Sidney Webb himself. Speaking as President of the British Labour Executive at the Party Conference in 1923, he said:

> Let me insist on what our opponents habitually ignore, and, indeed, what they seem intellectually incapable of understanding, namely the inevitable gradualness of our scheme of change. The very fact that Socialists have both principles and a programme appears to confuse nearly all their critics.

Webb continued:

> If we state our principles, we are told "That is not practicable". When we recite our programme the objection is "That is not Socialism". But why, because we are idealists, should we be supposed to be idiots?, For the Labour Party, it must be plain, Socialism is rooted in Democracy; which necessarily compels us to recognise that every step towards our goal is dependent on gaining the assent and support of at least a numerical majority of the whole people. Thus, even if we aimed at revolutionising everything at once, we should necessarily be compelled to make each particular change only at the time, and to the extent, and in the manner, which ten of fifteen million electors, in all sorts of conditions, of all sorts of temperaments, from Land's End to the Orkneys, could be brought to consent to it.

That was Webb in Britain in 1923. It is as relevant and true in Australia in 1984. For it represents an unchanging truth and a fixed principle for the Labor Party and social democrats everywhere. And I repeat and emphasise: it goes beyond pragmatism; it is the principle which flows from our fundamental commitment to democracy.

I suppose there is no greater hero in the pantheon of radical reform that Aneurin Bevan, who was also a great Fabian. He was never accused of selling out, or selling the cause short. He was never denounced as an opportunist or derided as a pragmatist.

Thirty years after Webb's analysis which I have just quoted, Bevan wrote of this magnificent confession of his faith:

> The philosophy of democratic Socialism is essentially cool in temper. It sees society in its context with nature and is conscious of the limitations imposed by physical conditions. It sees the individual in his context with society and is therefore compassionate and tolerant. Because it knows that all political action must be a choice between a number of possible alternatives it eschews all absolute prescriptions and final decisions.
>
> Consequently it is not able to offer the thrill of the complete abandonment of private judgment, which is the allure of modern Soviet Communism and of Fascism, its running mate … It accepts the obligation to choose among different kinds of social action and in so doing to bear the pains of rejecting what is not practicable or less desirable …
>
> It seeks the truth in any given situation, knowing all the time that is this be pushed too far it falls into error … Its chief enemy is vacillation, for

it must achieve passion in action in the pursuit of qualified judgements. It must know how to enjoy the struggle, whilst recognising that progress is not elimination of struggle but rather a change in its terms.

In this brief review, I have said enough to indicate the spirit, ideals, methods and objectives of the Society whose centenary we celebrate tonight …

There was another important idea – a method more than a principle – which became closely associated with Fabianism. Sidney Webb called it 'permeation'. Today it would be called 'consensus'. Webb put it this way:

Most reformers think that all they have got to do in a political democracy is to obtain a majority. This is a profound mistake. What has to be changed is not only the vote that is cast, but also the mental climate in which parliament and the government both live and work.

That I find, to be an accurate description of the approach I and my colleagues have tried to bring to the affairs of this nation in our first term of office …

For our reforms to endure, the whole mood and mind and attitudes of the nation must be permanently changed.

Certainly, we are proceeding to implement the policy on which we were elected and the platform of the party with a thoroughness, I believe, not excelled by any previous Labor government in our history. But that specific task must go hand in hand with the more general and deeper, longer range task – the task of establishing, in the mood and mind of this nation, permanent acceptance of the naturalness and inevitability of change and reform, as the authentic Australian way of life …

An occasion like this services to bring home to us all, one of the great truths about our cause in Australia – the cause of Labor and social democracy.

And that is the continuity of our movement and the continuity of our role in our nation. The party itself is a hundred years old in 1991. The Labor movement is already well over a century old.

One of the great paradoxes of Australian politics is that the parties and forces of conservatism and reaction – for all their self-proclaimed loyalty to tradition – have no real continuity and no true sense of continuity. And without a sense of continuity – in the case of individuals or parties or movements or nations – there can be no true sense of identity.

And I believe it is precisely because our adversaries lack that sense of their own continuity, and in a deep sense, their own identity, they are obliged to seek it outside themselves – in other institutions and even other nations.

And that I believe explains, at least in part, much of their current conduct – their lurches, not only in search of a policy, but in search of an identity.

It is, by contrast our own sense of continuity, as a government, a movement, a party, a cause which provides us with the stability and strength to overcome the countless setbacks we have suffered and, equally, in the days of triumph, to live up to the motto set for itself by the Fabian Society one hundred years ago:

> For the right movement you must wait, as Fabius did, most patiently, when warring against Hannibal, though many censured his delays; but when the time comes you must strike hard, as Fabius did, or your waiting will be in vain and fruitless.

Source: The Bob Hawke Prime Ministerial Library

JOAN CHILD

'Parliament as the instrument for the advancement of our cause'

The first female Speaker, Joan Child, identifies the essential
nature of the Labor Party as a parliamentary party

Joan Child was the first female Speaker of the House of Representatives.

In this speech, her last in Parliament, Child pays tribute to the Labor Party, first and foremost as 'a parliamentary party'. It is this belief in democracy over revolutionary means that distinguishes the Labor Party from other progressive movements for social and economic change. It is through the Parliament that Labor has sought to shape the Australian nation. Child argues that this belief in parliamentary democracy goes to the very ethos of the party itself: how it governs and operates within the parliamentary system. Parliament is seen 'as the instrument for the advancement of [Labor's] cause'. As a parliamentary party, Child defines Labor's 'cause' as one of 'reform, progress and equality'.

In *At Home in the House*, a book of speeches by Victorian Labor women, Child says that she selected this speech for inclusion because 'it was my last speech in the House of Representatives, and second, I wanted it on record that it is through the House of Representatives and the House of Representatives alone, that governments are formed. It is the peoples' House and it carries out the will of the people – not the Senate, but the House of Representatives'. In addition, Child said, 'a third reason would be my regard for Ben Chifley – a truly great Australian and Labor man'.

The speech remains an important reflection on the values, traditions and continuing and enduring importance of Labor as a parliamentary party. It is also a testament to a pioneering Labor woman.

'Parliament as the instrument for the advancement of our cause'

The House of Representatives, Canberra 30 November 1989

Many things distinguish the Australian Labor Party from not only our political opponents here in Australia but all other political parties in the world.

One of the most important of these is our special sense of our own history, that sense that we are part of a continuing movement in the working out of Australia's destiny, that sense of continuity and affinity with the men and women who have built up our party and movement for over a century.

Today I wish to deal with one of the most important aspects of Labor's continuing strength. It is the key to our continuing relevance and our central importance to the history and growth of this Australian nation. I refer to the role of the Australian Labor Party as, first and last, a parliamentary party.

I put forward three propositions.

First, there can be no true understanding of the nature, meaning or history of Labor except by understanding its central role as a parliamentary party.

Secondly, there can be no true understanding of the Parliament of Australia except by understanding the critical role of Labor in shaping the Australian Parliament. Just as the work of Labor for the past century has uniquely shaped the Australian nation, so its work in the Parliament has uniquely shaped our Parliament into a uniquely Australian one.

I make a third assertion: that it is the House of Representatives through which this great national work has been done, and it is through that House alone that Labor can continue its central task of shaping the destinies of our people and our nation.

Our present ascendancy in the Parliament of our nation has been won only by years of immense effort and dedication, often in the face of seemingly insuperable odds. Our continued success depends upon maintaining that effort and dedication.

The continuing struggle has always had two aspects: first, the resistance of the conservative Right, the men born to rule, against accepting Labor's legitimacy within the parliamentary system.

And second, the historic divisions of opinion within the Labor movement itself about the effectiveness of Parliament as the instrument for the advancement of our cause. This has always been one of the most fundamental questions for the Australian Labor movement.

The greatest challenge – though certainly not the first – to Labor's faith in the parliamentary system came in 1975. At the height of the crisis of 1975, Gough Whitlam summed up two aspects of Labor's struggle to establish itself as the pre-eminent party of parliamentary democracy. In his Curtin Memorial Lecture at the Australian National University he said:

> 'I would not wish to any future leader of the Australian Labor Party the task of having to harness the radical forces to the restraints and constraints of the parliamentary system if I were now to succumb in the present crisis. '

It is clear that the basic attack which has been mounted against the Labor government was not an attack on its competence or its effectiveness but on its very legitimacy – the legitimacy of any reformist government now or in the future.

It is a remarkable testimony to the strength of the Labor Party as a parliamentary party that, despite all that happened in 1975, we stand where we do today.

In the final analysis, it occurred because the Labor Party itself – the membership, the rank and file-sustained faith in the parliamentary system despite all that had happened to threaten that faith.

But sustaining this faith has to be a two-way process. The faith and loyalty shown by the rank and file deserve and demand a matching response from Labor governments which owe their election to that faith and loyalty.

That means that Labor governments have a responsibility to show that their faith in the parliamentary system is justified, to show that Labor's cause of reform, progress and equality can be truly advanced within the parliamentary system, and I deeply believe that all our Labor governments are striving to do just that, despite the great difficulties and challenges of the times through which we are passing.

I come now to my second point – the impact of the Australian Labor Party upon the parliamentary system itself. Australian Labor's unique contribution to parliamentary democracy has been the development of the caucus system.

In the past, our conservative opponents have violently attacked this approach from the beginning. But, in the end they have virtually adopted it. The heart of the Labor system at every level is the principle of majority rule.

With the coming of the pledged Labor parliamentarians, party politics took on an altogether new meaning. The sentiment behind the pledge was, in fact, a logical extension of the basic ideas of the Labor movement on political questions generally. It merely applied to parliamentary practice two fundamental doctrines: majority rule and solidarity …

Labor's caucus system has had three results of immense importance and value.

First, it ensures that the executive government is answerable to the whole parliamentary party.

Second, it strengthens the control of the elected government over the bureaucracy. But, above all, the discipline of the caucus system has given Australia a strong, effective, two-party system-the indispensable position for stable government in a modern parliamentary democracy.

I come now to my third and most important point.

The House of Representatives is the key to parliamentary democracy in Australia and the whole future of the Australian Labor Party is centred upon the dominant role of the House of Representatives if the effective two-party system is to survive in our nation. I will give three illustrations, from Chifley to Hawke.

In the first place, we must never forget that Chifley, in his great partner- ship with John Curtin, came to power through the House of Representatives and the House of Representatives alone. Australia's greatest government at the time of Australia's greatest danger depended wholly and solely upon the House of Representatives. Curtin did not come to power in 1941 by an elec- tion. He came to power to win the war because two members of the House of Representatives changed their votes to defeat the Fadden government and install the Curtin-Chifley government.

In the most terrible period in Australia's history the Curtin government was sustained by a razor-thin majority in the House of Representatives and throughout that period until the general election in 1943 the Curtin government never had a majority in the Senate. That is, the Curtin-Chifley partnership relied entirely on the confidence of the members of the House of Representatives. That is how Australia survived the worst crisis in our history.

The second illustration is the double dissolution election of 1974, the election in which I first had the honour to be elected to the House of Representatives. Except for those of us who were so deeply involved, the 1974 election is in danger of becoming, in the eye of history, the election that never was.

But in truth it was one of Labor's greatest successes, because it was a triumph for the legitimacy of the reform program of the Whitlam Labor government, as expressed by the people – and that was the issue which lay at the heart of Gough Whitlam's mighty struggle in 1975 ...

My third illustration is the 1987 election, in many ways the most remarkable of all. No election has better illustrated the role of the House of Representatives as the true expression of the will of the people on the central question: who shall govern?

There was something quite majestic about the way the people of Australia went about achieving exactly what they wanted to achieve, just as they did in South Australia last week. In many electorates where they could afford to do so, they took the opportunity to deliver a warning … But wherever it counted and was necessary for achieving their central purpose of returning a strong government, the people made sure that that was what Australia would get …

I emphasise that such a result, such a vindication of parliamentary democracy, could only be achieved through the House of Representatives operating on the basis of single member constituencies.

By contrast in the Senate we remain a minority and increasingly the Senate will become a chamber for registering public opinion on a range of issues, very often single issues. That may be a legitimate function for an upper House, but I do not think that was what was envisaged by the Constitution.

The registration of temporary public opinion is not the same thing as the expression of the will of the people about who shall govern. That is always the central question for parliamentary democracy and governments can only be formed through the House of Representatives. That will always be the central role of the Australian House of Representatives – it is the people's House carrying out the people's will.

The greatest source of strength which the House of Representatives has in fulfilling its true role remains the enduring commitment to parliamentary democracy on the part of the Australian Labor Party.

It is a commitment based upon our recognition of the House of Representatives as the best instrument available to us for the advancement of our cause of change and reform.

Long may both the commitment and the cause endure.

Source: Commonwealth of Australia Parliamentary Debates (Hansard).

Joan Child became the first female Speaker of the House of Representatives in 1986. In her final speech to Parliament, Child made the important point that Labor exists first and foremost as a parliamentary party, which reflects the purpose and ethos of the party. Labor's cause is, Child says, to achieve 'reform, progress and equality'.
Source: Newspix

BOB HAWKE

'The engine room of national renewal, the generators of change, the pioneers of reform'

In the twilight of his prime ministership, Bob Hawke urges the true believers to keep faith with Labor's cause

When the delegates met in Hobart for Labor's Centennial National Conference, Labor's most successful Prime Minister, Bob Hawke, was in the twilight of his prime ministership and his government was facing several challenges.

Hawke faced a resurgent opposition led by Dr John Hewson. There was a divisive battle for the party's presidency between Barry Jones and Stephen Loosley. Weeks earlier, Paul Keating had challenged Hawke for the party leadership, Hawke surviving by 66-44 votes. Hawke sought to stabilise his leadership, rally the Labor faithful and chart a course for victory at the next election. *The Australian* said the speech was 'crucial to the reestablishment of his leadership'.

Hawke's speechwriter, Stephen Mills, recalled in *The Hawke Years* that 'after multiple drafts' on the eve of the conference 'none hit the mark'. Kim Beazley drafted 'the introduction to the speech' and the peroration was written by Hawke himself. 'Seated at his desk in the bedroom of his (hotel) suite, wearing his tracksuit', Mills remembered, 'Hawke produced, in fluent, virtually uncorrected single-spaced long-hand, a testament of his identity within the Labor Party'.

Hawke had held the party together during a period of far-reaching change and reform that had, nonetheless, unsettled some Labor supporters. In an interview in mid-2010, Hawke said his task was to 'blend the continuity of our existence as a labour movement with the need for accommodation to changing circumstances'. He says: 'There were certain fundamental principles that were unchangeable, but there were a lot of historical sacred cows that needed to be slaughtered. And so it was a process of culling the herd. We were part of an extremely rapidly changing world. If we were going to optimise our prospects for growth, we had to be prepared to change'.

'The engine room of national renewal, the generators of change, the pioneers of reform'

ALP National Conference, Hobart 26 June 1991

I know that you all share with me a sense of privilege on this special occasion. As delegates to this centenary conference, we meet as the representatives of Australia's most important and enduring force for change and progress – an institution uniquely Australian in its creation and character, uniquely Australian in its values and in its achievement – the Australian Labor Party.

A proud name and a proud achievement over one hundred years – one hundred years of cooperation with the Australian union movement which brought it into being; one hundred years of commitment to the cause of parliamentary democracy; one hundred years of struggle and service on behalf of the people of Australia.

We meet as the representatives of Australia's greatest political party – the engine room of national renewal, the generators of change, the pioneers of reform.

We are the party that built Australia's system of social justice; the party that created an industrial relations and wages system in the early years of this century; the party that founded great institutions of our public life, not least the Commonwealth Bank; the party that first provided the means by which Australia could defend itself; that led Australia through its most perilous days; the party that after the Second World War rebuilt Australia and laid the foundations of modern Australian society; the party that inaugurated a program of mass immigration that has changed and enlarged and enriched the very character of our nation; the party that in the 1970s gave new impetus to the quest for social justice.

Our party fixed its course by the light on the hill – never wavering in our determination to reach that goal, but never fearing to modify our means and abandon old methods if that was necessary to make us more relevant and more effective in the service of the people of Australia.

And delegates, your Labor government today stands foursquare in this, our grand tradition of nation building.

Created by the trade union movement, the Labor Party has forged with the modern trade union movement an Accord partnership that is rebuilding the Australian economy. We have opened a new era in industrial relations, delivering in exchange unparalleled improvements in the social wage – not least Medicare and the Family Allowance Supplement. We have secured the future of the steel industry and turned around our national export performance. We have made taxation fair and efficient. We have offered new opportunities to young Australians through expanded education and training. We are dedicated to justice for Aborigines and Torres Strait Islanders. We protect the environment from short-sighted destruction. We have engineered national self reliance in defence and, at a time of unprecedented change in our region and the world, we have sought constructive and cooperative paths in foreign policy.

Ours has been a ministerial team of unrivalled quality.

Our partner has been a trade union movement of unrivalled commitment.

And it has been Conferences such as this over the last decade that have underpinned our success with drive, vision and unity …

So we are rightly proud of our past and we rightly celebrate it.

But I use that past to speak now of the future. We are the party of Australia's future. And never in our party's history has our responsibility for the future been greater. It has fallen to Labor, once more, to set the agenda for the future of Australia – to set the goals which will determine the nature and quality of the Australia we take into the 21st century, and to set the course by which the Australian people will attain those goals.

That is our task at this centenary conference – to ensure Labor's platform expresses that agenda, sets that course, and ensures our organisation is in every respect ready for the next great electoral challenge we must face.

Delegates, the next federal election is still some two years away. But in a real sense we begin the campaign now – a two-year campaign not just to win the election, but to win the future for Australia.

Over this two-year campaign, we will conduct the fight on two fronts. First, we will continue the tasks of reforming and rebuilding Australia:

- to maximise for the people of Australia the gains which will come with sustained low-inflation economic recovery;
- to continue building a more competitive Australia;
- to continue building a more compassionate and sensitive Australia.

And our second task is to expose the real character and purpose of the opposition – to ensure that the Australian people have no illusions or misunderstandings about the fundamental choice they will have to make in 1993.

For this Liberal opposition is unlike any that has preceded it in the forty-odd years since the foundation of that party. Collectively in its leadership, it represents the most ideological and the most divisive alternative presented to the Australian people in the post-War era. And in its program it is, more than any before it, obsessively determined to entrench privilege at the expense of fairness and compassion ...

No one regrets more deeply than I the pain that has been suffered by many Australians through the tightening of monetary policy. But Australia is beginning to emerge from the pain and hardship. We have brought interest rates down over the past eighteen months by seven and a half percentage points. And now, the first signs of renewed activity and confidence are starting to emerge ...

Under Labor, and only under Labor, Australia can make that a secure and permanent gain. Because under Labor, and only under Labor, can an effective wages policy be pursued – a wages policy based on the agreement by the trade union movement not to exercise its power to maximise nominal wage increases, and on the complementary agreement by the Labor government to deliver improvements in the social wage ...

And, delegates, through this recovery, your Labor government will continue the broader agenda of economic reform – just as, through the recession, we never lost sight of the long-term goal of a more competitive Australia.

We will be implementing the reforms that flow from the decisions we have already taken:

- to make housing more affordable through the national housing strategy;
- to ensure cheaper and better services in the telecommunications and airlines industries;
- to cut tariffs – while providing significant associated labour adjustment assistance;
- to implement an active and effective competition policy for the benefit of consumers;
- to expand our new network of Cooperative Research Centres as an important part of creating the clever country;
- to develop and implement the policy of ecologically sustainable development; and
- to continue our vigorous engagement in the current trade round, at this critical time, to win a fair go for Australia's efficient and competitive farm producers ...

Behind the discipline of our significant reduction in Commonwealth outlays as a proportion of GDP, lies an achievement of immense significance for us of the Labor Party; it has cleared the way for us to deliver Labor's social priorities in a way that has surpassed the pioneering social reforms of previous Labor governments.

How have we done that? We have done it the Labor way … I make this assertion, not in any boastful spirit, but as an assessment of solid fact: no Labor government has applied the spirit of Labor ideals with greater fidelity. No Labor government has been more faithful to Labor's true traditions.

And it has been our special challenge to apply those ideals, follow those traditions, in this era of the most rapid change in the whole of recorded history. It is the mark of our strength that we have had the courage to change …

Now in my 45th year of membership of our party – the best part of half its existence – I have been afforded unique opportunities to feel its history; to understand the passions and commitment that drive it – sometimes in upon itself; to see its capacity for adaptation; but at all times to be nourished by the steadfastness of that commitment to its fundamental goal – the welfare of the Australian people.

I have, through leadership of the industrial and then the political movement, come not just to understand the relationship between the trade unions and the Labor Party, but in my own life, for a generation, to live out that relationship.

I have never needed to be reminded that our party was formed by organised working men and women. That history is imbued in me and has become part of me. That same history tells me how ruthlessly the bastions of privilege in this country will fight to destroy the challenge they see in a strong, united and committed labour movement …

Source: The Bob Hawke Prime Ministerial Library

PAUL KEATING

'Down the time tunnel to the future'
'Cracker Night'

*Paul Keating, in the arena, the statesman turned political
brawler, skewering his political opponents*

Paul Keating had a unique and unrivalled sense of the power of language in politics. He could destroy his opponents with words shaped as political spears launched across the dispatch box in Parliament. Then, in an instant, he could switch to statesmanship and speak eloquently about matters of great national importance.

When asked in an interview in June 2010 about reconciling the political gladiator with grand orator, Keating said, 'I proselytised about things that I believed would reshape Australia and make it stronger. I was always indignant at reactionaries who either sought to diminish or attack those views. So I always saw the Parliament as the central cockpit of politics; the central square in the ideas market, where intellectual hegemony had to be mastered and kept'.

Keating's great strength was his ability as an advocate. He used colourful analogies and powerful metaphors. He employed charm, persuasion, wit and intelligence. He could bully, harass and cajole his audience. He drew on Labor sentiment, tradition and historical imagery. His attacks boosted party morale and demoralised the opposition.

Edna Carew wrote that 'his form of argument is to attack and, with a tongue that wounds like a verbal machine-gun, to cut the enemy down'. He described Leader John Hewson as a 'feral abacus', a 'craven coward', a 'creep' and a 'clown'. He branded Alexander Downer as 'Shirley Temple' and 'the Christmas turkey'. He called John Howard a 'small thrifty shopkeeper', a 'part-time thinker' and a 'tawdry opportunist'. Before the 2007 election, he urged voters to 'change course' by 'driving a stake through the dark heart of Howard's reactionary government'.

Here are two speeches which exemplify Keating the statesman turned political brawler

'Down the time tunnel to the future'

House of Representatives, Canberra 27 February 1992

In the past week we have had one of those rare philosophic outbursts from the opposition. We had some remarks from the Leader of the Opposition and the honourable member for Bennelong at a philosophical level which could not have made the differences between the government and the opposition clearer than they did.

They started off with the Leader of the Opposition, with his back turned as usual, talking about, 'I never learned respect at school'. You see, I should never have said in front of Her Majesty the Queen of Australia that Australia was now trading with the Asia-Pacific area. I should never have said that we have independence from Britain and Europe, as Britain joined the Common Market and as Australia trades now 70 to 80 per cent of its imports and exports with the Asia-Pacific area. I should never have made that remark about independence to the Queen of this continent. I should have had more respect. How dare I even reflect modestly on the old links with Britain, on the British bootstraps stuff?

Of course we then had a flurry of comment by the honourable member for Bennelong about the 1950s and what a very good period that was – he said it was a very, very good period, a golden age. That was the period when gross domestic product per head was half what it is now; when commodities occupied 85 per cent of our exports; when telephones were half what they are now; when there were half as many cars per thousand people of population; when pensions were half their real value of today and when 10 children per 1,000 went to university instead of 30 per 1,000.

That was the golden age when Australia stagnated. That was the golden age when Australia was injected with a near-lethal dose of fogeyism by the conservative parties opposite, when they put the country into neutral and where we very gently ground to a halt in the nowhere land of the early 1980s, with a dependency on commodities that would not pay for our imports. That was the golden age when vast numbers of Australians never got a look in; when women did not get a look in and had no equal rights and no equal pay; when migrants were factory fodder; when Aborigines were excluded from the system; when we had these xenophobes running around about Britain and bootstraps; and that awful cultural cringe under (Robert) Menzies which held us back for nearly a generation.

I said today at the Press Club that one of my colleagues, the Minister for Administrative Services, Senator Bolkus, has always been at the Cabinet about the future development of the old Parliament House and about whether it ought to be a constitutional museum or museum of Australian cultural history. We thought we could basically make the changes and put some of the cultural icons of the 1950s down there ... the Morphy Richards toaster, the Qualcast mower, a pair of heavily protected slippers, the Astor TV, the AWA radiogram.

And, of course, the honourable member for Wentworth and the honourable member for Bennelong could go there as well. When the kids come and look at them they will say, 'Gee, mum, is that what it was like then?'. And the two Johns can say, 'No, kids. This is the future'. Back down the time tunnel to the future – there they are.

I was told that I did not learn respect at school. I learned one thing: I learned about self-respect and self-regard for Australia – not about some cultural cringe to a country which decided not to defend the Malayan peninsula, not to worry about Singapore and not to give us our troops back to keep ourselves free from Japanese domination.

This was the country that you people wedded yourself to, and even as it walked out on you and joined the Common Market, you were still looking for your MBEs and your knighthoods, and all the rest of the regalia that comes with it. You would take Australia right back down the time tunnel to the cultural cringe where you have always come from ...

These are the same old fogies who doffed their lids and tugged the forelock to the British establishment; they now try to grind down Australian kids by denying them a technical school education and want to put a tax on the back of the poor. The same old sterile ideology, the same old fogeyism of the 1950s, that produced the Thatcherite policies of the late 1970s, is going to produce *Fightback!* We will not have a bar of it. You can go back to the fifties to your nostalgia, your Menzies, the (Richard) Caseys and the whole lot. They were not aggressively Australian, they were not aggressively proud of our culture, and we will have no bar of you or your sterile ideology.

Source: Commonwealth of Australia Parliamentary Debates (Hansard).

'Cracker night'

Greek Club, Brisbane 16 May 1994

Thank you very much indeed for that tremendously warm welcome …

I can tell you, quite sincerely, that it was in this room, this crowd, two years ago, more than at any other time in the period that I had been prime minister, that I got more cheer and more zest and more support than in any other place. I was doing it hard at the time, and I needed a kick along, and I had had a good couple of days in North Queensland and I came down here to one of the best dinners I have ever been to, and certainly then, the best of my time as prime minister …

And I think it was here in this room that Labor's journey to victory in 1993 really started to roll. Because it was here that I said, that the difference between the Labor Party and its opponents was a matter of heart. It was here that I first said, if some group drops back we will lean out our caring arm and pull them up … the Leader of the Opposition at the time (John Hewson) said that when the prime minister talks about pulling people up, doesn't he realise he will drag the rest of us down? …

So, this night two years ago was a turning point in Labor's re-election in 1993. But, the fact is, we have done what we said we would. We kept the promise and we kept the faith. Faith in ourselves, faith in Australians and faith in Australia, faith in the enduring values of our traditions as a country, of fairness, of egalitarianism, of a fair go, and a capacity for tolerance, and a great capacity for change.

And, perhaps it is the last, which is as important as any of the others, and that is the capacity to change. For change we have. Change as a nation we have. Australians, I think, are entitled to be proud of the change of the last ten years. For we have made big economic and social changes in Australia to ensure our economic future and to change from an inward looking country to an outward looking confident society going out to trade with the rest of the world.

It has been our lot, as Labor people, as a Labor government with now eleven years in office to fashion Australia in an image of the Labor Party. Modern, progressive, caring, to become a country which is economically strong and robust, and efficient and dynamic, and which at the same time is socially cohesive …

Now, this year our white paper (on employment) and Budget are met with a scowling reassertion of the principles of Fightback! … Now, this week,

263

it's back to what they do best – exclusion. Exclusive. See, they always regard themselves as exclusive and their supporters as exclusive, so the whole notion of inclusion is alien to them. It's only the Labor Party that believes in inclusion …

Peter Reith blew the whistle on them on the weekend and he said, 'Fightback! was as good a package after the election just as it was a good package before the election'. Oh, it was a terrific package, Peter, terrific package. But there was more. He said, 'Fightback! should form the framework of the opposition's next election policy'.

And, yesterday, Dr Hewson agreed with him … But, he's returning to Fightback! Like Wiley C Coyote, he's returning to the scene of the accident. He said, 'The essential philosophy of Fightback! has to be preserved' – like the coyote waiting for the anvil to drop from the sky.

But, they are an unhappy lot, these days, our opponents. No, they are – no, they are an unhappy lot. They've got positively no regard for one another.

And, we saw over the weekend Hewson and (Andrew) Peacock reported as referring to (John) Howard as 'The Rodent' and (Jeff) Kennett referring to (Peter) Costello as, 'Dog'. Not 'The Dog', just plain, 'Dog'.

And, of course, Bronwyn (Bishop), who enjoys almost universal contempt in the party – well she's had a rough couple of weeks – and after the government presented the white paper I was cruising down the corridor … and I heard this great roar of laughter come from the office, and I put my head in just as the camera was panning away from Bronwyn's press conference. There she was, talking to the camera – all by herself. You know, how a budgie talks to itself in the mirror. Well, there she was, up, talking to herself …

I always remember something Jack Lang said to me, and of course whenever I mention Jack Lang they always hate it, because they hate the memory of Lang, you know. He said to me, 'Look, I'll tell you this, Paul, never be worried about the skyrockets of politics. At first a shower of sparks and then a dead stick falls to earth'. And I thought, in fact, the fireworks analogy fits this lot well …

Some of you are old enough to remember cracker night … and I've seen this bunch sitting on the front bench, crackers as crackers, with Hewson the Skyrocket and Howard, Howard always with such promise. He always reminded me of that thing called the Flower Pot. Now, I don't know if any of you remember the Flower Pot, but that was the one where it always promised a dazzling performance. And you'd light it up, and it had multi-colours and it did a show for you but, often, when you lit it up it went 'ffffft', you know, a bit of a spark and there was a bit of a show, and then there'd be a bit more, and a bit more, then, finally, it fell away to nothing. And that's really, basically, very typical of his contribution.

Then there's (Ian) McLachlan, our establishment friend, who was supposed to have come to Canberra and really go off with a big bang. I always think of him as the Bunger, you know, the big red bungers: the strong and silent type capable of the big bang. You light it up, everyone stands back and then the wick sort of goes down, and everyone's waiting, and they keep on waiting, and that's it, it doesn't go off.

And then there's Bronwyn. She reminds me of the Catherine Wheel. We used to nail them to the fence and they'd go off and they'd take off, spreadeagle the kids, burn the dog, run up a tree and then fizzle out going round in circles.

So, that's them: bitter, burnt out and accident prone.

Nevertheless, we can never be complacent about them. And we won't be … So, I hope that with the support of you people in the Queensland Labor Party we'll be able to chart a course forward, not worry about our opponents, leave them in our wake and go on to make the changes which will make this a great and powerful, but really decent and nice, place to live …

Source: Editor's personal files.

PAUL KEATING

'We are the reform party in this country'

*Paul Keating presents the case for Labor amid the clash
of political ideologies over the past century*

Paul Keating always had a profound sense of the Labor Party's history, tradition and philosophy.

In an interview with Keating in June 2010, he said: 'The Labor Party, as Arthur Calwell said, is a party of conviction. The Liberal and National parties are parties of convenience: they know what they are against; they've often described themselves as anti-Labor groupings, but they rarely know what they are for. The Labor Party is the great building force in Australian public life, but it is poorly organised and scatty. It is also ideologically uncertain. It comes into is own when it is led and shaped'.

Three months into his prime ministership, trailing in the opinion polls and with the economy still emerging from recession, Keating addressed the Victorian Labor Conference and spoke of Labor's philosophical moorings and of the case for reform. He drew on Labor's historic mission to animate the purpose of his government. Michelle Grattan wrote in *The Age* that this was Keating's 'first significant speech to a party forum as leader'. He was keen to 'tap traditional party sentiment' and make a 'rallying speech' to the party faithful. It was a largely extemporaneous address.

Well before the 'third way' philosophy of Tony Blair and Bill Clinton, Keating placed his government within the context of the competing theories of Karl Marx and Adam Smith, Margaret Thatcher and Clem Atlee, Franklin D Roosevelt and Ronald Reagan. He speaks almost of a third way framework for Australian Labor, amid the clash of political ideologies of the past century.

As 'the builders' with the 'vision', Keating said, Labor believes in 'imagination, opportunity, inclusion, togetherness, cooperation, cohesion, pride'. In contrast, the Liberals were 'a party of primitives, throw-backs to 19th century robber-baron capitalism', he said.

'We are the reform party in this country'

Victorian ALP State Conference, Melbourne 21 March 1992

These are challenging times and it's nice to be amongst friends and I haven't always been amongst friends this week. But in engaging times like these we need to know where we are and where we're going. We have to have a very good fix on what out political policy and strategy is because parties sometimes lose their way and many parties have in the past. But fortunately that has not happened to us. Not in recent times.

You might have heard me say that we've been working in this century between two competing ideas in politics. One has been that private reward and private initiative was the main spring of all endeavour and human progress, and on the other hand, state socialism and government intervention was the way forward. We have seen these philosophies, Adam Smith on the one hand, (Karl) Marx on the other and various shades in between from the polarity of public life in the twentieth century.

We saw it in the United States with conservatives like Calvin Coolidge, articulating the policies of reward for the wealthy and the swing to the reaction against it in the Depression, to the need for government involvement which came with Franklin Roosevelt's New Deal. We saw the swing back to the years of (Dwight) Eisenhower, where again, we saw the same conservative incantations. And then the swing back as Americans wanted better with Lyndon Johnson's Great Society and support for blacks. And then again back to the Ronald Reagan years of 'greed is good', the notion that private initiative and private reward is all that matters.

We saw it in Britain, with (Winston) Churchill after the war and the swing to the government initiative was regarded as being important. And then the swing back to the dry radicalism of Margaret Thatcher where basically again the strong prospered and the weak were left in their wake.

Federal Labor came to office in 1983 against that tide. When we came to office the political tide was away from government intervention, government involvement, government engaging problems in society and the economy. But we stood against that tide, against the tide of Reaganism and Thatcherism, which was then the international trend. We dragged the pendulum back, not to state socialism which we knew was not working, and had never worked, and wouldn't work, or to massive central planning, but to a peculiarly and proudly Australian policy …

And we came up with a policy which was about opening Australia up, about economic restructuring, of letting markets have a role in the country, keeping a focus on efficiency, but at the same time looking at the needs of people trying to fashion a social wage which made the lot of Australians better.

Of course, we had big objectives, we had to come out of the recession of the early '80s, we had to bring Australia back up, we had to restart investment, we had to get employment going, we have to overcome inflation and put a suture on our debt.

But we did all of that within a growth model, in partnership with the trade unions under the Accord. In other words, Labor included people. We brought in the unions. Which have always been a strength of Labor and said let's do this together, let's devise a policy which is Australian, which deals with Australian problems. That is, a role for government but without suffocating creativity, without suffocating the role of the sensible operation of the market and with a focus on things we knew it had to be on – economic efficiency, getting companies going again, rebuilding our old industrial structure, turning our industrial museum back into a modern, sophisticated industrial society.

We never accepted the Thatcher view that employment was a residual, that if the rich got their go the crumbs that would fall from the table would go to the working and middle classes. We never accepted that view. Nor did we accept the puritanical market view of the New Zealand Labour Party, of David Lange and Roger Douglas.

We absorbed Thatcherism and Reaganism, took it in our strides, used those precepts about markets and efficiency as we wanted to use them in the Labor context in the Labor model and followed a Labor policy and talked to our friends in the trade unions as the New Zealand Labour Party didn't, and as the British Labour Party couldn't. And that's what made us different.

In the '80s we freed up savings for investment, but we developed this enormous social wage which started caring about things like:

Health – with Medicare – the right to health insurance whether you were sick, sore or sorry, rich or poor, single or with a large family, you had health protection under us. That was an important part of the social wage.

Women's issues – which we promoted strongly all the way from the 1980s, whether they be equal opportunity, or affirmative action or access to superannuation.

Pensioners and lifting up the age pension, which had fallen in real terms under Fraser, and which we have improved dramatically through the '80s.

Aged care – we're the first government to develop a comprehensive policy towards the aged. That is from geriatric assessment through to Home and Community Care through to the Hostel program.

Income support for the low paid – with a family allowance supplement directed to low paid, low income families, or support to families generally with the family allowance payment.

Increased retention rates in school – because we knew that not only was it unfair to our children not to give them the opportunity to complete secondary school but we would never make it as an advanced country we took the view that 3 kids in 10 completing secondary school was good enough. It is now 7 in 10 and we then created the equivalent of a dozen universities and now, we're building TAFE up behind it.

Child care – giving women the opportunity to go to work, and giving those who are at home relief with occasional day care in the course of the day or week.

Superannuation – giving Australian workers a chance to have a standard of living in retirement greater than that which can be provided by the Commonwealth through the aged pension. Building on the age pension, but something better, and at the same time develop a pool of savings for the nation to employ in terms of its capital restructuring.

We made a smaller public sector a better public sector, by targeting spending to those in real need.

So that was our '80s model. We rejected all these international fashions, we rejected the hard-hearted view of the Right. We took our policy, we opened the economy up, we let the market forces work in many respects, but we had a Labor stamp on it.

And now we've developed it further with 'One Nation' (Keating's 1992 post-recession policy blueprint) … It sets out a clear role for the public sector beyond the social wage and income support. It gives the public sector a further role, a policy of engagement of national problems not a policy of withdrawal, not the policy of withdrawal of Dr Hewson who wants to tear everything out of the way to let the wealthy push their way through the economy.

'One Nation' is about making markets work sensibly. It's not about trying to set up state socialism or government planning but sensibly letting the creative elements of people and organisations work.

It's a policy of inclusion, of bringing people together, lowering the drawbridge, letting people in, to participate, to become more cohesive. And the concept encompasses the Accord where Australia's workers are part of the process, part of the conversation with a Labor government. And partnerships for progress between government and business, government and unions, business and unions, the Commonwealth and the States, political government and the public service …

The only way we can prosper as a nation is working this way. Having respect for our institutions, the arts, the public institutions like the public service, our central bank with its balanced objectives of employment and development against inflation and price stability, or the public service which carries out the functions of government. The policy of inclusion goes to those institutions.

And it is about having a national identity. About understanding that we are able to make our own way, that we are Australians and we're whole hearted about it and the policy is an Australian policy. It's not an American policy or a British policy. It's not like Professor Hewson's, who is borrowing from the late '70s of Margaret Thatcher. It's not like Labour in New Zealand. It's ours. It's Australian Labor, it's Australian and it's ours …

We are the reform party in this country. We're the creators of the new concept. And we're the people holding our hand out in friendship to workers, to business, to minorities, to Aborigines and to anyone else that needs a hand. In friendship and in expectation, and hope, hope for Australia, hope for one nation, one proud nation, one independent nation.

Comrades, I ask you to contrast this with the Liberal Party, now a party of primitives. A party of primitives, throw-backs to 19th Century robber-baron capitalism, those who believe that what we should do is make way for the wealthy because in their slipstream the rest will pick up something on the way through. Survival of the fittest – if you're not a millionaire there is something wrong with you and therefore those who have got money should be given the opportunity to make their way. It's called, in Liberal parlance, 'freedom to achieve' …

What do they want to give us as their philosophy? Well they want to lower the drawbridge and run out with the GST and levy it on everyone's food and clothing and then run back in. That's their idea of inclusion, that's their idea of cohesion, that's their idea of making Australia one nation. Go and put a flat tax on everybody regardless of income, don't compensate them, let the wealthy get the big break.

A barren, sterile, ancient view of managing a modern society. The selfish, nark view of the world. The nark view of the world, the drawbridge up, the wealthy inside, the government withdrawing from the social equation. That's their policy. They are fundamentally different from us, but they always have been. We imagine Australia's future, determined by imagination, opportunity, inclusion, togetherness, co-operation, cohesion, pride. They imagine it determined by cost accounting and privilege. That's them.

Now Dr Hewson is totally limited in his thinking. Ideologically hamstrung, ideologically divisive, politically barren – a cold fish washed ashore by the recession, a primitive species we have not seen before in this country. We've seen it in Thatcher, and Reagan and Coolidge and others but not here. Australia can't afford Dr Hewson, or his party, or his policies ...

We offer something better and brighter. We offer breadth, as we always have, vision, opportunity. We are, as we've always been, the builders. And whether it be the rail network, or the highways, or the ring roads, or the electricity grids, or the ports, or the TAFE, or the universities, or the Family Allowance Supplement, or family allowance, or superannuation or Medicare, it is always Labor doing the building.

And we will go on doing the building.

Source: P Keating, The Major Speeches of the First Year, *ALP, Canberra, 1993.*

KEVIN RUDD

'A progressive party of the centre'

To be a progressive party of the centre is Labor's mission, says Kevin Rudd

Most Labor Party leaders seek to articulate the philosophy of their party to reflect their own personal policy and political goals. Party leaders have often sought to draw from the party's history to craft a narrative which simultaneously draws strength from this past but uses language to orient the party towards the future.

In 2001, speaking on the ABC1's *Lateline* program, Kevin Rudd argued that Labor should position itself as a party of 'the radical centre'. Previous Labor leaders and thinkers have advocated a 'middle way' or 'third way' for the party, consistent with its traditions. In several articles in *The Monthly* in 2006, Rudd wrote about how the party could deal with the key policy challenges for Australia and challenge the ruling orthodoxy of the Howard government.

In May 2007, at a birthday party celebrating the magazine's second year, Rudd spoke of Labor's mission: 'Labor has always been a progressive party of the centre with a keen eye on the challenges of the future. Always working to marry economic growth with social improvement, always striving to enlarge and uplift the nation's people, always looking to the future, and at our best Labor has been a navigator of the nation's future'. He also sought to define his opponents as narrow extremists who had betrayed their legacy of social liberalism.

Rudd received a warm response to this speech, which was covered in the media at the time. This speech was also later reprinted in *The Australian Financial Review* following Labor's election victory, offering a window into Rudd's philosophy and his conception of Labor's mission.

'A progressive party of the centre'

The Monthly's Second Birthday Party, Melbourne 14 May 2007

Last year John Howard used his infamous *Quadrant* speech to claim an ideological victory over all who dare to take a different view. This was intellectually arrogant in the extreme.

He went to Quadrant's dinner party not to praise the socially and economically liberal strands of his own party, but to bury them and thereby bury his party's history of social liberalism.

From (Edmund) Burke to (Benjamin) Disraeli, from (Alfred) Deakin to (Robert) Menzies, and to (Malcolm) Fraser, the other side of politics has almost invariably had a socially liberal wing to moderate their support to the individual in the capitalist system.

But today what I see on the other side is a political party which believes in both a market economy and a market society.

Just a few weeks ago on ABC Radio National, Malcolm Fraser described his party under Howard's leadership: 'I don't think it's a Liberal government. It is in name, but it's not a Menzies kind of Liberal.'

Fraser is right. Today's Liberals are neither the party that was founded in 1944 nor the party of Fraser in 1983.

Indeed, today's Liberals are rejoicing: at least one self-promoting young Liberal believes Fraser should resign from the Liberal Party and join The Greens.

Again, intellectual arrogance creeping across a once great political party.

The Monthly provided me with a forum to respond to Howard's triumphalism in my essay on market fundamentalism.

The market fundamentalism which has no answer to the great challenge we face on climate change.

The market fundamentalism which sees employees not as people but as commodities in the workplace.

The market fundamentalism which has no interest in providing public goods like health and education unless you are prepared to pay for them, and able to pay for them.

The market fundamentalism which believes a fair go is a part of Australia's past but has no place in Australia's future.

The market fundamentalism this country can do without.

On our side of politics we have sought to find a middle way.

Labor has always been a progressive party of the centre with a keen eye on the challenges of the future.

Always working to marry economic growth with social improvement, always striving to enlarge and uplift the nation's people, always looking to the future, and at our best Labor has been a navigator of the nation's future.

And, with all these things, a party which has sought, despite its failures, to reach out and embrace the great tradition of compassion still alive in the Australian soul – to hold it, hug it, breathe life into it and to keep it alive.

That's been our mission.

Source: Editor's personal files and The Australian Financial Review.

PART 5
War and Conflict

WILLIAM HOLMAN

'The most iniquitous, most immoral war ever waged'

William Holman opposes, most stridently, the Boer War

In 1899, to assist the British fight the Boer War in South Africa, the NSW government decided to send a contingent of troops.

Labor MP William Holman joined the debate in the NSW Parliament, outlining his opposition. He gave a courageous, brave and well argued speech, in which he mustered all of his talents as a speechmaker.

He spoke of his 'emotions of shame and indignation' at the actions of the British. Controversially, and in response to an interjection from Edmund Barton, he said, 'this is the most iniquitous, most immoral war ever waged with any race'. He then stunned the Parliament with this comment: 'I hope that England may be defeated'. There were howls of 'shame' and the Parliament was in uproar. 'It is the duty of every man who values human progress', Holman said, 'to build up more and more an understanding between the peoples of the world; to turn the human race into one gigantic nation, with a community of laws and of intellect, so that questions of difference, instead of being settled by the sword, may be settled by the humane and peaceful method of arbitration'.

The storm of protest which followed the speech forced Holman to clarify his remarks. He later said that his comments were aimed at the British South African Company being defeated, not Britain.

The Sydney Morning Herald, like other newspapers around the nation, reported on the debates over the war in great detail.

However, Holman's view was not widely shared. Some Labor MPs supported the contingent of troops being sent to South Africa. But Holman's courage and foresight would be vindicated by history.

Holman was one of the party's greatest orators and a leading figure in the party's early decades. He would become Labor's second NSW Premier but later split with the party over his support for conscription in the First World War.

'The most iniquitous, most immoral war ever waged'

NSW Parliament House, Sydney 18 October 1899

… We are asked to arm and equip 375 of our fellow-colonists, and to send them to another country to shoot men down. A very bitter responsibility will rest upon the head of every man in this Assembly if a single man is killed by our action in sending away this contingent, and it can be shown afterwards that we were mistaken, and throw in our weight with the wrong side in an unjust and unrighteous quarrel …

The Hon Member for Hartley asked me would I assert that there were no grievances? I say that there are no people in the world who have no grievances, and I admit that the Uitlanders have grievances. Their grievances amount to this: that the Transvaal government refuses to permit the Uitlander, the alien, the stranger within its gates, to take any part in the political life of the country until he becomes naturalised.

But the grievance exists in full force in our midst today. There are men in my own electorate who, although they have been in this country for fifteen years, have never had a vote and never will have a vote, no matter how long they may live in the colony, or how industrious may be their share in the work of the colony, unless they throw off their allegiance to their native land and swear allegiance to the Queen of Great Britain and Ireland. But they do not want to do that, and, therefore, we, as a self-governing colony, refuse to allow them the political rights that we enjoy. The position is the same in the Transvaal …

The time has now come to speak plainly, and to throw all the pretence that this is an affair of the empire to the winds. I do not know whether it is necessary for me to say that I am loyal to the empire … Whilst I am loyal to the empire, I see with emotions of shame and indignation which I can hardly express, the name and reputation of that empire being dragged in the dust at the behest of a little gang of swindling speculators on the Rand.

We know that this affair is no movement of the empire at all. We know how the whole trouble between the Dutch and the British races at the Cape has been stirred up since that masterly and statesmanlike pacification was brought about by the greatest Englishman of the century. Every time there has been a rift in the lute at Cape Colony a revival of the old hatred between the Dutch on the one side and the English on the other – every time it has been possible to create trouble there at once we trace the hand of Cecil

Rhodes pulling the string that sets everything in motion. I say that he is the man at whose behest we are now asked to send our gallant but misguided men to fight in the Transvaal …

… every patriot in the House, swelling into importance with the jingo emotions which possess his little twopenny-halfpenny soul, feels called upon in the interests of humanity and freedom to go to the relief of his oppressed and down-trodden countrymen.

There was a time indeed when to belong to the English race and to fight under the English flag was an honour … that was a time when England stood up … and alone withstood in the interests of freedom the might of conquering France. In those days it was, perhaps, a fair thing to say that England did stand up on behalf of liberty and freedom …

But today the English race has fallen on a time when apparently the utmost it can do is to bully weak and struggling powers. England can threaten a country like Venezuela; it can send an expedition into the Sudan. It can fight the Zulu; and it can now, after a long process of negotiation, finally draw the sword against the Boer …

Whilst my country is fighting in a just cause I hope I shall be as ready to support its claims as any other member. But as I believe from the bottom of my heart that this is the most iniquitous, most immoral war ever waged with any race, I hope that England may be defeated …

(Following interjections)

I may say that I expressed myself in a manner which carried somewhat more than I altogether intended. My anxiety is, and has been all through this fight, that in this long duel which has been taking place between the independent burghers on the one hand and the marauders of the chartered company on the other, that the Boers may win. That has been my wish ever since I have been capable of understanding the morals of the case …

The English empire has done much, and is undoubtedly a large civilising factor. That is a fact which we delight in, and which none of us deny. But the Englishman has no rights in the world peculiar to himself. The heaven-born Englishman is entirely an invention of the jingo press. We are not called upon to set right the other countries of the world, and to instruct them in the management of their affairs, and to dictate to them in their own internal concerns.

No doubt we have a right to interfere on behalf of our fellow-subjects when those fellow-subjects are really oppressed, when those fellow-subjects have no other hope or redress of grievances under which they languish save the armed intervention of their country. But that that is the case in the present instance will not be alleged for an instant by the other side. The majority of the Uitlanders have not asked for assistance, they are under no grievances which are not common to all aliens living in foreign countries. These men are not oppressed, they are not slaves, they are not robbed. It is free to them to find shelter in friendly British territory not 100 miles away. They do not wish to do so, they elect to stay there, because on the whole they are better off in the Transvaal in spite of all their disabilities than they would be in Natal ...

The man who survives in the struggle for existence today is not the man who goes forth, as Dr Jameson went forth on his raid, with his pistols in his belt and his sabre at his side, prepared to ride roughshod over humanity, but the man who conforms to the usages of society; and the fittest nation to survive is that nation which, in all its dealings with its fellow nations, is actuated by the highest regard for every jot and tittle of international law.

Just as today the robber, the burglar, and the bushranger, in spite of their courage and energy, are held down and thrust into the outer darkness, and have to meet the punishment which justly waits upon them at the bidding of society at large, so, with nations, the day of buccaneering has gone by; and it is the duty of every man who values human progress to build up more and more an understanding between the peoples of the world; to turn the human race into one gigantic nation, with a community of laws and of intellect, so that questions of difference, instead of being settled by the sword, may be settled by the humane and peaceful method of arbitration.

Source: NSW Legislative Assembly Debates (Hansard).

ANDREW FISHER

'To our last man and our last shilling'

Andrew Fisher declares his support for King and country

The assassination of Archduke Franz Ferdinand on 28 June 1914 – the day after the Australian Parliament was dissolved for the elections – was the first in a sequence of events which led to the First World War.

During the election campaign, and as the world edged closer to war, Prime Minister Joseph Cook pledged Australia's support for Britain in any likely war. Speaking at Horsham in Victoria, Cook said that 'when the empire is at war, so is Australia at war'.

To avoid the war becoming an election issue, Labor leader Andrew Fisher matched Cook's support for the war, on the same day, but with a more memorable flourish: 'to our last man and our last shilling'. The comment was made at a campaign rally in Colac in Victoria, with more than 1000 eager supporters in attendance. Britain had not yet formally declared a state of war, and did not do so until 5 August 1914.

Fisher's speech, like that of Cook's, was prominently reported in the nation's newspapers. As Les Carlyon notes in his book *Gallipoli*, Fisher reiterated his support at Benalla three days later, saying that 'in a time of emergency there are no parties at all. We stand united against the common foe, and I repeat what I said at Colac, that our last man and our last shilling will be offered and supplied to the mother country'.

There was virtually no difference between the major political parties or within the parties themselves on supporting a war. Many were energised by the ideal of fighting for freedom and democracy.

Fisher's Labor Party won the 1914 election and he secured his third non-consecutive term as Prime Minister.

Fisher's words were often repeated and were widely remembered at the time of his death in 1928.

'To our last man and our last shilling'

Victoria Hall, Colac, Victoria 31 July 1914

Turn your eyes to the European situation and give the kindest feelings toward the Mother Country at this time.

I sincerely hope that international arbitration will avail before Europe is convulsed in the greatest war of any time.

All, I am sure, will regret the critical position existing at the present time, and pray that a disastrous war may be averted.

But should the worst happen after everything has been done that honour will permit, Australians will stand beside our own, to help and defend her, to our last man and our last shilling.

Source: The Canberra Times, 25 October 1928.

THOMAS JOSEPH (TJ) RYAN

'I am opposed to conscription'

TJ Ryan fights Billy Hughes' plans for conscription in the First World War

The attempt by Labor Prime Minister Billy Hughes to introduce conscription for service in the First World War divided the nation and split the Labor Party.

Hughes wanted a greater contribution of soldiers from Australia to support the war effort. But many in the Labor caucus, the party organisations and unions were opposed. Although caucus had supported a referendum on conscription, which was lost on 28 October 1916, caucus would not support Hughes's proposal for another. Hughes left the party as a debate of no confidence in his leadership was underway, on 14 November 1916. He was expelled from the party.

A special conference in December affirmed the party's opposition to conscription. At that conference, future party leader James Scullin argued that Hughes had violated 'the spirit of the labour movement'. Hughes formed a new government with conservative support and pushed ahead with his plans for a second referendum.

Queensland Premier TJ Ryan became the leading opponent of conscription. Determined to succeed, Hughes used wartime powers to censor any opposition. Newspaper reports of Ryan's speech opposing conscription at Centennial Hall in Brisbane on 19 November 1917 were censored. Ryan told Parliament on 21 November that the censorship was 'one of the gravest issues ever'. On 22 November, Ryan said his speech published in the press had 'an entirely different meaning'. A special edition of Hansard, known as *Hansard 37*, containing Ryan's full speech was published by the government.

However, Hughes instructed that copies be confiscated. But the censor was met at the printing office by State police and Ryan himself, wearing only his pyjamas. The censor later returned with armed soldiers and copies were seized (three were secretly hidden). Ryan then organised the printing of a Government Gazette Extraordinary. Hughes could not stop him. People would learn of Ryan's opposition to conscription and the unscrupulous methods of Hughes.

In Sydney, 200,000 people cheered Ryan's arrival at the conclusion of the campaign against conscription and, on 20 December 1917, Hughes' second referendum failed.

'I am opposed to conscription'

QLD Legislative Assembly, Brisbane 22 November 1917

The premier moved the following motion:

> That this House emphatically protests against the manner in which the censorship is being abused to suppress reports of the views of those opposing the Commonwealth Government's conscription proposals, and condemns it as an unwarrantable interference with the rights of free discussion on the platform, and in the Press, upon one of the gravest issues ever submitted to the public, and a flagrant infringement of the time honoured rights of a free people.

... In addressing myself to the motion before the House, I regard the matter that we are about to discuss as one of the very greatest importance ...

The censorship no doubt is necessary, but it should only be purely for purposes connected with the successful carrying on of the war. It should be utilised for the prevention of information getting to the enemy or for any other purpose that is intended for securing the public safety and the defence of the Commonwealth ...

But when these powers are used for an entirely difference purpose; when they are extended to be utilised for political purposes, they are then beyond the ambit, not only of the War Precautions Act, but of the whole for which the censorship is established ...

In short, in my opinion, the exercise of the powers in a manner in which they are being exercised is entirely unlawful ...

But the censorship during this campaign is being used for the purpose of suppressing the views of those who are opposed to the conscription proposals of the Commonwealth.

The issue that is before the country is of the very gravest importance; it is a proposal to take power over the life and liberties of the people, and it is imperative that there should be the greatest freedom both in speech and to the press ...

I have no hesitation in saying that, in my opinion, the form in which this question is submitted to the people is misleading. It is calculated to give a wrong impression, and to induce people to vote for the proposals perhaps who do not fully understand what those proposals are. The form of the question is this:

> Are you in favour of the proposals of the Commonwealth government for reinforcing the Australian Imperial forces overseas?

Now everybody is in favour of reinforcements. We are all in favour of rein-forcements, but … the question is put in a form that it should not be. I saw a cable from London appearing in the press both in Sydney and Brisbane – *The Sydney Morning Herald* and the *Brisbane Courier*. This is the cable, dated 19th November, 1917:

> There are general complaints among the soldiers regarding the vagueness of the referendum question, they being asked to vote for the government proposals but the nature of the proposals is not disclosed. Voters are solely dependent upon fragmentary newspaper cables. The government is urged to cable an explanatory statement.

So that you can see that even the soldiers in England – probably the soldiers at the front – have evidently been complaining about the form in which this question is being put, and consequently that cable is being sent to Australia …

I propose now to put before the House, with regards to the manner in which the proposed report of my remarks made in the Centennial Hall on the 19th November were treated by the censor …

I will take an extract from my speech. This is the way it reads, as allowed to be published:

> Now, five divisions are 100,000 men and since the beginning we have recruited 383,000 men in Australia. Of that number, they tell us 60,000 have not left Australia's shores. Very well, there have been only 114,000 casualties. Yet you are asked to sanction the proposal for the compulsory deportation of the single men of the country – the single men between twenty to forty-four.

That is as they allowed it to be published – an entirely different meaning from what I said. This is what was left out:

[Note – The portions struck out by censor are indicated by the bold type.]

> **Very well; I put these two together, and take them from 383,000, which leaves 209,000. As five divisions are 100,000, I take them away, and 109,000 men are left for the purposes of reinforcements. So that on these figures, without any further recruiting, you could go on from twelve to sixteen months. (Loud and prolonged applause.) And, if we continue the volun-tary system at the rate they say we are now doing, we would go on for over two years; able to reinforce on these numbers at the rate of 7,000 men per month.**

… that portion of my speech was omitted, was cut out by the censor. Now, I ask any intelligent member of this House … was he justified in taking out the main portion of my contention, leaving in words that conveyed an entirely different meaning from what I said? You see the impression he leaves me making on the public. He leaves me saying this:

Very well, there have been only 114,000 casualties. Yet you are asked to sanction the proposals for the compulsory deportation of the single men of the country.

An absolutely and entirely different statement from the statement I made, calculated to mislead the public and certainly to convey a meaning that I never intended to convey and that I never did convey. Does anybody think for a moment that I would get up on a platform and say that 'You are asked to sanction the proposals for compulsory deportation'? No.

I argued that on the numbers that has enlisted – 383,000, less the casualties 114,000, less 60,000 men they told us had not left Australia, there would still be 209,000 left, and that five divisions were 100,000, leaving 109,000 for reinforcements. I said that the 109,000 could reinforce them without any further recruiting for twelve to sixteen months. I understated it. I could have increased it. I could have told them that they were sufficient for more than twelve to sixteen months, but I did not want to overstate it; I preferred to err on the other side. And then I continued to say that if recruiting went on at the same rate at which we are now told it is going on, there would be a sufficient number of men recruited during those months to keep the five divisions re-enforced, with the 109,000 I mentioned, for two years.

Now Mr Groom writes a letter which appears in today's *Daily Mail*, bearing on this same subject, and I propose to quote it, because it proves the truth of my contention that the censor disallowed. This is what Mr Groom writes to the paper this morning;

> To the Editor.
>
> Sir, – I would be glad if you would permit me to amplify a passage in the necessarily condensed report of my speech last night. I am reported as having said, 'Calculated by the casualties coming out now, in eighteen months there would not be a division of Australians fighting in France'. I referred to the statement made that there were 109,000 men available at present, in addition to the 100,000 men in the five divisions in France. I pointed out that many of the 100,000 were young men in training, and that General Birdwood and other said that 7,000 per month were necessary to keep up the full strength. I added that if reinforcements were not sent and the casualties continued, we could not keep up the reserves, and that in eighteen months we would not have reserves for the five divisions, and that being so, we would in eighteen months not have the men to reinforce a division now fighting in France.
>
> Yours, etc
>
> LITTLEON E GROOM
>
> Brisbane, 21st November, 1917

His letter proves the truth of my conclusion, and yet what I said was struck out by the censor from the report submitted! The people are not to be trusted! They are not to be allowed to get such information on such an important matter as this! Well, I quote that letter by Mr Groom in corroboration of the truth of what I said and I ask, 'Why was that passage struck out of my speech and why was it allowed to appear in a form in which it was never delivered?'

I ask, 'Are the people of Australia going to tolerate that sort of thing; are they going to allow the censorship to be used for a thing of that sort?' If I understand the spirit of fairplay of the people of Australia – and I speak entirely apart from the political beliefs they have – they will not tolerate that sort of thing.

Now, let me take another illustration; an illustration with regard to the question to be submitted. I hope that the whole of the passages I quote may be printed in Hansard, showing the portion that was allowed to be published and the portion that was excised, so that Hon Members may be really able to distinguish what was cut out by the censor. Now, this is what I am allowed to be reported to have said on that matter:

> The question Mr Hughes put is this – 'Are you in favour of the proposal of the Commonwealth Government for reinforcing the Commonwealth forces overseas?' I don't care whether you are for 'Yes' or for 'No'. To get them to vote for reinforcements? We are all in favour of reinforcements. (Great applause).

This is what I did say:

> The question Mr Hughes put is this – 'Are you in favour of the proposal of the Commonwealth Government for reinforcing the Commonwealth forces overseas?' **How misleading that question is!**

That last sentence is struck out:

> I don't care whether you are for 'Yes' or for 'No' **But is that a fair form of question? No. And does not the Prime Minister know that the people of Australia know it is unfair; that it is intended to mislead?**

All words after 'No' in the first sentence are stuck out. This is also struck out:

> **But not only are they misleading those in Australia, they are keeping the men at the front in the dark. Is there anything more reprehensible, more to be condemned, than the attempt on the part of your own government to deceive the men who are fighting for you at the front? (Hear, hear!) That is what is being done by the form of the question, and I appeal to all fair-minded Australians to gauge these proposals by the way in which they are brought forward and by the manner in which the question is being asked. (Applause.)**

That is all struck out. The public are not allowed to hear that from me …

I consider that I have never spoken in my life on a more important question than that on which I am speaking now, because here it is shown that we have a military censorship that can with a stroke of the pen strike out something that does not agree with the views of the Commonwealth government …

I am appealing to the intelligence of the whole people of Queensland with regard to this matter. Are they not to be allowed to hear the truth? …

I am opposed to conscription; Hon Members are supporting it. They are entitled to put their views, and I am entitled to put mine. But with the system being adopted at present, there is only one side allowed to put its views; and anyone who dares say otherwise, the military censorship is upon him and he is shut up, closed down …

It is a most important question. It is involving the question of freedom of speech and the freedom of the press. It is dealing with the most important issue that has ever been before the people. I am one of those who believes that, if conscription were carried in this country, the efficiency of Australia as a factor in bringing about a successful conclusion of the war, would not be increased …

All the more I do believe that, if under any circumstances conscription were to be carried by the adoption of such methods as these; because, although they may keep the people in the dark while this campaign is going on, they won't be able to keep them in the dark much longer …

They may think to get a temporary advantage of having an affirmative vote carried on the 20th December; but they must bear in mind that the people will eventually find out that information has been suppressed from them, and that they will resent it …

Source: QLD Legislative Assembly Parliamentary Debates (Hansard).

JOHN CURTIN

'The tribute which a grateful country pays to those who have served it'

John Curtin speaks at the opening of the Australian War
Memorial and pays tribute to the fallen

A month after John Curtin was sworn in as Prime Minister, he spoke at the opening of the Australian War Memorial, on Armistice Day.

It was only a little over two decades since the guns had fallen silent at the end of the Great War. Curtin had been a pacifist and anti-conscription campaigner during that war. Now, he was leading the nation during another war.

In this speech, at the foot of Mount Ainslie, in front of 5000 people, Curtin spoke of the 'matchless courage' of those whose 'innumerable acts of heroism' that were recorded in the archives of the memorial.

Watched by politicians, foreign dignitaries and 18 Victoria Cross winners, according to *The Canberra Times*, Curtin drew inspiration from the 'continuity' of the 'ANZAC tradition' when describing the 'struggle' in which the nation was now engaged. He noted the symbolism of the War Memorial and Parliament House being located so nearby; the latter a reminder of 'a free people' and the 'unifying purpose' of defending that liberty. Curtin said the memorial was the 'tribute which a grateful country pays to those who have served it so steadfastly'.

His biographer, Lloyd Ross, argued that this speech was one of Curtin's best. While noting the 'sustaining power' and 'fiery convictions' expressed in his speeches, Ross said that for many he 'was possibly still most effective on those occasions when sentiment could be given full release and he was harmonising his thoughts with some aspects of the environment that he loved'.

In the beautiful surrounds of Canberra, opening the nation's most important, most revered and most loved public building, this is indeed Curtin at his best.

'The tribute which a grateful country pays to those who have served it'

Australian War Memorial, Canberra 11 November 1941

The Australian War Memorial contains the complete records of the first great crisis in Australian history. There is, in the memorial, the accounts of innumerable acts of heroism. There is the story of an unquenchable faith and there, in itself, can be said to exist the sanctuary of Australian tradition.

It is, I believe, extraordinarily appropriate that the place where this tradition is housed should be in sight of the building which is the seat of ordered government. The Parliament of a free people deliberates day-by-day and cannot but be inspired and strengthened in the performance of its great duty by the ever present opportunity to contemplate the story that has gone before them, of the deeds that helped to make the nation, and of the unifying purpose which links the ordered ways of a free people with that matchless courage which inspires its sons to maintain it …

And just as the War Memorial is a treasure house containing the records of what occurred 25 years ago, so is it to be a treasure house for all that takes place in the struggle in which we are now engaged …

It gives continuity to the ANZAC tradition. It gives uninterruption to the basic impulses of this nation. It provides for all time to come to the generations that will inhabit this land, a place where they may have brought before them, in the most conspicuous way, the legends of their country, and come to know something of the deeds that kept their freedom unimpaired …

And it is also fitting that the land upon which each has been erected should be the property of men and women no matter where they may live in this great Commonwealth, just as the men of the fighting forces were Australians rather than the sons of a particular State.

So their memory is to be perpetuated in a building which is Australian and is not the property of any one State or subject to the rules and decrees of any government of a part of a State.

This is an Australian War Memorial. It is the tribute which a grateful country pays to those who have served it so steadfastly. It will house not only the relics of the last war, and the relics of the present war, but it will keep alive the unquenchable spirits of sacrifice and service which are the cornerstones of a people's greatness.

Source: Digest of Decisions and Announcements, No 5 / The John Curtin Prime Ministerial Library.

*Queensland Premier TJ Ryan was the most important advocate against
conscription in the First World War. It was a defining debate within Labor,
which led to Billy Hughes leaving the party and a subsequent split throughout
Labor's ranks. Ryan had been censored by Hughes over conscription and took
his fight to the people and Hughes' second referendum on conscription failed.
Source: Australian Labor Party (Queensland Branch)*

JOHN CURTIN

'We are at war with Japan'

John Curtin announces the beginning of the war in the Pacific

On 8 December 1941, the day after the Japanese attacked the United States at Pearl Harbour, Prime Minister John Curtin issued a statement saying that 'the thread by which peace was hanging has been snapped'. In 'the gravest hour of our history', Curtin said that Australia's 'security and vital interests' were 'at stake', and declared that Australia was at war with Japan. As David Black has noted, this was a separate, Australian, declaration of war.

Later, in this national broadcast, Curtin spoke directly to the people of Australia. 'Men and women of Australia', he began, 'we are at war with Japan'. The reasons were three-fold: the 'unprovoked attack' by the Japanese on Pearl Harbour, the imperilling of Australia's 'vital interests' and 'because the rights of free people in the whole Pacific are assailed'. He explained how the Japanese had 'struck like an assassin in the night'.

As a nation, which Curtin said 'has freedom and liberty as its cornerstones', this 'free way of living' would be defended in war. But with the nation 'in peril', he readied Australians for a long and hard fight. He made it clear that everything Australians held dear was at stake. 'Let there be no idle hand', he said, 'the road of service is ahead'. He quoted poetry and summoned his people 'to meet the external aggressor'.

'We are at war with Japan'

Broadcast, Canberra 8 December 1941

Men and women of Australia,

We are at war with Japan.

That has happened because, in the first instance, Japanese naval and air forces launched an unprovoked attack on British and United States territory; because our vital interests are imperilled and because the rights of free people in the whole Pacific are assailed.

As a result, the Australian government this afternoon took the necessary steps which will mean that a state of war exists between Australia and Japan.

Tomorrow, in common with the United Kingdom, the United States of America and the Netherlands East Indies governments, the Australian government will formally and solemnly declare the state of war it has striven so sincerely and strenuously to avoid.

Throughout the whole affair, and despite discouragement, the Australian government and its representatives abroad struggled hard to prevent a breakdown of discussions. Australia encouraged the United States to retain the diplomatic initiative on behalf of the democratic Powers.

We did not want war in the Pacific. The Australian government has repeatedly made it clear – as have the governments of the United Kingdom, the United States and the Netherlands East Indies – that if war came to the Pacific it would be of Japan's making. Japan has now made war.

Since last February it has been the constant aim and endeavour of the democracies to keep peace in the Pacific … Yet, when the President of the United States had decided to communicate direct to the Japanese Emperor a personal appeal for Imperial intervention on the side of peace, the war government of Japan struck. That war government, set on aggression and lusting for power in the same fashion as its Axis partners, anticipated the undoubted weight of the President's plea and shattered the century-old friendship between the two countries.

For the first time in the history of the Pacific, armed conflict stalks abroad. No other country but Japan desired war in the Pacific. The guilt for plunging this hemisphere into actual warfare is, therefore, upon Japan …

By so doing, Japan chose the Hitler method. While its diplomatic representatives were actually at the White House; while all the democratic powers regarded the conversations as continuing; Japan ignored the convention of a formal declaration of war and struck like an assassin in the night.

For, as the dawn broke this morning … guns from Japanese warships; bombs from Japanese aircraft; shots from Japanese military forces struck death to United States citizens and members of its defence forces; to the peaceful subjects of Great Britain and her men on ships and on the land. The Pacific Ocean was reddened with the blood of Japanese victims. These wanton killings will be followed by attacks on the Netherlands East Indies; on the Commonwealth of Australia; on the Dominion of New Zealand; if Japan can get its brutal way.

Australia, therefore, being a nation that believes in a way of life which has freedom and liberty as its cornerstones goes to the battle stations in defence of the free way of living. Our course is clear, our cause is just – as has been the case ever since September, 1939, when we stood in the path of Hitlerism and declared that we would stand out to the end against ruthless and wanton aggression.

I say, then, to the people of Australia: give of your best in the service of the nation. There is a place and part for all of us. Each must take his or her place in the service of the nation, for the nation itself is in peril. This is our darkest hour. Let that be fully realized. Our efforts in the past two years must be as nothing compared with the efforts we must now put forward.

I can give you the assurance that the Australian government is fully prepared … This afternoon, the full cabinet met … Tomorrow, the war cabinet will meet again, as will the Australian Advisory War Council, when the Leader of the Opposition and his colleagues will be fully appraised of every phase of the position. The Parliament of the Commonwealth will assemble on Tuesday of next week.

One thing remains, and on it depends our very lives. This thing is the cooperation, the strength, and the will-power of you, the people of the Commonwealth. Without it we are, indeed, lost.

Men and women of Australia: the call is to you, for your courage; your physical and mental ability; your inflexible determination that we, as a nation of free people, shall survive. My appeal to you is in the name of Australia, for Australia is the stake in this conflict. The thread of peace has snapped – only the valour of our fighting forces, backed by the very uttermost of which we are capable in factory and workshop, can knit that thread again into security. Let there be no idle hand. The road of service is ahead. Let us all tread it firmly, victoriously.

We here, in this spacious land where, for more than 150 years, peace and security have prevailed, are now called upon to meet the external aggressor …

We Australians have imperishable traditions. We shall maintain them. We shall vindicate them. We shall hold this country and keep it as a citadel for the British-speaking race and as a place where civilisation will persist.

Men and women of the Commonwealth of Australia: It is my solemn duty to sound a tocsin! I proclaim a call unto you. I do it in the words of Swinburne:

> Come forth, be born and live,
> Thou that has help to give,
> And light to make man's day of manhood fair,
> With flight outflying the sphered sun,
> Hasten thine hour
> And halt not till thy work be done.

Source: Digest of Decisions and Announcements, No 10 / The John Curtin Prime Ministerial Library.

JOHN CURTIN

'Men and women of The United States'

John Curtin looks to the United States in this historic broadcast abroad

The Japanese bombing of Pearl Harbour on 7 December 1941 was the opening battle in the Pacific theatre of the Second World War. John Curtin, Prime Minister for less than two months, was concerned about the defence of Australia.

In a New Year message, published in the Melbourne *Herald* on 27 December 1941, Curtin said that 'Australia looks to America, free of any pangs as to our traditional links or kinship with the United Kingdom'. This appeal to America was reiterated in this landmark speech.

It is now remembered as the springboard for the creation of the Australian-American alliance. However, it was not a decisive break with the bonds of Empire. Curtin continued to speak of Australia's close relations with Britain and advocated greater Empire government collaboration. But Curtin's call to the United States did strike a resonant chord with the Australian people.

He said that Australia was the last best hope between the Japanese and the western coast of America. 'If Australia goes, the Americas are wide open', he said. The speech is thick with metaphor, purple prose and powerful sentences characterising the 'great struggle'. He appealed to sentiment, tradition and history. It is a brilliantly composed speech for radio that is infused with words that animate and energise Curtin's appeal.

The Sydney Morning Herald said it was 'stirring' and 'high-spirited'. The *Argus* doubted whether Curtin had ever made a speech 'as vigorous, as logical, as frank and as eloquent'.

The speech was also broadcast to Canada, South America, Britain and in Europe. No Australian had ever had a larger audience for a speech. *The Washington Post* said that Curtin's call could not be ignored.

General Douglas MacArthur would arrive in Australia to take command of the Allied forces four days later and the foundations of the alliance would cement itself through 1942.

'Men and women of The United States'

Broadcast to the People of America, Canberra 14 March 1942

Men and women of The United States,

I speak to you from Australia. I speak from a united people to a united people, and my speech is aimed to serve all the people of the nations united in the struggle to save mankind.

On the great waters of the Pacific Ocean war now breathes its bloody steam. From the skies of the Pacific pours down a deathly hail. In the countless islands of the Pacific the tide of war flows madly. For you in America; for us in Australia, it is flowing badly.

Let me then address you as comrades in this war and tell you a little of Australia and Australians. I am not speaking to your government. We have long been admirers of Mr (Franklin) Roosevelt and have the greatest confidence that he understands fully the critical situation in the Pacific and that America will go right out to meet it. For all that America has done, both before and after entering the war, we have the greatest admiration and gratitude.

It is to the people of America I am now speaking; to you who are, or will be, fighting; to you who are sweating in factories and workshops to turn out the vital munitions of war; to all of you who are making sacrifices in one way or another to provide the enormous resources required for our great task …

Japan, behind her wall of secrecy, had prepared for war on a scale of which neither we nor you had knowledge. We have all made mistakes, we have all been too slow; we have all shown weakness – all the allied nations. This is not the time to wrangle about who has been most to blame …

Who among us, contemplating the future on that day in December last when Japan struck like an assassin at Pearl Harbour at Manila, at Wake and Guam, would have hazarded a guess that by March the enemy would be astride all the south-west Pacific except General MacArthur's gallant men, and Australia and New Zealand. But that is the case …

It was, therefore, but natural that, within twenty days after Japan's first treacherous blow, I said on behalf of the Australian government that we looked to America as the paramount factor on the democracies' side of the Pacific.

There is no belittling of the old country in this outlook. Britain has fought and won in the air the tremendous battle of Britain. Britain has fought, and with your strong help, has won, the equally vital battle of the Atlantic. She has a paramount obligation to supply all possible help to Russia. She cannot, at the same time, go all out in the Pacific. We Australians, with New Zealand, represent Great Britain here in the Pacific – we are her sons – and on us the responsibility falls. I pledge to you my word we will not fail. You, as I have said, must be our leader. We will pull knee to knee with you for every ounce of our weight.

We looked to America, among other things, for counsel and advice, and therefore it was our wish that the Pacific War Council should be located at Washington. It is a matter of some regret to us that, even now, after 95 days of Japan's staggering advance south, ever south, we have not obtained first-hand contact with America.

Therefore, we propose sending to you our Minister for External Affairs (HV 'Doc' Evatt), who is no stranger to your country, so that we may benefit from his discussions with your authorities. Dr Evatt's wife, who will accompany him, was born in The United States. Dr Evatt will not go to you as a mendicant. He will go to you as the representative of a people as firmly determined to hold and hit back at the enemy as courageously as those people from whose loins we spring – those people who withstood the disaster of Dunkirk, the fury of Goering's blitz, the shattering blows of the Battle of the Atlantic. He will go to tell you that we are fighting mad; that our people have a government that is governing with orders and not with weak-kneed suggestions; that we Australians are a people who, while somewhat inexperienced and uncertain as to what war on their own soil may mean, are nevertheless ready for anything, and will trade punches, giving odds if needs be, until we rock the enemy back on his heels.

We are, then, committed, heart and soul, to total warfare. How far, you may ask me, have we progressed along that road? I may answer you this way. Out of every ten men in Australia four are wholly engaged in war as members of the fighting forces or making the munition and equipment to fight with. The other six, besides feeding and clothing the whole ten and their families, have to produce the food and wool and metals which Britain needs for her very existence … From four out of ten devoted to war, we shall pass to five and six out of ten. We have no limit.

We have no qualms here. There is no fifth column in this country. We are all the one race – the English speaking race. We will not yield easily a yard of our soil. We have great space here and tree by tree, village by village, and town by town we will fall back if we must. That will occur only if we lack the means of meeting the enemy with parity in materials and machines. For, remember, we are the Anzac breed. Our men stormed Gallipoli; they swept through the Libyan desert; they were the 'rats' of Tobruk; they were the men who fought under 'bitter, sarcastic, pugnacious Gordon Bennett' down Malaya and were still fighting when the surrender of Singapore came. These men gave of their best in Greece and Crete; they will give more than their best on their own soil, when their hearths and homes lie under enemy threat.

Our air forces are in the (Charles) Kingsford-Smith tradition. You have, no doubt, met quite a lot of them in Canada; the Nazis have come to know them over Hamburg and Berlin and in paratroop landings in France. Our naval forces silently do their share on the seven seas.

I am not boasting to you. But were I to say less I would not be paying proper due to a band of men who have been tested in the crucible of world wars and hallmarked as pure metal. Our fighting forces are born attackers; we will hit the enemy wherever we can, as often as we can, and the extent of it will be measured only by the weapons in our hands ...

We fight with what we have and what we have is our all. We fight for the same free institutions that you enjoy. We fight so that, in the words of (Abraham) Lincoln, 'government of the people, for the people, by the people, shall not perish from the earth'. Our legislature is elected the same as is yours; and we will fight for it, and for the right to have it, just as you will fight to keep the Capitol at Washington the meeting place of freely elected men and women representative of a free people.

But I give you this warning: Australia is the last bastion between the West Coast of America and the Japanese. If Australia goes, the Americas are wide open. It is said that the Japanese will by-pass Australia and that they can be met and routed in India. I say to you that the saving of Australia is the saving of America's west coast. If you believe anything to the contrary then you delude yourselves.

Be assured of the calibre of our national character. This war may see the end of much that we have painfully and slowly built in our 150 years of existence. But even though all of it go, there will still be Australians fighting on Australian soil until the turning point be reached, and we will advance over blackened ruins, through blasted and fire-swept cities, across scorched plains, until we drive the enemy into the sea. I give you the pledge of my country. There will always be an Australian government and there will always be an Australian people. We are too strong in our hearts; our spirit is too high; the justice of our cause throbs too deeply in our being for that high purpose to be overcome.

I may be looking down a vista of weary months; of soul-shaking reverses; of grim struggle; of back-breaking work. But as surely as I sit here talking to you across the war-tossed Pacific Ocean I see our flag; I see Old Glory; I see the proud banner of the heroic Chinese; I see the standard of the valiant Dutch.

And I see them flying high in the wind of liberty over a Pacific from which aggression has been wiped out; over peoples restored to freedom; and flying triumphant as the glorified symbols of united nations strong in will and in power to achieve decency and dignity, unyielding to evil in any form.

Source: Digest of Decisions and Announcements, No 22 / The John Curtin Prime Ministerial Library.

JOHN CURTIN

'A great naval battle is proceeding'

*John Curtin announces to a hushed Parliament that
the nation faces the threat of invasion*

It was late on Friday afternoon and the House of Representatives was about to adjourn. Only a few MPs were left in the chamber. The public gallery was empty. A few journalists watched from the press gallery. Prime Minister John Curtin entered the House, waited, and then at 3.59 pm formally moved the adjournment.

He had received a message from General Douglas MacArthur that a major naval battle was underway in the Pacific. Japanese ships were heading south, planning to invade Port Moresby to launch attacks on Australia and cut off America's communication lines with Australia.

'I have received a communiqué from the commander-in-chief of the Allied forces in the South-west Pacific area', Curtin said, 'stating that a great naval battle is proceeding in the south-west Pacific'.

Suddenly MPs flooded into the chamber. The public gallery and the press gallery quickly filled. 'The events that are taking place today are of crucial importance to the whole conduct of the war in this theatre', he said. He drew on Abraham Lincoln when he said Australia's forces were giving their 'last full measure of devotion' to the war. He called on all Australians to do 'their duty to the nation'.

His press secretary, Don Rodgers, said in an oral history that it was Curtin's 'finest speech'. There were 'tears on both sides of the House and even among hardened members of the press gallery', Rodgers said.

Although the invasion was repelled and the Japanese were probably never going to invade Australia, this was unknown at the time. Curtin used the Coral Sea battle to urge a greater contribution from all Australians to the war effort and increased Commonwealth powers to prosecute the war.

'A great naval battle is proceeding'

The House of Representatives, Canberra 8 May 1942

I have received a communiqué from the Commander-in-Chief of the Allied Forces … stating that a great naval battle is proceeding in the south-west Pacific area …

The events that are taking place today are of crucial importance to the conduct of the war in this theatre.

I have no information as to how the engagement is developing, but I should like the nation to be assured that there will be, on the part of our forces and the American forces, that devotion to duty which is characteristic of the naval and air forces of the United States of America, Great Britain and the Commonwealth.

I should add that at this moment nobody can tell what the result of the engagement may be. If it should go advantageously, we shall have cause for great gratitude and our position will then be a little clearer.

But if we should not have the advantages from this battle for which we hope, all that confronts us is a sterner ordeal, a greater and graver responsibility …

I ask the people of Australia, having regard to the grave consequences implicit in this engagement, to make a sober and realistic estimate of their duty to the nation.

As I speak, those who are participating in the engagement are conforming to the sternest discipline and are subjecting themselves with all that they have – it may be for many of them the last full measure of their devotion – to accomplish the increased safety and security of this territory.

In the face of an example of that description, I feel that it is not asking too much that every citizen who today is being defended by these gallant men in that engagement should regard himself as engaged in the second line of service to Australia.

This is today the front line; it needs the maximum support of every man and woman in the Commonwealth … I put it to any man whom my words may reach, however they may reach him, that he owes it to those men, and to the future of the country, not to be stinting in what he will do now for Australia.

Men are fighting for Australia today; those who are not fighting have no excuse for not working.

Source: Commonwealth of Australia Parliamentary Debates (Hansard).

JOHN CURTIN

'The compass of the labour movement'

*In this spellbinding performance, John Curtin invokes
Labor's values to win support for the war effort*

When John Curtin arrived in Sydney for the NSW Labor Party's 1943 conference, the poisonous forces aligned to former Premier Jack Lang were bracing for a showdown on conscription. Curtin had spent the previous few days in Sydney attending the War Cabinet. It was a cold winter. After he spoke to the conference, Curtin would be bed-ridden for several days, having succumbed to a virus. This fiery performance would strain his already weakened constitution.

In his speech, Curtin made the case for limited overseas conscription 'for our own security'. This was personally very difficult for Curtin as he had opposed conscription during the First World War. He also spoke of the things which made up 'the compass of the labour movement'. They were: 'to keep the country free for a free people', 'a better social order' and 'opportunities for treating the common man fairer and squarer'.

On conscription, Lang was rebuffed, with delegates voting 231-118 to support Curtin's proposal. This victory ensured that Curtin would prevail at the party's forthcoming federal conference.

There were ovations and cheers, before, during and after the hour-long speech. Curtin was a dynamic orator. He would raise and lower his voice. He would punch the air with his hands and sweep them from side to side as he pivoted to look at one section of the audience or another. He would button and unbutton his jacket as he spoke. David Day writes in his biography of Curtin that the journalist Edgar Holt reported: 'His voice rasped in emphasis, sobbed in emotion. He shouted. He whispered. He spoke of the greatness of the Labor Party's past, the grandeur of its future. Hard-bitten delegates fell into a trance – and when he stopped they cheered'.

The Sydney Morning Herald said it was 'Curtin's finest speaking effort as Prime Minister'. At the 1943 elections, the Herald argued, 'We could not choose a better leader today'.

'The compass of the labour movement'

Trades Hall, Sydney 6 June 1943

I propose to make some general observations about the labour movement, the country, the war and the state of the world ...

I feel that we have now reached the stage when a new page of the book of this war can be turned ...

The war has gone on and not until quite recently could it be said that the initiative, which had rested with the enemy, has now decisively parted from him ...

I leave out politics, I leave for the time being policy for the future, for upon success or failure of the war, as a war, depends things which are even more than policy – the survival of the country and the preservation of the right to frame policy let alone give effect to it ...

The position in the Pacific is that the Japanese are consolidating their positions and building air bases in the arc to the north of Australia extending from Timor to the Solomons. Their strength is growing. The system of bases and landing strips developed by the Japanese gives them great mobility and power to concentrate anywhere along the arc. The aim must be to pierce the arc of bases held by the Japanese to force their withdrawal or to isolate them in sections for later destruction ...

What part is Australia to play in thrusting the enemy away from the Commonwealth and in joining in the ultimate offensive for the defeat of Japan? There have been two major concepts as to the best way to defend Australia. One was held by the Menzies and Fadden governments, in which the primary military consideration was cooperation in overseas theatres. The other, for long advocated by the Labor Party, was that which, while fully endorsing cooperation in the scheme of Empire defence, placed the main emphasis on the government's responsibility for the local defence of the Commonwealth by all the resources in its power ...

Neither the Menzies government nor its military advisers provided for the contingency that Singapore might fall or that the British fleet might not come. Both these things happened and Australia lay almost impotent at the feet of the enemy. The perilous situation with which Australia was confronted has been greatly altered by the battle of the Coral Sea and the campaign in New Guinea.

The Labor Party's opposition to compulsory service outside Australia had all along been based on the Menzies government's conception that expeditionary forces to other parts of the world came first. With Labor in power and able to implement its defence policy of priority for local defence, there was a new basis for an entire transformation of Labor's attitude towards compulsory service in those regions essential for ensuring effective defence of the Commonwealth. It was from this angle that the government decided that the Defence Act should be amended to enable the Militia forces to serve outside Australia in the South-Western Pacific Zone.

When General MacArthur unfolded his plan of operation in the South-West Pacific Area to ensure the security of Australia as a base and to push the Japanese back, it was evident that the Australian land forces must be able to be disposed in any of the islands adjacent to Australia in accordance with the Commander-in-Chief's plan …

Let it be quite clear that there is no future for Australia with its white population, and no prospect of an increasingly higher standard of living, if the Japanese are to remain in possession of south-eastern Asia and the islands surrounding Australia …

The destiny of Australia and its future security may well be determined by the distance we are prepared to go in using our forces to defeat the Japanese. If the experience of this war has shown that the future security of Australia requires greater guarantees in regard to the security of islands adjacent to Australia, Australia cannot demand such guarantees if it is unwilling in war to use its forces in the ejectment of the enemy from these threatened points of attack …

There is still a long and difficult road to travel before victory over Japan is won and the journey will have its dark passages. Australia's effort must not be relaxed, but intensified, where possible, to an even higher degree. Australia must be satisfied with nothing less than the utmost of which it is capable. Anything less may make all the difference in the results for which we are fighting and working.

The people – the masses of this country – have rallied wholeheartedly, notwithstanding bad patches here and there. As a nation, the Australian people, for the first time in history attacked by an invader, has risen to the occasion and has supported any projects which the government has found necessary to provide for the conduct of the war …

This Labor government – as if it were by fate – was called upon to execute the major responsibility that any Australian government has had imposed upon it in the history of this country. Many, of course, may dislike the way this, that or the other has been done. I said that that is relatively unimportant. The problem was to keep the country free for a free people.

Over long years, the labour movement has been constantly engaged in reviewing the situation so that there might be a better social order; so that there might be a freer community; so that there might be opportunities for treating the common man fairer and squarer and more hopefully than was the case. It was engaged in the evolution of a nation. That has been the compass of the labour movement. As a result, the Labor Party of this country has been incorporated into the very soul of the Australian nation. It is integral with what is accepted as the true welfare of the people of Australia.

Over the years men have worked in the labour movement, officers have been elected; men have come in and men have gone out, and some have been pushed out. But no man has ever been pushed out because he had an idea to advance on which the governing body of labour could give its opinion and who sought authority for it.

When Japan struck against the security of Australia, there happened to be in the Commonwealth parliament a Labor Party in office which did not have a majority in the House of Representatives of its own party, nor a majority in the Senate of its own party. Any one of the regulations which this government has formulated for the conduct of the war had to be formulated in the sure and certain knowledge that it had not only to be good in itself but had to withstand the possibility of being disallowed before it could be applied. Not a piece of legislation could be framed by the cabinet with the certainty that it would be passed in the form in which the government framed it. This government not only had a war to fight but it also had to manage a parliament which no previous prime minister – and there had been two in this parliament – was capable of managing ...

The world can never be the same in the years to come – politically, governmentally, in transportation, in problems of defence and security as it was in the years before this war started. I say that the world is constantly changing. I say that the platform of twenty years ago will not meet the problems of today. I should hate to see the man who would say that the Labor platform, because it stood in 1902, or 1905 or 1908, must be the Labor platform today ...

I believe the inspiration for change, for progress, for all that demonstrates the best in the Australian people lies in the labour movement because it is the people's movement – it has no concern with big business and it stands for humanity as against material gain – and has more resilience, more decency and dignity and the best of the human qualities than any other political movement. I believe that the labour movement is vital to the good government and progress of Australia.

But I also believe that for that very reason the labour movement has a greater responsibility for the maintenance of Australia as a free people, for the defence of Australia as a land worth defending, than any other political party. This is our country. It will be the country of our sons and daughters.

It was the country where our forefathers came to broaden the constitution, to make the laws more amenable to the common man than the authority of the ruling classes. They came here because the old world was too despotic and unjust. They hoped to evolve a country where they would be free. We have to live up to it. We have to maintain this country as free people, but freedom has to be fought for, not only internally against those who would destroy it for wealth but to restrain the aggressor from without ...

I say to this labour movement, as one who has been a member for 36 years and who has been raised to the highest place in this Commonwealth – that it cannot stand still. It has to march with the advancing forces of the world ... I ask the labour movement for maximum cooperation with the government of Australia ... The Commonwealth government can get cooperation from Labor governments and it has also had cooperation from the constituent elements of the labour movement and I express my thanks.

It would have been a double strain without the support of my colleagues and this gives me an opportunity to pass on the debt of gratitude in my heart for the counsel and support of my friends who are in the labour movement and some men who are not in the labour movement. I have found this period not only a strain but a trusteeship which has remained in me. Many may not agree with all that has been done but all my actions have been induced by circumstances which no man can push aside. I have not faced a problem with a prejudice nor with a bias. I have endeavoured to find the correct answer. For any government that does not make mistakes will be a government of inertia and inaction and therefore, as there will be nothing for which to condemn it, there will be nothing for which to praise it.

I say that the use of Australian forces, resources, capacities, wealth and manpower in those areas and places where the struggle for Australia's security has to be faced, was as valid a use by this government as it will be in the years to come. I ask support for what the government has been called upon to do militarily and economically.

I ask for at least a kindly thought for the difficulties, politically. I ask the labour movement, with all the possibilities inherent in the situation in the years to come, to stand together because the true interests of the men and women of this country; their immediate problems, their future hopes are all bound up in the re-election of this government.

Source: The John Curtin Prime Ministerial Library.

Two of John Curtin's greatest speeches were delivered in London in 1944. In this photo, addressing the Guildhall, he was presented with the Freedom of the City. With his health rapidly fading, Curtin spoke with great force and conviction about freedom, democracy and social and economic advancement as the purpose behind the war. Those who were present said it was one of the finest speeches they had ever heard.
Source: John Curtin Prime Ministerial Library

JOHN CURTIN

'The cause of freedom will be victorious'
'Those 22 yards of turf'

John Curtin speaks movingly about the importance of
freedom and democracy to London audiences

When John Curtin went to London in May 1944, he was not a well man. He had travelled from the United States where he had met with Franklin D Roosevelt, but due to illness had to cancel several other engagements. In London, he held several meetings and visited the House of Commons to watch Winston Churchill speak.

A ceremony was held at the Guildhall in London, where Curtin was presented with the Freedom of the City by the Lord Mayor, Sir Frank Newson-Smith.

Lloyd Ross writes in his biography of Curtin that, as Curtin 'rose to speak, he stumbled, and had to be guided forward'. At the microphone, he discarded his notes and extemporised, with an eloquence rarely surpassed. He spoke of the 'struggle' of the war, the cause of freedom and democracy, and 'the true dignity of man'. He spoke of the poor, whose 'hopes of betterment and of improvement' were at 'stake'. He spoke of Britain as 'the very cradle of liberty', defended parliamentary democracy, the clash of ideas and the contestability of the party system.

Later, the Corporation of the City of London hosted a luncheon, held at Mansion House. Many politicians were present, including British Labour leader, Clement Atlee.

There, Curtin spoke passionately about Australia's British heritage. 'Australia is a British people', he said, 'Australia is a British land'. Curtin said that both countries shared an 'unconquerable spirit which refuses to acknowledge defeat' at cricket. He declared that 'Lords is to Australia what it is to this country' and, in prosecuting the war, 'we are helping to defend those 22 yards of turf'.

Curtin would visit Lords three days later, for the first time.

'The cause of freedom will be victorious'

The Guildhall, London 10 May 1944

My Lord Mayor, your Grace, my Lords, Ladies and Gentlemen, it is a very great honour that has been paid to my country today and others. As its servant I cannot but feel a high sense of personal pride that I should be the human instrument whereby the City of London indicates to the people of the Commonwealth of Australia that what they have done and will continue to do has the respect of this august city.

Many men in the past have sought and many are seeking now by violence to get for themselves the City of London, but that they can never do. Conquest is not the title that aggressors can employ in order to achieve the great honour that has been freely given to the people of Australia today. Not by war can freedom be attained; but by war all too often it has to be maintained. And the struggle that we are now engaged in cannot end until those who have sought to destroy the world have been defeated and deprived of the strength that they now employ. Not until then can it be said that freedom can be maintained by us for ourselves and for the world at large. Nor it can be gained by those who have drawn the sword.

The crucial issue in the world today is that freedom is at stake. If the British nation, its Allies, and the freedom loving peoples are defeated then freedom disappears from the entire world and it is because our own rights have been struck at and that our rights involve the rights of others equally with ourselves, that the people of this country, which is the very cradle of democratic liberty, where it has been nurtured and evolved and set the model for the world at large, here there is a keen perception of the innate nature of the struggle. But that perception is as clearly realised by the men and women of the Dominions as it is realised here …

In all the theatres the struggle is still raging furiously as has been said earlier today. Nations have been subjugated, their institutions have been destroyed, their people reduced to the status of helots in the labour service of those who conquered them. What they can do in the way of production and service ministers to the strength that we and our Allies have yet to overcome.

And therefore it is demanded by the very nature of the struggle, not by the mere proclamations of the Prime Ministers, but by the character of the war, that the complete resources of all the Allies and those who hope that they will succeed, every bit of that is not too much to use in order that victory may be assured and in any event to make certain that the time when it will come shall not be indefinitely prolonged.

I have stated to you what I know and believe to be the conception that the people of Australia have of the nature and consequences of this war. We are to win or lose it all. There can be no half way to the termination of this struggle. This world cannot stand repetitions of these colossal calamities every twenty-five years or so and thus it is requisite that having been given no alternative but to defend ourselves, we shall go on until such time as it will be impossible for malignant forces to re-incubate the conditions which will compel the world to resort to war.

The freedom of this City cannot but mean much to the minds of men which you have already had described to you as indicating at least some part of the sort of man I have been. Yes, I was a printer's devil and I, of course, like many others of my fellow countrymen and countrywomen have had what has been described as 'humble origins'. Yes, the poor have a stake in this struggle, the very very poor equally with the very very rich. The rich may have that which they now possess to maintain, but the poor have all their hopes of betterment and of improvement, one of the crucial issues of this conflict for the enemy commenced his campaign of world denial of liberty by destroying such institutions as he had in his own country which rested upon the same postulate of liberty. He denied the right of association to the workers. He burned the Parliament so that the free people would not have representative spokesmen in the places where laws were made.

There was at once an indication of complete antagonism between the conception of life as held by the aggressor and the conception of life which is the very foundation upon which the great Empire has been evolved – the right of people to quarrel with their own government, to criticise it, to defeat it, to provide an alternative to it, one which would undertake as it were some legislation after their own heart's desire.

These things may not be related intimately to the material world, but they are inherently part of the true dignity of man. They have in themselves, at any rate, the ingredients upon which the very essentials of liberty find subsistence …

There are times in the history of man's episodical life in which only by being strong can he be certain that he can be preserved. There is no orderly evolution that man has undergone. There are occasions in which the exercise of the strongest authority is necessary to preserve the greatest liberty. This is such an occasion. It is not the first occasion, but we do hope that it will be the last. That is the prayer of the Dominions.

But prayer alone is not sufficient, it has to be accompanied by work. It has to be made clear to the enemy that in the unity of labour and the gallantry of the forces and the steadfastness in the factories, and workshops, and in the places where tools of war are being fabricated there is not one moment being lost. There is full devotion to the task of providing the men of the forces, whether they be the land forces, the air forces, or the men on the sea, with all that is requisite, mechanically and materially, for the work and service that they render, so that they are given the greatest possible aid …

Just as, one hundred and forty years ago, someone in this City, the prime minister of that day, said that it was the exaltation of the people of Britain to have withstood everything that despotism and ambition could attempt, and it was their greater exaltation to hold out the prospect to subjugated peoples of an early liberation, so today we echo those words.

We say that, having withstood for ourselves the attack which the enemy has made upon us, so we hold out the prospect of early liberation to the nations now ground under the oppressor's heel.

'Those 22 yards of turf'

Mansion House, London 10 May 1944

The references which the Lord Mayor has made to Australia as having done something in the defence of Britain and the British Empire are references which no doubt he feels warranted in making. But we would feel very negligent if there had not been on our part that readiness to act which has been referred to in such appreciative terms.

You see, Australia is a British people. Australia is a British land, and the 7,000,000 Australians are 7,000,000 Britishers. They are located in the antipodes, but they are not a bit different from those in any part of the country …

But it is the stock from which Australia has come which gives to it its fibre, its physical stamina, the endurance of its people in adversity, and that unconquerable spirit which refuses to acknowledge defeat.

You have had some evidence of that at Lord's now and again. Lords is to Australia what it is to this country. We would refuse to contemplate a world in which there would be a jurisdiction over Lord's which would prohibit the playing of test matches. While we may argue about whether or not the game is played according to the rules, we most certainly decline to permit some intruder to decide what the rules should be.

We are helping to defend this historic city of London and those 22 yards of turf which we hope will be used time and time again, so that the motherland and Australia can decide whether the six-ball over is better than the eight-ball over …

We entered upon this struggle for the same reasons and the same high purpose as animated you. That purpose has yet to be vindicated. We shall be inflexible in our resolve to achieve that end.

It is true that we do not like wars. They take too much from the inadequate resources which we have for the promotion of the welfare of the people. But there obviously were to be no limits to this conflagration, and once the King of England was at war the King of Australia was at war. Paying homage to the one King, regarding themselves as part of a union, Australians knew quite well that, as the whole was greater than the parts, you could not defend the whole by allowing any of its parts to be ravaged by an aggressor.

There is no difference of opinion as to how our communities should be governed. They should be governed by the people themselves. That belief we have inherited from your own struggle. We have modelled our political system on the system which your forebears fought for and evolved, and now in the British Commonwealth we have a fraternisation of equals.

Source: The John Curtin Prime Ministerial Library.

BEN CHIFLEY

'The war is over'

Ben Chifley announces to the nation that the Second World War has ended

Ben Chifley was the fifth Prime Minister to lead the nation during the Second World War. He had succeeded John Curtin only a month before the war ended. He had been intimately involved in the war effort, particularly the plans for post-war reconstruction, and he was determined to avoid an economic depression when the war ended.

The Second World War had been fought in far away battlefields abroad and on the nation's doorstep. The war had impacted greatly on the home front with almost all sectors of the economy focused on supporting the war effort. The war in the Pacific came to a close a week after atomic bombs were dropped on the Japanese cities of Hiroshima and Nagasaki in early August. The war in Europe had ended months earlier.

When the Allied terms for peace were accepted by the Japanese, Chifley announced to the nation, in his characteristic raspy voice, 'Fellow citizens, the war is over'. In this nationwide broadcast from the ABC studios in Canberra, made at 9.30 am on 15 August 1945, Chifley announces the end of the war. *The Canberra Times* reported that the broadcast was made almost simultaneously with other world leaders.

He offers, first, thanks to God. He remembers those who have given their lives in the service of their nation. He thanks those who supported the war effort at home. He recognises the service of military leaders and recalls the deaths during the war of Franklin D Roosevelt and Curtin. 'And now', he says, 'our men and women will come home'. He calls upon all Australians to celebrate 'this great victory and deliverance' and to look longer term, and 'join together in the march of our nation to future greatness'.

'The war is over'

Broadcast, Canberra 15 August 1945

Fellow citizens, the war is over.

The Japanese government has accepted the terms of surrender imposed by the Allied nations and hostilities will now cease …

At this moment, let us offer thanks to God.

Let us remember those whose lives were given that we may enjoy this glorious moment and may look forward to a peace which they have won for us. Let us remember those whose thoughts, with proud sorrow, turn towards gallant, loved ones who will not come back.

On behalf of the people and government of Australia, I offer humble thanks to the fighting men of the United Nations, whose gallantry, sacrifice and devotion to duty have brought us the victory. Nothing can fully repay the debt we owe them, nor can history record in adequate terms their deeds from the black days that followed September 1939, and December 1941, until this moment.

We owe, too, a great debt to those men and women who performed miracles of production, in secondary and primary industries, so that the battle of supply could be won and a massive effort achieved …

I am sure that you would like me to convey to the commanders of the fighting forces the warmest thanks for their skill, efficiency and great devotion. Especially do I mention General Douglas MacArthur, with whom we had so much in common and with whom we shared the dangers when Australia was threatened with invasion.

In your name, I offer to the leaders of the United Nations our congratulation and thanks. We join with the United States in a common regret that their inspiring leader, the late Mr (Franklin) Roosevelt, did not live to see this day. We thank his successor, President (Harry) Truman, for the work he has done. Australians, too, will feel their happiness tinged with sorrow that another man, who gave his all, was not spared to be with us today. That man was John Curtin. To Mr (Winston) Churchill, Generalissimo (Josef) Stalin and Generalissimo Chiang Kai-shek go the unstinted thanks of free people everywhere for what they have done for the common cause. Especially do we honour Mr Churchill, with whom in the dark days – to use his own words – we had the honour to stand alone against aggression.

And now our men and women will come home; our fighting men with battle honours thick upon them from every theatre of war. Australians stopped the Japanese in their drive south, just as they helped start the first march towards ultimate victory in North Africa. Australians fought in the battles of the air everywhere and Australian seamen covered every ocean. They are coming home to a peace which has to be won.

The United Nations Charter for a world organisation is the hope of the world and Australia has pledged the same activity in making it successful as she showed in the framing of it.

Here in Australia, there is much to be done. The Australian government, which stood steadfast during the dread days of war, will give all it has to working and planning to ensure that the peace will be a real thing. I ask that the state governments and all sections of the community should cooperate in facing the tasks and solving the problems that are ahead. Let us join together in the march of our nation to future greatness.

You are aware of what has been arranged for the celebration of this great victory and deliverance. In the name of the Commonwealth government, I invite you to join in the thanksgiving services arranged, for truly this is a time to give thanks to God and to those men against whose sacrifice for us there is no comparison.

Source: AW Stargardt, Things Worth Fighting For: Speeches by Joseph Benedict Chifley, *Melbourne University Press, Melbourne, 1952.*

ARTHUR CALWELL

'On the side of sanity and in the cause of humanity'

Arthur Calwell delivers his finest speech, opposing the Vietnam War, and promises that Labor will be vindicated

In this speech, Labor leader Arthur Calwell responds to the ministerial statement by Prime Minister Robert Menzies announcing the decision to send combat troops to Vietnam.

It is a decision, Calwell says, which Labor opposes 'firmly and completely'. Calwell outlines the folly of the Vietnam War, how it does not address 'the Communist challenge', that it is not in the interests of Australia or the United States, and prophesises its eventual failure. He believes that the United States will withdraw after 'becoming interminably bogged down in the awful morass of this war'. He predicts an increase in Australian forces over time and the likely conscription of young Australians.

Graham Freudenberg, who drafted the speech, argues 'the later reputation of this speech rests mainly on the accuracy of its predictions'. It also shows a deep understanding of the Vietnam conflict, of the nature of jungle warfare, the history of the Vietnamese people and the strategic challenges facing Australia.

Calwell addresses part of his speech to the Labor Party: 'I also offer you the sure and certain knowledge that we will be vindicated; that generations to come will record with gratitude that when a reckless government wilfully endangered the security of this nation, the voice of the Australian Labor Party was heard, strong and clear, on the side of sanity and in the cause of humanity, and in the interests of Australia's security'.

Labor suffered a heavy defeat at the subsequent 1966 elections.

In his memoir, *Be Just and Fear Not*, Calwell said some in the party did not want to oppose the war so strongly. But, he argued, 'there are great issues that demand that every politician should stand up for the truth as he sees it and take the consequences'.

'On the side of sanity and in the cause of humanity'

The House of Representatives, Canberra 4 May 1965

The government's decision to send the First Battalion of the Australian Regular Army to Vietnam is, without question, one of the most significant events in the history of this Commonwealth …

The over-riding issue which this parliament has to deal with at all times is the nation's security. All our words, all our policies, all our actions, must be judged ultimately by this one crucial test: what best promotes our national security, what best guarantees our national survival? It is this test which the Labor Party has applied to the government's decision …

Therefore, on behalf of all my colleagues of Her Majesty's Opposition, I say that we oppose the government's decision to send 800 men to fight in Vietnam. We oppose it firmly and completely …

It is not our desire, when servicemen are about to be sent to distant battlefields, and then war, cruel, costly and interminable, stares us in the face, that the nation should be divided. But it is the government which has brought this tragic situation about and we will not shirk our responsibilities in stating the views we think serve Australia best. Our responsibility, like that of the government, is great but, come what may, we will do our duty as we see it and know it to be towards the people of Australia and our children's children. Therefore, I say, we oppose this decision firmly and completely.

We do not think it is a wise decision. We do not think it is a timely decision. We do not think it is a right decision. We do not think it will help the fight against Communism. On the contrary, we believe it will harm that fight in the long term.

We do not believe it will promote the welfare of the people of Vietnam. On the contrary, we believe it will prolong and deepen the suffering of that unhappy people so that Australia's very name may become a term of reproach among them.

We do not believe that it represents a wise or even intelligent response to the challenge of Chinese power. On the contrary, we believe it mistakes entirely the nature of that power, and that it materially assists China in her subversive aims …

We of the Labor Party do not believe that this decision serves, or is consist-ent with, the immediate strategic interests of Australia. On the contrary, we believe that, by sending one quarter of our pitifully small effective military strength to distant Vietnam, this government dangerously denudes Australia and its immediate strategic environs of effective defence power.

Thus, for all these and other reasons, we believe we have no choice but to oppose this decision in the name of Australia and of Australia's security.

I propose to show that the government's decision rests on three false assumptions: an erroneous view of the nature of the war in Vietnam; a failure to understand the nature of the Communist challenge; and a false notion as to the interests of America and her allies. No debate on the government's decision can proceed, or even begin, unless we make an attempt to understand the nature of the war in Vietnam.

The government takes the grotesquely over-simplified position that this is a straight-forward case of aggression from North Vietnam against an independent South Vietnam …

The government then takes this theory a little further by cleverly pointing to the undoubted fact that just as Communist North Vietnam lies north of South Vietnam, so Communist China lies north of North Vietnam. Thus, according to this simplified, not to say simple, theory, everything falls into place and the whole operation becomes, in the prime minister's words 'part of a thrust by Communist China between the Indian and Pacific Oceans' …

But is this picture of Chinese military aggression thrusting down inexorably through Indo-China, Malaysia and Indonesia to Australia a true or realistic one? … I believe it does not …

That there has long been, and still is, aggression from the North and subversion inspired from the North, I do not for one moment deny. But the war in South Vietnam, the war to which we are sending this one battalion as a beginning in our commitment, is also a civil war and it is a guerrilla war. The great majority of the Vietcong are South Vietnamese. The object of the Vietcong in the war – this guerrilla war – is to avoid as far as possible direct entanglement with massed troops in order that by infiltration, subversion and terrorism, they may control villages, hamlets, outposts and small communities wherever these are most vulnerable …

To call it simply 'foreign aggression' as the prime minister does, and as his colleagues do, is to misrepresent the facts and, thereby, confuse the issue with which we must ultimately come to terms …

What support has the present government, the eighth of ninth regimes since the murder of Diem 18 months ago? It has no basis of popular support. It presumably has the support of the Army, or the ruling junta of the Army. It will fail and be replaced when it loses the support of the ruling junta, or when that junta itself is replaced by another. That has happened eight or nine times in the past year and a half …

The government of South Vietnam does not base itself on popular support. Yet this is the government at whose request, and in whose support, we are to commit a battalion of Australian fighting men … And we are told we are doing this in the name of the free and independent government and people of South Vietnam. I do not believe it, and neither does anybody else who considers the matter with any degree of intelligence …

Our men will be fighting the largely indigenous Vietcong in their own home territory. They will be fighting in the midst of a largely indifferent, if not resentful, and frightened population. They will be fighting at the request of, and in support, and presumably, under the direction of an unstable, inefficient, partially corrupt military regime which lacks even the semblance of being, or becoming, democratically based. But, it will be said, even if this is true, that there are far larger considerations – China must be stopped, the United States must not be humiliated in Asia …

Humiliation for America could come in two ways – either by outright defeat, which is unlikely, or by her becoming interminably bogged down in the awful morass of this war, as France was for ten years. That situation would in turn lead to one of two things – withdrawal through despair, or all out war, through despair. Both these would be equally disastrous …

I cannot refrain from making an observation about Australia's trade with China … The government justifies its action on the ground of Chinese expansionist aggression. And yet this same government is willing to continue and expand trade in strategic materials with China … The government may be able to square its conscience on this matter, but this is logically and morally impossible.

Finally, there is the question of Australia's immediate strategic concern … We are the only country in the world fighting on two fronts in South East Asia. America is committed to Vietnam. Britain is committed to Malaysia. Australia, with its limited resources, with its meagre defences, has obligations in Vietnam, Malaya, Borneo and New Guinea. The commitments are apparently without end, in size and in number.

How long will it be before we are drawing upon our conscript youth to service these growing and endless requirements? … If the government now says that conscripts will not be sent, this means that the 1st Battalion is never to be reinforced, replaced or replenished. If this is not so, then the government must have a new policy on the use of conscripts – a policy not yet announced …

I cannot close without addressing a word directly to our fighting men … Our hearts and prayers are with you. Our minds and reason cannot support those who have made the decision to send you to this war, and we shall do our best to have that decision reversed. But we shall do our duty to the utmost in supporting you to do your duty. In terms of everything that an army in the field requires, we shall never deny you the aid and support that is your right to expect in the service of your country.

To the members of the government, I say only this: If, by the process of misinterpretation of our motives, in which you are so expert, you try to further divide this nation for political purposes, yours will be a dreadful responsibility, and you will have taken a course which you will live to regret.

And may I, through you, Mr Speaker, address this message to the members of my own party – my colleagues here in this parliament, and that vast band of Labor men and women outside: the course we have agreed to take today is fraught with difficulty. I cannot promise you that easy popularity can be bought in times like these; nor are we looking for it. We are doing our duty as we see it. When the drums beat and the trumpets sound, the voice of reason and right can be heard in the land only with difficulty. But if we are to have the courage of our convictions, then we must do our best to make that voice heard.

I offer you the probability that you will be traduced, that your motives will be misrepresented, that your patriotism will be impugned, that your courage will be called into question. But I also offer you the sure and certain knowledge that we will be vindicated; that generations to come will record with gratitude that when a reckless government wilfully endangered the security of this nation, the voice of the Australian Labor Party was heard, strong and clear, on the side of sanity and in the cause of humanity, and in the interests of Australia's security …

Source: Commonwealth of Australia Parliamentary Debates (Hansard).

Arthur Calwell's finest speech as party leader was when he outlined Labor's opposition to the Vietnam War. It was a position that cost Labor dearly at the 1966 election. But as Calwell predicted in 1965, the war would end in failure and the party's opposition to the conflict would be 'vindicated' by history.
Source: Australian Labor Party (Victorian Branch)

JIM CAIRNS

'Government by the people demands action by the people'

The leader of the Vietnam War Moratorium Movement, Jim Cairns, calls on the government to listen to the people

As opposition to the Vietnam War intensified, Jim Cairns became the unofficial leader of the Victorian Vietnam Moratorium Campaign (VMC), seeking to end Australia's involvement in the war. He advocated public protests and defying unjust laws as a legitimate form of political agitation.

In Parliament, the Gorton government's Attorney-General, Tom Hughes, argued that the VMC was a violent, anti-democratic, communist-controlled insurgency.

During this important debate in Parliament, Cairns recounted the history of Vietnamese occupation and defended those engaged in peaceful protest. Cairns said those who protest do not need 'to explain their conduct'. Declaring that 'times are changing', Cairns said the right to peaceful protest is as central to democracy as Parliament itself, which he labelled as a 'fossilised institution'. 'Democracy is government by the people', Cairns argued, 'and government by the people demands action by the people'.

Shortly after this speech was given, Cairns would lead more than 100,000 protestors through the streets of Melbourne in the first of several great marches opposed to the Vietnam War.

In an interview with Barry Cairns, Jim's son, for this book in 2010, he said that the family had grave concerns for Cairns' safety, but knew that what he was trying to achieve was important, and so the family supported him in those efforts.

When Cairns died in 2003, his colleague Tom Uren said 'never in my life have I heard or seen an audience give so much respect to a public figure – they showed their love for him. It was his enormous courage that made him such a magnificent individual. He drew great strength from the warmth of an audience, and they drew strength from him'.

For the message of peace, the defence of the right to protest, the integrity, courage and convictions of Cairns, and the ultimate vindication that his cause was right, this is a great Labor speech.

'Government by the people demands action by the people'

The House of Representatives, Canberra 14 April 1970

The argument by the Attorney-General is that the Vietnam Moratorium Campaign is not genuine – that it is not made up of people who genuinely feel strongly about what they are doing: they do not really know what they are doing. His argument is that it is the result of influences from overseas without which, in effect, there would be no campaign at all.

The Minister may not know how people feel about this war in Vietnam.

He may not even know how people feel about conscription, but there is a very deeply felt opposition to what is happening in Vietnam and to conscription of young Australians without a fair principle of conscientious objection …

I concede the minister may not even know this but there is a very deeply felt opposition in the community to the government. There is a deeply felt opposition in the world to what is happening in Vietnam …

Nothing that the Attorney-General has said is based on fact or evidence. No facts or evidence have been given by himself or any of his predecessors to support their assertions of links with Peking or some other place.

There is no need for any conspiracy theory to explain the opposition to what is being done in Vietnam. It exists all round the world. It is only in Australia that this communist conspiracy theory is ever put forward by responsible people. In most other countries a person is given credit for his views on any matter at all and these views are examined on their merits. But that does not happen here …

Vietnam is a small peasant country that has suffered foreign occupation for over 130 years and a movement to resist it has existed unbrokenly for all those long years. That movement resisted and fought French occupation from 1847 to 1941 and suffered severe and appalling casualties. Perhaps 500,000 people were killed by bullets and bombs and millions died directly as a result of the war. The Vietnamese were deprived of human dignity, even of human identity, and were demeaned and depraved by the war.

Then between 1941 and 1945, Vietnam was treated as a mere pawn in the game of big power by the Soviet Union, China, America and Britain. There was no Atlantic Charter for Vietnam.

Then when the Vietnamese movement for national independence had become so strong that the French were forced to recognise it, they immediately began a campaign to undermine and destroy it. In this campaign from 1946 to 1954 about 550,000 Vietnamese, mostly civilians, were killed and as many were maimed and wounded.

But the Vietnamese won their battles against the French and for a short time they appeared to have won their independence. Then they were deprived of it by a big power arrangement at Geneva

Then the world's greatest industrial and military power, America, stepped into the shoes of the French – with the expressed intention of holding as much as possible of Vietnam under its control.

And so the fighting went on.

Between 1946 and 1970, perhaps as many as 250,000 armed Vietnamese have been killed and 350,000 civilians have also been killed by bullets and bombs in South Vietnam alone. As many as 90,000, mostly civilians, in North Vietnam have been killed. Much of the rest of the country has been burned and bombed half-way back to the Stone Age. In South Vietnam what is not some kind of den of corruption is a brothel.

That is what has been done for Vietnam and that is why the opposition to the war is natural and understandable.

There is intense and widespread opposition to the death and destruction. It needs no messages or control from Hanoi or Peking. Is it surprising that there is intense opposition to what has happened in Vietnam from students, workers and all sorts of people all around Australia and in every country of the world?

There is surely a limit to the number of human beings anyone will kill – even if they are coloured, foreign and Communist – to achieve any particular purpose. What is the limit in Vietnam? Is there any limit?

It is not those who oppose the war who are in such a strange position that they should be asked to explain their conduct.

It is not those who oppose the war who need some international system of obedience and orders, or rewards and benefits to explain their conduct

It is the supporters of the war in Vietnam who need to explain what they do.

It is not they who are responding to orders from abroad …

A question now arises: What is such a person expected to do if he feels this way? Is he expected to retire into apathy and disinterest?

The answer to this question requires an understanding of what democracy is. Some people seem to think that democracy is just parliament alone. They seem to think that all the ordinary citizen has to do is vote once every two or three years and then leave everything to the constitution and those who happen to be elected to parliament.

But times are changing. A whole generation is not prepared to accept this complacent, conservative theory. Parliament is not democracy. It is one of the manifestations of democracy and it can become a most important manifestation of democracy if people are prepared to come out of their apathy and do something about it.

What has to be done is not merely to refuse to talk politics or religion, as is almost the general custom, to vote once every two or three years and leave everything to those who win seats in parliament. This is the way to make parliament a hollow ritual and a fraud, which it has recently been called by leading journalists who observe its proceedings …

Democracy is government by the people, and government by the people demands action by the people. It demands effective ways of showing what the interests and needs of the people really are. It demands action in public places all around the land. The authorities of today are not accustomed to that. The laws restrict this action, and governments panic and even stimulate fear and insecurity.

I believe that in normal circumstance action by the people should be peaceful, inoffensive and dignified. We can guarantee that only if fair and reasonable outlets are available for protest and dissent. They are no available today, and so no-one can guarantee that results in those circumstances. I deplore violence and repudiate anyone who initiates it or deliberately uses it …

I will oppose the war in Vietnam with anyone who opposes it. I will not be deterred from doing so by threats or pressures or intimidation. I sincerely hope that no-one else will be deterred …

I will not be deterred from reasonable public political actions by fears that something might go wrong. I will do everything in my power to prevent it from going wrong – but I am not going to work within the limits imposed by my political opponents …

On 1st June 1951 JB (Joseph Benedict) Chifley said:

> I can only hope that you will be inspired by the same things which inspired the pioneers of this movement, and that you will not be frightened … over to the 'right' because of the whispered word 'Communist'. I could not be called a young radical. But a thing it worth fighting for, no matter what the penalty is, I will fight for the right, and truth and justice will prevail.

Ben Chifley had no intention of being frightened over to the right because of the whispered word 'communist' …

I do not think that anyone must be deterred from working against the immoral and unjust military invasion by Vietnam by the Australian government and its allies. I hope that every Australian citizen will realise that if he is to govern himself he cannot perform that task by leaving it to others. He must perform that task himself.

Democracy begins on the farms, in the factories and in the streets, and if people will not, often at risk to themselves, stand up for their rights in those places there will be no democracy. I do not think the generation over 35 years of age realises the significance of how thoroughly this thinking has gripped the younger generation …

Of course, unless there is a change there will be difficulties in the future development and extension of democracy, because democracy is government by the people. What is being done in the Vietnam Moratorium Campaign is an example of government by the people; it is an example of people taking action about issues that are important to them, actions which they believe will be influential in the making of national decisions that are open to them and in the ways in which they can make their decisions effective.

The important thing for us, to my mind, is to work for a proper, peaceful and dignified expression of that activity and not endeavour to blackguard it, as the minister did by his statement this evening, or to drive it into corners so that it would become the problem that the minister seems to think it is already.

Source: Commonwealth of Australia Parliamentary Debates (Hansard).

In this photo taken in 1970, Jim Cairns leads 100,000 activists through the streets of Melbourne protesting against the Vietnam War. Cairns, who was also a federal Labor MP and later served as Treasurer in the Whitlam government, was the undisputed leader of the Victorian Vietnam Moratorium Campaign. Few speakers could electrify an audience like Cairns.

Source: National Library of Australia

BOB HAWKE

'These hills rang with their voices and ran with their blood'
'We do not come here to glorify war'

*Bob Hawke recalls the Anzac legend, born at Gallipoli,
on the 75th anniversary of the battle*

In 1990, Bob Hawke travelled to Turkey to speak at a ceremony commemorating the 75th anniversary of the landings at Gallipoli in Turkey, during the First World War. Joining him on a chartered RAAF jet were 58 veterans of the war.

Hawke spoke briefly at a dawn service at Anzac Cove and then later at Lone Pine. The speech was drafted by Graham Freudenberg, whose father was a stretcher-bearer at Gallipoli. On the RAAF plane to Turkey, Hawke read passages from the journal written by Freudenberg's father.

At the Lone Pine ceremony, Hawke reflected on the sacrifice of the soldiers and drew on the wider 'meaning of the ANZAC tradition, forged in the fires of Gallipoli'. He spoke of the 'heroism and human waste' of Gallipoli, the 'untold sacrifice and suffering' and the 'terrible forces unleashed upon the world' by war.

There are echoes of Abraham Lincoln: 'hallowed ground' and how we cannot 'dedicate' an already 'sacred' battlefield of war but, rather, we must 'dedicate ourselves' to the larger meaning of their sacrifice.

'It was one of the most memorable experiences of my prime ministership', Hawke said in an interview for this book in July 2010. 'I can remember there were two extraordinary aspects of the day', Hawke recalled. When the diggers saw the young Australian backpackers, 'they just embraced one another', Hawke said, 'bringing tears to the eyes'. When the Australian veterans met the Turkish veterans, 'they also embraced one another'.

Freudenberg says the Lone Pine speech was the best speech that he ever wrote for Hawke.

'These hills rang with their voices and ran with their blood'

Dawn Service, Gallipoli, Turkey 25 April 1990

The Anzacs who came ashore at this place, at this hour, on this day, seventy-five years ago, and their comrades who followed them here during the eight long months of the dreadful combat that ensued, were not, despite all their efforts, to achieve their military objectives.

But because of the courage with which they fought, because of their devotion to duty and their comradeship, because of their ingenuity, their good humour and their endurance, because these hills rang with their voices and ran with their blood, this place Gallipoli is, in one sense, a part of Australia.

So we return to this remote peninsula today, privileged in the company of some of the diggers who fought here, and proud to identify in their exploits the very character of our nation.

We have not come in order to dedicate this place – it is already sacred because of the bravery and the bloodshed of the Anzacs.

We should instead dedicate ourselves to keeping bright the memory of those men who so unstintingly did what was asked of them on our behalf and to ensuring that the freedom and peace for which they so ardently yearned, for which they so bravely fought, and for which so many of them so selflessly gave their lives, shall not pass away.

Let us remember too, in respect, the valour of those Turkish soldiers who died here in defence of their country.

As dawn broke on this day in 1915, a terrible slaughter began.

Today, as dawn emerges from the blackness of night, let us hope that the nations of the earth are emerging from the self-destructive practices of enmity and will build, in sunlight, a world of peace.

Source: The Bob Hawke Prime Ministerial Library.

'We do not come here to glorify war'

Lone Pine, Gallipoli, Turkey 25 April 1990

The landings on Gallipoli seventy-five years ago were followed by eight months of untold sacrifice and suffering, which were to claim the lives of more than one hundred thousand men of the armies of Turkey, Germany, France, Britain, India, Canada, New Zealand and Australia.

No place on the Gallipoli Peninsula was more fiercely contested than these few acres where we now stand – known to the Anzacs who captured it as Lone Pine, and to the Turkish soldiers who defended it to the last, as the Ridge of Blood.

In three days of literally hand to hand combat, in August 1915, more than two thousand Australians and five thousand Turks died here. Seven of the nine Victoria Crosses awarded to Australians at Gallipoli were won here.

In a unique act of honour to fallen foes, the people and government of Turkey have dedicated this ground as a memorial to the eight thousand seven hundred Australians who died on Gallipoli.

In making this pilgrimage today, we first pay the tribute of honour to the fallen of Turkey, fighting on their own soil, dying in defence of their home-land, inspired by the indomitable leadership of a Man of Destiny, Mustafa Kemal – known to history as Kemal Ataturk.

Let it be said at once: for us, the people of Australia and New Zealand, the heirs to Anzac, the meaning of Gallipoli can never be measured by mere numbers of the slain. In those terms, Gallipoli was but an initiation to the killing fields of France and Flanders.

And let it be said also that we do not come here to glorify war.

For us, no place on earth more grimly symbolises the waste and futility of war – this scene of carnage in a campaign which failed.

It is not in the waste of war that Australians find the meaning of Gallipoli – then or now.

I say 'then or now' for a profound reason. For the meaning of the Anzac tradition, forged in the fires of Gallipoli, must be learned anew, from genera-tion to generation …

In the continuing quest for the real meaning of Anzac, our way is lit by the shining presence here today of the little band of first Anzacs, who have returned.

This is, for all of us here, and for all our fellow Australians at home, an honour, an experience, an emotion, which goes beyond words. These men know the truth of Gallipoli. They would be the last to claim that they were heroes – but indeed they were.

They did not pretend to fathom the deep and immense tides of history which brought them to these shores, at the crossroads of civilisation, so far from home, so far from all they knew and loved.

They did not see themselves as holding in their hands the destiny of six mighty Empires – all now vanished.

Nor could they begin to imagine that the vast and terrible forces unleashed upon the world in 1914 would still be working their way through human history 75 years on.

But they knew two things: they had a job to do; and they knew that in the end, they could only rely on each other to see it through – they knew they depended on their mates …

In that recognition of the special meaning of Australian mateship, the self-recognition of their dependence upon one another … there lay the genesis of the Anzac tradition.

And at the heart of that tradition lay a commitment. It was a simple but deep commitment to one another, each to his fellow Australian. And in that commitment, I believe, lies the enduring meaning of Anzac, then and today and for the future.

It is that commitment, now as much as ever – now, with all the vast changes occurring in our nation, more than ever – it is that commitment to Australia, which defines, and alone defines, what it is to be an Australian. The commitment is all …

In all the story of heroism and human waste that was Gallipoli, nothing is more honourable than the custodianship of this hallowed ground by the people and government of Turkey for seventy-five years.

Australia does not forget.

At the going down of the sun and in the morning we will remember them.

Source: The Bob Hawke Prime Ministerial Library.

PAUL KEATING

'These battles were fought, not for the glory of war, but for humanity'

*Paul Keating enlarges the Anzac legend at Kokoda, a
place of hallowed ground for Australians*

Paul Keating's first trip abroad as Prime Minister, to Indonesia and Papua New Guinea, coincided with the 50th anniversary of the battles that took place in Papua New Guinea during the Second World War.

In book *Engagement*, Keating wrote that 'the deeds and courage of Australians who had defended their country in Papua New Guinea ... had not been sufficiently acknowledged'.

So in the stifling tropical heat at Ela Beach in Port Moresby on Anzac Day 1992, Keating described the battles as 'the most important ever fought' because the Australian soldiers had 'fought and died not in defence of the old world, but the new world'.

It was an important statement for a nation accustomed to the Anzac legend born at Gallipoli. It was not designed to denigrate Gallipoli – far from it – but equally to recognise that the legend was 'revisited' in the Second World War by Australian soldiers who 'believed in Australia – in the democracy they built, in the life they had made there, and the future they believed their country held'.

The following day, Keating flew to sites along the Kokoda Track, and later described how he 'felt with overwhelming emotional force how hallowed this ground had been'. At a ceremony in the Kokoda town square, Keating stunned the assembled guests by falling to his knees and kissing the base of the memorial. Keating described this day as 'one of the most moving of my public life'.

While 'Keating's effort to elevate Kokoda was overdue', Paul Kelly writes in *The March of Patriots*, it was 'the most contentious Anzac Day speech ever given by an Australian prime minister'.

'These battles were fought, not for the glory of war, but for humanity'

Kokoda, Papua New Guinea 25 April 1992

Today marks the 77th anniversary of the most famous battle in Australia's history ... On this day through all those years we have repeated the words 'Lest we forget'. And we have not forgotten.

The message has always been – remember their bravery and sacrifice, their willingness to lay down their lives for their country, and for their friends.

Gallipoli and the history of the Australian nation are indissoluble. It is inscribed in legend. The legend was cemented in the terrible battles in Europe and the Middle East between 1915 and 1918. It was sustained between the wars when the monuments were built and the rituals of the nation born at Gallipoli were defined.

The spirit of Anzac became the canon of Australian life: the ideals to which we aspired, the values by which we lived.

The legend was re-visited in 1939 when Australian troops again left for the Middle East, again fought heroically, again with New Zealanders – and again, some might say, too often against the odds.

Sixty thousand young Australians died in the First World War; 30,000 in the Second.

The great majority of them lie buried on the other side of the world. In France and Belgium, Libya, Syria, Turkey, Greece, Crete. They also lie in Singapore and Malaysia, Burma, Borneo and other countries of this region, including of course, Papua New Guinea ...

War has shaped Australia's history in the twentieth century like nothing else. Shaped and twisted it. At times it has stifled it.

We will continue to hold the memory of those who served and died as inextinguishable and sacred. We will continue to remind ourselves – 'Lest We Forget'.

Legends bind nations together. They define us to ourselves. But they should not stifle us. They should not constrain our growth, or restrict us when we have to change. Anzac is a commemoration of the most universal human values. But it does not confer on us a duty to see that the world stands still.

The Australians who went to two World Wars, or to Korea, Malaya, Vietnam, went to secure a place in the world for their country and its ideals … We all should know the story better than we do.

We should remember not only the battles which were fought here in Papua New Guinea, or in Malaya, or at El Alamein, Tobruk, or Greece and Crete: or those who suffered and died in prison camps in Singapore, Burma and elsewhere in the world.

We should remember all those, but we should also remember the battle fought out in Canberra and London and Washington – for in large part it was that battle which made success here in Papua New Guinea possible.

In that battle John Curtin defied those people Australia had never before defied. He insisted to his counterparts in London and Washington – his friends, our friends – that Australian troops then serving in the Middle East should return home and defend Australia … Curtin was right.

Just as he was right when he declared that in the hour of crisis, after the fall of Singapore, Australia looked to the United States – free, he said 'of any pangs as to our traditional links of kinship with the United Kingdom'. 'We know that Australia can go and Britain still hold on' he said. 'We are therefore determined that Australia shall not go'.

In doing this he took the Anzac legend to mean that Australia came first – that whatever the claims of Empire on the loyalty of those who died in the Great War, the pre-eminent claim had been Australia's. The Australians who served here in Papua New Guinea fought and died, not in the defence of the old world, but the new world. Their world. They died in defence of Australia and the civilisation and values which had grown up there.

That is why it might be said that, for Australians, the battles in Papua New Guinea were the most important ever fought.

They were fought in the most terrible circumstances … They were fought by young men with no experience of jungle warfare. By the very young men of the militia with no experience of war at all. They were fought by airmen of outstanding courage, skill and dedication. They were fought against a seasoned, skilful and fanatical enemy.

At Milne Bay the Australians inflicted on the Japanese their first defeat on land … On the Kokoda Trail it was again the young and inexperienced militia men … who fought gallantly – and eventually won … These were the heroic days of Australia's history.

It would be wrong to let this day pass without paying tribute to the people of other countries whose bravery and selflessness helped win the day

– Including the British and other Commonwealth servicemen and women who fought in the war against Japan.

While Australians fought the enemy here in Papua New Guinea, the United States forces held them out at sea and on Guadalcanal. What they did then created the enduring bond between Australia and the United States.

Today we must also pay tribute to the servicemen of Papua New Guinea who fought and died under Australian command.

And, perhaps above all, we should honour and express our profound admiration for the Papua New Guinean carriers whose stalwart support was crucial to the final victory. The support they gave to Australian soldiers, the terrible conditions and dangers they endured with the soldiers, the illness, injury and death many of them suffered, constitutes one of the great humane gestures of the War – perhaps the great humane gesture of our history. It has never been forgotten, and never will be forgotten.

It is the best possible reminder that these battles were fought, not for the glory of war, but for humanity.

And it, too, created an enduring bond – between Papua New Guinea and Australia.

Ladies and gentlemen, these days there is a relatively new memorial to the Anzac legend in Australia. Sitting on the hill near the new Parliament House, it is a modest monument inscribed with these words: 'Look around you – these are the things they believed in'.

In the end they believed in Australia – in the democracy they had built, in the life they had made there, and the future they believed their country held.

Not all generations are called on to risk and sacrifice their lives for their beliefs – but all generations need to believe.

On this Anzac Day it seems appropriate to remind ourselves of our responsibility to renew that faith and loyalty.

There can be no better way, surely, to honour those who so gallantly fought and died here.

Source: <www.keating.org.au>.

PAUL KEATING

'He is one of us'

Paul Keating delivers a moving eulogy for the unknown Australian solider

'They were words as simple and powerful as any prime minister has spoken for a very long time', said *The Sydney Morning Herald.* Paul Keating's eulogy for the Unknown Australian Solider, returning from Villers-Bretonneux to be interred at the Australian War Memorial, was eloquent, powerful and deeply moving. The eulogy was one of the events to mark the 75th anniversary of the end of the First World War.

On Remembrance Day 1993, thousands of people lined Anzac Parade in Canberra, joined by veterans, dignitaries and politicians. Cannons fired, military bands played and church bells rang. The sky was blue and the sun was shining.

'We do not know this Australian's name and we never will', Keating said. He placed the soldier's service among all who had served their nation and the 100,000 Australians who had died in war. Although unknown, 'he has always been among those we have honoured', Keating said, 'and he is one of us'. 'The Unknown Australian Solider we inter today', Keating said, 'was one of those who by his deeds proved that real nobility and grandeur belongs not to empires and nations but to the people whom they, in the last resort, always depend'.

The speech echoes Lincoln's Gettysburg Address. Its genius is in the arrangement of words that are so simple and yet so powerful, which join together to build an argument and meaning that is inescapable by its conclusion.

Writing a decade and a half later, the veteran journalist and speechwriter for Bill Hayden, Alan Ramsey, said it was 'one of this country's few genuinely great speeches'. It is perhaps the greatest speech made by an Australian Prime Minister since John Curtin held that high office.

'He is one of us'

Australian War Memorial, Canberra 11 November 1993

We do not know this Australian's name and we never will.

We do not know his rank or his battalion.

We do not know where he was born, or precisely how and when he died.

We do not know where in Australia he had made his home or when he left it for the battlefields of Europe.

We do not know his age or his circumstances – whether he was from the city or the bush; what occupation he left to become a soldier; what religion, if he had a religion; if he was married or single.

We do not know who loved him or whom he loved.

If he had children we do not know who they are.

His family is lost to us as he was lost to them.

We will never know who this Australian was.

Yet he has always been among those we have honoured.

We know that he was one of the 45,000 Australians who died on the Western Front.

One of the 416,000 Australians who volunteered for service in the First World War.

One of the 324,000 Australians who served overseas in that war, and one of the 60,000 Australians who died on foreign soil.

One of the 100,000 Australians who have died in wars this century.

He is all of them. And he is one of us.

This Australia and the Australia he knew are like foreign countries. The tide of events since he died has been so dramatic, so vast and all-consuming, a world has been created beyond the reach of his imagination.

He may have been one of those who believed the Great War would be an adventure too grand too miss. He may have felt that he would never live down the shame of not going. But the chances are that he went for no other reason than that he believed it was his duty – the duty he owed his country and his King.

Because the Great War was a mad, brutal, awful struggle distinguished more often than not by military and political incompetence; because the waste of human life was so terrible that some said victory was scarcely discernible from defeat; and because the war which was supposed to end all wars in fact sowed the seeds of a second, even more terrible, war – we might think that this unknown soldier died in vain.

But in honouring our war dead as we always have, we declare that this is not true. For out of the war came a lesson which transcended the horror and tragedy and the inexcusable folly. It was a lesson about ordinary people – and the lesson was that they were not ordinary.

On all sides they were the heroes of that war: not the generals and the politicians, but the soldiers and sailors and nurses – those who taught us to endure hardship, show courage, to be bold as well as resilient, to believe in ourselves, to stick together.

The unknown Australian soldier we inter today was one of those who by his deeds proved that real nobility and grandeur belongs not to empires and nations but to the people on whom they, in the last resort, always depend.

That is surely at the heart of the Anzac story, the Australian legend which emerged from the war. It is a legend not of sweeping military victories so much as triumphs against the odds, of courage and ingenuity in adversity. It is a legend of free and independent spirits whose discipline derived less from military formalities and customs than from the bonds of mateship and the demands of necessity.

It is a democratic tradition, the tradition in which Australians have gone to war ever since.

This unknown Australian is not interred here to glorify war over peace; or to assert a soldier's character above a civilian's; or one race or one nation or one religion above another; or men above women; or the war in which he fought and died above any other war; or of one generation above any that has or will come later.

The unknown soldier honours the memory of all those men and women who laid down their lives for Australia.

His tomb is a reminder of what we have lost in war and what we have gained.

We have lost more than 100,000 lives, and with them all their love of this country and all their hope and energy.

We have gained a legend: a story of bravery and sacrifice and with it a deeper faith in ourselves and our democracy, and a deeper understanding of what it means to be Australian.

It is not too much to hope, therefore, that this unknown Australian soldier might continue to serve his country – he might enshrine a nation's love of peace and remind us that in the sacrifice of the men and women whose names are recorded here, there is faith enough for all of us.

Source: <www.keating.org.au>

SIMON CREAN

'I don't believe that you should be going'

*On the deck of a naval ship, Simon Crean tells the troops
departing for Iraq why he opposes the Iraq War*

After the terrorist attacks on 11 September 2001 and the subsequent invasion of Afghanistan, several countries, including Australia, also committed forces to an invasion of Iraq because they believed that it possessed weapons of mass destruction. No weapons were subsequently found. Although Iraq's ruler, Saddam Hussein, was a brutal dictator, and his removal from power was perhaps justified on that basis alone, the case for war rested on an assumption that was false and it did not have the support of the international community or the sanction of The United Nations.

The Labor Party opposed the invasion of Iraq. In this speech, Labor leader Simon Crean stood on the deck of *HMAS Kanimbla* in front of 350 Australian troops about to leave for Iraq, and told them bluntly that he opposed their deployment. He said, 'I don't support the deployment of our troops in these circumstances'. But he praised them as 'a magnificent fighting and defence force', and made it clear that his opposition was to the government, not them.

Via correspondence with Crean in September 2010, he said that this speech was 'unscripted'. In developing the argument, he said he 'was drawn to the comparison with the Vietnam War', a war that he had 'opposed'. He said, 'I also knew people who fought in that war and were vilified for their service – this was wrong'.

So in this speech, Crean said that he 'wanted to remind the Australian people that it was possible to voice opposition to a war, without in anyway diminishing our respect and support for men and women called upon to serve their country'.

'Not since Calwell', *The Sydney Morning Herald* declared, 'has Labor risked such a speech'. But unlike Calwell, the *Herald* reported, no leader opposing a deployment 'has ever said so to the departing troops'.

At that time, the war enjoyed public support. The speech required great courage. And like Calwell, 40 years earlier, Crean was right.

'I don't believe that you should be going'

HMAS Kanimbla, Garden Island, Sydney 23 January 2003

Governor-General, Prime Minister, Head of Defence Forces, Head of the Navy, men and women of the Kanimbla and their families who are gathered here today for us to farewell you and to wish you God Speed and a safe and speedy return.

I don't want to mince my words because I don't believe that you should be going. I don't think that there should be a deployment of troops to Iraq ahead of The United Nations determining it. But that's a political decision, that's an argument that the Prime Minister and I will have, no doubt, over coming weeks and months.

But having said that I don't support the deployment of our troops in these circumstances. I do support our troops and always will, and that distinction is fundamentally important. The men and women of our fighting forces in a democracy are expected unquestioningly to accept the orders of the government of the day. You don't have a choice and my argument is with the government, not with you.

I know that you will give, through service and through your training, the best of your ability. You are a magnificent fighting and Defence Force, you have been trained for it …

I also believe that it's fundamentally important in this complex world that more and more we've got to resolve these issues through The United Nations collectively …

Understand this again, and I repeat it, the people going on our behalf don't have a choice. But in the circumstances I wish them God Speed and I will be doing everything that I can, everything possible to ensure that they are returned safely and quickly …

Source: Commonwealth Parliamentary Library.

Labor leader Simon Crean had the courage to oppose Australia's involvement in the Iraq War and didn't hesitate to tell US President George W Bush or the Australian troops departing for the war did he did not support their deployment. Source: Australian Labor Party

PART 6

Australia and the World

HERBERT VERE 'DOC' EVATT

'Real peace is not merely the absence of war'

Doc Evatt reports to Parliament on the creation of The United Nations

As Minister for External Affairs in the Chifley Government, HV 'Doc' Evatt was part of the Australian delegation to the San Francisco conference on the establishment of The United Nations, beginning in April 1945. Over several months, Evatt emerged as the undisputed champion of the small and middle-power nations, working to ensure that their voices would be heard.

After returning from San Francisco, Evatt presented a Bill to Parliament seeking to approve the Charter of The United Nations. In his Second Reading speech, Evatt summarised the aims of The United Nations – 'the maintenance of world peace and the promotion of human welfare by international cooperation'. He outlined the various 'organs' of the organisation and how they would operate.

He urged Australia to continue to work for peace, economic prosperity and progressive social advancement. 'Real peace', Evatt said, 'is not merely the absence of war'. The United Nations, he said, must 'promote not only peace but also welfare, international justice, observance of human rights, and the progressive development of friendly relations between nations, based on economic and social security'.

It was a long speech – lasting more than two hours – frequently interrupted with questions and comments by the opposition.

Evatt led several Australian delegations to The United Nations. He became president of the Atomic Energy Commission, chaired a committee on the future of Palestine and represented Australia on the Security Council. The capstone of his international career was serving as the president of the third session of the United Nations General Assembly in 1948-49. In this role, he presided over the adoption of the Universal Declaration of Human Rights. Evatt was the voice of a new Australia in a new world.

'Real peace is not merely the absence of war'

The House of Representatives, Canberra 30 August 1945

The purpose of this Bill is to ask the Parliament to approve the Charter of the United Nations. The Charter takes the form of an agreement between governments. It was duly signed at San Francisco on behalf of no fewer than 50 nations, including Australia …

The proposed world organisation will be called the 'United Nations'. Its purposes and principles cover the maintenance of world peace, and the promotion of human welfare by international cooperation …

The Charter provides for the establishment of six main organs for the realisation of the purposes and principles of the United Nations. They are: the General Assembly, the Security Council, the Economic and Social Council, the trusteeship Council, the International Court of Justice and the Secretariat …

The General Assembly is composed of all member States of the United Nations working together on the principle of sovereign equality. It will meet in annual and special sessions in which each State, whether large or small, will have one vote. The assembly will be a world convention in which each member State will have the right to discuss any question within the scope of the Charter …

The two main limitations on the Assembly's powers are, first, that it has no power to make recommendations on its own initiative on any matters relating to the maintenance of security while those matters are being actively dealt with by the Security Council, and, secondly, that it has no direct executive power …

The central organ of the proposed security system is the Security Council. The council has the responsibility of composing disputes between nations, of dealing with threats to peace, and of quelling aggression should it break out. The council consists of eleven members – five permanent and six non-permanent. The five permanent members are the United States of America, Great Britain, the Soviet Union, France and China. The six non-permanent members will be elected by the General Assembly for a period of two years …

The Charter has approved the principle that world security depends not only on the machinery for settling disputes, but also on creating economic and social conditions which should remove the underlying causes of war. Accordingly, member States pledge themselves jointly and severally to promote higher standards of living, full employment and economic progress, and to cooperate in dealing with international economic and social problems ...

Another major organ for settling international disputes is the International Court of Justice. The Court can play an important part in the development and strengthening of international law ...

The matter of voting procedure in the Security Council was one of the most controversial of the conference ... To us, it was a matter of principle that while the unanimity of the great powers could be justified as a prerequisite for enforcement action, no more justification existed for the right of veto on measures designed for the peaceful settlement of a dispute ...

Therefore, we pressed strongly our amendment for the removal of an individual veto which could block the council's conciliation jurisdiction. Finally, the voting went against us by twenty to ten, with fifteen abstentions, but only after a plain intimation by the great powers that they would not sign the Charter if our amendment were carried ...

Having the Security Council consisting of the great powers, and the veto applicable in the manner which I have mentioned, obviously some balancing authority was required in the interest of a democratic working constitution. The Australian view was that the assembly of the new organisation should have the right to discuss freely and fully any matter of real international concern ...

On every occasion, it was evident that a great majority of nations strongly supported the principles of the Australian proposals ... Finally, a formula was adopted giving to the assembly the right to discuss 'any questions or any matters within the scope of the present charter or relating to the powers and functions of any organisations provided in the present charter' ...

Another important debate arose out of the Australian amendments that were designed to elevate the stature and improve the functions of the Economic and Social Council. Against the strongest preliminary opposition, we were able to secure an amendment of the purposes of the organisation to include this clause:

> The United Nations shall promote . . . high standards of living, full employ-
> ment and conditions of economic and social progress and development.
> ... We ourselves put forward an amendment to make clear that the only
> permissible intervention of the organisation in matters of domestic jurisdic-
> tion should be in the case of actual enforcement measures by the Security
> Council, that is, to prevent aggression or to defend the victim of aggression
> ... After prolonged discussions, we secured an alteration of the amendment
> moved by the sponsoring powers, which fully covered our objective. In the

result, internal matters such as the migration policy of a state will not fall within the scope of the organisation …

Of the 38 amendments of substance which Australia proposed, no fewer than 26 were either adopted without material change or adopted in principle. The Australian proposals which were accepted included the following:

1. Amendment to lay down a governing principle aimed at protection of territorial integrity and political independence of member States.
2. Provision that peaceful settlement shall proceed not arbitrarily but in conformity with the principles of justice and international law.
3. Inclusion of a specific provision that the only permissible intervention of the organisation in matters of domestic jurisdiction shall be in the case of actual enforcement measures by the Security Council.
4. The most vital amendment to extend the assembly's right of discussion and recommendation to all matters and questions within the scope of the charter (which necessarily includes preamble purposes, principles, and all the activities of the organs).
5. Amendment preventing freezing of disputes in the Security Council as occurred in the League of Nations by requiring the Security Council to report to the assembly or the member States immediately it has ceased to deal with the dispute.
6. Amendment designed to ensure that all the special military agreements to place forces and facilities at the disposal of the Security Council, shall be made not by members *inter se*, but by the Security Council with each member or group of members.
7. Amendment to secure that in the election of non-permanent members of the Security Council special regard shall be had, first, to proven ability to contribute to international security and then to geographical representation.
8. The substance of Australia's amendment specifically providing for the right of self defence in case of inaction by the Security Council was incorporated in the agreed formula on regional arrangement.
9. Amendments to the economic and social chapter to include the promotion of full employment and higher living standards within the purposes of the Economic (and Social) Council.
10. Inclusion of a definite pledge by each member to take action to promote, inter alia, the objective of full employment by joint and separate action in cooperation with the organisation.

11. An amendment designed to secure that the objective of the organisation will be that fundamental human rights shall not only be respected, but observed.

12. Amendments to enlarge the powers of the Economic and Social Council to enable it to call conferences, to prepare conventions, to coordinate agencies, and generally to act as a coordinating economic body.

13. Contribution to the new chapter on trusteeship. Seven Australian amendments were adopted, including a general declaration of trusteeship in relation to all non-self-governing countries and the specifying of obligations of the trustee as including:
    a. Just treatment of the peoples concerned;
    b. Their protection against abuses;
    c. The promotion of constructive measures of development;
    d. Encouragement of research;
    e. Full cooperation with other international bodies and, most important;
    f. The transmission regularly to the world organisation of full statistical information relating to economic, social and educational conditions of the native peoples.

14. The removal of the individual veto on constitutional amendments was not obtained; but in cooperation with other small nations the opportunities of special constitutional review were facilitated.

One of the outstanding features of the conference was the part played by smaller nations, particularly the 'middle powers' … The Australian delegation, working closely in cooperation with that of New Zealand, always adopted an independent approach. We did not belong to any bloc of nations …

It will be plain to honourable members that we cannot expect to reap the advantages held out by the Charter without incurring our fair share of the responsibilities … an undertaking to settle all disputes by peaceful means, to refrain from the threat or use of force in international relations, and to give the organisation every assistance in any action it takes in accordance with the present Charter …

Australia, and every other member, agrees to accept and carry out all decisions of the Security Council. We shall undertake when we ratify the Charter, to make available to the Council on its call, and in accordance with a special agreement, armed forces, assistance and facilities, including national air force contingents, for use in the event of aggression …

Under article 56 of the Charter, Australia, along with every other member, pledges itself to 'take joint and separate action in cooperation with the organisation' for the achievement of certain basic purposes which include higher standards of living for their respective peoples, full employment, solutions of international social, economic, health and related problems, international, cultural and educational cooperation and respect for, and observance of, human rights and fundamental freedoms for all without distinction as to race, sex, language or religion.

Concerning dependent peoples, there is a general obligation in article 73 of the Charter to recognise that the interests of such peoples are paramount in the eyes of powers having control over the territories in which they live, and to develop their political, social and economic well-being …

As a member of the United Nations, Australia will ipso facto, be a party to the statute of the International Court of Justice, and will undertake to comply with the decisions of the court in any case to which we are a party.

Finally, Australia must share in bearing the expenses of the organisation as they may be apportioned by the General Assembly …

There is offered to us an opportunity, which certainly will never recur, of taking an active and energetic part in an organisation which, if the obligations are properly carried out, should be able to stamp out any resurgence of fascist aggression, and also set in motion practical steps for achieving freedom from want, as well as freedom from fear …

Real peace is not merely the absence of war. The small nations look to the world organisation to promote not only peace but also welfare, international justice, observance of human rights, and the progressive development of friendly relations between nations, based on economic and social security …

The Charter is still in the making. The organisation has yet to be set up and made to work. It will come into force when the five sponsoring powers and a majority of the other 45 nations which signed the Charter adopt it.

There are many stepping-stones to world prosperity, world justice and world peace … the attainment of the ultimate goal depends, not on any document, but upon the steadfast determination of governments and even more upon their peoples …

If we are as resolute in the future in the interests of peace as we have been in the prosecution of the war, we can win peace. It is our duty to make this organisation worthy of those who fought to make victory possible and for those who have died for us.

Source: Commonwealth of Australia Parliamentary Debates (Hansard).

BEN CHIFLEY

'For the preservation of peace'

Ben Chifley makes the case for Australia to join the international economy

The Bretton Woods conference of 45 nations, held on the slopes of New Hampshire in 1944, established the post-war international economic structure that largely exists today.

These Bills allowed Australia to ratify the Bretton Woods International Monetary Agreement, joining Australia to the international economy. It enabled Australia to join the International Monetary Fund (IMF), the International Bank for Reconstruction and Development (now the World Bank) and the global trading system (now the World Trade Organisation).

Despite the move towards international cooperation and the desire for peace and prosperity in the years after the Second World War, there was some hostility and scepticism about these proposals. It fell to Ben Chifley as Prime Minister and Treasurer to persuade the Labor Party and the Parliament, to support these Bills. They would help bring Chifley's vision of the post-war world to fruition. He believed that the Agreement was vital for employment, economic growth, higher living standards and economic stability.

Cabinet first considered the Bretton Woods Agreement in 1944, under John Curtin's prime ministership, but did not support it until November 1946. The party's federal executive also debated it for some time and caucus support was not initially supportive. Eventually, in March 1947, caucus agreed after much effort by Chifley to persuade them of the Agreement's merits.

Chifley argued that it would 'constitute an attempt for the first time in history to grapple with world economic problems by concerted action on a world scale for the common good'.

The Bill passed the House of Representatives by 55-5 votes in March 1947. However, two independent Members and three coalition Members voted against the Bills. Transport Minister Eddie Ward abstained.

'For the preservation of peace'

The House of Representatives, Canberra 13 and 20 March 1947

13 March 1947

The purpose of the Bill is to seek approval by the Parliament of Australia becoming a member of the International Monetary Fund and of the International Bank for Reconstruction and Development. These institutions form part of the general structure for peace, security and welfare in the post-war world in the building of which Australia has taken a most active part, and towards which the Minister for External Affairs (HV 'Doc' Evatt) has made no small contribution.

The United Nations is the apex of this structure, but, recognising that economic welfare is a fundamental basis for peace and security, there has been developed within and around the United Nations special machinery for world economic collaboration. The broad object of this machinery is to promote throughout the world expanded production, employment, trade and higher standards of living ...

Australia has consistently maintained the view that the successful working of international economic organisations, and the expansion of internal investment and trade, depend to a very great degree on the achievement and preservation of full employment in the major industrial countries.

After a long series of formal and informal discussions ... we finally succeeded, at San Francisco in June 1945, in amending the purposes of the United Nations to include the promotion of 'high standards of living, full employment and conditions of economic and social progress and development' ...

But employment and trade undertakings can be defeated by exchange manipulations, and it is the special object of the International Monetary Fund to avoid the recurrence of these evils. Competitive exchange depreciation, discriminatory exchange controls and the blocking of currencies were destructive weapons in the economic warfare which raged throughout the thirties and contributed to the outbreak of armed conflict in 1939.

Their effect was to deprive international trade of a stable basis, and, by greatly diminishing its volume, to impoverish people in all countries, especially in those which, like Australia, depend largely upon external trade.

By providing a permanent institution to promote international monetary cooperation, it is hoped to avoid these evils, to facilitate the expansion and balanced growth of international trade and to contribute thereby to the promotion and maintenance of high expansion and balanced growth of international trade and to contribute thereby to the promotion and maintenance of high levels of employment and real income.

The International Monetary Fund represents an attempt to avoid the errors of the past ... The Fund is an inter-governmental organisation and is wholly controlled by governments ... Broadly, the Fund comprises on the one hand an international pool of gold and currency reserves to meet emergencies, and, on the other hand, a code of rules to regulate exchange relationships between members.

Each member joining the Fund is assigned a quota which measures two things: first, its obligation to contribute to the pool of gold and local currencies; and, secondly, its right to draw foreign exchange from the Fund ... if our overseas funds should run down, for instance, as the result of drought. It would also assist overseas loan obligations in times of difficulty ...

The undertakings which a member gives regarding exchange stability and the convertibility of its currency in respect of current transactions are clearly important commitments. There are, however, adequate safeguards to ensure that reasonable exchange stability shall not become excessive exchange rigidity, and that movements in exchange rates required for employment reasons shall be achieved ...

Like ourselves, the United Kingdom government is pursuing a full employment policy, and as a further and final safeguard, the United Kingdom government sought and obtained from the Fund a ruling that 'steps necessary to protect a member country from chronic or persistent unemployment arising from pressure upon its balance of payments are among the measures necessary to correct a fundamental disequilibrium' ...

Further, in return for the exchange undertakings given, a member is assured of assistance from the Fund in time of need and is freed from the fear of its external trade being disrupted by fluctuations in the exchange rates of other countries and by the restrictive currency practices which caused so much trouble in the past ...

The par value of the currencies of members is to be expressed in terms of gold as a common denominator or in terms of the United States dollar, and this has been described as equivalent to the gold standard. But that is not so. The central feature of the gold standard was rigid exchange rates, with currencies so linked to gold that countries were compelled to expand or contract the volume of credit within their territories as gold flowed in or out of their reserves. In contrast, the monetary fund envisages controlled flexibility of exchange rates and also, by providing additional currency reserves for members, seeks to avoid the need for contractions of credit where members are subject temporarily to an adverse balance of payments.

The purpose of the International Bank for Reconstruction and Development is to provide a source of capital funds for the reconstruction of countries devastated by war and for the development of industrially backward countries ...

A feature of these Bretton Woods organisations which commends them to the government is that, taken with related bodies in the United Nations scheme, they constitute an attempt for the first time in history to grapple with world economic problems by concerted action on a world scale for the common good. They recognise the vital fact that the complex and ever-changing problems of international trade, finance and economic relations generally can no longer be allowed to drift as they did formerly when individual nations followed separate and often discordant policies. They represent a bid to pull the world situation together, get it under control and set it upon a steady and coherent course ...

Just as political isolation in the world would be an impracticable policy for Australia, so do I think that economic isolation would be disastrous.

20 March 1947

During the last 30 years the world has experienced two major wars and a serious depression. I believe that every reasonable man hopes that the misery and suffering of those years will never be repeated ...

I have been an ardent advocate of all international organisations, because I believe that through them we are engaging in a great human experiment, which is designed to prevent the catastrophes that result from wars and financial and economic depressions ...

This is the first time in the history of the world that the governments of many countries have made an attempt to create economic stability.

Great issues are at stake, not perhaps tomorrow, next year or even five years hence. We all must give encouragement to international organisations for the preservation of peace. In doing so, we must have economic stability, because many of the conflicts in our history have been due to economic causes.

If we are able to cure one of the fundamental causes of war, we shall have made substantial progress, and a contribution to the welfare of not only Australia and its people, but also the people of the whole world, for generations to come ...

Perhaps the experiment will fail; but every country which has any regards for the cause of humanity cannot, for some selfish reason, or because some ghosts of the past happen to walk, or because of fears created by their experiences of a financial and economic depression, refuse to become parties to this Agreement.

If we have any love for mankind and a desire to free future generations from the terrible happenings of the last 30 years we must put our faith in these international organisations …

It is true that some of the mechanics of this Agreement may have to be changed; but that is no reason why any country should not help the world to achieve the great objective and ideal behind the United Nations organisation.

It is for those reasons only, and not for any national, personal or political reason, that I have always believed that the Parliament, and the people of this country, in their own small way, are justified in their own interests in entering into this Agreement.

Source: Commonwealth of Australia Parliamentary Debates (Hansard).

It was Ben Chifley who announced to the nation that the Second World War had ended. But the war did not signal the end of his government's involvement in foreign policy. With HV 'Doc' Evatt as External Affairs Minister, they worked together to see Australia adopt the Bretton Woods Agreement which linked Australia to the international economy and to see the United Nations established, providing an important voice for the small and middle-ranking powers like Australia.
Source: Australian Labor Party

GOUGH WHITLAM

'We give primacy to The United Nations'

Gough Whitlam outlines a bold new vision for Australia in the global community

At his first media conference as Prime Minister, Gough Whitlam said that his government intended to develop a 'more constructive, flexible and progressive' approach to foreign policy. He wanted 'a more independent Australian stance in international affairs, an Australia which will be less militarily oriented and not open to suggestions of racism, an Australia which will enjoy a growing standing as a distinctive, tolerant, cooperative and well regarded nation not only in the Asian and Pacific region, but in the world at large'.

In his memoir, *The Whitlam Government*, he could declare that 'foreign policy was one of my government's strongest and most successful areas of achievement'.

In those early, invigorating, salad days of the Whitlam Government, several momentous foreign policy decisions were made, including: the complete withdrawal of forces from Vietnam; a ban on racially selected sporting teams; independence for Papua New Guinea; the purchase of new F111 planes; the appointment of new representation at the International Labour Organisation (ILO); talks regarding the diplomatic recognition of China; the closure of the Rhodesian Information Centre in Sydney; and the recalling of Australia's ambassadors to the United Nations, Washington and Taiwan.

International treaties, covenants, conventions and courts were used to give effect to Labor's goals in human rights, racial discrimination and nuclear non-proliferation.

Whitlam's speech to the United Nations represents a faithful distillation of the foreign policy approach and achievements of the Whitlam Government. Whitlam described his government as 'social democratic' and affirms his faith in the United Nations as a forum for international collaboration and cooperation, important to Australia's domestic and international interests. 'In seeking a better international order', Whitlam said, 'we give primacy to the United Nations'.

'We give primacy to The United Nations'

The United Nations General Assembly, New York, 30 September 1974

… As head of the first Australian social democratic government since Australia helped to found The United Nations and to frame its Charter more than a quarter of a century ago, I re-affirm our loyalty to both. Such pledges are easily enough given; yet no nation makes them more sincerely, more earnestly today than Australia.

No country needs more than Australia the fulfilment of the international objectives of The United Nations to reach the fulfilment of her own national objectives. There are few countries in which the paradox is demonstrated with such force that true national independence depends upon international interdependence. There are few nations to which the mirage of national self-sufficiency can be made so tempting; yet there are few nations for which that mirage can be so easily shattered.

Australia, fortunate in possession of great resources, confident in the ability of her own people to develop those resources, is nevertheless not ashamed to admit her interdependence with her neighbours and her partners across the world and her dependence upon them.

We are a people without illusions; we Australians neither falsely exaggerate our strengths nor fearfully exaggerate our weaknesses. It is precisely because we make a rational assessment of our strengths and weaknesses that we recognise that we depend upon a better international order to preserve those things we most value about our national independence. In seeking a better international order, we give primacy to The United Nations.

It is therefore with growing concern that we witness what can only be called a drift away from international order and international cooperation at present occurring in world affairs. Australia's concern springs not just from the real difficulties created by recent events but, even more, from the feeling that there has been a weakening of will, a loss of momentum in international determination to meet and overcome those difficulties …

The task of this Assembly should be to help stop that drift. Our natural preoccupation with our national problems – and for most of us they are very great indeed – must not lead to a loss of international concern and involvement. We cannot turn inwards …

No nation, no group of nations, no bloc, no alliance, can live alone, can live entirely to itself in this new world. We are all internationalists now – by necessity. Australia is internationalist by necessity – and by choice. Each of us has our bilateral arrangements and our regional arrangements. Many, like Australia, through treaty or trade or tradition, have honourable alignments and valuable associations.

It is however through this organisation, its Assembly and its councils, and through the specialised agencies, that the enduring international settlements must ultimately be sought and the drift away from international cooperation must be arrested.

So there must be no loss of nerve, no loss of will here. If we here lose our nerve, if we here allow that drift to continue unchecked, we face the breakdown of the Nuclear Non-Proliferation Treaty, the breakdown of world economic order, the breakdown of all our high hopes and high words about closing the gap between the developed and developing nations and the breakdown of any claims of The United Nations organisation to be an effective peace-keeper and peace-maker ...

We continue to urge upon the superpowers the need for them both to maintain the utmost mutual restraint in their relations between themselves – and towards us. They can, of course, easily destroy each other; they can also destroy all of us. We are entitled to ask them to move forward to a stage of complete detente where their tremendous power can be used jointly for the betterment of the whole civilization ...

For our part, the Australian government pledges that it will neither develop nor acquire nuclear weapons.

Our first aim must be to strengthen the Non-Proliferation Treaty and work for its acceptance everywhere ...

Secondly, we should make a comprehensive treaty to ban nuclear weapons testing an urgent priority ...

Thirdly, we need effective international arrangements to govern and control nuclear experiments for peaceful purposes ...

Another approach to the goal of disarmament worth serious exploration is the concept of peace zones. They are of course no substitute for comprehensive disarmament and no substitute for an effective Non-Proliferation Treaty. Australia, however, takes a particular interest in the agreements and proposals embodying this concept, because most of them affect our continent and our region directly ...

For the Australian government, these initiatives not only represent ends in themselves but, we believe serve to stimulate progress on other important measures intended to bring to fulfilment the hopes of mankind to live in security, free from the threat of nuclear war ...

In this difficult, complicated, crowded world we all are creating for ourselves, the causes of conflict multiply. Nuclear brinkmanship, ideology, border disputes, race hate, religious bigotry, national ambitions, foreign exploitation – all provide actual or potential sources of tension, conflict, bloodshed and war. Yet there remains for the future one of the oldest of all the causes of war – the threat of war for the possession of resources.

Huge population increases, the revolution of rising expectations, the enormous and often wasteful demands our technological civilization makes upon the world's resources, have increased the pressures on our world civilization to the very threshold of the tolerable …

There is no place in our thinking for 'economic nationalism' in its crudest sense. We do, of course, wish to ensure steady markets at fair prices for what we produce. We recognise the great scope for increased cooperation between producers of raw materials and for groups of exporting countries to associate to build a better framework for orderly and rational development of production and trade …

Of all the changes which have occurred in the international community since World War II none has more profoundly altered the face of the world than the accession to independence by those peoples and states formerly under colonial rule. The process is not yet complete, but we look to a time in the near future when no territory will be controlled against its choice by a metropolitan power with whom it has no geographical, social, racial, cultural affinity …

Papua New Guinea became self-governing on 1 December, 1973. It will become fully independent as soon as the House of Assembly of Papua New Guinea decides … The Australian government made its own decision long ago – we utterly reject a colonial role for Australia …

There is to me, I must say, a most satisfying symmetry in the march of events by which Portugal the oldest, and Australia the newest, of the colonial powers are acting at the same time towards the liquidation of colonialism. Across the distance of 400 years the new world in Australia clasps hands with the old, in ending a false, demeaning, unworthy power over others …

The dramatic and welcome progress made towards the dissolution of the oldest and last of the colonial empires now enables The United Nations to direct even more concentrated attention upon the twin evil of racism – particularly its post-colonial manifestations in Southern Africa. We must be unremitting in the efforts sanctioned by the Assembly to break the illegal regime in Rhodesia, to end South Africa's unlawful control over Namibia and to end apartheid …

My government – conscious that Australia's own record is seriously flawed – is determined to remove all forms of racial discrimination within our own shores, notably now, as notoriously in the past, against our own Aboriginals.

While racism remains as cruel as any example of man's inhumanity to man, we should not, however, overlook the existence of other forms of discrimination which rob men and women of their right to live in dignity and peace of mind. Throughout the world political prisoners languish in jails or are otherwise deprived of their civil liberties. There are thoroughly unacceptable constraints on the right of political asylum. Religious and ethnic minorities are persecuted, workers are denied the protection of ILO Conventions, women are denied equal opportunities …

Refusal to recognise the inalienable rights of all people to freedom and independence produces tension and conflict not only between the oppressed and the oppressors but between them and other nations which become associated or involved in these just and legitimate struggles.

Now more than ever, we look to The United Nations. It has the experience, the stature and the capacity to help us identify the sources of tension between nations, to prescribe collective measures to mitigate and eventually remove the causes of conflict, and to anticipate and prevent situations developing which have the potential for disturbing world peace …

As the challenge of The United Nations to provide a genuine and continuing source of leadership, of hope and purpose for the world is more urgent, the opportunity more real, than at any time in the organisation's history.

In the response we here make to that challenge, we shall be judged – as nations, as representatives of our nations and as men and women – not by our power or size or wealth, but by the honesty of our efforts to promote and practice the principles of the Charter of this United Nations.

Source: The Whitlam Institute.

As External Affairs Minister in the Chifley Government, HV 'Doc' Evatt played an important role in the formation of the United Nations in 1945. He served as president of the General Assembly and saw the UN as vital not only for peace, but for economic prosperity and social progress. Source: National Archives of Australia

BOB HAWKE

'The spirit of men and women yearning to be free'

*Bob Hawke urges Commonwealth leaders not to ignore
the cry for freedom in apartheid South Africa*

As Bob Hawke wrote in his memoirs, by the 1980s, many regarded the Commonwealth Heads of Government Meeting (CHOGM) as *passé*. But Hawke believed the forum could be used 'as an instrument to give effect to Chifley's philosophy of Labor's universal mandate', which was to work 'for the betterment of mankind ... anywhere we may give a helping hand'.

At the 1985 meeting in the Bahamas, Hawke saw an opportunity to progress the goal 'of a free and democratic South Africa from which discrimination based on colour had been eliminated'.

Recalling the speech to CHOGM leaders in an interview for this book in July 2010, Hawke said that 'the total repugnance of apartheid' was 'fundamental to my thinking'. 'If the regime [in South Africa] could not be persuaded by the moral argument', against apartheid, he said, 'then it would have to face the impact of harsher international sanctions'.

In a powerful summoning of CHOGM's history and capacity, Hawke called for action. 'The spirit of men and women yearning to be free, to have that right to determine their own destiny will not be extinguished. It will not be extinguished, however brutally that arsenal is unleashed upon them', Hawke said.

With the support of India's Rajiv Gandhi and Canada's Brian Mulroney, and others, they agreed to take a stand against apartheid. British Prime Minister Margaret Thatcher opposed sanctions. So did Australia's then Opposition Leader John Howard.

Soon, the economic, sporting and diplomatic isolation of South Africa intensified.

In 1990, Nelson Mandela was released from prison after 27 years, and South Africa began to dismantle apartheid.

This speech, with its words beautifully composed, carefully arranged and logically argued, is a powerful reminder of the importance of Labor's universal mandate.

'The spirit of men and women yearning to be free'

Commonwealth Heads of Government Meeting,
Nassau, The Bahamas 16 October 1985

We Commonwealth leaders assembled here at Nassau are the inheritors of a great tradition. It is the tradition of a Commonwealth emerged from empire; like most great traditions it is not without flaw or blemish.

But the very fact that we are a Commonwealth that has emerged from empire with a greater measure of common purpose is itself a measure of the strength of this tradition.

Let us at the outset of this meeting ask ourselves the question – what have been the elements, the secret if you like, of that strength? And let us ask that question seeking to find in the answer a guide in discharging our high responsibilities.

If I could put it in a simple phrase, I believe the essence of that strength has been in understanding of the limits of power.

Let me be precise. In the immediate post-war period, it would have been possible for Britain to maintain for longer than it did the colonial status of the Indian sub-continent. It had the instruments of power to do so, but it understood the limits of that power.

And those limits were understood through a proper perception of the force of other rights and interests which together constitutes a countervailing power. These included the right and determination of peoples to be free to determine their different destinies; and it included an enlightened self-interest on the part of a Britain which understood that, in the long term, its own economic, political and strategic concerns would be better protected by accommodating the new realities.

This countervailing power is not as susceptible to measurement as the power that can be accounted in battalions, squadrons and the elements of military and economic weaponry. But all our history as a Commonwealth has shown that it is no less real for that reason.

It has an inexorable capacity to grow and ultimately to overcome those who would take refuge in this sterile accounting of conventional power.

Some would argue that, at times, the limits of power have not been understood sufficiently early. It has been argued of Britain. It has been equally argued of Australia, in relation to Papua New Guinea.

But I repeat, we assemble as a unique institution representing a quarter of the world's population, one third of its sovereign and independent nations, meeting as equals because, however falteringly at times, we have together learned the limits of power.

And that learning process has given the Commonwealth a particular capacity to recognise in time the need for change; to discern civilised directions for change; and, at important moments, to be an effective agent for change.

If my answer then to this question – what is the secret of the strength of our Commonwealth tradition? – is correct, I believe it can usefully inform our approach to the major issues before us in the coming week.

Without doubt, the predominant of these is, and should be, South Africa – an issue of historic concern to the Commonwealth. If ever there was a regime which should have learnt from our experience the lesson of the limits of power, it is that in South Africa.

They are the sterile accountants of our day who would measure their capacity to insulate themselves against the pressure of inevitable change by the size of their military arsenal. They are wrong.

For the force of that countervailing power is growing, it is inexorable and it is unquenchable. The spirit of men and women yearning to be free, to have that right to determine their own destiny will not be extinguished. It will not be extinguished, however brutally that arsenal is unleashed upon them.

The world that is witness to events in South Africa is becoming increasingly impatient. I believe it is looking to us to draw upon our tradition, to seek to apply to South Africa the lessons we have learned from our own experience.

This will require us to strengthen, by our decisions, the countervailing power that is growing by the day within and outside South Africa.

This will require us to examine and to be prepared to implement the option of further effective economic sanctions.

But just as importantly, it will require us to sustain the flame of an enlightened self-interest that has now been lit in South Africa, and is manifest in the recent talks in Lusaka between representatives of South African business and the ANC.

For the fact is that all the economic capacity that has been established in South Africa and which now disproportionately benefits the few, will only endure and be available for the benefit of all if a new, free and just South Africa is created …

We have learned from our experiences, we reflect in our tradition, that conflict can give way to harmony.

We rightly accept as an article of shared faith that the colour of people's political skin is as irrelevant as the colour of their eyes to their political, economic and social rights.

Let us by our approach to our task in the coming days, and by the decisions we take, not only confirm this article of faith within the Commonwealth but seek to make it a reality for all those who look to us for help.

Source: The Bob Hawke Prime Ministerial Library.

BOB HAWKE

'Our economic futures are interlinked'

Bob Hawke proposes the creation of APEC to an audience in Seoul, South Korea

Just as it was Paul Keating who expanded and elevated the Asia Pacific Economic Cooperation (APEC) forum into a major regional economic institution, it was Bob Hawke who gave birth to the idea.

In this speech, Hawke speaks passionately about his government's policy of greater 'enmeshment' with the Asia-Pacific region, including closer ties with South Korea. He argues that the opportunity presented by closer engagement through multilateral forums can achieve greater economic outcomes, and specifically trading outcomes, for all nations. Hawke proposes the establishment of the APEC regional forum, including a 'meeting of ministers', to focus on trade liberalisation and expand regional cooperation.

It was a further demonstration of Hawke's belief in consensus, by working together in the common interest to achieve mutually beneficial outcomes. 'Our economic futures are interlinked', he told his South Korean audience, but spoke to the wider region.

Modelled initially on the Organisation for Economic Cooperation and Development (OECD), Hawke's speechwriter, Stephen Mills, said that the idea faced strong resistance in the Canberra bureaucracy. But Hawke had won the support of South Korean President Roh Tae Woo, so he pushed ahead.

In his memoirs, Hawke labelled this speech 'as one of seminal importance'.

'Our economic futures are interlinked'

Korean Business Associations Luncheon, Seoul, 31 January 1989

Australia and Korea lie near the northern and southern extremities of the most dynamically growing region in the world: the Asia-Pacific region.

This region generates more than one third of the world's trade, and is likely in the next decade to create more than half the world's economic output. This extraordinary growth gives nations such as ours tremendous opportunities and new responsibilities.

Whether we can fulfil the predictions of those who see us entering a 'Pacific Century', with all that would mean for rising living standards for our people, is in our own hands.

But these opportunities cannot fully be exploited unless we are prepared, as individual nations and as a region, to do the hard work that will be involved.

Today I want to discuss one focus for that work – how we as a region can better cooperate so that our future, individually and regionally, is a secure and prosperous one ...

If one had to isolate the single key factor underpinning the growth of all the dynamically performing nations of the region, it would surely be their capacity to take advantage of a relatively open and non-discriminatory international trading system.

The multilateral system of global trade, under the auspices of the GATT, has provided more than four decades of growth for the world's economies ...

Given this centrality of trade to our region, we have cause for concern about our economic future. Serious cracks are appearing in the international trading system which have major implications for the future health of both our region and the world economy.

First, you will all be aware of the bilateral trade pressures associated with the significant trade imbalances between a number of regional countries and the United States.

Second, there is a trend towards the formation of bilateral or regional trading arrangements which run the risk of undermining a truly multilateral trading system.

Third, there are fundamental tensions within the GATT framework of multilateral trade, of which the recent Montreal deadlock is but the latest manifestation.

Each of these problems has prompted calls for some sort of regional action.

But they are not the only driving forces behind calls for closer regional ties. It has long been recognised – especially as the region's economic importance continues to grow – that the countries in the region are essentially interdependent; our economic futures are interlinked.

That realisation led in 1980 to the creation of the Pacific Economic Co-operation Conference – PECC – of which Australia was a co-founder and of which we remain a consistent supporter.

PECC's work has illuminated large areas of common interests within the region. But its informality, which has helped to broaden its membership, has also made it difficult for it to address policy issues which are properly the responsibility of governments …

I believe the time has come for us substantially to increase our efforts towards building regional co-operation and seriously to investigate what areas it might focus on and what forms it might take …

We want to assess what the region's attitudes are towards the possibility of creating a more formal intergovernmental vehicle of regional co-operation. A meeting of ministers from throughout the region would be a useful forum to investigate the question.

What we are seeking to develop is a capacity for analysis and consultation on economic and social issues, not as an academic exercise but to help inform policy development by our respective governments. I see merit in the model provided, in a different context, by the OECD …

Let me spell out three areas in which I believe the Asia-Pacific region could profit from closer cooperation through such an institution.

First, effective regional cooperation can greatly improve the chances of success of the Uruguay Round and could thereby give a vital boost to the liberalisation – and therefore the preservation – of the GATT-based trading system …

Second, we must be prepared openly to discuss obstacles to trade within our region … Australia's view is that the essence of a properly functioning trading system is, of course, that countries should seek multilateral trade balance, not bilateral balance with all countries …

The third area in which we could benefit from regional cooperation is through identifying the broad economic interests we have in common …

Australia's support for non-discriminatory multilateral trading solutions in the GATT framework is clear, long-standing and unambiguous …

The Asia-Pacific region is at a pivotal point in history. And the region is located at a pivotal point in the global economy.

We have much to offer each other. We have substantial shared political and economic interests, and a powerful complementarity in our economic skills, resources, and business, cultural, and political links.

Cooperation offers the region the opportunity to influence the course of multilateral trade liberalisation, avoid alternative approaches which would undermine this objective and enable us to enter the next century with confidence that our potential will be fulfilled.

Source: The Bob Hawke Prime Ministerial Library.

PAUL KEATING

'Sure of who we are and what we stand for'

Paul Keating outlines his vision for Australian engagement in the Asia-Pacific region

Paul Keating's dominant focus as Prime Minister was foreign policy. No 'prime minister', Greg Sheridan argued in his book, *Tigers: Leaders of the New Asia-Pacific*, 'had ever put Asia, specifically East Asia, so much at the heart of Australian life'.

A major achievement of Keating's regional diplomacy was his elevation of the Asia-Pacific Economic Cooperation (APEC) trading forum. APEC was proposed by Bob Hawke as a regional trading forum in 1989. Keating saw greater potential for APEC if it facilitated meetings at a heads of government level, providing 'the locomotive drive to a more ambitious APEC agenda', Keating wrote in *Engagement*. The region lacked such an institutional apparatus for regular dialogue between leaders.

Keating suggested it to United States President George HW Bush on a visit to Australia in 1991. He also proposed it to Bill Clinton, Indonesia's President Soeharto and Japan's Prime Minister Miyazawa. 'It was a masterful and effective performance – one of the few occasions in Australia's diplomatic history when an Australian prime minister has engaged in effective shuttle diplomacy', wrote Sheridan.

In this, his first foreign policy speech as Prime Minister, Keating canvassed the idea of regional leaders' meetings. Moreover, this speech represents the nub of Keating's approach to Asia – an ambitious attempt to recast the relationship, building on the efforts of Gough Whitlam and Hawke, to better reflect Australia's independent identity and outlook, and to benefit from the economic growth in the region.

But 'we don't go to Asia cap in hand', Keating said, 'with the ghost of empire about us. Not as a vicar of Europe, or as a US deputy. But unambivalently. Sure of who we are and what we stand for'.

'Sure of who we are and what we stand for'

The University of NSW, Sydney 7 April 1992

In 1935, the magazine Australian Quarterly carried a long article entitled 'Australia's Place in the Empire'. It was the text of an address delivered in London by Robert Gordon Menzies. An address delivered in the circumstances he loved, to the audience he loved ...

The virtues of the English race and Australia's filial loyalty were the themes of his 1935 address. 'The thing that sticks firmly in the mind of the average Australian is that he is British', he said. He told them that they should recognise our relationship was a 'blood relationship' before it was a mercantile one. And he asked them a question which he said would determine our relationship with Britain not merely for the next five years, but for the next five hundred. 'Does Great Britain feel that its sons and brothers ... are its own flesh and blood, or does it regard them as remittance men?'

Now, in my view, Winston Churchill gave Menzies the answer a few years later. 'Australians', he told Lord Moran, 'come of bad stock' ...

Nothing I say tonight, and nothing I have said in recent weeks, can reasonably be interpreted as criticism of the British people, and least of all those British men and women who fought and suffered and died in the war against Japan and Germany.

My criticism is directed at those Australians – or, more accurately, that Australian attitude – which still cannot separate our interests, our history, or our future, from the interests of Britain.

It seems to me an attitude which still exercises at least a subliminal influence on our thinking – persuading us that someone or something will do it for us ... I say that this attitude has long been, and remains, debilitating to our national culture, our economic future, and our destiny as a nation in Asia and the Pacific.

I spent the last decade attempting to make the necessary changes to the Australian economy – facing it toward the world and opening it up, to make us more competitive and give us a chance ...

We've altered a lot of the practices and habits of mind which emanated from that way of thinking – at least as far as the economy goes. We've also gone a very long way towards getting rid of the industrial culture of hostility.

But altering our political perspective, which includes regenerating our spirit, pulling us together as a nation, focussing our sense of ourselves – all these things, I believe, remain tasks for the nineties.

These things, I assure you, are not meant as a distraction as some people have suggested. They are central. They are central to our developing relationship with Asia and the Pacific …

It might be said that Menzies was a man of his time and should not be judged with hindsight. But Menzies is a man of our time too. His unnaturally long political era – made possible by the split in the Labor Party – his endless, and almost endlessly regressive, era sunk a generation of Australians in Anglophilia and torpor …

My responsibility is to this generation and succeeding ones, and these echoes of Menzies cannot be allowed to get in the way. We cannot pretend to ourselves that we are insulated from change in the world.

In any event, the old traditions of Australia will remain with us. We are not about disloyalty but its opposite. We are about nationhood, and the democracy which is at the centre of it.

That is something I think Australians must realise: that we don't go to Asia cap in hand, any more than we go, like Menzies went to London, pleading family ties. We go as we are. Not with the ghost of empire about us. Not as a vicar of Europe, or as a US deputy. But unambivalently. Sure of who we are and what we stand for.

If we are to be taken seriously, believed, trusted, that is the only way to go …

We might learn something from the geophysics of the situation. Geophysically speaking this continent is old Asia – there's none older than this. It's certainly not going to move, and after two hundred years it should be pretty plain that we're not going to either …

It is sometimes argued that Australia's democratic institutions and traditions of tolerance and open debate somehow disqualify us from forming successful relationships in Asia. My starting point is that Australia's democratic institutions and traditions are non-negotiable.

Many things have changed and will change in Australia – our ethnic composition and, with it, our culture; our economic and industrial practices; our world view – a great deal will change. But traditions of democracy, fairness and personal liberty which we have fought wars to defend, will remain this country's guiding principles …

I cannot accept that this deeply rooted democracy is a disadvantage in dealing with Asia. It is a region, after all, which contains stable democracies like Japan and India, and a number of societies whose economic advance has opened the way to political liberalisation. South Korea and Taiwan to name just two …

What is true politically is also true economically. It is important for Australians to realise that this country's economic weight is considerable. Our GNP is third in the West Pacific and equal to the combined GNP of all the ASEAN countries. We have much of what the countries in the region need – resources, space, a skilled work force, education services. We have the English language, and a rapidly increasing number of young Australians who are competent in Asian languages ...

The success of multiculturalism in Australia, and increasing immigration from Asia, have stimulated our awareness of Asian societies and improved our standing in the region ...

During the 1980s, North-East and South-East Asia constituted the fastest growing region in the world, expanding at approximately twice the world average growth rate. Together these countries account for about 1.7 billion people. That is change on a grand scale.

We do not yet know what the shape of Asia – geopolitically, or economically – will be. But we do know that the key question for Australia is how to position ourselves to take maximum advantage of the changes ...

As we seek the strategy most likely to succeed in this generally favourable environment, three key questions confront us.

First, what level of strategic and economic engagement with the Western Pacific will the United States sustain over the medium to long term?

Second, what quality of international leadership will Japan achieve in the period ahead?

Third, depending on the outcome of the Uruguay Round of multilateral trade negotiations, what type of trade alignments are likely to evolve in the Asia-Pacific region over the next decade? The questions are obviously inter-related. The issues have been much discussed and I don't wish now to add to the available body of analysis and speculation. Let me offer, instead, some comments on Australia's preferences in each case ...

US strategic engagement in the Western Pacific, and the maintenance of existing US bilateral alliances, make a vital contribution to regional stability and confidence ...

Japan's impressive economic achievements are widely recognised, but their translation into international influence has been uneven ... Our firm preference is for a more active Japanese role internationally ...

... concern is often expressed that the international trading system will gradually degenerate into three trading blocs – one in Europe, one in the Americas, and the other in East Asia ... In the modern globalised trading environment, it is not inevitable that the Americas and East Asia would separate into rival trading blocs ... even if they did, Australia would still have viable trade policy options – though undoubtedly inferior ones to those a multilateral system offers ...

Just as Australia's economic engagement with Asia is more advanced than is sometimes realised, so too we have more scope to contribute to regional political affairs than is commonly appreciated at home.

We start from the best possible position, having no historical or fundamental conflict of interest with any country in the region. We have institutional strengths to draw on. We have well-developed foreign policy expertise in the government and academia. We must be careful not to overplay our hand, but if our timing is good and we choose things which genuinely serve the wider interest, we can help shape the regional agenda.

Our role as a catalyst in the Cambodia peace process is one good example. We have also played a useful role in launching and helping advance the APEC process, and in encouraging regional security dialogue in Asia.

As I see it, the quality of Australia's future relationship with Asia very much depends on what happens with regard to trade alignments in the Pacific ...

All this points to the wisdom of Australia's effort since 1989 to establish and develop APEC. The general virtue of the process is its promotion of regional economic cooperation within a framework which embraces North America and East Asia ... the objective should be to promote an open regionalism which is compatible with a wider multilateral trading system.

Another way of promoting cooperation in the Asia-Pacific region would be to establish a process of periodic heads-of-government meetings, say every two or three years. The absence of such a process is conspicuous in a region whose weight in global affairs is steadily increasing ...

I discussed this general idea with President Bush when he visited Australia. I hope to pursue it as opportunity allows with other Asia-Pacific leaders ...

We have come a long way in the last decade: there is every chance of a quantum leap in the next. We won't make that leap in the way Bob Menzies might have tried to make it. Blood will not determine it. To do it, we need to recognise that we have become a player in these affairs – and have a stake in them – not by accident, but by initiative. The key to our success now rests with ourselves. In initiatives we have taken abroad. And in the ones we have taken at home ...

We'll never get anywhere but into trouble if we drift – as we did in the fifties.

In the eighties, we took hold of the rudder and set about an essential economic transformation which leaves us able to hold our own in Asia in the nineties …

I have spent much of the past decade engaged in structural reform. That has also meant something equally as difficult – perhaps more difficult. I mean cultural reform, the reform of our outlook. Success at home depends on this change. Success in Asia depends on it too. It depends on the individual and collective faith of Australians. It depends on establishing beyond doubt:

- that Asia is where our future substantially lies;
- that we can and must go there;
- and that this course we are on is irreversible.

What John Curtin said in 1942 is right for us in 1992: 'On what we now do depends everything we may like to do'.

Source: <www.keating.org.au>.

PAUL KEATING

'Those lessons we learn from Ireland'

Paul Keating, the grandson of Irish immigrants, addresses the Irish Parliament

When Paul Keating went to Ireland in 1993, he said it was as if he 'never left'. Keating is an Irish Catholic. His grandparents had arrived in Australia in 1855 from Ireland to make a new life. He had grown up in the predominantly Irish Catholic community of Bankstown.

He led a party that has strong Irish Catholic roots. More Labor leaders claim an Irish heritage than any other, including James Scullin, John Curtin, Frank Forde, Ben Chifley and Kevin Rudd.

By the end of the 1800s, around half a million Irish had made Australia their home. Today, over six million Australians claim an Irish heritage.

Few foreign leaders have addressed the Dáil Éireann. Keating followed only five others: John F Kennedy, Ronald Reagan, François Mitterrand, Bob Hawke and Nelson Mandela.

As he was introduced, Keating was told 'how truly proud your Irish grandparents would be if they could see their grandson today'. Keating spoke of the immigrant experience and his own history, linking them both with the transformation of Australia under Labor. He drew on the Irish spirit: the boldness, the sense of adventure and imagination, seeking new opportunities and broader horizons. He received a standing ovation.

Don Watson, Keating's speechwriter, said in *Recollections of a Bleeding Heart*, that it 'was a speech from the dreaming of Paul Keating'. Deeply personal, it is a testament to his political philosophy and to his legacy, his leadership and his commitment to reform.

At a dinner at Dublin Castle, Laura Tingle reported in *The Australian* that Keating said the Irish sense of 'nationhood, folklore, egalitarian values, values of fairness and values of decency' were more important to Labor 'than any ideology'.

'Those lessons we learn from Ireland'

Dáil Éireann, Dublin, 20 September 1993

Ceann Comhairle (the Speaker or chairman), let me say it is a pleasure to be in the great city of Dublin; a rare feeling, as ever, to be in Ireland whence came my own people, so many of my fellow-Australians and so much of my country; and an honour to address the Dáil …

Both our countries are now players in the international economy and inevitably we have overlapping economic interests. … necessarily, I want to talk about related social issues, particularly unemployment which is a problem afflicting both our countries …

I am also here for the less tangible but utterly inescapable and irresistible attraction of history. I have a feeling the people in this Chamber may inwardly groan every time a politician of Irish ancestry comes here and signals that he or she is going to give them a history lecture. It would not surprise me if you are thinking – here we go again, he is going to tell us about our Irish past or our literary tradition; he is bound to quote Yeats at us; tell us about 1798 again or give us his views on our character. I would dearly like to spare you this and I will.

As a post-colonial country ourselves, some of us remember the presumptions of visitors. Yet, the fact remains that Ireland is possibly unique in the world in the hold it has on the consciousness of other countries. I know when my predecessor, Bob Hawke, addressed this Parliament several years ago he spoke about the feeling he had when he arrived at Shannon airport — he said he felt as if he had come home. Bob Hawke is nowhere near as Irish as I am; if Bob felt at home, it must be I never left …

Australians feel uncannily at home with the Irish. They feel a great affinity which apparently transcends ancestral connections and this seems to me to speak of the immense power and importance of history, memory, language and culture.

I am not talking about some quaint showcase of the past, of museums, of curious glimpses of faded agrarian life or even Georgian architecture, although I could look at Georgian architecture all day, myself. The attraction of Ireland is an elemental thing; it fulfils a need in us. It is almost as if one can say that if Ireland did not exist countries like Australia would have to invent it, and perhaps we should.

Politicians or governments of all complexions, bureaucrats and business people, all those of us in a position to influence policy, should know what it means to ignore history, heritage, language and culture. Yet, there is always a tendency in political thought towards orthodoxy rather than those broad and less readily defined concerns.

On the way here via the United States and Britain I was reading Seán Ó Faoláin's book *The Irish*. At one point, writing about Wolfe Tone, he says:

> One feels that his laughter and his humanity would have blown all these away, would have defined political liberty not merely in terms of comfort but of gaiety and tolerance and a great pity and a free mind and a free heart and a full life.

Ó Faoláin, of course, was talking about Ireland, which I do not mean to do; I mean to talk about my own country.

Many of the Irish who played leading parts in Tone's rebellion of 1798 were transported to Australia, among them prominent leaders of the rebellion like Michael Dwyer, Joseph Holt, James Meehan and Michael Hayes.

I might add, inter alia, that a concentration of 1798 veterans took up land to the south-west of Sydney in such numbers as to earn the place the name of Irishtown. It is now called Bankstown and it is where I was born, grew up and spent most of my life. It is my hometown and the heart of my political constituency, and the most obvious ethnic groups these days are Lebanese and Vietnamese.

The curious thing about the 1798 convicts is that in the colony of New South Wales the expectation that these rebels would rebel was never really met. The profound opportunities for economic independence which Australia provided for men and women of ordinary means, combined with the liberal humanity of individuals like Governor (Lachlan) Macquarie, put paid not just to their rebelliousness, but to the notion that the Irish were born rebels, that they were irredeemably hostile to society, or at least it should have put paid to the notion …

One hundred years later a huge sign was erected in London's Aldwych near the site of Australia House. It said:

> Go to Australia. You will have a hearty welcome, a generous return for your energy and enterprise and a climate that is the healthiest in the world.

Australia has always held out this great promise, that it could take the poor and the oppressed and give them liberty, economic independence and the material comforts denied them in their own country and, beyond that, by these 'blessings' winnow from their hearts and minds all the ancient bitterness and unreason, as if Australia could do what a Wolfe Tone might have done.

If there has been a continuous theme to Australian history, one mission, it is perhaps this one. If there is one standard we have set ourselves, it has been how well we have lived up to this promise.

The theme begins with the British and Irish convicts and it follows the trail of migration through to the present day. It includes not just the Irish but the Italians, the Greeks, the Lebanese, the Jews, the Latvians, the Vietnamese, the Chinese and the Cambodians — people from more than 150 countries of the world.

It has been a difficult ambition to live up to. Consider the appellations given to the country over the years. It has been known as the 'better country'; the 'land of the better chance'; the 'working man's paradise'; the 'social laboratory of the world'; 'Australia Unlimited' and, although it was originally meant ironically, 'the lucky country'.

Occupying a land so vast, with such bountiful resources, such a splendid climate, such free institutions, being heirs to a land seemingly so blessed, may be why Australians are sometimes rather severely self-critical. In fact, depending on which columnists one reads – and there seems to be no consensus even among the several of Irish extraction – one would think sometimes we live in a diabolically impoverished and inadequate place.

It is a constant theme of political and cultural argument in Australia that we have failed to deliver on our unlimited potential; indeed, that our great good fortune in possessing a vast continent has made us complacent. There is a view, which I do not share, that those things we have achieved might have been more the product of good luck than good management.

With rare exceptions, we have delivered liberty. If material prosperity has occasionally been hard to come by, and there have been enough instances of conflict to indicate that the resentments were not entirely swept away, Australia has always been and remains by any standards both a prosperous country and a tolerant one.

I do not know any way to measure the extent to which an immigrant culture has been responsible for this; how much it has both obliged us to practise tolerance and provide opportunity, or to what extent we can say that a migrant culture, of its nature, will demand these things and value them.

A familiar question for Australians is how much we are a product of our circumstances, and how much we are what we have made ourselves to be. In truth, by the act of migration the country was made: by that voluntary act and by the emigrants' ambitions it was built.

As a politician, I know little of a lasting nature happens by virtue of some latent moral or political force. As a general rule we do not get blown where we want to go – we have to take ourselves there. In politics, as in much else, it requires imagination and a will to exercise political power. That depends on having not just the Irish rebel's feeling about injustice but the 19th century Irish emigrant's ability to imagine a better life, and to find it.

Indeed, I would like to think I had more of the qualities of the emigrant. Better a politician who not only confronts an unsatisfactory reality, but has the wherewithal, the will and the skill, to change it. Better one willing to go to sea – but, of course, not in a boat without oars.

In Australia in the 1980s we embarked on a voyage of economic reform. We deregulated the economy and opened it up to the world. In doing this we did what the emigrant does – we confronted necessity. Had we not done so, the modern world and the opportunities it offers would have passed us by. It took political will, persuasion and persistence and the ability to resist the temptation to turn back ...

Of course, we were not the only country in the world to reform our economy in the 1980s. Much that we did was done elsewhere as countries realised that in the modern era if they did not change they would fall behind ...

A large element of our improved international competitiveness was achieved by means of an accord between the government and the trade unions. The accord dramatically reduced industrial disputation, held wages to competitive levels, made a major contribution to reducing inflation to a rate among the lowest in the OECD and sponsored a creative and co-operative culture in the workplace which is radically increasing levels of productivity.

Implementing the concept of the social wage in the 1980s meant that in the 1990s we have a first-class health system; a social net as extensive and sophisticated as any in the world; legislation affecting the rights and wellbeing of women as advanced as any in the world; and through positive government programmes assisting ethnic groups and encouraging cultural diversity, a multicultural society of infinitely more richness and strength, including economic strength. In other words, as the Australian government has stepped out of the marketplace in many regards, it has stepped into its social responsibilities.

It is essentially for reasons of social unity and social justice that we have made the biggest effort in our history at last to deliver the basis of social justice for indigenous Australians, of extended opportunity which New World countries like ours are intended to provide.

The great casualty of immigration was Aboriginal Australia. The destruction of this extraordinary ancient culture, and the brutality and injustice inflicted on the first Australians can never really be set to right, any more than the injustice and dispossession which occurred in this country can be fully set to right …

If we have learned a lesson in the course of the journey, it is that the pace will be best maintained and the change will be more effective if the people are included. No political principle was so thoroughly confirmed for me in recent years as this one: that one succeeds best by trusting the people's best feelings. I believe that is the essential weapon of every political reformer. Change will never be made by heeding the negatives, the conservatism, myopia, prejudice or pedantry which exists in any society. Those prone to nervousness could not dictate a reform agenda. Change will be made by leaping over them – by talking of something better.

Of all the lessons of the emigrant, for the politician this is the most fundamental and I believe it is the lesson contained in those words I quoted about Wolfe Tone – that political reform means to enlarge life. It means offering an alternative to cant and narrow orthodoxy and all the debilitating constraints in which history is forever wrapping us and to which conservative self-interest always appeals.

Political reform means offering to the people what emigration offered to the Irish in the 19th century, to Europeans after World War II, to Cambodians and Vietnamese in recent times – quite simply, the prospect of a better life in a better country.

This takes me back, in turn, to those lessons we learn from Ireland: that if we are drawn to Ireland by the history, the language and culture – not to say the beauty of the place – then governments ignore these things at their peril.

For that reason there is a link between culture and reform, between the arts and reform, between the life of the mind and reform.

It is why, like the extension of social policy, the extension of policies encouraging cultural development is essential in times of dramatic economic change. They feed the national imagination, encourage people to contemplate alternatives and, of course, they soothe the savage beast in us.

You see what lessons can be drawn from Ireland: real, hard, political lessons. It is not that we were thinking of Ireland when we drew them. The parallels only begin to present themselves as we approach the old shores.

Nor were we thinking of Ireland when we thought of the republic … It seemed to us that a republic might acknowledge and enshrine the values of a people who have been willing to imagine something better, willing to confront the need to change, to make their way on a new frontier, and who have learned that these things are best done together.

To those who want to hold back, who fear change, who say it is not the right time to do this, we might say – what if our forebears had said that? What if they had lacked the imagination and the will? What if they had stayed put?

Well, I would not be an Australian nor would most of the 17 million others, and I would not have had the extraordinary opportunities my country has given me – among them the immeasurable privilege of coming to the land of my ancestors as prime minister of Australia and addressing this national Parliament.

Source: Houses of the Oireachtas, <www.oireachtas.ie>.

PAUL KEATING

'The shameful decision by France to test nuclear weapons'

*On the floor of the NSW Labor Party Conference, Paul
Keating speaks of a world without nuclear weapons*

In mid-1995, the French government announced that it would resume testing nuclear weapons in the South Pacific.

The reaction in Australia was profound. All things French were now considered toxic: baguettes, fries, French restaurants, Peugeot cars. There were protest marches in capital cities. In Perth, the French Consulate was fire-bombed.

The tests struck a chord within the Labor Party. The Hawke government pushed for the adoption of the Chemical Weapons Convention, helped to create the South Pacific Nuclear Free Zone, supported the Nuclear Non-Proliferation Treaty and the Comprehensive Test Ban Treaty, and appointed an Ambassador for Disarmament. The Whitlam government had also made nuclear non-proliferation a cornerstone of its foreign policy.

The Keating government reacted strongly to the testing. Defence contracts between Australia and France were frozen. Foreign Minister Gareth Evans led a delegation from the South Pacific Forum of nations to Paris to protest. The Australian Ambassador to France was recalled. Keating moved a motion of condemnation in Parliament, wrote articles in French newspapers and successfully pushed for the Commonwealth Heads of Government Meeting to denounce the move. At the International Court of Justice, Evans appeared in person to argue that the tests, and the very existence of nuclear weapons, were illegal. The high-powered Canberra Commission was established to recommend 'concrete and realistic steps for achieving a nuclear weapons-free world'.

At the NSW Labor Party conference later that year, Keating delivered a keynote address from the stage, mingled with delegates and served cups of tea to party members. He then moved a resolution from the conference floor condemning the French tests. When the party's president, Terry Sheahan, said 'I call delegate Keating to the microphone', the Sydney Town Hall erupted in cheers and applause. The conference was electrified. Here was the Prime Minister, standing among delegates on the conference floor, his vote and his voice worth no more than anybody else's. It was classic Keating: taking a moral stand while employing the language of a political street fighter.

The French eventually reduced the number of planned tests and they concluded in 1997.

'The shameful decision by France to test nuclear weapons'

Sydney Town Hall, Sydney 30 September 1995

Mr President, I thought I would take this opportunity of the conference to say something declaratory, to move a proposal which I urge the conference to adopt. It is about the role of the French in the Pacific and the shameful decision by France to test nuclear weapons there. It says this:

> Conference condemns the continuing program of dangerous and environmentally irresponsible nuclear testing being conducted by France in the South Pacific.
>
> Conference notes the destabilising adverse effects of the program on the region and the infringement of the rights of the indigenous people of the South Pacific.
>
> Conference expresses its outrage that France's nuclear testing program seriously impedes progress on the Comprehensive Test Ban Treaty and Nuclear Non-proliferation Treaty and the efforts to create a nuclear free world.
>
> Conference expresses its total opposition to all nuclear testing by all states in all environments.
>
> Conference calls on the federal government to continue its campaign to employ all practical measures at Australia's disposal to halt the French nuclear testing program, including through diplomatic efforts including resolutions of The United Nations General Assembly and other multilateral organisations and regional bodies such as the South Pacific Forum; taking every appropriate step in international law to secure the end of the testing program; encourage individual campaigns of protest by Australians.
>
> Conference states that no new contracts for Australian uranium sales to France be signed or approved until France signs the CTBT.
>
> Conference calls on the Australian government to take all actions in respect of existing contracts for uranium sales to ensure that such sales make no direct or indirect contribution to the French nuclear weapons program.

Mr President, the Australian Labor Party and this government has had a long and honourable history on arms control and disarmament issues …

Our objection to what is being done now is at a time when there should be a premium on non-proliferation, at a time when the world believed the Cold War had ended. A democracy. Not a totalitarian regime, but a democracy has come out and said that in its view, the nuclear weapons game is not over. That the premium on non-proliferation will be lowered and it have basically said it is competent for it and others to go out and test nuclear weapons, to refine them further or to develop them in a primary sense.

Now by President Jacques Chirac overturning President Francois Mitterrand's decision for a cessation of testing of nuclear weapons at Mururoa Atoll, what we have seen there is a nuclear weapon state telling all the would-be proliferators that it is basically okay to test weapons. The Irans, Iraqs, the Pakistans and all of the others who are out there mucking around with nuclear weapons, France is out there saying it is okay. That is our objection.

Our second objection is that because it is a democracy it ought to have respect for the people in the area in which it is testing. That is, it is not testing these weapons in its own territory, its own metropolitan territory, it is testing them in an area of the Pacific it calls its own.

And in debating this with one French newspaper, the editor upbraided me, he said this is French territory, this is France. I said, 'Yes I know, there are Polynesians all the way down the Loire Valley and Carcassonne and Aix-en-Provence, popping out behind the trees, down in the Dordogne, they are all over the place'.

The fact is, what France has done is call into question the legitimacy of its connections in the Pacific for its contempt and betrayal of the values that democracies have …

The biggest problem that we face in the post Cold War world is a cessation of testing of nuclear weapons and Australia will be at the forefront of the development of a Comprehensive Test Ban Treaty.

If some good comes from this we hope to pin France into it and it said it would support a zero threshold which would mean that we may have a treaty of substance.

But beyond the treaty and the Non-proliferation Treaty, of course, we still have the great stock pile of weapons out there, decaying weapon inventories.

I think what France has done is remind the world, remind everybody, that there are 50,000 nuclear warheads laying around the place, that we do have rotting submarines sitting in Vladivostok, that their reactors are overheating and they are being kept cool by pumps on the wharves and all of the other bits and pieces of industrial junk which has been appendages of that old desire to see a big Soviet maritime force

It is true still, unfortunately, that there are 14 reactors the same as Chernobyl, that they have the same inherent design faults, that they are sitting in the Ukraine and Belarus and these other places around Northern Europe, that they threaten continental Europe, that they have to be replaced and that the premium has to be upon non-proliferation on the disposal of these weapons stocks and on making these electricity programs safe.

This is what France should be interested in and it is engagement with these issues which will bring security to France. Not some notion that it should be developing a weapons program itself and one which in some way will guarantee its security in the past. This is all a throwback to 1940 and 1941. This is all about (Adolf) Hitler going down the Champs Elysees. It is all about Chirac saying never again.

Well, of course, we all know never again and anyone that owns nuclear weapons can say never again, but why must they refine their weapons and why must they add to the inventory and why can't they join the rest of us in cleaning the world up. This is what we want them to do.

Mr President, the good thing about this is we are having an impact on the French people themselves. I have placed articles in *Le Monde*, in *Liberation* and with other newspapers, we are winning the battle in France itself and President Chirac has just taken an enormous tumble in the opinion polls from an approval rating in the 50s – I think 58 – down to 32 per cent and a disapproval rating which has gone from 20 odd per cent to something like 45 per cent. It has been a complete reversal of his fortunes and that of his government.

Now, we have got 71 per cent of the opposition in the European Parliament, France's European allies – 71 per cent opposition to testing amongst the French people – and, of course, general support for the policies and processes that we have articulated and enunciated.

So, he is losing the battle in Europe, he is losing it at home, he is losing it in Germany which is a country that matters most to France in terms of public opinions, he is losing it, I think, all around the world.

We want to make it clear that our opposition is not an opposition to France itself. France has given the world so much in its history with the French Revolution, with democracy, with its culture, so our opposition is not an opposition to France or the French people; it is an opposition to the French President's decision and the French government. We object to this unprincipled decision, to this betrayal of the interests of the rest of us and those in the Pacific by a democracy.

We have worked with France in the past to do things. I had the pleasure in 1988 of meeting Prime Minister Michel Rochard and proposing to him that we not sign the minerals convention and that we make Antarctica a wilderness park and that is where the movement towards the 50 year wilderness declaration for Antarctica came from. Bob Brown was chewing on a muesli bar at the time, I think …

So, we are not against France or the French people, but we are against this decision. We want it reversed. We want to see no more tests. We want the French to clean up their act. We want then to apologise and we want them to join the rest of us in cleaning the world of these dreadful weapons. This is what we want.

President Chirac says I am anti-French, this you know Mr President, isn't true. All those antique dealers down the Rue de Bac and the Rue Madeleine and the Rue de St Honoré know it's not true too. But what is true is that we are going to keep on his wheel until he lets off. What is true is I'll keep after him until he gives up and I know the Australian people are going to keep after him as well. That we are not going to relent. That we do have good values and we do get indignant about these things and we did think the Cold War was over and there was no more need for it …

So, Mr President, I urge conference support for the resolution. I know there is a fair bit of bipartisan support for this. I welcome this, but I assure you the government will fight this right to the end. Gareth Evans is in New York at the moment, were we are now putting together the support at The United Nations for a resolution which is condemning this testing and process and calling it into question and seeking cessation of it. We will be using all of the forums we can to keep this pressure on and I know with the support of the Labor Party and the community of this country we can have a very big impact.

Source: Editor's personal files.

SIMON CREAN

'Australia still looks to America'

Simon Crean recalls the US-Australian alliance and tells
George W Bush that Labor opposes the Iraq War

George W Bush was the fourth United States President to visit Australia while in office. His 2003 visit came amid the global war on terrorism and while Australian forces served in Iraq and Afghanistan.

Labor had opposed the invasion of Iraq. Simon Crean had been Labor's leader for less than a year and had faced a protracted period of internal party division. He would resign a month after this speech. But on this occasion, Crean excelled.

In The House of Representatives, the mood was tense. Half the Labor caucus had signed a letter of protest over the invasion of Iraq, which was handed to Dr Condoleezza Rice, the US National Security Adviser, in the chamber. Bush's speech was heckled by Greens Senators.

Crean, who had met Bush privately, said that Labor's support for the alliance 'remains unshakeable', but the two countries 'must be honest with each other'. He said 'honesty is, after all, the foundation stone of that great Australian value, mateship'. He noted the differences over Iraq but acknowledged 'the strength of our shared values, interests and principles'. He spoke of John Curtin and Franklin D Roosevelt, and echoed the words of Abraham Lincoln and the Declaration of Independence.

Via correspondence with Crean for this book in September 2010, he said that he wanted to 'deliver a more fundamental interpretation of the alliance and the context for Labor's position'. The 'crucial' part was to state Labor's 'commitment to the alliance and to the relationship, but also our opposition to the war in Iraq'.

Paul Kelly, writing in *The Australian*, said that Crean 'handled a difficult brief with finesse'. The late Matt Price said it was 'easily the most impressive of his two-year term as leader'.

Graham Freudenberg, Labor's greatest speechwriter, was lured from retirement to help draft the speech.

'Australia still looks to America'

The House of Representatives, Canberra 23 October 2003

Mr President, I join with the prime minister in extending the warmest of welcomes to you and Mrs Bush. It is a pleasure to have you in our country.

We are especially pleased that you have come to this country following the meeting of APEC, because it is a source of great pride that a great former prime minister of this country, Bob Hawke, was instrumental not only in getting APEC going but also in insisting that, for it to be effective, the United States needed to be involved.

Your presence today reminds us all that the partnership between our two great nations is broad, deep and many sided. It is longstanding and, in its fundamentals, it is bipartisan. It is, above all, a partnership of peoples. It is something beyond political parties and beyond administrations.

More than 60 years ago another great Labor prime minister, John Curtin, and a great American president, Franklin Roosevelt, forged that partnership together in the crucible of World War II. Curtin famously wrote in December 1941: 'Australia looks to America, free of any pangs as to our traditional links or kinship with the United Kingdom'.

It is altogether fitting today that we should reaffirm that alliance in a world of rapid change …

We now also look to the future in our own region, as both a good friend and a good neighbour among the nations of Asia and the Pacific. We also look to our future in terms of our deep and enduring support for The United Nations and the principles of The United Nations Charter – as we did in East Timor. Above all, Australia looks to itself; to the self-reliance of a proud, a free, a strong and an independent people.

The Australian perspective is bound to differ from time to time from the perspective of the United States. Of course, on occasions, friends do disagree – as we did, on this side, with you on the war in Iraq. But such is the strength of our shared values, our interests and our principles that those differences can enrich rather than diminish, can strengthen rather than weaken, the partnership.

Our commitment to the alliance remains unshakable, as does our commitment to the war on terror. But friends must be honest with each other. Honesty is, after all, the foundation stone of that great Australian value, mateship.

Mr President, the world has changed, but there remains an essential truth in prime minister Curtin's words of 62 years ago: Australia still looks to America.

That is a truth not just for Australia but for democracies everywhere. It is a profound, historical truth which derives its power not from the might of America but from the democratic promise upon which America was brought forth, conceived and dedicated 227 years ago.

The equal rights of all nations, respect for the opinions of all peoples and the idea that all men are created equal: these principles, taken together, form the true and imperishable basis of the promise of, and the friendship between, our two great nations.

May they never perish from the face of the earth.

Source: Commonwealth of Australia Parliamentary Debates (Hansard).

JULIA GILLARD

'Your city on a hill cannot be hidden'

Julia Gillard urges global leadership from the United States

Julia Gillard was the third Australian Prime Minister to address a joint meeting of the United States House and Senate, following Bob Hawke in 1988 and John Howard in 2002. In 1950 and 1955, Robert Menzies addressed only the House.

The speech was to mark the 60th anniversary of the Australia-United States alliance formalised in the ANZUS treaty. Gillard's task was to give her own rendering of the history of the alliance, reaffirm the broader partnership and present her government's foreign policy priorities.

Gillard looked and sounded confident, resplendent in a bright orange jacket amid a sea of dull grey suits.

The speech was well delivered. Short sentences were crafted around carefully chosen words, relying less on a speechwriter's literary tricks, instead favouring direct and meaningful language. Apparently, Gillard wrote most of the speech herself.

The speech utilised historical analogies that stirred the emotions of the audience. Recalling the 'city on a hill' metaphor from the greatest speech of all – Jesus' Sermon on the Mount – Gillard called for 'bold' United States leadership. 'Your city on a hill cannot be hidden', she said. By saying 'the world always looks to America', Gillard was recalling John Curtin's famous December 1941 message. Gillard used several personal anecdotes to illustrate her themes. Watching the 1969 moon landing as a kid, Gillard believed that 'Americans can do anything'.

The effectiveness of a speech must, in part, be judged by the response from the audience. Clearly moved by the speech, Speaker John Boehner wiped a tear from his eye. The audience lapped up the warm tribute and Gillard received more than a dozen standing ovations.

'Your city on a hill cannot be hidden'

The United States Congress, Washington DC 9 March 2011

Since 1950, Australian Prime Ministers Robert Menzies, Bob Hawke and John Howard have come here.

Speaking for all the Australian people through you to all the people of the United States they each came with a simple message. A message which has been true in war and peace, in hardship and prosperity, in the Cold War and in the new world. A message I repeat today.

Distinguished Members of the Senate and the House: You have a true friend down under.

For my parents' generation, the defining image of America was the landing at Normandy. Your 'boys of Point-du-Hoc' risking everything to help free the world.

For my own generation, the defining image of America was the landing on the moon. My classmates and I were sent home from school to watch the great moment on television. I'll always remember thinking that day: Americans can do anything.

Americans helped free the world of my parents' generation. Americans inspired the world of my own youth. I stand here and I see the same brave and free people today. I believe you can do anything still.

There is a reason the world always looks to America.

Your great dream – life, liberty and the pursuit of happiness – inspires us all.

Those of you who have spent time with Australians know that we are not given to overstatement. By nature we are laconic speakers and by conviction we are realistic thinkers. In both our countries, real mates talk straight. We mean what we say.

You have an ally in Australia. An ally for war and peace. An ally for hardship and prosperity. An ally for the sixty years past and Australia is an ally for all the years to come.

Geography and history alone could never explain the strength of the commitment between us. Rather, our values are shared and our people are friends. This is the heart of our alliance.

This is why in our darkest days we have been glad to see each other's face and hear each other's voice. Australia's darkest days in the last century followed the fall of Singapore in 1942. And you were with us.

Under attack in the Pacific, we fought together. Side by side, step by bloody step ...

Distinguished Members of the Senate and the House, Australia does not forget.

The ultimate expression of our alliance, the ANZUS Treaty, was not signed until 1951. But it was anticipated a decade earlier. In the judgements – the clear, frank and accurate judgements – of an Australian Prime Minister. And in the resolve – the extraordinary, immovable resolve – of an American President.

In the decades since, we have stuck together. In every major conflict. From Korea and Vietnam to the conflicts in the Gulf.

Your darkest days since Pearl Harbour were ten years ago in Washington and New York. And we were with you. My predecessor John Howard was quite literally with you and he came to this Capitol when you met on September 12 to show you that Australians would be with you again.

And after fifty years, under a new Prime Minister and a new President, the ANZUS Treaty was invoked.

Within Australia's democracy, John Howard and I had our differences. But he was and is an Australian patriot and an American friend, a man who was moved by what he saw here in that terrible September.

When John Howard addressed you in 2002 we were already with you in Afghanistan. And we are there with you today ...

Just as our security alliance is one for war and peace, our economic partnership is one for hardship and prosperity ...

Our societies share a deep understanding of the human importance of work. We believe life is given direction and purpose by work. Without work there is corrosive aimlessness. With the loss of work comes the loss of dignity.

This is why, in each of our countries, the great goal of all we do in the economy is the same to ensure that everyone who can work does work.

In turn, this is why each of our countries took early and strong action in the face of the greatest threat to the world's economy since the Great Depression.

And we did not just act locally or individually. We worked together when hardship came. New global realities and the emerging economic weight of countries like China, India and Brazil meant the vital forum for the global response was the leaders of the G20 nations.

My predecessor Kevin Rudd worked hard to ensure this was so ...

Like you, I am a leader in a democracy. I know reform is never easy. But I know reform is right.

The global economic outlook remains fragile and uncertain. Global economic imbalances persist and we must address them or risk future instability. Your leadership in the G20 is still needed to ensure we make the reforms which will keep the global economy on the path to strong, sustained and balanced growth …

We worked hard with you during the global economic crisis to resist protectionist pressures. This only built on our decades working together to promote free trade in the world.

I know many of you worked hard to achieve the Australia-US Free Trade agreement. Thank you. Our FTA experience shows the benefits of free trade.

And we aim for even larger benefits from the Trans-Pacific Partnership, which is a great economic opportunity for our two countries and seven of our regional partners …

I am looking forward to your country hosting the APEC Leaders' meeting later this year. We will work closely together there. Australia is also working for an ambitious and balanced conclusion of the WTO Doha Round as soon as possible.

And we look forward to your Congress passing a 2012 Farm Bill that advances free trade rather than distorting it, and that through free trade, creates jobs.

We know the equation is simple: trade equals jobs …

And our societies share a deep commitment to the value of education. We understand education's transformative power. We know education is the future for every child who learns. We also know education is the future for our economies.

Our future growth relies on competitiveness and innovation, skills and productivity, and these in turn rely on the education of our people.

Australia and America are partners in a globalised world, where open societies flourish and competitive economies thrive …

Achieving prosperity while sharing its benefits requires far-sighted educational reforms.

In the same way, achieving growth while caring for our climate requires far-sighted economic reforms. Breaking the link between economic growth and emissions growth is a difficult challenge for our economies and we can only achieve it by working together.

Our cooperation in key international forums and in research and development is making an important contribution. We must work together to achieve an historic transition to high technology, high skill, clean energy economies …

Shared values are the basis of our security alliance and shared values are the basis of our economic partnership as well.

Through hard work and education, we can deliver a strong economy and opportunity for all.

Americans are great optimists and Australians will always 'have a go'.

So, conceived in the Pacific War and born in the Cold War, adapted to the space age and invoked in the face of terror, our indispensable alliance is a friendship for the future.

It is this year's sixtieth anniversary of the signing of our Treaty that occasions your invitation to me today. For that I am grateful. As I said to President Obama, it is an alliance sixty years young with so much future to share.

And this is a timely opportunity, not so much for reflection on our past, as for discussion of our future.

The bipolar world in which our Alliance was signed has long disappeared. I am not sad about its passing.

Hundreds of millions of people have a better life today, democracy and human dignity have spread wide in the world in the last twenty years. We have seen this from Eastern Europe to East Asia in recent years and we are seeing the hope of it in the Middle East now ...

The rise of the Asia-Pacific will define our times. Like you, our relationship with China is important and complex. We encourage China to engage as a good global citizen and we are clear-eyed about where differences do lie ...

When our alliance was signed sixty years ago, the challenges of the space age were still to come. The challenges of terrorism were still to come.

For sixty years, leaders from Australia and the United States have looked inside themselves and found the courage to face those challenges.

And after sixty years, we do the same today. To protect our peoples. To share our prosperity. To safeguard our future. For ours is a friendship for the future. It has been from its founding and remains so today.

You have a friend in Australia. And you have an ally. And we know what that means. In both our countries, true friends stick together. In both our countries, real mates talk straight.

So as a friend I urge you only this: be worthy to your own best traditions. Be bold.

In 1942, John Curtin – my predecessor, my country's great wartime leader – looked to America. I still do.

This year you have marked the centenary of President Reagan's birth. He remains a great symbol of American optimism. The only greater symbol of American optimism is America itself.

The eyes of the world are still upon you. Your city on a hill cannot be hidden.

Your brave and free people have made you the masters of recovery and reinvention. As I stand in this cradle of democracy I see a nation that has changed the world and known remarkable days.

I firmly believe you are the same people who amazed me when I was a small girl by landing on the moon. On that great day I believed Americans could do anything.

I believe that still. You can do anything today.

Source: <www.pm.gov.au>

Julia Gillard is the third Australian Prime Minister to address a joint meeting of the United States House and Senate. In paying tribute to the United States' role in the world, Gillard declared, 'Your city on a hill cannot be hidden'. Clearly moved by the speech, Speaker John Boehner wipes a tear from his eye.

Source: Fairfax

PART 7

Victory, Defeat, Love and Loss

BILLY HUGHES

'It is not fair – to Judas'

Billy Hughes launches an extraordinary attack on Alfred Deakin for his Machiavellian treachery

In 1909, the fusion of most of the non-Labor groupings in Parliament by the wily Alfred Deakin spelt the end of the first of three Labor governments led by Andrew Fisher.

It also prompted the most extraordinary scenes in Parliament. William Lyne labelled Deakin a 'Judas' – the apostle who betrayed Jesus and hung himself to atone for his sins. But it was then Deputy Labor leader and Attorney-General Billy Hughes who mauled Deakin like no other speaker, in speeches delivered in the evening of 27 May 1909 and the following morning.

With great vitriol and vituperation, fire and flare, Hughes condemned Deakin for his Machiavellian treachery. Politicians and journalists raced into the chamber to watch Hughes in full flight. Few had heard anything like this before. The face of Hughes was red hot with anger. The veins in his hands were bulging. His mind was calculating the most venomous invective to unleash. His voice was high-pitched, shrill and excitable.

He accused Deakin of duplicity and opportunism. Deakin, he said, had enjoyed Labor's support in the past, but was now destroying the Fisher government. He had already conspired to destroy the Watson and Reid governments. Deakin had 'assassinated governments, abandoned friends to the wolves, deserted principles, and deceived the people', Hughes said. Referring to the 'mention of Judas', Hughes said, 'It is not fair – to Judas, for whom there is this to be said, that he did not gag the man whom he betrayed, nor did he fail to hang himself afterwards'.

The recriminations continued for weeks and probably killed The Speaker, Sir Frederick Holder, who collapsed in Parliament amid another heated debate, suffering a cerebral haemorrhage and later dying. Deakin's third prime ministership would last only a year.

Hughes would later earn the epithet of a Labor 'rat' when he left Labor and formed a government with conservative support. But on this occasion, he was Labor's most effective advocate and staunchest defender.

'It is not fair – to Judas'

27 May 1909

'When we find men voting against proposals, the principles of which they say they approve, rather than allow opponents to get them on the statute-book, I think we have yet to learn what public spirit is'. Those are remarks uttered in a prophetic spirit by the honourable member for Ballarat (Alfred Deakin) on 31st October, 1906, and it is upon this very suitable basis that we may proceed briefly to consider the extraordinary situation in which we find ourselves today …

The Honourable Member has always, in this State, and throughout the Commonwealth, enjoyed a reputation for politeness, generosity, gentleman-liness of demeanour, and fair play, which, I regret to say, an examination of his career will hardly justify. While one under the glamour of his affability was very willing to forget many things, he has so timed his actions that we were barely able to forget the one before he managed to perpetrate a fresh enormity which recalled them all.

I may be permitted to congratulate some Honourable Members whom I see opposite, and who find themselves today where they always were. Those men have always opposed the Labor Party, and have every right to do everything they can to put the Labor Party out of office. To them, who are personal friends of mine, I can only say that I congratulate them now that they are one step nearer office than they were before, because in taking it I do not think they have sacrificed any political principle …

In the career of the honourable and learned leader of the opposition, since he entered this House, has there been an hour that he has enjoyed office and power save by the grace and help and aid of our party? Has he achieved anything in this country since Federation was established but by the help of this party? Is there one solitary law of importance that has been placed upon the statute-book by him save by our aid? Is there anything, in short, for which he takes credit which is not due to the support of the Labor Party? …

What, then, is the Honourable Member's record with regard to ourselves? A little while ago, the Honourable Member for Maribyrnong, in criticising the program of the Fisher government, declared it to be substantially that of the Liberal Party with a few extras … Yet a policy which he was content to support cheerfully for the nine years we have kept him in office he now declares himself unable to consider any longer.

We now find him undertaking to carry out what he terms a national policy, and I look around to see the gentlemen who are associated with him in that great work. I see among them the men whom he has always unsparingly denounced ... There is not a vested interest in this country now that does not acclaim him as their champion ...

What a career his has been! In his hands, at various times, have rested the banners of every party in this country. He has proclaimed them all, he has held them all, he has betrayed them all ...

The Honourable Member for Ballarat has thought fit to criticise the policy of this government. He has done so in a way of which, since he never was at a loss for words, it can only be said that there are no words even at this command, to explain his position and attitude. It is a thing beyond words ...

His new policy, hatched and fathered by the new Joshua, who does not bid the sun stand still, but gathers into one camp the hostile factions that for years have been at each other's throats, the Honourable Member for Ballarat will find indeed a boomerang that will hit him when he least expects it.

He sits there now and his new colleagues with him. There are no open signs of dissension in that camp yet. The spoils have not yet been allotted. There is an air of hopeful expectancy about these gentlemen. They conceive that the eternal laws of mathematics, which have governed numbers since the world began, can be set aside, and that eight portfolios will go into forty-three in the way that each desires. Their fond hopes are, in the majority of cases, not destined to be realised.

But what power has dragged these various factions into one camp? The Honourable Member for Ballarat, in the speech which he delivered in the Town Hall on Tuesday night, put forward the 'national' program. I have perused that program, and ... I find that, although he as referred to this list of measures in that speech as too long, covering legislation which is beyond the power of this parliament, there are only two measures which were not in the program which the late government set on the business paper ...

Let us take his conduct towards the Watson government. He, in a most public fashion, pledged himself to support that administration. He shook me warmly by the hand, at the corner of Collins and Spring streets – another kissed the man he was about to betray – and he assured me that he would extend to the Watson government that support which it deserved, and which it had given him. Yet a little later, as he himself has declared – I heard him with my own ears in this chamber – he drafted the amendment moved by Mr (James) McCay, which brought about the downfall of that ministry ...

The heads of the Reid-McLean Ministry were, we were told, equal in all things, and they suffered equally from the piratical sword of the Honourable and learned Member for Ballarat. It was his hand that slew them, and he then came again into power. Honourable Members will notice that he always comes into power after he has been entrapped into doing things of whose effect he had not the faintest notion. He frames an amendment, ignorant of the purpose for which it is to be used. He does so, good easy soul, to assist another over a difficulty in phraseology; but afterwards he invariably comes into office. He put the Reid-McLean government out of power and formed an administration of his own.

But in March, of last year, something happened. What that was is worthy of note, because, although he declares that he has never had any particular quarrel with the policy of the Labor Party, he has always objected to our methods … In the clearest way he accepted our programme of practical reform. It was our caucus and methods to which he took exception …

The Honourable gentleman, in March last, proposed a coalition with the Labor Party – not a loose alliance, but a definite coalition … they went to the point that he was prepared to even stand down and allow the leader of the Labor Party to be Prime Minister – although on that no actual agreement was arrived at – but there were to be four portfolios for the Deakin Party and four for the Labor Party …

They were prepared to swallow not only our policy but our methods. They prepared to contract an alliance with men whom we have lately been told practised the worst methods of Tammany. They were prepared to ally themselves with men whose methods are subversive of liberty, and which make democratic government in this country impossible. Even more, they were prepared to sacrifice four of their own men – to throw overboard anybody and everybody – so long as the Honourable gentleman, who has led in turn all parties, might have an opportunity of leading one more …

What matters the policy or fate of those who follow him, since he has never attempted to carry out any that was not the policy of those who stood behind him? When they altered he altered; when they halted he halted. When they ceased to be useful he deserted them. When their policy ceased to be popular he abandoned it …

If we have been guilty of maladministration of the public affairs of the country, or of corruption and rottenness such as has been hinted, but which none dare put in formal and precise terms, then, indeed, we deserve that every honest man shall range himself against us …

Let those Honourable Members who love liberty, and say that we are the foes of freedom and the people, put it to the issue of a struggle, and go before the people. Since they will not let us say here what is to be said in defence of our policy, but cover up in a way that is shameless and unprecedented, their attempt to oust from office a party whose policy they have approved, against whose administration they can say nothing, whose policy they were prepared to adopt, whose methods they have criticised, but have been, for years, in the habit of condoning, let them agree to go before the people …

The cause of Liberalism is hopelessly doomed when it depends upon the daily and hourly support of Honourable Members who have ever been its open and avowed enemies.

If the Honourable Member for Ballarat be gifted with even ten times the eloquence of Demosthenes there are damning facts that will refute him and stop the ears of the public when he tries to explain these matters away. How will he explain that a party with which for nine years, with one break of eleven months, he was in close association, and with which he was prepared to contract an actual alliance, upon which he had been dependent daily and hourly for office, has been treated as he has treated us? How will he explain his surrender of the citadel of Liberalism to the hosts of reaction?

They will say there could have been only one reason for this conduct and that it was perfectly plain. The vested interests of this country have been aroused and alarmed … The great vested interests needed a leader to protect them; and they have found one ready to their hand …

He has persuaded the reactionaries, for the time being, to cover their vulpine faces with the wool of the sheep. But the people, when they have an opportunity, will tear that cover off them, and disclose them as they are. And they will sweep into outer darkness, too, those who, professing democracy, have betrayed them …

28 May 1909

The Honourable and learned Member for Ballarat has just favoured us for the first time with some excuses for his present action. He has found that which we feared he had lost forever – his facility for explaining and excusing everything – and has given us fresh occasion for amazement, and for some little amusement.

The Honourable gentleman has been endeavouring to elevate political assassination into a fine art, and to place it upon a scientific basis. It appears now that the reason why he assassinated the Watson government was that he was inveigled under specious pretences to draft an amendment which he had not the faintest idea would have the result that followed its adoption …

Had (Thomas) De Quincey lived until now he would have been able to include in his delightful essay on *Murder as Fine Art* the methods of the Honourable Member for Ballarat, for no man has adopted such a variety of methods, and none has contrived to more successfully evade the consequences of his political crimes. His last assassination in some respects out-Herods Herod, but his former achievements ran it hard for first place.

Then there was the assassination of the Reid government, he pledged himself to support it, he destroyed it by a speech which the Right Honourable Member for East Sydney (George Reid) very properly assumed was not only the beginning of the end but the end itself. The Right Honourable Member therefore came down with a governor-general's speech of one paragraph; but did that save him from the wrath to come? We go out because our speech contains thirty-two clauses. He went out because his contained only one clause …

The Honourable and learned Member for Ballarat has told us that the Right Honourable Member for East Sydney was under a complete misapprehension. When at Ballarat he gave the Right Honourable Member notice to quit, he never meant it. At that very moment when the Right Honourable Member's political brains were falling over his shoulders, when his scalp was dangling at the Honourable Member's belt, the Honourable Member was really his best friend. God save us from such friends!

Last night the Honourable Member abandoned the finer resources of political assassination and resorted to the bludgeon of the cannibal. Having perhaps exhausted all the finer possibilities of the art, or desiring to exhibit his versatility in his execrable profession he came out and bludgeoned us in the open light of day. It was then that I heard from this side of the House some mention of Judas. I do not agree with that; it is not fair – to Judas, for whom there is this to be said, that he did not gag the man whom he betrayed, nor did he fail to hang himself afterwards …

… his is a program that changes to fit the bewildering circumstances of political warfare. It is the program of those who from time to time are whirled in violent gyration around the Honourable Member. He still remains the same. Parties change. Circumstances change. He alone remains constant and unshaken. But yesterday he was here. Today he is there. But the day before he offered to stand equal in all things with us … Indeed, he offered us the superior position. Now he leads the cohorts of the opposition …

There is surely some moral obliquity about a nature such as his. No act that he commits, no party that he betrays, no cause that he abandons, affects him at all. He regards himself as the selected and favoured agent of Providence. Everything that he does he does for the very best. He does it because there is nothing else that can be done to conserve the welfare of the people and the interests of the nation. To realise this noble ideal he has assassinated governments, abandoned friends to the wolves, deserted principles, and deceived the people ...

He is the political mercenary of Australia. He will lead any party – he will follow none! He is faithful to only one thing – himself. He is true to only one power, and he bends the knee to only one principle, and this is that which is at any time the most powerful ... he has abandoned his party, and he has applied the gag to those who were his friends and allies, and prevented them from explaining their policy, a policy which he declared – was it five or six or ten days ago – to be a good one for Australia and a policy which even now he is unable to attack successfully.

He sits there now and declares that he is content to leave everything to the cool judgement of the people. He means the refrigerated, the hypnotised judgement of the people. Let him get to the people, whilst the facts and the memory of his latest acts are fresh in their minds. When he says, 'We will sweep the country', the statement is perfectly true. The Honourable gentleman will sweep the country, but we shall be the men who hold the broom and he will be the broom with which we shall sweep it.

Source: Commonwealth of Australia Parliamentary Debates (Hansard).

Always colourful and controversial, Billy Hughes was a founding member of the Labor Party and one of its earliest MPs. While he later left Labor to lead a government in opposition to Labor, in his time he was a devastatingly effective advocate for the Labor cause. His speech condemning the treachery of Alfred Deakin stunned the Parliament. In this photo years later, he is opening the David Jones department store in Sydney in 1928.
Source: Fairfax

JAMES SCULLIN

'He ruled the destinies of Australia'

Jim Scullin remembers one of Labor's greatest leaders, Andrew Fisher

For the first five decades of Labor's existence, the party's greatest leader was undoubtedly Andrew Fisher.

Fisher became Labor leader in 1907, succeeding John (Chris) Watson, and led Labor to two election victories: in 1910 and 1914. He served as Prime Minister on three separate occasions – 1908-09, 1910-13 and 1914-15 – and presided over governments that enacted far-reaching reforms and legislative achievements that had long been part of Labor's platform. After resigning as Prime Minister in 1915, Fisher became Australia's High Commissioner in London. He remained in London for most of the remainder of his life, dying in 1928. Fisher was buried in Hampstead Cemetery. In 1930, a large obelisk memorial to Fisher at the cemetery was unveiled by British Labour Prime Minister Ramsay Macdonald.

Upon his death, although some journalists downplayed Fisher's achievements, *The Queenslander* newspaper, in describing Fisher's rise from coalminer to Prime Minister, said his career 'reads like a romance'. The paper recognised Fisher's 'earnestness of purpose', 'high sense of personal honour' and that he possessed 'the gift of leadership'.

Early the following year, Labor's then leader, Jim Scullin, seconded a motion in Parliament moved by Prime Minister Stanley Melbourne Bruce, which expressed 'profound regret' at Fisher's death and recorded 'its appreciation of the distinguished service rendered' to Australia.

Scullin had been a member of the Labor caucus during Fisher's prime ministership, from 1910-13 and was a great admirer.

In Parliament, Bruce said that Fisher was 'a man of great and wide sympathies, lofty ideals, great dignity and a most striking personality'. Scullin, who would become Prime Minister eight months after this speech was delivered, called Fisher 'one of the greatest men that ever rose to a public position in Australia'. Scullin said that, as Prime Minister, Fisher had 'ruled the destinies of Australia'. Billy Hughes, who succeeded Fisher as Labor's leader, said that 'No one did more for the Australian labour movement than Andrew Fisher; no man led it more successfully. He was the very incarnation of the ideals of Labor'.

'He ruled the destinies of Australia'

The House of Representatives, Canberra 6 February 1929

I second the motion of the Prime Minister (Stanley Melbourne Bruce), and desire to express my regret, and I believe the regret of every Honourable Member of this House, at the death of one of the greatest men that ever rose to a public position in Australia.

I can recall my early entry to the federal parliament at the time Mr Fisher became Prime Minister of Australia. The admiration that I then conceived for him as a great man grew with the knowledge that I subsequently gained of him.

I think probably that the most striking illustration I can recall of Mr Fisher's career and capabilities was a cartoon that appeared in the press on the day he became Prime Minister. That cartoon depicted a figure representing Australia speaking down the mouth of a mine and calling to Mr Fisher, 'Andy, come up, your country wants you'.

That was an incident in the wonderful career of a great man who came to Australia from Scotland, and started to win his way in Queensland.

He worked in the bowels of the earth in coal and gold mines, entered the public life of both State and Commonwealth, and was raised to the highest position that a public man can achieve.

In those memorable years when he ruled the destinies of Australia, he laid foundations upon which we have built to some extent. In those foundations he left monuments of work which has helped this country in many a dark hour.

That is a short history of the life of this man. Those who were privileged to know him are aware that his personality was lovable in the extreme. He had a deep affection for what was good and those who were good, but a strong detestation for what he believed to be wrong.

I well remember how when we sat in Melbourne, the chamber would resound with his denunciation, spoken with a rich Scottish accent, of the things which he believed to be wrong, and of the wrongs which he wanted to be righted in the interests of the people of Australia.

He aroused hostility amongst many but he never lost the respect of any person whose opinion was worth having.

I have received word that there is to be erected in the heart of Empire a monument to his memory, because of the great services that he rendered to the British family of nations.

I cannot help remembering that when he was Prime Minister of Australia, and returning from a memorable mission abroad, from a thousand platforms and by hundreds of newspapers he was denounced as one who would smash the Empire, as one who was against the Empire … But he lived down such abuse … and, for his life's work as a citizen of Australia and a member of the British Empire, we are proud of him and revere his memory.

I join with the Prime Minister in expressing our deepest sympathy with Mrs Fisher and her family in the loss of a good father and husband and a great Australian.

Source: Commonwealth Parliamentary Debates (Hansard).

After resigning as Prime Minister in 1915, Andrew Fisher became Australia's
High Commissioner in London. He remained in London for most of the
remainder of his life, dying in 1928. Fisher was buried in Hampstead Cemetery.
He was regarded as a pioneering centre-left political leader in the
British Labour Party and throughout the world. In 1930, a large obelisk
memorial to Fisher at the cemetery was unveiled by British Labour
Prime Minister Ramsay Macdonald.
Source: Author's photo

JOHN CURTIN

'One of the most eminent of the band of prominent Labor men'

John Curtin recalls the life and legacy of Labor's first leader, Chris Watson

John (Chris) Watson led a long and distinguished life.

He was one of the founding members of the Labor Party, a leading figure in the trade union movement, served in two parliaments, became Labor's first federal parliamentary leader and Labor's first Prime Minister, in 1904. Following his retirement from parliament in 1910, he remained involved in party and union politics, until 1917, when he was expelled from the party over his support for conscription in the First World War.

A month after he became Prime Minister, John Curtin informed the House of Representatives of Watson's death. Curtin described him as 'a great pioneer' and 'one of the most eminent of the band of prominent Labor men elected to the first parliament'. He paid 'tribute to the valuable services that he rendered to the movement of labour' and that he had used 'his natural gifts' in the service of the Commonwealth.

Billy Hughes, then Leader of the United Australia Party, and previously a member of Watson's cabinet, also offered a warm tribute. He said 'death has removed one of the public men who blazed the trail for Labor and democracy and played a great part in shaping the destinies of the commonwealth'.

After Curtin's motion of condolence was carried by the House, the sitting was suspended 'as a mark of respect to the memory of the deceased gentleman'.

At Watson's state funeral, held two days later at St Andrew's Cathedral in Sydney, the pallbearers included Curtin and NSW Premier William McKell and former party members and prime ministers Hughes and Joseph Cook.

Curtin's speech on the day of Watson's death was a fitting tribute to Labor's first leader, delivered by Labor's greatest leader.

'One of the most eminent of the band of prominent Labor men'

The House of Representatives, Canberra 18 November 1941

It is with feelings of deepest regret that I refer to the death today of the Honourable John Christian Watson, a former prime minister of the Commonwealth …

Born at Valparaiso in 1867, the late Mr Watson went to New Zealand as a child, and later came to Australia. His parliamentary career commenced in 1894 when he was elected to the Legislative Assembly of New South Wales as Member for Young, which constituency he represented until June, 1901, when he retired from it after election to the first Federal Parliament for the division of Bland, New South Wales, at the general elections of 1901. He was reelected for that division in 1903, and at the general elections of 1906 was elected to represent the division of South Sydney. He retired from parliamentary life at the expiration of the third parliament in 1910.

The late Mr Watson was the first leader of the federal Labor Party and, upon the defeat of the first Deakin ministry on the Conciliation and Arbitration Bill, was commissioned to form a ministry. His ministry held office from the 27th April to the 17th August, 1904, when it, too, was defeated on an issue affecting the Conciliation and Arbitration Bill. The Right Honourable Member for North Sydney (Billy Hughes) was a member of the Watson ministry, which was succeeded by the Reid-McLaren ministry. After his retirement from the Commonwealth Parliament, Mr Watson engaged in commercial activities He was a director of several companies, and for many years was an executive officer of the National Roads and Motorists Association of New South Wales. He also had wide sporting interests and rendered valuable service as a trustee of the Sydney Cricket Ground.

I had the great honour to know the late Mr Watson personally. Having been the first Labor Prime Minister of Australia, to him can be assigned, in the history of this federation, the role of a great pioneer. On several occasions of sadness, references have been made in this House to the passing one by one of that historical band of men who assembled in Melbourne when the first Commonwealth Parliament met, and tributes have been paid to the distinguished services which they rendered to Australia. That can be said in general of all of them; but I believe that it has special application to those who were leaders of the political parties.

The Australian Labor Party sent to that Parliament members from all of the States. At that period in the history of this country, although the colonies had engaged in a Federation campaign, they were still somewhat detached from each other. The men who gathered together as representatives of the different political parties may have known each other by name, but could not be said to have had that intimate acquaintance with each other's personality which has characterised the personnel of this Parliament in later years …

The late Mr Watson was regarded as one of the most eminent of the band of prominent Labor men elected to the first parliament and, as I have said, he was chosen as their leader. He essayed a very difficult task in the laying of the foundations upon which the Labor Party has since built.

I have said that there arose in the Parliament, on an industrial measure, issues which led to the defeat of the second Commonwealth government, led by the late Mr (Alfred) Deakin, who was commissioned when the first Prime Minister, the late Sir Edmund Barton, was appointed to the bench of the High Court of Australia.

The late Mr Watson, as leader of the Labor Party, was then entrusted with the task of forming the first federal government composed of Labor men. This must ensure him a permanent place in the history of Australia, and most certainly in the annals of Labor in this Commonwealth …

He made friends wherever he went, was an influence for unity, and endeavoured at all times to make Labor a great and, indeed, a permanent force in the political system of this country. I am sure that I shall be forgiven if, in emphasising the distinguished place which he held in the Parliament of this country, I, also on behalf of the great mass of people who support the Labor Party, pay tribute to the valuable services that he rendered to the movement of labour.

He was a man of fine public spirit. He had been a compositor, and like many other men in the printing trade, learned as he worked. Thus at his case he enriched his natural gifts, which, subsequently, he placed at the disposal of the Commonwealth. I move –

> That this House expresses its profound regret at the death of The Honourable John Christian Watson, a former member of the New South Wales and Commonwealth Parliaments, and Prime Minister and Treasurer of the Commonwealth from April to August, 1904, places on record its appreciation of his distinguished public service, and tenders its deep sympathy to his widow and daughter in their bereavement.

Source: Commonwealth of Australia Parliamentary Debates (Hansard).

Frank Forde served in the Scullin, Curtin and Chifley Labor governments.
He was Labor's deputy leader for 14 years and served as Prime Minister for
eight days following John Curtin's death. His eulogy for Curtin was one of
the finest ever delivered in Parliament. In this picture, he addresses a rally
in Sydney in 1942 in the middle of the Second World War.
Source: Fairfax

FRANK FORDE

'The captain has been stricken in sight of the shore'

Frank Forde pays tribute to Australia's greatest Prime Minister, John Curtin

John Curtin's death was a shattering blow to a nation at war.

One of Curtin's final public speeches was a tribute to United States President Franklin D Roosevelt, who had died in April 1945 – another wartime leader who did not live to see the end of the conflict. Shortly after, Curtin was hospitalised for several weeks seeking treatment for congestion of the lungs and was not regularly attending Parliament or cabinet meetings. He died at The Lodge, just after 4.00 am, on 5 July 1945.

Just 10 hours after Curtin's death, at 2.30pm the following day, Acting Prime Minister Frank Forde told The House of Representatives that the Prime Minister had died. In his eulogy, he paid 'a tribute of affection' to 'this common man, this son of the people'. Acknowledging that Curtin would not see the end of the war, Forde said, 'the captain has been stricken in sight of the shore'. He called him 'a gallant, happy warrior', a great Labor leader and 'Australia's greatest son'.

In the presence of five former Prime Ministers, *The Canberra Times* said that Forde had given 'the most moving speech he has ever made'.

Curtin's body lay in state at Kings Hall in Parliament House. After a short memorial service, his casket was taken by gun carriage to Fairbairn Airport and departed for Perth. He was buried at Karrakatta Cemetery on 8 July 1945. Treasurer Ben Chifley was too distraught to attend.

Labor MP Fred Daly recalled that 'thousands of people marched to the graveside in an inspiring and solemn tribute to a great Australian'. Arthur Fadden, the Leader of the National Party, recalled that when Robert Menzies said to him, 'I don't want all this fuss when I go, Artie', Fadden replied, 'don't worry, you won't get it'.

'The captain has been stricken
in sight of the shore'

The House of Representatives, Canberra 5 July 1945

It is my melancholy duty formally to inform Honourable Members of the tragic death early this morning of the prime minister, the Right Honourable John Curtin.

Today, the Australian nation mourns and offers to this common man, this son of the people, a tribute of affection, gratitude and honour, which has been offered rarely, even to kings. For this man was truly one with the masses who populate our country. He had striven and struggled among them, and when he came to the highest place in the land he was still one of them.

John Curtin is as one today with those fighting men of our race who have given their lives that we might live. For them, interposing, as he himself put it, their bodies between us and the enemy, he worked day and night for many weary months and years that they might have the strength to hold out. For the British race and for the cause of The United Nations, he did everything that was in his power to shape policies that would produce the maximum effort on the part of this country.

As I said earlier today, the captain has been stricken in sight of the shore. His memorial stands around us – a free land, a free people. And I feel that he has chosen his own epitaph – in the words of Swinburne, which he quoted to the Australian people on that momentous day, the 8th December, 1941, when Japan struck. They were:

> Come forth, be born and live,
> Thou that hast help to give,
> And light to make man's day of manhood fair,
> With flight outflying the sphere sun,
> Hasten thine hour
> And halt not till thy work be done.

John Curtin's work was done, well and faithfully done. Nothing remained for fulfilment, but the laurel wreath of victory and the benefaction of peace. And so he was called home to rest.

It may be said that the call came before its time. But I think I interpret the feeling of all men when I say that I am thankful that he was spared for so long during this dreadful struggle to guide our nation's destiny. It is true that he had dreams for the future. He had an abiding faith in the future national greatness of Australia, and I recall the vivid picture he painted of what he could see for the future in a speech that he made in Sydney in June, 1943, when addressing the New South Wales conference of his political party. But it was not to be for him. For those of us who remain, he has set a course to follow, and the best tribute we can pay to his memory will be to do as he would have wished us to do.

In this regard, his faith in Australia was expressed by himself on that day in April, 1939, when in this place, he offered the sympathy of his party to the family of the late Mr JA Lyons. Mr Curtin said then: 'We believe that the country that yielded such a man can continue to produce such men'. When the hour arrived, Australia produced John Curtin, and now that he has gone this country is without his leader. In this moment of grief, I am sure he would, if he could, say to us to have faith in ourselves and to carry on the task of building our nation to greatness.

We, in this parliament, here and in another place, have lost a colleague. We have lost, too, a guide and a friend. And parliament, as a democratic institution, has lost one of its staunchest adherents, who revered it, and did much to uphold its dignity and influence.

We of the Federal Parliamentary Labor Party cannot assess our loss in a measure of words. His period of leadership, extending over the record term of nine years, nine months and five days, commenced at a time of trouble in the party's fortunes. His untiring work, shining example, and high ideals raised it to its zenith, and today it has a strength unapproached at any time in its history. All of us will treasure those rare moments when, with the informality of which he was suddenly and spontaneously capable, he would chat with us individually or in groups. To those of us who had the honour and privilege to sit under his chairmanship in the cabinet room, he gave a wealth of knowledge which will stand us in good stead ...

The tributes paid by the world to our great Australian reflect John Curtin as a world figure. That is very fitting, for John Curtin worked for all humanity. In the course of my recent visit to England and America I found that on his tour abroad last year he had made a profound impression upon the statesmen and people of both those countries.

And so we now bid farewell to a man for whom, I am confident, history will mark a place as Australia's greatest son. It is a consolation to everyone to know that this gallant, happy warrior passed on without pain. He faced the last great crisis, fortified by the philosophy which had seen him through so many personal and political crises, both before and after he became Prime Minister. His last words were spoken to his dearly beloved wife, his constant and never failing help-mate and counsellor ...

Mr Curtin was prime minister continuously for a longer period than any previous holder of that office from his party – three years, nine months and a day. The late Mr Andrew Fisher held the office for a greater period, but during three cabinet terms.

Those are the biographical details of a career about which many volumes could be written. Death has written 'finis' but death can never take from our hearts and minds the memory of John Curtin.

It is now my sad task to submit the following motion:

> That this House expresses its deep regret at the death of The Right Honourable John Curtin, Member of the House of representatives for the Division of Fremantle, and for more than three years, Prime Minister of the Commonwealth of Australia; places on record its appreciation of his distinguished public service; and tenders to his widow, his son and daughter, and all relatives, its profound sympathy in their bereavement.

Source: Commonwealth of Australia Parliamentary Debates (Hansard).

NICHOLAS MCKENNA

'To know Ben Chifley was to love him'

Nick McKenna eulogises Labor's most loved leader, Ben Chifley

Ben Chifley delivered his last major political speech to the NSW Labor Party conference on 10 June 1951. It was, as historians have said, tantamount to a final political testament from the political veteran.

The following day, 11 June 1951, the Labor caucus met in Canberra. At that meeting, the first after the 1951 election, Chifley was re-elected as Labor's leader. On 12 June, Chifley attended a State Dinner to commemorate the 50th anniversary of the Parliament, and spoke of the virtues of parliamentary government. On 13 June, Chifley declined to attend the State Ball, instead retiring to the Hotel Kurrajong, 'to read a couple of bloody westerns', he told Labor MP Fred Daly. Later in the evening, he suffered a seizure and subsequently died.

At the Jubilee Ball, just before midnight, Prime Minister Robert Menzies announced that Chifley had died. He encouraged all to 'leave quietly, with sorrow in our minds and hearts for the passing of a fine Australian'.

On 15 June, Chifley lay in state in Kings Hall in Parliament House, before he was taken by gun carriage to Fairbairn Airport and transported to Bathurst for a state funeral, held on 17 June.

On 19 June, Menzies informed the House, officially, of Chifley's death. Menzies said that Chifley was 'the undisputed leader of a great movement'. HV 'Doc' Evatt, Labor's acting leader, spoke of Chifley's 'pursuit of justice'.

The most eloquent speech was delivered by Labor's Senate Leader, Nicholas McKenna. He spoke of 'the man whom we of the Australian Labor Party, and many others beside, knew and loved'. He sought to reveal the inner most character of the man. Party members, he said, 'looked on him as father, brother and mate all at the one time'. 'To know Ben Chifley', McKenna said, 'was to love him'.

426

'To know Ben Chifley was to love him'

The Senate, Canberra 19 June 1951

… The finest and truest tribute that has been, or ever will be, paid to Joseph Benedict Chifley was uttered only last week by the lady who was his wife and is now his widow: 'he loved everything and every one' she said. That might well be his epitaph, but it is more, far more than that …

I suggest that when we pray for the repose of the soul of Ben Chifley we say just that 'he loved everything and every one'. The hearts of the widowed, the deserted, the unemployed, the disabled and the sick of Australia will join with us in that prayer. He it was, more than any one in all Australia, who strove and legislated to relieve their plight.

I do not propose to speak of Joseph Benedict Chifley, the trade union leader, the Australian Labor Party leader, the Federal Treasurer, the Prime Minister of Australia, or the statesman with the international outlook. I leave those aspects to popular, if inadequate, knowledge, and as rich fields to be explored by the historian in due course.

I propose to speak of Ben Chifley, the man whom we of the Australian Labor Party, and many others besides, knew and loved.

The key to the character of Ben Chifley was his true, great and abiding interior simplicity. From that interior simplicity stemmed his gentleness and his great strength, his love of everything and every one, his honesty, uprightness, single-mindedness of purpose and steadfastness, his high sense of duty, his courage, his loyalty, his vast tolerance, his unselfishness, his modesty, his tranquillity, his all-pervading sense of humour, his love of country and, indeed of all humanity.

That, too, led him to choose austerity rather than soft-living.

It accounted for the absence of vice in him and for his scorn of anything dishonourable.

It led him on in a never-ending search for knowledge and truth, a search that made him equally at home in subjects as diverse as literature, religion, the arts, sport, finance and history.

It accounted for his great wisdom and for the fact that every member of his party looked on him as father, brother and mate all at the one time.

He never entertained a thought or did a thing that was mean, paltry or vindictive. He was not capable of it. He always defended those criticised in his presence …

Ben Chifley was deeply interested in those whom he met and knew. He shared with them their little joys and sorrows and interests. He was, I suppose, the repository of more personal confidences than were ever entrusted to any man in public life. That explains why each of thousands of people throughout Australia on learning of his death, felt that he had lost his best friend.

As the leader of the government (Robert Menzies) has said, to know Ben Chifley was to love him, and the extent of one's regard for him was the measure of one's knowledge of him.

By virtue only of the patent qualities inherent in him, Ben Chifley effortlessly won the loyalty of and extracted the best from all those who were near him in his work. Lightly, even casually, he imposed responsibilities on them. Their knowledge that without a word being spoken he trusted them to discharge that responsibility faithfully, led them to superhuman efforts so that they would not fail him. That, Mr President (Ted Mattner), is the mark of the true leader.

There were some who, in the heat of controversy, vilified him. In sorrow, I leave them to their remorse and to the stirrings of their consciences. I offer them the consolation that their barbs did him no hurt; he rode, serene, above them.

All that Mr Chifley accomplished for Australians and Australia would never have been done if his sacrifice of himself had not been accompanied by the sacrifice of Mrs Chifley. For many long years she bore the loss of his cheerful presence and society …

Ben Chifley, in giving so unstintingly of himself, in asking nothing for himself, got everything worthwhile in return …

We, of the Federal Parliamentary Labor Party, can now say what we could never say to him during his life, 'We loved him' …

Ben Chifley, if he could speak to us today, would tell us that he got all that he desired from life, and that death was merely the door opening to that which above all, he sought – knowledge and truth …

There is no need of tears for Ben Chifley.

The poet might well have been thinking of him when he penned these lines:

> Tho' Duty's face be stern, her path is best.
> They sweetly sleep who die upon her breast.

And so, for my Labor colleagues – Ben Chifley's friends and colleagues – I say from this Parliament: 'Goodbye, Ben Chifley. May God grant to your soul eternal rest and happiness'.

Source: Commonwealth of Australia Parliamentary Debates (Hansard).

HERBERT VERE 'DOC' EVATT

'An elder statesman of great wisdom and experience'

*Jim Scullin, an elder statesman of the Labor Party and a former
Prime Minister, is fondly remembered by Doc Evatt*

Following the short and tumultuous three years of Jim Scullin's
government, he stayed in Parliament for nearly two more decades
and mentored many Labor MPs.

Scullin was a trusted adviser to John Curtin during the period of
his government, helping to rally caucus support for conscription and
more generally for his leadership. When Curtin died, Scullin encouraged Ben Chifley to nominate for the party leadership, which he did,
and won. Scullin's parliamentary office was located between Curtin
and Chifley's.

Scullin died in January 1953, after several years of illness. A
state funeral was held at St Patricks Cathedral in Melbourne, with
Archbishop Daniel Mannix leading the service. Thousands of mourn-
ers attended the requiem mass and lined the route to Melbourne's
General Cemetery where he was buried.

The Argus remembered Scullin as a 'man of the people' and a
'distinguished' Prime Minister.

HV 'Doc' Evatt had been appointed by the Scullin Government as
a judge on the High Court – the youngest judge appointed. He had
also served in the Labor caucus with Scullin, from 1940, when Evatt
entered Parliament, to 1949, when Scullin retired. Evatt was now
Labor's leader.

Evatt's eulogy for Scullin was given during the first session of the
20th Parliament. It was also the very first day that a future Prime
Minister would be sworn-in and sit in Parliament. Gough Whitlam
had just won the seat of Werriwa in a by-election and was taking his
seat on the backbenches.

Whitlam would hear Prime Minister Robert Menzies move a motion
recalling Scullin's 'meritorious public service' and Evatt remember 'an
elder statesman of great wisdom and experience' who 'contributed
much to the life of this country'.

'An elder statesman of great wisdom and experience'

The House of Representatives, Canberra 17 February 1953

I behalf of the Opposition, I second the motion.

I am sure that I am speaking for the whole House when I say that we greatly appreciate the spirit in which the prime minister has summed up some of the salient features of the public career of that great Australian, Jim Scullin.

As the prime minister has correctly pointed out, the late Mr Scullin came to high office at perhaps the most critical period economically of our history, and undoubtedly, the anxieties which beset him during that period left their mark on him physically. He appeared to be a man of frail physique, and certainly the anxieties of the depression period weighed very heavily upon him.

The prime minister also mentioned that the late Mr Scullin was a great public speaker. I regarded him as an orator when he addressed great meetings, but perhaps he was at his bet as a parliamentarian in this House.

Among the great debaters whom it has been my privilege to hear, I have not heard a greater debater than Mr Scullin on his subject. He did not often intervene in a debate, but, on his subject, he debated superbly. He did not underestimate the argument against him, and tried to grapple with it. He was always listened to with rapt attention in this House.

Mr Scullin, in his political life, showed great chivalry. He looked beyond the immediate conflict of politics towards greater objectives.

The prime minister put his finger on another important point vital to an understanding of the character of Mr Scullin when he referred to the humility of the late Right Honourable gentleman. This spirit of humility sprang from the fact that he was a man of the deepest religious convictions.

I hope that the tributes paid to the memory of Mr Scullin will be some additional comfort to his widow and family, and his friends, because no one stood higher in the opinion of the Parliament than he did.

I refer particularly to the years of World War Two. It will be left to historians to describe what he contributed to Australia's security. They will tell what he did for Australia's great secondary industries as the prime minister of this country during the early 1930s. Only when World War Two came was his work in that field fully appreciated.

Mr Scullin took part in a very important imperial conference at which the principles of dominion self-government were defined and extended. One result of that was the appointment, on his recommendation, of Sir Isaac Isaacs, the first Australian to be governor-general of the Commonwealth. That was an important development.

On matters of finance, Mr Scullin was a recognised authority in this House. During World War Two, by which time he had ceased to be an official of the Labor Party, he was a valued adviser of two Labor prime ministers, Mr (John) Curtin and Mr (Ben) Chifley. Indeed, as the present prime minister will recall, Mr Scullin was, on certain occasions, the adviser of the wartime Menzies administration.

He was always available in the service of the Parliament and of the nation. He was an elder statesman of great wisdom and experience, and he was able to lighten considerably the great burdens that fell upon the wartime prime ministers of this country.

We shall remember him as we should remember him, with pride and affection, as a great Australian who contributed much to the life of this country, and showed to people in all parts of the world how democracy could work.

Source: Commonwealth Parliamentary Debates (Hansard).

Jim Scullin led Labor for three tumultuous years as Prime Minister. He was a mentor to John Curtin and Ben Chifley in the two decades following his prime ministership. On his death, the media praised him as a distinguished Prime Minister and as 'a man of the people'. In his day, Scullin was regarded as one of Labor's greatest orators.
Source: National Library Australia

GOUGH WHITLAM

'Nothing will save the Governor-General'

Just hours after he was dismissed as Prime Minister, Gough Whitlam addresses the crowd from the steps of Parliament House

The dismissal of the Whitlam Government is one of Australia's most significant political events.

On 11 November 1975, Prime Minister Gough Whitlam and Opposition Leader Malcolm Fraser met at 9.00 am to try to resolve the deadlock over the failure of the Senate to pass the Budget, but no agreement was reached.

At around 10.00 am, Whitlam advised the Governor-General, Sir John Kerr, by telephone that he would see him at 1.00 pm to recommend a half-Senate election to resolve the deadlock. According to Fraser's advisers, Dale Budd and David Kemp, Kerr then phoned Fraser to ask for guarantees if he was appointed Prime Minister. This contradicts Kerr's claim in his memoirs that these guarantees were put to Fraser *after* he was appointed prime minister.

At 1.10 pm, Whitlam was dismissed by Kerr. He retired to The Lodge to phone his wife, Margaret, consult his colleagues and eat a steak.

At 1.30 pm, Fraser was appointed 'caretaker' Prime Minister and advised that Parliament be dissolved.

At 2.23 pm, the Senate passed the Budget.

At 3.14 pm, the House passed a no-confidence motion in Fraser as Prime Minister.

At 4.45 pm, the Governor-General's secretary, David Smith, read the official proclamation dissolving Parliament to a large crowd outside Parliament House. Whitlam stood behind Smith as he spoke. Prompted by Smith's 'May God save the Queen' at the conclusion his statement, Whitlam seized on these words. 'Well may we say God save the Queen', Whitlam said, 'because nothing will save the Governor-General'.

On ABC Radio, Hugh Evans described Whitlam's speech as 'a dramatic and bitter attack' on Kerr.

Many Australians were shocked and outraged by the dismissal. But just weeks later, the Whitlam Government was soundly defeated at an election and the Whitlam era in Australian politics was over.

'Nothing will save the Governor-General'

Parliament House, Canberra 11 November 1975

Ladies and Gentlemen,

Well may we say 'God Save the Queen', because nothing will save the Governor-General.

The proclamation which you have just heard, read by the Governor-General's official secretary, was countersigned 'Malcolm Fraser', who will undoubtedly go down in Australian history from Remembrance Day 1975 as Kerr's Cur.

They won't silence the outskirts of Parliament House even if the inside has been silenced for the next few weeks.

The Governor-General's proclamation was signed after he had already made an appointment to meet the Speaker at a quarter to five.

The House of Representatives had requested the Speaker to give the Governor-General its decision that Mr Fraser did not have the confidence of the House and that the Governor-General should call me to form the Government.

Maintain your rage and enthusiasm through the campaign for the election now to be held and until polling day.

Source: Australian Broadcasting Corporation.

The dismissal of the Whitlam government was an event that shocked the nation. Just hours after he was removed from the prime ministership by the Governor-General, Gough Whitlam stood on the steps of Parliament House in front of a large crowd and declared, 'Nothing will save the Governor-General'.
Source: Australian Labor Party

PAUL KEATING

'For the true believers'

Paul Keating claims victory for the true believers

In 1993, Paul Keating won the so-called 'un-winnable' election. Longevity, the recession, the removal of Bob Hawke as Prime Minister, didn't matter. The victor was now Prime Minister in his own right; the government's mandate was refreshed. The boyhood ambition which fuelled his political rise had been realised. In the campaign, he had led a spirited defence of Labor values and a slashing attack against his opponents.

On election night, Labor supporters at the Bankstown Sports Club celebrated with expectation of the moment when Keating would claim victory. The stage was dressed in a striking cobalt blue curtain designed by Baz Luhrmann. In the auditorium, the crowd started to chant, 'We want Paul'.

When he finally walked out onto the stage, Keating was met with enthusiastic cheers. He waved and held his hands aloft in victory. 'Thank you, ladies and gentlemen' he said, 'well, this is the sweetest victory of all'. An almighty cheer erupted. Keating continued: 'This is a victory for the true believers'.

Keating knew how to use a political speech to furnish a historic moment. The language is steeped in Labor lore. By labelling it 'the sweetest victory', he had borrowed from NSW Premier Neville Wran, who had used the phrase after his fourth election victory in 1984. In using the phrase, 'the true believers', he invoked Labor's soul – a phrase repeated throughout the Bible and is part of Labor lingua franca.

Via correspondence with Keating in mid-2010, he said that the media had 'completely written off the Labor government'. So the election result 'underlined the staying power of those people in the community who believed in a bigger agenda', he said. 'The true believers', he said, were those who had 'kept the faith'; the keeping of the faith was the expression of the belief of the believers.

Some commentators have suggested this speech only spoke to Labor supporters and not the wider Australian community. But in reading the speech in full, Keating acknowledged the need to govern for all Australians and that his victory was, in part, due to the hostile reaction to the policies of his political opponents.

'For the true believers'

Bankstown Sports Club, Bankstown 13 March 1993

Well, this is the sweetest victory of all – this is the sweetest. This is a victory for the true believers – the people who in difficult times have kept the faith – and to the Australian people going through hard times – it makes their act of faith all that much greater.

It will be a long time before an opposition party tries to divide this country again. It will be a long time before somebody tries to put one group of Australians over here and another over there. The public of Australia are too decent and they are too conscientious and they are too interested in their country to wear those sorts of things.

This, I think, has been very much a victory of Australian values, because it was Australian values on the line and the Liberal Party wanted to change Australia from the country it's become – a cooperative, decent, nice place to live where people have regard for each other.

And could I say to you that I wanted to win again, to be there in the 1990s to see Australia prosper, as it will.

The thing is, I said to the Australian people 'we've turned the corner'. Can I say now, after the election, let me repeat it: we have turned the corner. The growth is coming through. We will see ourselves as a sophisticated trading country in Asia and we've got to do it in a way where everybody's got a part in it, where everyone's in it.

There's always cause for concern, but never pessimism and Australia, wherein for the first time in our history, located in a region of the fastest growth in the world, and we've been set up now, we are set up now as we've never been set up before to be in it, to exploit it, to be part of it. It offers tremendous opportunities for Australians and now we have to do it, and we have to do it compassionately.

I give an assurance to the people that this victory won't go to the heads of the government or the Labor Party. We'll take it seriously, we'll take it thankfully, and we'll do a great deal with it.

The people of Australia have taken us on trust and we'll return that trust and we'll care about those people out there, particularly the unemployed – we want to get them back to work …

I can assure you the government will now be redoubling its efforts to be as good a government as you hope and expect we can. To be as conscientious with this mandate as we possibly can be, to give it our every effort, our every shot, to see that we recover quickly and we get going and we put this recessionary period behind us and we get this country of opportunity off and running.

But keeping the opportunity for everybody – keeping those great nostrums of access and equity. Getting people into the game. The policies of inclusion. The policies of One Nation (his 1992 post-recession economic policy blueprint). And that's what it's got to be about.

So can I say again, this is a tremendous victory. It's a tremendous victory for all those who have imagination and faith. The people who believe in things, who are not going to let good beliefs be put aside for essentially miserable ideas to divide the place up.

I mean, I think the Australian people have always had such remarkable sense to spot the value and to cut their way through it. Now part of this victory … is them spotting what they think were the dangers in the Liberal Party's policies. What I hope is that in the next election the victory is 100 per cent due to the good government of Labor.

Now, I'd like to start thanking some people and the first person I'd like to thank is my wife, Annita, who has helped me right through the campaign …

And can I also say, can I give an extra special note of thanks to the women of Australia, who voted for us believing in the policies of this government …

I want to pay particular thanks to the architects of this victory, my personal staff. Don Russell, Mark Ryan, Don Watson, my press secretaries and the rest.

And most particularly to those people in the Labor Party who have never lost faith, never lost heart, and are there at the polling booths to work and to fight for the good thing. Thank you. The people who never give up but are always there no matter how heavy the travails may be … Thank you again and thank you for believing.

But could I most particularly, and again finally, thank the Australian people without whose faith and decency and commitment to what's fair and what's reasonable and what is decent in this country, without whose conscientious judgements, this victory could not have been consummated and put together …

And I conclude on this note, to say we thank you, we appreciate it, we won't let you down.

Source: <www.keating.org.au>.

KIM BEAZLEY

'There are dark angels in our nation but there are also good angels'

Kim Beazley lifts Labor's spirits after losing the 2001 'Tampa' election

The 2001 election was one of the most difficult for the Labor Party.

Boats of refugees seeking asylum in Australia had escalated. In August 2001, a Norwegian transport ship, the *MV Tampa*, rescued 433 asylum seekers. Before it could offload its human cargo, it was taken over by SAS officers and denied landfall on Australian shores. The events prompted tough border protection laws and provided the setting for the election campaign.

As Paul Kelly writes in *The March of Patriots*, John Howard's actions 'created its own demand, igniting elements of nationalism, populism and racism, all given prime ministerial sanction'.

Against this backdrop, on 11 September 2001, the United States was attacked by terrorists.

With fear and security issues dominant, Labor was defeated. Tampa 'helped to win Howard an election victory', wrote Kelly, 'but its extremism bequeathed the legacy that there must be a better way'.

On election night, flanked by his family, Labor leader Kim Beazley addressed his supporters. He conceded defeat and resigned as leader.

Acknowledging the challenges of terrorism and security, he also talked of the need for security in education, health and aged care. His peroration drew upon Abraham Lincoln: 'Like any nation, there are dark angels in our nation but there are also good angels as well. And the task and challenge for those of us in politics is to bring out the generosity that resides in the soul of the ordinary Australian'.

In mid-2010, Beazley said via correspondence for this book, 'The 2001 election saw one of the most divisive campaigns in Australian political history' and 'those events still haunt Australian politics'. He said that 'when I made these remarks, I expected them to be the last I would make as a party leader'. But he would return to the Labor leadership in 2005.

'There are dark angels in our nation but there are also good angels'

Rockingham, Western Australia 10 November 2001

I am very proud of the Australian Labor Party, its Members of Parliament, its workers in the field tonight for a magnificent campaign … but I have to, tonight, I'm afraid for all of you, I have to concede defeat …

And I congratulate Mr (John) Howard on his re-election. I hope, as prime minister of this country for some time, that he has and does bear in mind the concerns and needs of all Australians, whatever their background …

Can I say this, five weeks ago it looked as though we in the Labor Party faced one of the most devastating defeats in our history. It is an extraordinarily difficult thing to conduct an election campaign against the background of an ongoing war, and in circumstances where people feel that great sense of insecurity.

Governments all around the globe have been the beneficiaries of massive public support as the people of the nation turn to the leadership of the government of the day in order to get themselves a sense of comfort and security …

I am so proud of the way we fought. We have fought for the security of the Australian people. But we have also offered more.

We've looked down through the fog of war to the kitchen table of the average Australian family. To those who sit around it, we've listened to their hopes and their dreams, the aspirations that they have for their young folk that they get a decent education, the aspirations and concerns that they have to ensure that they have access to affordable health care. Their love of the future of this nation, the determination they have to see it as a constructive and creative nation, a nation where people don't leave when they have bright ideas, but come here when they have bright ideas.

We alone in the Labor Party brought these issues to the campaign table and let me let you in on a secret – they're not going to go away. I am afraid to say, that crisis in aged care, health, the problems in our public schools, they'll all be there tomorrow. They'll all be there as a massive challenge to governments.

There will be a broader challenge to government, too. How are we going to be able to draw upon all our people, whatever their background, whatever racial group they come from, whatever cultural background they have, whatever religious background we may have, how are we going to draw on the strength of all our diversity to ensure that we as a nation survive and prosper? ...

We don't stand these days where we did once in the high regard of the nations in the region around us. And yet, in that high regard lies crucial elements of our security. This is the future challenge for government – how we address these things and deal with these things. It cannot be said that the election process that we have just been through necessarily assists that.

But what can assist it is the natural coming together of the Australian people after a great political contest, to think about the things which unify all of us and the gratitude we ought to have for being able to share in the prosperity of this lovely land ...

It is a challenge for all of you, but it's a challenge that I will be joining you in as a humble backbencher shortly. It is not my intention to remain as leader of the Australian Labor Party.

It has been an enormous privilege for me to lead this great party, this 100-year old party, this party that has so much of Australian history bound up in it. The greatest political party and one of the greatest Australian political parties still there fighting and battling for the needs and concerns of the ordinary Australian through every hardship that they confront and for every political difficulty that we confront.

So, I bow out of Labor Party history now and, to all of you, ordinary members of the Australian Labor Party ... I thank you for your support ...

But tonight I just bow out by thanking the Australian people. We are a great nation. We have a nation with a capacity to be better. We have a nation with a capacity for a generosity of heart. Like any nation, there are dark angels in our nation but there are also good angels as well. And the task and challenge for those of us in politics is to bring out the generosity that resides in the soul of the ordinary Australian, that generosity of heart, so that we as a nation turn to each other and not against each other in the circumstances which we have.

There is one key thing to all of this, I do believe, and that is this ... understand what an ordinary Australian family feels, and that if we look to security internationally, you look further to security in the hearts and minds of those around the kitchen table because there's no doubt at all that the sense of generosity in the hearts of an average citizen often starts with a sense of security at home. And if they do not feel a sense of security then their capacity to feel a generosity is often marred.

Now, that has always been a challenge that we in the Australian Labor Party have understood. A great 100-year history of the Australian Labor Party continues ...

Source: Australian Broadcasting Corporation.

Labor leader Kim Beazley was the first federal Labor leader to deliver an apology to the stolen generations of Aboriginal Australians. On election night in 2001, he told Australians there are 'dark angels' and 'good angels' in our nation.
Source: Australian Labor Party

JULIA GILLARD

'A day of courage, tragedy and sheer luck'

Acting Prime Minister Julia Gillard expresses sympathy
for lives lost in the Victorian bushfires

The 'Black Saturday' bushfires, which unleashed a rage of terror, destruction and death in Victoria on 7 February 2009, were the worst in Australia's recorded history. 173 people were killed. Thousands were injured and homeless. Towns and villages were destroyed. Over 2000 homes, and their priceless possessions, were incinerated. Thousands of native and livestock animals were lost. Businesses and farms were ruined.

But amid all of this, the response from emergency services, individual volunteers, community organisations, businesses, governments and Australians from all over the nation was overwhelming. Donations to bushfire victims reached into the hundreds of millions of dollars.

Parliament reconvened on the Monday following 'Black Saturday'. Prime Minister Kevin Rudd was in Victoria consoling the families and seeing the carnage first hand. It fell to Julia Gillard, as Acting Prime Minister, to formally move a motion of condolence in Parliament.

In a moving and eloquent speech, Gillard described it as 'a tragedy beyond belief, beyond precedent and, really, beyond words'. But in the words that followed, Gillard described the destruction and retold stories of tragedy and loss, courage and resilience, and warned the nation that 'more bad news' was ahead.

Gillard's eyes were red with tears and her voice wavered, as she struggled to hold back the emotion. The mood of the House was solemn. Parliamentary business was suspended. The flag flying over Parliament House was lowered to half-mast. The speech was widely praised for its empathy, understanding and heartfelt delivery.

'A day of courage, tragedy and sheer luck'

The House of Representatives, Canberra 9 February 2009

I move:

That the House:

(1) extends its deepest sympathies to families and loved ones of those Australians killed in the weekend's tragic bushfires in Victoria;

(2) records its deep regret at the human injury, the loss of property and the destruction of communities caused by the weekend's fires;

(3) praises the work of emergency services, volunteers and community members in assisting friends and neighbours in this time of need; and

(4) acknowledges the profound impact on those communities affected and the role of governments and the Australian community in assisting their recovery and rebuilding.

I offer the deepest and most sincere condolences of this House and our nation's Parliament to those families suffering most, to the communities lost and to a state that will never be the same.

It is a tragedy beyond belief, beyond precedent and, really, beyond words.

7 February 2009 will now be remembered as one of the darkest days in Australia's peacetime history.

The beautiful towns and hamlets of Kinglake, Marysville and Narbethong are no more. At least 640 homes and their irreplaceable contents, like the photographs of children and the memories of family life, have been destroyed.

The weekend's fires and particularly 7 February 2009 are surely Victoria's blackest time.

Whilst as yet it does not have a tragic name, it is blacker than the human tragedies of Black Friday of 1939 and Ash Wednesday of 1983, and in this dark time there has been a human cost without comparison.

7 February 2009 will be remembered as the day when more than 400 fires burned across the state during the most severe weather conditions ever recorded.

It will be a day remembered for the lives lost – 107 at last count – and families and communities were changed forever.

It will be remembered as the day when the fires raged across the state from Horsham in the west, Bendigo and Beechworth in the north and, in an arc of destruction, from West Gippsland to Kinglake and Kilmore.

It will be remembered as a day of tragedy, courage and sheer luck …

Victorian authorities inform us that 107 people are confirmed as deceased. This total has already outstripped those of Ash Wednesday of 1983 and Black Friday of 1939, and the grisly reality is that the record number of lives lost will continue to rise.

More bodies will be found and identified by our emergency services. Burns victims will sadly succumb to their severe injuries despite the intensive efforts of our health professionals. We need to brace ourselves for the increase in fatalities and be mindful of the grief and circumstances of those families and communities.

To be clear and frank, it will get worse and Australians need to prepare themselves for more bad news.

All Australians, whether they are in Victoria or the capital cities and regional and rural communities around our nation, have been hit hard by these events and are at one in supporting our emergency services. To each person who fought these fires we say thank you.

Most importantly, as a nation and as a community we need to extend a helping hand to rebuilding these towns and lives in the weeks and years ahead.

The Australian government stands shoulder to shoulder with the Victorian government in this emergency response and rebuilding effort … The Prime Minister (Kevin Rudd), the cabinet and the government as a whole will do what is required to assist the individuals, families, local organisations, businesses and communities affected by these tragic events …

The support of employers is also needed to ensure the release of volunteer fire-fighters and other emergency personnel to attend these efforts. Their continued support is crucial to allow these volunteers to continue their emergency services work. More generally, the community response in the regions that have felt the full force of these fires has been extraordinary but it is also consistent with our national character.

This commitment to helping our neighbours and fellow citizens needs to be a national and ongoing one. I encourage all Australians to make a contribution to the appeals that are underway.

The rebuilding of these lives and communities will take months and years rather than days and weeks. Just as the strength of our communities ensured many survived these very devastating events, it will be that strength and resilience of the Australian community that will help our fellow citizens rebuild.

Every one of us here today will do everything that we possibly can to respond, to rebuild and to make certain that, to the extent that we can ever combat nature's might, such tragedies cannot happen again. That will not be easy.

There will be a time for analysis when we seek to understand what happened, how it happened and why it happened, but our immediate task is to pull together as a family, to provide comfort and to heal.

Today, on behalf of the Prime Minister, the members of this Parliament and the nation, I want to grieve for those we have lost, pay tribute to the victims and praise the courage of those without whose help the death toll and the physical destruction would have been much, much worse.

I commend the motion to the House.

Source: Commonwealth of Australia Parliamentary Debates (Hansard).

Epilogue

Troy Bramston

In May 1904, a newly appointed Prime Minister rose in the House of Representatives to announce the ambitious program of the first national Labor government. Chris Watson learnt his craft as a trade unionist representing the workers, but as the head of a government he pledged to lead 'for the benefit of the whole of the people of Australia'. Labor's most successful leaders have used language that appealed to all Australians by linking the party's core values and policies with an aspirational belief in the ability of government to expand opportunity, reduce inequality and support a growing economy.

As Graham Freudenberg argues, 'The essence of the style and approach' of the Labor speech has been 'a continuing quest for practical idealism'. While Labor's finest orators have often used elevated rhetoric to energise the ambitions of its supporters, in government the party has almost always favoured pragmatic and achievable goals. In advancing the Labor agenda, no form of communication has been more enduring or important than speechmaking. 'The Australian Labor Party was built on speeches', Freudenberg says.

Today, as Labor struggles to reconnect with the community, its leaders have often chosen rhetoric that undermines this legacy. From its earliest days, Labor knew that appeals to class, militancy and radicalism did not appeal to the mainstream voters that Labor needed to form government. The new world of Australia was different from the old; the narrative of social class has never run as strongly here as it once did abroad. As the early Labor MP George Black understood, the party represented 'those who labour with either hand or head, with either mind or muscle'.

Watson's government did not last long, but he understood the need for a young party to appeal to all voters, not just some. In the years ahead, language will be a critical factor in determining whether Labor can win back the trust of voters. While Labor's strength has always been to renew itself, there are elements of continuity, such as language, that have endured. In the finest traditions of political oratory, Labor's most successful leaders understood the need to articulate core values rather than sectional values and place the party in the vital centre of politics, not on the fringes. In winning the support of voters and inspiring them to join the Labor cause, nothing has been more important than the art of great Labor speechmaking.

(P) As one ~~Canadian~~ has been said
elsewhere: " we are the bearers of
many blessings from our ancestors, and,
therefore, we must also bear their burdens?
as well "

The Apology

(P) Therefore, for the nation, the course
of action is clear.

(P) Therefore, for our people, the course
of action is clear.

(P) And that is to deal now with ~~this~~
that has become one of the
darkest chapters in the nation's
history -

(P) In doing so, we are doing more
than contending with the facts, the
and evidence and the often
rancourous debate.

(P) In doing so, we are wrestling with
our own soul.

(P) This is not the black armband of
history